Crucial Issues in
Contemporary Education

Goodyear Education Series

Theodore W. Hipple, Editor
UNIVERSITY OF FLORIDA

Edited by **THEODORE W. HIPPLE**
University of Florida, Gainesville

Crucial Issues in Contemporary Education

Goodyear Publishing Company, Inc.
Pacific Palisades, California

Library of Congress Catalog Card Number: 72-89589

Current Printing (last digit):
10 9 8 7 6 5 4 3 2 1

Y-1877-3
ISBN: 0-87620-187-7

Printed in the United States of America

Contents

198693

Preface

This book is intended for those who are interested in education, especially those who are pursuing or are intending to pursue a career in this changing and exciting profession. It is a book about issues in education; about those concerns that seem destined to shape education in the years ahead.

I have tried to identify those issues that are, as the title indicates, crucial: shifting philosophies of education (including attention to alternative schools or to none at all), accountability, teacher education, student unrest, urban education, racism in American education, and the future of education. Moreover, I have included very recent articles that present opposing positions on some of these concerns or that deal with them in some depth. Finally, I have utilized a variety of authors and sources; people and journals whose names are known to all in education as well as those with rather limited professional readership. In all of the articles, however, I sought commitment, scholarship, and lucidity. Though the readings must speak for themselves, I am pleased with the results.

The organization of this book posed some difficulties. A number of the articles discussed several crucial issues and their placement ultimately became somewhat arbitrary. The reader I am sure will see how these articles relate to the others, regardless of their placement in the book. To this end, I have concluded each section with some questions about the articles. Very few of these questions have easy answers, if, indeed, they have answers at all. The existence of a problem does not imply the existence of a solution. Instead, the questions are designed to make the reader think, perhaps more broadly and more deeply, about what he has read. A number of the questions are also intended to provoke the reader to think about his own beliefs about education.

The help of many went into the making of this volume. My wife Marjorie, presently an all-but-dissertation doctoral candidate in education, provided valuable ideas both on the selection of issues and on the choice of articles to illuminate the issues. My very able secretary, Mrs. Pam Malone, handled the voluminous correspondence to and from the editors of journals and the authors of articles with her usual capable skills. Most of all, of course, I am indebted to the authors whose works are included herein. Ultimately, their contributions, their thoughtful ideas and powerful insights made this book. I owe them much and I thank them.

Crucial Issues in
Contemporary Education

Chapter one
The Shifting Sands of Educational Purpose and Practice

From its earliest days, education has been rooted in philosophy. People like Plato, Aristotle, Locke, Rousseau, and Dewey, among a host of others that could be listed, have provided theoretical foundations for schooling which rest upon particular assumptions about the nature of man and his learning. Sometimes the philosopher is important in his own lifetime in shaping means and ends in education (as was John Dewey). In other times, his work has a delayed reaction and makes its impact long after he has died (as is the case with both Rousseau and Locke). Sometimes, too, one particular philosophical posture dominates the contemporary education scene. At others several rather discrete positions may be inferred from educational principles and practices.

In contemporary American education the philosophical foundations may be said to be shifting, if indeed they are not crumbling entirely. Neither a particular philosophy nor a particular philosopher holds sway, providing a pivotal point around which educational purpose and practice can be structured. Instead, purpose and practice seem more the result of expediency than of theory, more a consequence of a "wanting to get by, somehow" mentality than an effort derived from a consistently held and implemented set of beliefs. In short, and to put the matter kindly, education is in a state of ferment.

Some will argue that out of such a state of ferment and disorder, out of what temporarily appears to be chaos, will emerge a new synthesis which will provide present focus and future direction. Others, however, will argue with equal cogency that the contemporary inadequacies in education, the obvious failures, the demonstrable mindlessness so carefully documented in Silberman's *Crisis in the Classroom,* call for a vast rethinking about education, its purposes and practices, even its relevance. The articles in this section discuss such crucial issues as these.

The opening article by Marland expresses his optimism. "The American education system," he writes, "is too vital for us to ignore or abandon because it has faults." Yet hope and faith alone will not solve the problems of education. Rather, what is required is a commitment at all levels of education — federal, state, and local — and among all educators.

Shane notes that "something seemed to go awry with the once-sustaining purposes of U.S. education in the years between 1920 and 1970" and calls for a "rediscovery of educational purpose." His discussion of the requisite societal framework for such a rediscovery and his sample of eight kinds of "neglected or minimized learnings" crucial for national survival are penetrating and provocative. They also are challenging to anyone concerned about education. And who among us can morally afford not to be concerned?

If there is one basic tenet of contemporary American education, it is that all children ought to be educated. Schooling is not the private domain of the privileged few. Yet, as Hencley and Parsons note in the third article, even this principle is now open for reconsideration: "There is now a widespread and rather outspoken feeling that attendance at a public school is no longer necessarily a benefit."

In the next selection Fantini also notes the ills of today's education, but he is not ready to scrap the present system. Instead, he describes "public schools of choice" in which both the supply of education and the demand for it are so wedded that the consumers — the parents, students, and teachers — have options available to them to select the kind of education they deem most appropriate. A most innovative idea, it calls for thoughtful consideration.

One unmistakable outgrowth of the public dissatisfaction with education has been the defeat of bond and tax measures to finance education. (More appears on this crucial issue in Section Four.) A second movement has been the rise in number and scope of alternative schools. Often called "free" schools, these alternatives provide a vastly different kind of education from that offered in the majority of public schools. Morse describes these schools and notes their important link with what he calls an "alternative media."

The final article in this section is by Ivan Illich, whose name has become almost synonymous with "deschooling." (One of Illich's books, in fact, is called *Deschooling Society* and has had an enormous impact on American educational thinking.) In the selection presented here, Illich asserts his belief that "the disestablishment of the school has become inevitable." Yet, he argues, "this end of an illusion should fill us with hope."

The Condition of Education in the Nation

S. P. Marland, Jr.

The time seems propitious for a report on the condition of education in the nation. The long swell of history appears at this moment to have lifted us above the turbulence of recent years and positioned us to appraise with some reasonableness the present condition of the educational enterprise. It is a commanding view, a prospect at once gladdening and disturbing.

We can take legitimate satisfaction from the tremendous progress of recent years. The sheer size of the American commitment to education is amazing, with over 62 million Americans—more than 30 percent of the population—actively engaged as students or teachers. More than three million young men and women will graduate from high schools throughout the country in June 1971, as contrasted with fewer than two million 10 years ago. Nearly 8.5 million students are enrolled in higher education as contrasted with slightly more than four million 10 years ago. Size apart, our educational enterprise is also far more nearly equalized, with academic opportunity extended for the first time in our history to large numbers of black, brown, and Spanish-speaking people. Total black enrollment in colleges and universities, for example, has more than doubled since the mid-60s to nearly 500,000 today, though much remains to be done for the advancement of our minority young people before we can rest.

We can be proud of the willingness and rapidity with which education has begun to move to meet the extensive and unprecedented demands being made upon it. Ten or 20 years ago education was almost wholly limited to academic matters carried on within the conventional confines of the classroom and the curriculum. Today educators are dealing with the whole range of human concerns—academic, economic, social, physical, emotional—and education has burst out of the classroom through such efforts as "Sesame Street" with its succinct lessons for preschoolers in an attractive and exciting television format.

But, viewed objectively, the great flaws of the educational system, the great voids in its capacity to satisfy the pressing requirements of our people press us to set aside our pleasant contemplation of our successes. Sadly, the

From S. P. Marland, "The Condition of Education in the Nation," *American Education* 7 (April 1971): 3–5 by permission of the author and the U.S. Office of Education.

quality of education a person receives in this country is still largely determined by his ability to pay for it one way or another. As a consequence, "free public education" has a connotation in, say, Shaker Heights far different from what it has in the city of Cleveland, and a boy or girl from a family earning $15,000 a year is almost five times more likely to attend college than the son or daughter in a household of less than $3,000 annual income.

We know that ours is the greatest educational system ever devised by man. But it falls short of our aspirations. We must improve it.

• Like our system of representative government, the American education system is too vital for us to ignore or abandon because it has faults. It is time to set about, in an orderly fashion, making the system work better so that it will accomplish what we want from it.

DECADE OF DISCONTENT

American education has undergone over the past 10 years probably the most wrenching shakeup in its history. Education has been charged with inefficiency, unresponsiveness, and aloofness from the great issues of our society, perhaps even lack of interest in these issues. These charges, in some instances, have undoubtedly been true. But in most cases, I insist, the schools and those who lead them and those who teach in them are deeply, painfully, and inescapably concerned with the great social issues of our time and the part that the schools must play in resolving them.

The depth of the schools' contemporary involvement becomes strikingly apparent when it is compared with the false serenity of education as recently as 15 years ago, when it was in the very absence of stridency and criticism that our real problems lay. Public discontent with the education of 1970 was bred in the synthetic calm of the 1950s and before.

This movement from serenity to discontent, from complacent inadequacy to the desire for vigorous reform, has not been accomplished easily. Some reform efforts, conceived in an atmosphere of hysteria, have failed while others have succeeded splendidly, But after many stops and starts, false expectations and disheartening letdowns, we have arrived at a time and place in which, I judge, educational reform at all levels is the intent of all responsible educators. As a consequence, truly equal educational opportunity for all young Americans is now a feasible goal.

We are going through a period of intensive concern with the poor and the disadvantaged. Since 1965 under one program alone, title I of the Elementary and Secondary Education Act, the Federal Government has invested more than $7 billion in the education of children from low-income families. A number of States have made significant companion efforts. Admittedly, our success in increasing the academic achievement of the disadvantaged child has been marginal. But prospects for future success are increasing because the education profession itself, at first prodded into this work by such outside forces as the drive for civil rights, is now substantially dedicated to the redress of educational inequality wherever it may be found. This is a dramatic turnaround from the early and mid-60s when we tolerated the fact that certain of our citizens were not profiting to any measurable extent from the schools' conventional offerings and when we were content to permit these citizens to become the responsibility of unemployment offices, unskilled labor pools, and prisons. This time has passed, and we now accept the proposition that no longer does the young person fail in school. When human beings in our charge fall short of their capacities to grow to useful adulthood, *we* fail.

Rough events of the past decade, then, have brought the educators of this nation to a beginning appreciation of just what thoroughgoing education reform really means. A giant institution comprising 60 million students, 2.5 million teachers, and thousands of administrative leaders cannot remake itself simply because it is asked or even told to do so. Tradition has enormous inertia, and wrong practice can be as deeply rooted as effective practice. The past decade, in sum, has been a time of trial and error, a time in which we have plowed and harrowed our fields. Now we must plant deeply to produce the strong roots of a new American education.

WHY ARE WE EDUCATING?

As we look to 1972 and beyond, we are able to state with far greater clarity the reasons why we are educating our citizens than we could 10 or 20 years ago. We are educating a total population of young people in the elementary and secondary schools and we are no longer satisfied that 30, 40, or 50 percent of it should not really expect to complete high school. And if we are educating for the fulfillment of all the people of our land, we certainly cannot halt at the secondary level, or even the level of higher education, but must look to the arrangements for continuing adult education over the years. Increasingly, we are persuaded as a nation that education is not reserved for youth but is properly a lifelong concern. In the past half-dozen years, for example more than two million adult Americans have been given the opportunity to obtain an eighth grade education under the Office of Education adult education program. Many millions more have continued to grow professionally, culturally, and intellectually, as adults, through formal and informal institutions of education.

We must be concerned with the provision of exciting and rewarding and meaningful experiences for children, both in and out of the formal environment of classrooms. When we use the word "meaningful," we imply a strong obligation that our young people complete the first 12 grades in such a fashion that they are ready either to enter into some form of higher education or to proceed immediately into satisfying and appropriate employment. Further, we now hold that the option should be open to most young people to *choose* either route.

We must eliminate anything in our curriculum that is unresponsive to either of these goals, particularly the high school anachronism called "the general curriculum," a false compromise between college preparatory curriculum and realistic career development. If our young people are indeed disenchanted with school—and more than 700,000 drop out every year—I suspect that it is because they are unable to perceive any light at the end of the school corridor. They cannot see any useful, necessary, and rewarding future that can be assured by continued attendance in class. The reform to which we must address ourselves begins with the assurance of meaningful learning and growth for *all* young people, particularly at the junior high and high school levels. Students frequently ask us why they should learn this or that. We who schedule these courses and we who teach them should ask ourselves the same questions and have the wisdom and skill and sensitivity to produce good answers.

Courses of instruction, books, materials, and the educational environment—all should relate to the student's needs, answering some requirement of his present or future growth, irrespective of custom or tradition. We as teachers in today's educational setting cannot win the response of our young people by perpetuating formalized irrelevance in classrooms. Seemingly irrelevant expectations must be made relevant by the teacher. This is the nature of teaching.

EDUCATION RESEARCH

We are obliged not simply to provide education but to provide very good education. The success of our efforts to find ways to teach more effectively will depend upon the quality and application of our educational research, a pursuit that has absorbed more than $700 million in Office of Education funds over the past decade and will, I am determined, take an increasing share of our budget. We need to know how we can develop the child of deep poverty, the minority child, the child who has been held in economic or ethnic isolation for generations, the child without aspirations in his family or in his environment, the child who comes to school hungry and leaves hungrier. We must discover how to develop the five million American children who bring different languages and different cultures to their schools. They need special help. Nor can we ignore the gifted child, possessed of talents that we know frequently transcend the ability of his teacher.

If we would find the answers to these questions, let us set aside the traditional boundaries of learning, the days, the hours, the bells, the schedules. Let us find ways to free ourselves from administrative strangleholds on what teaching should be and teachers should be. Research must open wide the windows of learning, and teachers must listen carefully to the counsel of the researchers.

Let us find ways to keep more schools open 12 to 15 hours a day and 12 months a year to make sensible constructive use of our multibillion-dollar investment in facilities and personnel. Let us construct a school environment sufficiently systematic to be responsive to young people, yet informal enough to enable youngsters to come and go in a spirit of freedom and honest interest, rising above their present circumstances and reaching joyfully for all that the schools can give them.

NEED FOR HUMANENESS

Above all, let our schools be humane once more. With the possible exception of those who tend the ill, teaching is the first of the humane professions and it seems especially appropriate at this time to return to that tradition.

Teachers want to bring excitement to the classroom. They want to bring fulfillment to the lives of the children in their charge. But to achieve excitement and fulfillment in the classroom, teachers need a new freedom from administrative protocol and an increased competence in reaching each learner and touching his life deeply and compassionately.

Titles I and III of the Elementary and Secondary Education Act have taught us sound lessons in creative teaching techniques. Now let us set aside the mechanics of testing and the excessive formalities of school organization, and let us put these new techniques to work in all the classrooms of America.

Let us find ways for teachers to concern themselves wholly with students. We must use our technology and the other resources of this half of the twentieth century—resources that we have barely touched—to multiply the effectiveness of the teacher, to increase greatly the teacher's efficiency and productivity. Let technology extend the hand of the teacher through such efforts as "Sesame Street" discharging the routine tasks of instruction while preserving for the teacher those things that enliven the human spirit.

THE FEDERAL ROLE

I believe the federal role in education should be one of increasing the effectiveness of the human and financial resources of our schools, colleges, and universities. The present overall level of federal assistance to education is something less than seven percent of our total investment. I envision the federal share rising eventually to three or four times that level. But first the federal government must conduct centralized research into the learning process and deliver the results of that research convincingly and supportively to the educational institutions. We are constructing a nationwide educational communications network to disseminate proven new practice in order to move the art of education from its present condition to one of the increased quality that we demand of ourselves. We must proceed more swiftly to implement the products of research without stopping to redefine every goal and every process at every crossroad in the country.

The federal role calls for greatly increased technical assistance to states and local school systems to insure the delivery of new and better ways to teach and learn. As conductor and purveyor of educational research the U.S. Office of Education will, I hope, earn the faith and trust of the States and communities so that newly researched and validated program models stamped "O.E." will be swiftly and confidently put to use in our cities and towns, creating the overall climate of change that we ask.

Most of all, I ask that the Office of Education provide national leadership. Services, yes; supporting funds, yes. But I hold that this office, made up of nearly 3,000 people, must have a larger and more effective role. If our situation changes over the next year or two as I hope it will, and we are able to diminish substantially our preoccupation with administration and paperwork, hundreds of Office of Education staff members will be freed to bring leadership, technical assistance and stimulation to the States and localities. The dedicated, creative, and talented people who staff this office will be instantly available to help where the problem is, whether it be a question of racial discrimination, curriculum, improved ways to teach, introduction of new technology, evaluation, or whatever. This office will then be what it has long desired to be, a respectful and willing companion to the States and communities in serving the educational needs of the nation.

EDUCATION AND THE BICENTENNIAL

The United States of America will celebrate its 200th birthday in 1976. I would suggest this bicentennial year as a useful deadline against which we can measure our capacity to effect change and our sincerity in seeking it. The five years remaining before the bicentennial constitute a relatively brief time in the history of the American educational enterprise. Yet it is a particularly crucial time in which, I am persuaded, we can accomplish as much as—and more than—we have managed to achieve in the past 20 years, or perhaps the past 100. My reason for optimism resides in my belief that, big as this nation is, it is *ready* for change.

Our search for the education of 1976 is well begun. We know it will be innovative and efficient, yet characterized by good schoolteacher common sense. We know it will be flexible, responsive, and humane, that it will serve all the children of America, preparing them to meet universal standards of excellence, yet treating each in a very individualized and personalized way. We know that in 1976 our system of education will be considerate of the differences among us, adaptable to our changing expectations, and clearly available and clearly useful to all who seek it.

More than ever before, the substance of America's future resides in our teachers. The enormous success of our system of schooling in the past 195 years has brought our nation to a pinnacle place among nations. The next five years should be viewed as the time in which the educational successes and satisfactions that have enlightened and undergirded the lives of the great majority of our people must now be extended to enlighten and undergird the lives of all. More than ever, this is the time of the humane teacher.

The Rediscovery
of Purpose in Education

Harold G. Shane

Something seemed to go awry with the once-sustaining purposes of U.S. education in the years between 1920 and 1970. By the late 1960s there was even the gloomy prospect that our instructional landscape might be on the way to becoming a littered ideological junkyard.

As we entered the 1970s there undoubtedly were more than a few Americans who uneasily speculated, and not without some reasons, that we were moving into a confused, "Twilight of the Goals" interval which foreshadowed a social and educational Armageddon that was likely to occur in the next decade or two.

THE REDISCOVERY OF BASIC PURPOSE

Because of contemporary educational problems too well known to need recounting, it is suggested here with a sense of urgency that the need for a rediscovery of educational purpose is becoming frighteningly obvious. After 10,000 years we appear to have come full circle and once again need to rediscover the purpose of primitive man's education—human survival in the face of a dangerous, implacable environment.

From a life-and-death battle with a hostile nature early in our history we have cycled back to a point at which we face an analogous struggle to protect ourselves from an environment—a *biosphere* to use fashionable terminology—which has been made dangerous *for* man *by* man. Among the present, clear dangers are our propensity for overbreeding, our ingenuity in devising deadly weapons, the careless release of poisonous technological wastes, and the thoughtlessly accumulated mountains of "indisposable" trash which crowd our living space.

From Harold G. Shane, "The Rediscovery of Purpose in Education," *Educational Leadership* 28, no. 6 (March 1971): 581–84. Reprinted with permission of the Association for Supervision and Curriculum Development and Harold G. Shane. Copyright © 1971 by the Association for Supervision and Curriculum Development.

It is simple to propose that learning to survive has become a new central goal of education; it is decidedly less simple to conjecture about how to go about approaching such an objective.

ATTAINING NEW "SURVIVAL BEHAVIORS"

At least two paths of action present themselves if we accept the concept that survival in a meaningful world is an immediate goal for education. One of these is a reinterpretation of what *constitutes* "survival behaviors." The other is an educational reformation which will not only permit but which will begin to *ensure* that children and youth in our schools put together valid "behavioral survival kits." Such kits will help them not only to make it into the next century but, in the process, to begin to recast the world so that it promises to remain a nutritive bioenvironment suitable for mankind to inhabit. Let us look first at survival behavior.

From earliest times, the notion of survival was associated with attaining and staying at the apex of a socioeconomic pyramid. At least until the nineteenth century, about 15 percent of Western Europe's population—aristocrats, soldiers, ecclesiastics, scholars—was supported by the laborers, agrarians, and artisans making up the other 85 percent. Man fought like Duke William at Hastings to get to the top of the pile and schemed like King John at Runnymede to stay there. Indeed, through the ages, history has defined the one who survives as "successful" and has bestowed its worldly favors on those caesars who proved to have the highest "survival quotients" in life's arenas!

In the past century, however, science, technology, and democracy have combined to invert the human pyramid. Today in the United States, no more than 7 percent of the population is needed on our mechanized farms to produce food for the remaining 93 percent. Theoretically, one-third of our adults, by 1985, would not even need to be productive workers. The remaining two-thirds of the U.S. population doubtless could meet not only their own material needs but those of tens of millions of others who would produce nothing. This is a projection of a repugnant possibility, however, and not a prophecy!

Despite the reversal of our human pyramid, a 50,000-year interval of deep-rooted survival behavior is not quickly forgotten. For the most part, society and its schools have both failed to teach and failed to understand that man is becoming more capable of surviving by living *with* his fellows rather than by living *on* his fellows. Conjecture clearly suggests that there is not only "room at the *top*" but room *everywhere* for self-realization and for a better life for all in the inverted social pyramid of the present century *if we can discipline ourselves to make the needed "survival decisions."* To put it bluntly, a 180-degree reversal is needed in the traditional concept of "get-ahead behavior" that man has learned to accept during the past 500 centuries. We now need to learn how to stop behaving like troglodytes in trousers and take the steps that lead from being the scattered members of insecure tribes to becoming a secure mankind.

NEW PURPOSE AS A SOURCE OF DIRECTION FOR EDUCATIONAL CHANGE

Educational reforms of a sweeping and significant nature rarely have come about through the action of the schools in and of themselves. Educational practice tends to reflect what a majority or at least a plurality of society chooses to support in the classroom. Under such circumstances it seems reasonable to argue that *society itself must make itself accountable* for changes that are needed in the fabric of teaching and learning in order to bring us closer to a new central purpose for education.

Below is a sample of the kind of neglected or minimized learnings that a society interested in the survival and in the physical and psychological health of the children and youth should mandate that its schools recognize:

1. that we need to begin to lead less wasteful, extravagant lives, to do with less, and to rediscover enjoyment in simpler activites, objects, and pleasures so that our posterity will not live a marginal existence in a world stripped half-naked of its inheritance;

2. that the despoilation of our forests and the pillage of our pure air and clean water shall cease along with the poorly managed exploitation of fuels, fertile soils, and metals. Such abuses must be terminated by group consensus and by the legislation to which it leads;

3. that no one has the right to befoul or poison the earth with chemicals or radiocative wastes or poorly removed sewage and garbage;

4. that unless we exercise prudence and personal responsibility, we will suffer badly from the malignant consequences of changes that affect man's relationships with his environment, as in faulty city planning, random dam building, or unwise land use;

5. that there is a need to understand the immediate danger of irresponsible and uncontrolled human breeding as the world's population builds up toward the 4,000,000,000 mark;

6. that the folly of conflict is becoming more and more incongruous in a world grown capable of self-destruction;

7. that mass media need to become more positive agents for reinforcing the educational guidance of the young, for producing less misleading advertising, for more thoughtful and less strident news, and for a more accurate and dignified portrayal of life in the global village;

8. that we must learn to be more personally responsible for the participation and earned support that are needed to ensure an

increase in the number of able, dedicated public servants in elective and appointive governmental offices.

THE DEEPER MEANING OF "RELEVANCE"

What we mean by "relevance" in education is implicit in the previous eight points. "Relevance" is more than teaching subject matter and providing experiences that the young say they find immediately meaningful, more interesting, and more useful to them. A relevant education, an education for survival, is one which introduces children and youth to participation in the tasks that they and adults confront together in the real world of the 1970s.

Furthermore, if we are to make rapid progress toward the successful attainment of a new central purpose for education, society must not only encourage but *require* that the schools work to produce a generation of hardheaded young people committed to survival yet remembering the meaning of compassion; persons who have been taught the *Realpolitik* of life with honesty but who are nonetheless untainted by cynicism because they believe that it is not yet too late to cope with man's threat to himself.

THE FIRST STEP IN REFORMATION

Making a beginning in reform is not up to "society" as an abstract entity but to each of us as the individuals who make up society. It is through a new sense of imprescriptible personal responsibility that we can dispel the threatening twilight that recently has shadowed our goals.

In the process of creating a more benign environment, some of our sensate pleasures and much of our conspicuous consumption must diminish. Also, today's thoughtless waste of human and material resources must first be decreased and then ended as quickly as possible. In the process, our lives will perforce become not only simpler and less hedonistic; they will become more people-centered and less thing-centered. This necessary redirection can bring us far more gain than loss. The satisfactions of 40 or 50 years ago were not necessarily less warm or less desirable because feet, bicycles, or street cars transported an older generation to shops, schools, or theatres!

Furthermore, the short and long range changes that an endangered world requires for its future well-being should also involve fewer tensions, less erosive competition, and a clearer, more relaxing perspective with regard to what is most worth doing and most worth having.

A CONCLUDING CONJECTURE

Assuming we do avoid extinction, there would seem to be two levels or kinds of survival for man: as a biological *species* and as *humans*. The eight survival learnings itemized here should help to ensure that the species is around for some time to come. If nothing else, sheer panic seems likely soon to motivate us to diminish the interrelated problems of ecology, of hunger, of waste, and of conflict.

To survive in a truly *human* context rather than a merely biological one is something else! Here we come to a more subtle aspect of a "survival kit" for young learners. Our rediscovery of purpose and of personal responsibility for the social and educational reforms that are prerequisite to physical survival is but one side of the coin.

There is the concomitant task of helping the young of each generation to discover for themselves a moral, aesthetic, intellectual, and scientific heritage that they see cause for making a part of themselves. Does it not then seem reasonable that our success in guiding this freshening, continuing rediscovery by the young of *what makes us human* is what gives the real meaning to "education for survival"?

And may one not rightly conjecture that as a society-of-the-individually-responsible accepts this task, it simultaneously could become its own best hope for survival through the rediscovery of sustaining purpose in education?

The Necessity for Every School-Age Child to be Educated

Stephen P. Hencley and Michael J. Parsons

Is there really a need for every child to be educated? Why should school-age children go to school? What is the future of the public schools? Honest answers to questions like these require more attention than they would have twenty, and even ten, years ago. For recently the legitimacy of the public school has been challenged with a seriousness that has not occurred since they were first instituted.

The story of the American public school in the first half of this century, as every schoolman knows, is a story of triumph. The public school promoted democracy, improved individuals, and was good for business besides. If this was not wholly and always true, at least it was widely believed to be true! This belief was seldom debated, though often

From Stephen P. Hencley and Michael J. Parsons, "The Necessity for Every School-Age Child To Be Educated," *High School Journal 54* (February 1791): 321–30. Reprinted by permission of the authors and the University of North Carolina Press.

proclaimed. Everyone, it seemed, had faith in the public school system—employers, parents, citizens, educators, and even the students.[1]

Unfortunately, this is no longer the case. There is now a widespread and rather outspoken feeling that attendance at a public school is no longer necessarily a benefit, and an even more widely diffused sense of dissatisfaction among students, parents, and citizens. Of course, every teacher today will be familiar with the virtually new genre of school protest literature associated with names like John Holt, Edgar Friedenberg, and Paul Goodman. The development of the movement toward national assessment is symptomatic.

The sixties have also witnessed the development of a number of alternatives to the public school, and the serious advocacy of many more. A number of large industrial corporations have begun to set up their own schools—for example, the Singer Company in New Jersey. Companies such as Westinghouse and General Learning have begun to provide teaching on contract on a large scale. There has been a large swing to private schooling in the South because of desegregation. At the opposite end of the political spectrum is the enormous and accelerating growth of the Free Schools movement. Educational and training models provided by the Job Corps, Peace Corps, Neighborhood Youth Corps, even the Army, are being considered with increasing seriousness. And men as far apart politically as Kenneth Clark, the activist black psychologist, and Milton Friedman, the Goldwater economist, have advocated the deliberate promotion of further alternatives, such as parent- or trade union-run schools. Proposals to provide parents with vouchers so that they may seek and purchase educational opportunities of their own choosing for their children are further indications of malaise in the public school system.

What should we make of all this? Certainly we should not conclude that the public schools have failed, nor that they are less worthy of our energy and commitment than before. But, equally, we cannot ignore the fact that the questions asked at the beginning of this paper have become genuinely open issues for the first time in this century. Serious and open-minded proposals and formulations are much needed.

For this purpose we shall reformulate our opening questions, and ask instead: What are the reasons why all children should be educated? What goals should education seek? And, are these reasons and goals sufficient for compelling all children to go to school?

THE GOALS OF EDUCATION

Let us begin by summarizing the commonly accepted goals for public education during the last one hundred years. They might be divided for brevity into four major kinds, which we will call personal, productive, social, and intellectual. In addition, each was regarded as offering advantage both to the individual and to society at the same time. One might portray this in a chart such as the one shown which indicates that eight cells are generated for discussion purposes, though not every cell will be considered in the discussion to follow.

	1 Advantages to Individuals	2 Advantages to Society
1. Personal	A	E
2. Productive	B	F
3. Social	C	G
4. Intellectual	D	H

The personal goals of education rest simply on the notion that education promotes both personal development and individual self-fulfillment. These are among the simplest and most important goal statements to be made about education. They provide one avenue of justification for schools—especially if there is confidence that schools are paying off handsomely in goal achievement. Until recently, there has been little questioning of the importance of the school's contribution to the personal development of learners in terms of the following basic dimensions: (a) physical (bodily health and development), (b) emotional (mental health and stability), (c) ethical (moral integrity), and (d) aesthetic (cultural and leisure pursuits). Until the last decade, most Americans believed that the schools were doing well in promoting personal development and individual self-fulfillment for all children—regardless of social class, color, and individual abilities.

/ The idea behind the productive goals of schooling is that universal education is necessary to ensure a working population with the skills and understanding necessary for a growth economy fueled by constant technological advance. The level of these skills and understandings has constantly risen, until we are told that it will not be long before training and retraining will be a lifelong need for many people. One should notice that, despite the universal faith in the public schools already alluded to, it was not important until recently that everyone should finish high school. Society invented the "dropout problem" sometime in the fifties, when it became unlikely that a dropout could be reasonably employed throughout his lifetime. And, curiously, the development of facilities for lifelong education may relieve this situation again, as an early dropout will be able to pick up his education later in life as he sees the need. It seems that the economic need for universal education will in the future be as much a matter of learning to consume wisely as of learning to produce efficiently. This will be for the health both of society and the individual.

The importance of careful planning (and clarity in relation to productive goals in education) in periods of rapid transition and change were highlighted several years ago by Michael:

The long-range stability of the social system depends on a population of young people properly educated to enter the adult world of tasks and attitudes. Once, the pace of change was slow enough to permit a comfortable margin of compatibility between the adult world and the one children were trained to expect. This compatibility no longer exists. Now we have to ask: What should be the education of a population more and more enveloped in cybernation? What are the appropriate attitudes toward and training for participation in government, the use of leisure, standards of consumption, particular occupations?[2]

The social goals of education are more complex. Generally speaking, schools have delineated learnings related to social goals in terms of four basic dimensions: (a) man-to-man relationships (cooperation), (b) man-to-state relationships (civic rights and duties), (c) man-to-country relationships (loyalty and patriotism), and (d) man-to-world relationships (inter-relationships of peoples).[3] Moreover, it has always been assumed that universal education, especially in the public school, would promote democracy in a great variety of ways. Thus it would tend to provide an intelligent electorate, able to make more objective choices at the polls; it would give everyone more of an equal chance economically, and so promote social mobility; it would foster the arts and promote a healthy popular culture; and it would ensure common understandings by mixing the classes. At least this latter, it will be noticed, could only be done by the public schools, and it remains one of the strongest arguments public schoolmen can urge against the free schools. Nevertheless, if we cast a critical eye over these items and bear in mind the typical developments of the sixties, we find ourselves in doubt whether the schools have succeeded with any of these items. More on this later.

In addition to the above social goals, it is also well to note the unifying function of the school, promoting an awareness and love of America (especially among the immigrant groups early in the century). Thus the public schools taught patriotism and were an essential part of the "melting pot." To these has been added (from the fifties on) the notion that the schools should provide a supply of scientists and technological experts for the national defense effort, and later for the national economic competition with Russia. Today we are all familiar with the language of the National Defense Education Act.

The last comment above leads us naturally to the fourth set of educational goal dimensions: Those encompassing the intellectual domain. Among the important outcomes sought by schools in this area are the following: (a) possession of knowledge (a fund of information and concepts), (b) communication of knowledge (skill to acquire and transmit), (c) creation of knowledge (discrimination and imagination), (d) desire for knowledge (a love of learning). Recent developments cited earlier (the contract system, the voucher system, training of dropouts, etc.) tend to indicate a measure of dissatisfaction with schooling outcomes even in this (the most important?) area of learning outcomes associated with public education.

These are, according to our categorization, the four kinds of goal areas which have been variously stated and lengthily elaborated in many different ways. They are all reasons for advocating the education of all school-age children, and some of them (especially in category three) are also reasons for wanting that education to take place in the public schools. As we have said, it was not usual to make this distinction earlier in the century, since it was widely assumed that, if education was to be supported, it would best be in the public schools. This faith has now weakened and the position today needs to be supported by rational argument if it is to be maintained.

CONTEMPORARY SEARCH FOR GOALS

Another way of looking at the goals enumerated above is to think of them as statements of ideals for the public school system. That is to say, it was probably never supposed that they were to be perfectly achieved; rather they represent tendencies that the schools should try to promote, and are accepted as goals or guides as long as they seem both plausible and worthwhile. In the United States they have long seemed both plausible and worthwhile. They have constituted in effect the core of the philosophy of the public schools in this century. The question that our present social situation raises is this: Which of these qualities have these goals lost in part—plausibility or attractiveness?

The optimistic answer is the first—that the present dissatisfaction with the public schools is due to a sense that these goals, though valuable, are not being met in sufficient degree. This is optimistic because the problem is then largely one of finding better ways of meeting them, and the alternatives springing up can be construed as diverse experiments from which the public schools can learn. The pessimistic answer is that the traditional goals of schooling outlined above have lost their attractiveness and that the alternatives are really setting themselves quite different goals. This is pessimistic because we know that in the present political atmosphere the chances of reaching consensus about traditional old values, or emerging new ones, are small. The most plausible answer, in our judgment, is a mixture of the two, but heavily stressing the first. We think that, although some groups in some places are rejecting some of these goals, most current dissatisfaction with the public schools springs from a sense that they are not being successful in terms of these goals. This is in one sense a healthy sign, since it implies a reaffirmation of the goals, though *not* of the public schools.

If one puts this in terms of systems analysis, one might say that we have increasingly held up our products against the statements of objectives, and found serious discrepancies. This has, for most people, cast doubt on the means and processes (i.e., the typical public school procedures) rather than on the objectives. There is an increasing clamor that we take our traditional objectives more seriously, by questioning our traditional methods—a position which, it will be seen, is essentially conservative in the best sense. The question then becomes our second: Are there good reasons for supposing that the public schools can provide that education for the majority of our youth? Again, on this question we will advance some reasons for cautious optimism.

Before doing this, however, we must offer some justification for our optimism with regard to the first question. This can only be brief, but we hope it will be suggestive. With regard to our third category of aims, for example, there has, it is true, been some outright rejection of the use of the schools as instruments of the Cold War or for economic competition. This is especially true of college students. At the same time, however, conceptions of what the national goals are have been changing at all levels; and, though the debate continues, one may reasonably claim today that it is as much in the national interest to work for international peace as it is to prepare for war, as much to help wipe out poverty as it is to enlarge the Gross National Product. And, one is tempted to add, the schools have probably done as much with the former of these pairs as with the latter. The schools, in other words, have in general been moderately flexible in interpreting these objectives, enough not to have alienated large numbers in this area.

Consider also category two where again the question of flexibility of interpretation arises. Increasingly, as we have said, the pressure has been rising to get more schooling so as to have a better job. As this pressure has increased, so has the reaction to it, a reaction which might be interpreted as an outright rejection of this set of economic motives, springing from a sense that categories one and two are not truly compatible. One of the assumptions of the Public School Movement[4] was that these four kinds of goals were compatible with each other, and were even complementary. This is best spelled out and justified in the work of John Dewey. Today that happy conjunction seems, to some, to have fallen apart. Thus, the Organization Man does not seem a good model for the self-actualizing person, any more than the work of Madison Avenue seems likely directly to further a democratic society. In the same way, given the economic motive for grading and the way schools have of mirroring the important features of society, the achievement of good grades in school is no longer a necessary sign of significant learning. But, of course, this is not the whole story. The Organization Man has been the target of many attacks. The artificiality of his reward system has been mirrored in the artificiality of the school grade system, but at the same time there have been numerous attempts to revitalize or remove the grading system. This indefinitely stratified status system has been copied in complex tracking and streaming systems and in the peer group structures of high schools, but there are also movements that cut across this. The same may be said of the impersonal, secondary group behavior (appropriate to bureaucracies) that our high schools have been teaching. The schools have been at least as flexible as the larger society in interpreting economic and productive goals, and they cannot easily be blamed for being no more decisive. Moreover, as the productive aspect of the economy begins to require a lifelong education, the severity of the pressure to graduate from high-school may relax. One can hardly doubt that this will be to the schools' advantage.

One area where our third category of traditional aims of the schools seems to have been challenged is in relation to minority groups. The traditional thought seems to have been to promote democracy by assimilation, and to destroy diversity of people. The schools, for example, have made deliberate efforts to foster English instead of the native tongues of Spanish-Americans, Indian-Americans, French-Americans, Chinese-Americans, and so forth. Of course, the policy of the melting pot has now been openly rejected by many groups (notably including rednecks, and many suburban white parents and some of the minority groups themselves). But this is also true of many school men and even schools. The debate between integrationists and separatists continues both within and without the schools, and here again the public schools seem capable of reinterpreting the notion of democracy to include diversity of culture and language, and perhaps even of class. What this amounts to is that the country as a whole is debating these issues and values, and that the schools also are, generally, uncertain. But they do not appear to be inflexibly wedded to one set of interpretations, as they might have been.

CAN THE PUBLIC SCHOOLS RESPOND?

So, much as an indication of what is meant by the claim that the traditional goals of education are being reinterpreted rather than rejected, we pass to the question whether it is plausible to suppose that the public schools will be able to meet these goals, however interpreted. We start by noticing that for many it is not clear that the public schools are any longer actually promoting traditional American ideals of democracy. The various minority separatist movements are fueled by our failure to achieve a meaningful integration in the schools, and in society in general.

To many, the schools appear to have been perpetuating class and ethnic barriers, and we are only slowly coming to understand the mechanisms involved in this. The curriculum, for example, has been heavily dominated by white middle-class concerns, and needs heavy injections of bicultural materials such as Black history, Spanish language, Indian cultures, etc., if it is not to disadvantage every one but the white middle class. Again, concepts of the neighborhood and of local control seem increasingly to separate rather than to mix different classes and ethnic groups as the differences between the suburb and the inner city grow. Equally, the doctrine of local tax support has the effect of maintaining the gap between rich and poor school systems. In like manner, it may be questioned whether the public schools really promote the development of an informed, critically-minded, citizenry. With the rise of the mass media, manipulative psychology, and the consumer society, political elections look more (and not less) like popularity contests. Authority patterns in the schools have tended to produce conformists. Often, teaching methods have produced acceptance rather than critical questioning. School peer groups have been a powerful influence in promoting uncritical consumer-mindedness, and so on.

But as one mentions these various points, it is clear that a great deal is already happening in the public schools to remedy them, and the vigor of the public schools is displayed in the great variety of experiments currently going on along these lines. Tendencies here that are relevant include the nongraded school, the individualization of teaching, the use of new media, T-grouping, self-evaluation, team-teaching, increasing involvement of the school with the community and vice versa, and accountability procedures. All of these tend to make the achievement of self-actualization goals possible while promoting both social and national interests. For, in the long run, it is no more possible than in the days of John Dewey to regard these various categories of goals as normally in conflict. Only specific and too narrow interpretations of them can be incompatible, for it cannot be in the national interest to have anyone less skilled or competent than he might be since the economy needs more and more highly developed skills. For parallel reasons, the social and political scenes need more self-actualizing, non-neurotic, critically-minded citizens. The actual achievement of this harmony involves not only reconceptualizing theory, but the successful establishment of school practices such as these. We do not doubt that some combination or variation of practices like these will eventually come to be accepted as the norm in the public schools. The questions seem rather to be, exactly what combination or variation, and when?

Here again, we find ground for optimism, especially in the conception of educational change as consisting of the supplanting of one normative model by another.[5] Educational change is often thought of as a gradual, evolutionary process of slow adaptation. It is more plausible, however, to see it as a process in which a model of educational practice dominates the schools for a while and is then supplanted by another with relative suddenness. During the reign of such a model, it provides a framework for thinking about methods in the fields, set limits to change within it, and relies on a number of unspoken assumptions. The model that has been reigning for the most part of this century is one where one teacher is assigned to a classroom, sets the goals within it, performs the evaluations, and relies heavily on talk and books.

We have been discussing some of the assumptions that this model relies on, though there are many more specific ones that do not relate directly to goals. The continued dominance of such a model obviously depends on a widespread confidence in it, which our model has now clearly lost. It will not be decisively replaced, however, until its successor has emerged with sufficient definition and promise to capture the imagination of large numbers of educators. This has not yet happened. The present is a kind of interregnum, in which we may expect a great deal of experimentation, dissatisfaction and even defection, while the old model remains the basis of practice in many places. Yet when the new model emerges (as it surely must do) promising to fulfill our previous goals in the new conditions, it may rally support with surprising speed. This is a hopeful theory, in that it explains the present conjunction of growing dissatisfaction and apparent lack of solutions as a normal, if not necessary, part of the process of educational change.

To sum up our discussion, we have said that perhaps more than ever, there is reason for all children to be educated in America today, and that this need can be elaborated in terms of personal, productive, social, and intellectual benefits. These terms are largely still the traditional ones in which the public schools have set their goals. It is more doubtful that the public schools are presently doing well in terms of these goals, and this explains much of the current dissatisfaction with them. At the same time, we have given some indication of reasons for believing that the public system can be more successful, if it is willing to change enough. The threat of defection, therefore, should be seen more as a challenge than a threat. Numerous responses have been made already to this challenge, and the continuing vigor of the public school system is evident in them. Alternatives have been, and will be, increasingly offered and suggested, but we think there is reason for confidence in the long run in our public school system.

NOTES

[1] Historians of education have begun to re-evaluate these beliefs. *See,* for example: Henry Parkinson, *The Imperfect Panacea, American Faith in Education, 1865-1965* (New York: Random House, 1968).

[2] Donald N. Michael, *Cybernation: The Silent Conquest* (Santa Barbara, California: Center for the Study of Democratic Institutions, 1962), p. 41.

[3] Further research elaboration of dimensions discussed in this article may be found in Lawrence Downey, *The Task of Public Education* (Chicago: Midwest Administration Center, 1960).

[4] *See* James E. McClellan, *Toward an Effective Critique of American Education* (New York: Lippincott, 1968), ch. 1.

[5] This conception derives from T. S. Kuhn's work in the history of science: *The Structure of Scientific Revolutions* (Chicago: University of Chicago Press, 1962), and is more fully spelled out in Ch. 3 of Hencley, S. P., McCleary, L. E., and McGrath, J. H.: *The Elementary School Principalship* (New York: Dodd, Mead, 1970).

Public Schools of Choice and the Plurality of Publics

Mario D. Fantini

The ills of our public schools are now common knowledge. Why they are in trouble is still a matter of debate and inquiry. The major attempts of the 1950s and 1960s for educational reform—desegregation and compensa-

From Mario D. Fantini, "Public Schools of Choice and the Plurality of Publics," *Educational Leadership* 28 (March 1971): 585-91. Reprinted by permission of the Association for Supervision and Curriculum Development and the author. Copyright©1971 by the Association for Supervision and Curriculum Development.

tory education—have had disappointing results, while problems continue at an accelerated rate, for example: absenteeism, dropouts, academic retardation, drug addiction, unrest, and defeated school bond issues. Further, the latest batch of public school critics has projected an almost macabre tone to the public schools: *Our Children Are Dying, Death at an Early Age, Murder in the Classroom, The Classroom Disaster.* While it is imperative that we emphasize the critical nature of the educational problem, to continue lashing out at the public schools at this time serves little useful purpose, resulting mainly in ill feelings from those trying to make schools work.

We should all realize that education in America is organic to individual, group, and societal *survival.* We have entered the Age of Education. Modern education should be instrumentally tied to the needs of society, of groups, and of individuals, and to the encompassing growth and development of all of these. An obsolete educational institution handicaps *all* learners, teachers, administrators, communities, and the larger society. Thus, we are all disadvantaged.

DIVERSITY IS IMPORTANT

In a pluralistic society, diversity is an important value that our educational institutions should express. Yet, our public schools as presently structured cannot meet the growing demands that are being thrust upon them from virtually every sector of our society. Students are demanding that schools become relevant to them and help close the generation gap. Minority parents are demanding a quality of education that guarantees equality of educational performance. Business and industry are increasingly demanding an educational product who is prepared for a technological, service-oriented economy.

We are asking the schools to deal with such societal problems as poverty, alienation, delinquency, drug addiction, pollution, and racism. The result is that, while these demands are legitimate, the schools cannot as presently structured satisfy them. The consequences to our public system of education are loss of confidence, frustration, disconnection, and retaliation by the consumer. It is little wonder that President Nixon started his Education Message of March 3, 1970, with: "American education is in urgent need of reform."

In our society when a major societal institution such as the school is in need of basic reform, the public *participates* in the process. Participation is the heart of an open political system. Thus far, the push for increased participation has come from our urban centers, through school governance patterns such as decentralization and community control. These patterns appeal strongly to minorities that have been shortchanged through poor education: Black, Chicano, Puerto Rican, etc.

Participation under decentralization can mean that parents and other citizens *share* educational decision making with professionals, at the local level and with central school authority. Participation under decentralization is limited for each citizen to voting *for* representatives *to* a local school board. The locally elected board then is responsible for trying to *represent* the interests of those who voted for him. Decentralization can mean a federation of local school boards, each with a limited authority over part of the total school system.

Participation under community control shifts the bulk of authority to a local board elected by the community. In an extreme form of decentralization, a local subdistrict may actually *secede* from the rest of the school system to assume an independent status with the state department of education. Again, participation in direct decision making for *each* citizen is limited to voting for a representative in the local election.

We need a process today in which *each* user of our public schools can make a decision concerning the type of education which makes the most sense for *him. This means giving parents, students, teachers, and administrators a direct voice in educational decision making.* Parents, teachers, students, and school administrators—those closest to the learning front—have traditionally been those farthest from participation in educational decision making. We are all familiar with the "top-down" flow of authority which characterizes our educational institutions, in which those farthest from the learner are making decisions about his nature and nurture.

The rise of the parties closest to the action—teachers, parents, and students—during the sixties has signaled the beginning of a new flow of decision making from the "bottom-up."

However, the plurality of publics which now relate to the school in direct, vested-interest ways makes the school an arena for power politics. That is, since each public—teachers, parents, and students—wants the school to be responsive to its own concerns and needs, each has had to organize politically in order to have its interests realized.

Competing for power in order to meet group needs can result and, indeed, has resulted in direct confrontation among the "new" publics. We are witnessing collision between parents and teachers—between students and teachers. Ironically, parties who should be natural allies have been trapped into conflict because the current institutional arrangements literally compel this type of behavior. Parents have blamed teachers for the poor quality of education and for the high costs of schooling—teachers have blamed parents for being apathetic and unreasonable about holding teachers accountable without realizing that teachers themselves are constrained by the institution.

The point is that the key publics are blaming one another and losing track of the real "enemy"—the outdated nature of the institution we call the school. The parties need to have access to a new form of participation during this period of school reform if we are to avoid the group power game in which we are presently engaged. (How can we enter a new stage of participation in which the demands and the rights of the various publics are protected? What is the direction of reform? It is to these basic questions that we now turn.)

THE NEW REFORM EFFORTS

The major task before school reformers now is to offer constructive suggestions and proposals, ones which provide some hope, which are attainable, and which affect the lives of many children, not just a few. What will be the new reform efforts of the seventies? Two movements which started at the tail end of the sixties offer us some signs for the seventies.

The first of these is the movement of alternative schools *outside* the public school system. These new schools have increased in number over the past few years as conditions in *urban* public schools—especially urban—continue to decline. It is reform by retreating from public schools into the realm of private schools. New schools took various forms: prep-academic, mini, so-called "open" or free schools (in contrast with "closed" public schools), and others.

The second movement is an attempt to reach the educational consumer directly through a tuition voucher which can be used to purchase quality education. This latter form attempts to generate needed change by altering the economic structure of American education, that is, by increasing the power of the educational consumer to purchase different forms of education in a type of free market enterprise.

Both these movements are extremely significant, not so much for what they offer as programs, but for what they reveal about the fundamental nature of the reform problem and the desperation stage that many of our educational consumers have reached. Alternative schools have pointed out that educational options to conventional public schooling exist and can be vastly superior. However, this movement suffers from the fiscal constraints which victimize new schools. Most new schools have good ideas but find it difficult to "stay alive" financially without resorting to high tuitions (thereby denying many citizens access to this alternative). The tuition voucher approach points out the need for providing the educational consumer with opportunities to make more educational choices.

Together they reveal a need for a new political-economic educational system—that is, a participatory-governance system on the one hand, and a new *supply* and *demand* system on the other. In one sense, the alternative new schools movement has generated attention on the *supply* side of the new economic educational system and the tuition movement has stimulated development on the *demand* side. Each, however, is now largely separated from the other and from the public school system which they usually view as the "enemy."

What is needed is to bring these two developments—supply and demand—and individual decision making into the context of *public schools* where the majority of students are enrolled. What we propose is a new system of Public Schools of Choice. Before outlining our conception of Public Schools of Choice, we should emphasize more fully the shortcomings of dealing with just the demand side of the educational supply and demand question.

Attempts to change the realm of demand do not guarantee that the supply side will also change. In fact, what can happen is that the supply which exists can be further tightened, that is, current alternatives can be strengthened, with marginal increases in new alternatives (and these often are reflected in a compromise with quality).

Those who have reviewed attempts to change the demand structure of other institutions—say health and higher education—have made the assessments that have important implications for us at this time. Medicaid, for example, is a voucher system which provides increased medical purchasing power for the citizen. This health system has not affected the supply system appreciably. The consumer has increased opportunity to purchase what exists. In the case of health services, therefore, some would agree that the real services for the consumer have not been ignored—the service problem being the one that is most crucial to patient welfare.

Another attempt to influence the demand market was the GI Bill which provided opportunities for millions of returning servicemen to enter higher education. This demand structure connected many educational consumers with the *existing* supply of colleges and universities. Many of these colleges were not relevant to the varying needs of the adult populations being served. Of course, we are all familiar with the "fly-by-night" suppliers who, seeking a "fast buck," provided mediocre services to the citizen.

In our opinion, the problem is *not* the *demand* but the *supply* system. Public schools already have a built-in demand system—a voucher system if you will—through taxation. Further, increasing numbers of parents and students are dissatisfied with the educational services being provided them, that is, with the supply system. The problem is to provide more alternatives for those dissatisfied educational customers who are demanding more choices, not to increase further the demand capability. As we have suggested, increasing the demand capacity does not necessarily guarantee a renewed supply capacity.

On the other hand, creating a new supply system outside the public school system in the long run accomplishes little. In this case, the supply system—new educational options—exists outside the demand structure of the masses who need these options and are requesting them most. Moreover, those leading the new school movement find themselves in continuous fiscal difficulty and must ultimately turn to public support.

The trick is to get a system of educational options with consumer choice to take place *inside* the public school system.

LESSONS FROM THE PAST

Certainly we now have a backlog of experience in dealing with public school improvement. It is now time for us to review the lessons of the past and apply them directly to the present.

From our perspective, the pertinent lessons from the past, including the voucher plan and alternative schools, are:

1. Any reform effort *cannot be of a superimposed variety,* that is, the days of a small group planning *for* or doing *to* others are fading out.

2. Reform considerations *must respect the rights of all concerned parties and must apply to everyone*—they cannot appear to serve the interests of one group only. Thus, for instance, if decentralization plans of urban school systems are interpreted to serve only minority communities, then the majority community may very well oppose such efforts. Similarly, if plans appear to favor professionals, then the community may be in opposition.

3. Any reform alternative *must demonstrate adherence to a comprehensive set of educational objectives*—not just particular ones. Proposals cannot, for example, emphasize only emotional growth at the expense of intellectual development. The converse is also true.

4. Reform proposals *cannot substantially increase the per-student expenditure* from that of established programs. To advance an idea which doubles or triples the budget will at best place the proposal in the ideal-but-not-practical category. Further, an important factor for reformers to bear in mind is that the new arena will deal with wiser use of *old* money, not the quest for add-on money.

5. Programs *cannot advocate any form of exclusivity*—racial, religious, or economic. Solutions cannot deny equal access to any particular individual or group.

6. *There is no single model answer,* no blanket panacea to the educational problem. Attempts at uniform solutions are almost never successful.

7. *The process of change must be democratic and maximize individual decision making.* Participation by the individual in the decisions which affect his life is basic to comprehensive support.

The above "learnings" become not only the criteria for developing any new proposal, they are the ground rules for the operation of any new plan. Using them, we can see, for example, how such current proposals as big city decentralization and community control are in trouble. Both these reform efforts collide with the criteria. Consequently, unless new reform alternatives can adhere to these criteria, there is no reason to assume that these will be any more successful.

At present, those who aspire to influence the schools must of necessity resort to the political process based on representative government, that is, officials elected or selected to govern the local schools. While such tactics as decentralization and community control do increase the voice of communities in educational affiars, they do not guarantee that *each* parent, student, or teacher can make decisions, or indeed have options. Further, the decisions reached by the elected representatives usually do not reflect the desires of important segments of their constituency.

PUBLIC SCHOOLS OF CHOICE

A Public Schools of Choice model provides the opportunity and the means for developing alternative education forms within the framework of the public educational system. Let us illustrate: one set of agreed-upon educational objectives has to do with mastery of the basic skills and academic proficiency in history, reading, writing, and mathematics. The chief means for achieving these objectives is the standard age-grade mode presently offered in public schools. We are familiar with the normal sequences of separate grades one through twelve. Students who do not meet their expected grade "norm" are usually forced to keep "down" with the others.

One option to the age-graded system is the ungraded, continuous progress approach. In this scheme, the learner proceeds at his own rate, and there are no age grades as such. How can this option be made available to the parents and teachers who might be interested? The ungraded alternative may be known only by *one* of the parties of interest, the professionals.

Awareness of such alternatives is achieved by reading professional publications or attending professional conferences. These are more available to administrators than to teachers. Administrators have more time to pursue professional activities. Students and parents usually have no access to professional information. Consequently, those farthest from the action are most knowledgeable about alternatives. Teachers, students, and parents, closest to the action, are the least likely to be aware of existing alternatives.

Providing information about alternatives to all concerned must be a key function in public school systems of choice. Hence, based on sufficient information, teachers, parents, and students could make a thoughtful choice of continuing the present graded system or developing an ungraded system.

We now come to a critical aspect of our discussion. Suppose 10 percent of the parents, students, and teachers in a school wanted to explore an ungraded system. Under normal circumstances, the 90 percent would simply overrule the 10 percent. The 10 percent might possibly impose their will on the 90 percent by manipulating them, or, if influential, they might convince the board of education to make the change they desire. It is all-or-nothing for both sides. Imposition either way makes for much hostility and little good sense. All suffer since the discontented—whether parents, teachers, or students—will, even unwittingly, undermine the unity and harmony in the school. Under a Public Schools of Choice system, both can have their programs implemented. This point deserves further explanation.

Under the present structure a program develops when a new educational means or approach is "pushed" by a particular group or an influential administrator. If there is opposition to the new approach, a struggle develops. Someone must win; therefore, someone must lose. The idea we are proposing displaces this obsolete winner-take-all process. It channels energies aroused by conflicting views into the constructive action of building new educational possibilities side by side with the existing program. The choice process legitimizes various options, each geared to a common set of established objectives.

Further, alternative approaches need not take place at different schools. American education already has a broad, successful experience with "schools within a school." Consequently, if the ungraded approach has sufficient support, then those teachers, parents, and students in the school who have chosen this alternative would be free to develop a "nongraded school within a school."

Choice must be seen as a basic human right. Enabling people to make informed, intelligent choices must become a basic responsibility of school systems. What this free choice process does is to go beyond making choices legitimate; it succeeds in making them operationally possible. Also, each new approach becomes an opportunity for community learning. Those involved must decide whether it really is what they wanted. Those not involved may decide whether or not it would be better for their children. This learning would take place without stress or antagonism since no one can be imposed upon. This process is extremely important in terms of protecting the rights of people in our educational system.

ACCESS TO OPTIONS

Public Schools of Choice can only work when all interested parties have adequate access to educational options. Unless they are aware of the great variety of educational alternatives, they are left with only those few with which they are already familiar. Thus, they are very effectively forced to "play" by the ground rules established by the existing system. Hence, in a public school system based on choice, a key responsibility of the board of education and the central office staff is community education and information about educational possibilities. Since the system has freed them to act on their beliefs constructively, such information becomes vital without becoming disruptive. We would anticipate that the thirst for information would lead to innumerable meetings, small and large, informal and formal, of parents, teachers, and students, alone and together.

We hardly need stress the irreplaceable role of professional educators in developing alternatives. They have, and only they can really carry out, the responsibility for the substance of the curriculum. The choice of school, however, is another matter. Parents must be responsible for determining the kind of education they want for their children. They must be provided, therefore, with the opportunity and conditions to enable them to perform this crucial policy role. Consequently, a new standard of professional and lay cooperation would evolve. Under this model, parents, teachers, and students, aided by educational experts, could develop harmonious conceptions of quality education.

The schools we envision, then, could create and develop their own characteristics and styles. Some may ask, as examples, whether a Nazi School, or a school for blacks that advanced the notion that all white people were blonde-haired, blue-eyed devils and pigs, could exist within the framework of a public system of choice. Plainly, no. Our concept speaks to openness; it values diversity; it is nonexclusive; it embraces human growth and development and is unswerving in its recognition of individual worth. Within these bounds, however, is an infinite spectrum of alternative possibilities in creating new educational and learning forms.

Among the alternatives available are many which already have a substantial number of supporters. The following are only a few examples:

School #1. The concept and programs of the school are traditional. The school is graded and emphasizes the learning of basic skills—reading, writing, numbers, etc.—by cognition. The basic learning unit is the classroom and functions with one or two teachers, instructing and directing students at their various learning tasks. Students are encouraged to adjust to the school and its operational style. Students with recognized learning problems are referred to a variety of remedial and school support programs. The educational and fiscal policy for this school is determined by the central board of education.

School #2. This school is nontraditional and nongraded. In many ways it is very much like the British (Leicestershire) system. There are lots of constructional and manipulative materials in each area where students work and learn. The teacher acts as a facilitator—one who assists and guides rather than directs or instructs. Most student activity is in the form of different learning projects done individually and in small groups rather than all students doing the same thing at the same time. Many of the learning experiences and activities take place outside of the school building.

School #3. This school emphasizes learning by the vocational processes— doing and experiencing. The school defines its role as diagnostic and prescriptive. When the learner's talents are identified the school prescribes whatever experiences are necessary to develop and enhance them. This school encourages many styles of learning and teaching. Students may achieve equally through demonstration and manipulation of real objects as well as by verbal, written, or abstractive performances. All activity is specifically related to the work world.

School #4. This school is more technically oriented than the others in the district. It utilizes computers to help diagnose individual needs and abilities. Computer assisted instruction based on the diagnosis is subsequently provided both individually and in groups. The library is stocked with tape recording banks and "talking," "listening," and manipulative carrels that students can operate on their own. In addition, there are Nova-type video retrieval systems in which students and teachers can concentrate on specific problem areas. This school also has facilities to operate on closed circuit television.

School #5. This school is a total community school. It operates on a 12- to 14-hour basis at least six days a week throughout the year. It provides educational and other services for children as well as adults. Late afternoon activities are provided for children of varying ages from the neighborhood, and evening classes and activities are provided for adults. Services such as health, legal aid, and employment are available within the school facility. Paraprofessionals or community teachers are used in every phase of the regular school program. This school is governed by a community board which approves or hires the two chief administrators, one of whom is in charge of all other activities in the building. The school functions as a center for educational needs of all people in the neighborhood and community.

School #6. A Montessori school. Students move at their own pace and are largely self-directed. The learning areas are rich with materials and specialized learning instruments from which the students can select and choose as they wish. Although the teachers operate within a specific and defined methodology, they remain very much in the background, guiding students rather than directing them. Special emphasis is placed on the development of the five senses.

School #7. Patterned after the Multi-Culture School in San Francisco, the seventh school may have four or fine ethnic groups equally represented in the student body. Students spend part of each day in racially heterogeneous learning groups. In another part of the day, all students and teachers of the same ethnic background meet together. In these classes all learn their own culture, language, customs, history, and heritage. Several times each week members of one ethnic group share with the others some event or aspect of their cultural heritage that is important and educational. This school views diversity as a value. Its curriculum combines the affective and cognitive domains and is humanistically oriented. Much time is spent on questions of identity, connectedness, powerlessness, and interpersonal relationships. The school is run by a policy board made up of equal numbers of parents and teachers and is only tangentially responsible to a central board of education.

Distinctive educational options can exist within any *single* neighborhood or regional public school. The principle of providing parents, teachers, and students with a choice from among varying educational alternatives is feasible at the individual school. In fact, this may be the most realistic and pervasive approach, at first. For example, in early childhood a single school might offer as options: (a) an established kindergarten program; (b) a Montessori program; (c) a British Infant School program; (d) a Bereiter-Englemann program.

The high school could offer: (a) a prep "school"; (b) a community "school"; (c) a "school" without walls.

Again, parents, teachers, and students will have to "fully understand" each program.

Daily, fresh educational alternatives are offered to the public. Conferences on "new schools" are in constant session in one city or another. In
one instance, a conference was heralded as a "Festival of Alternatives in
Education." Some alternatives are certain to be transient flashes in the
pan. More seriously, if not tragically, many fine alternatives are likely to
be ignored because there exists no process for their orderly introduction or
testing by public school systems.

We think that a Public Schools of Choice system can assume this task
and contribute significantly to a process for renewing our public school
system without imposition on parents, teachers, or children. In making
their choice, these publics will accept the risks and the possibilities of their
dreams. Should it be any other way?

The Alternative

David Morse

A child is fastening words into a sculpture . . . a poem-tree. Others are
constructing an inflatable. Another group lounging on sofa cushions argues
the merits of adding tadpoles or watercress to the aquarium. At the
potter's wheel the potter's silent hands teach a child how to form the
shoulder of a vase: silence even while *Jesus Christ Superstar* issues from
the next room. "Shut the fucking door," one of the tadpole people yells,
and in a moment stalks over and slams it himself. Silence of the boxwood
stick pressing against the whirling clay, then the wet sponge: dull to shiny,
back to dull. The vase is severed neatly from the wheel, and the small
hands take over.

This is a "free school," or "alternative school." Alternative to the
monolith of public instruction. Springing up by the hundreds all over the
country. Where before only a handful existed, patterned mainly after
Summerhill, the number has doubled every year for the past three years,
until now free schools total roughly 1000 and the trend gives every
indication of continuing its phenomenal growth.

The rise of the free school closely parallels the proliferation of
"underground" media, chiefly in the form of magazines, newspapers and
films during the 'sixties, and now including local small-scale "block" radio
broadcasting and shoestring productions in "free" video aimed at breaking

From David Morse, "The Alternative," *Media and Methods* 7 (May 1971): 28–34.
Reprinted by permission of the author and the publisher.

the monopoly of public broadcasting—until now it is accurate to speak of "alternative media."

Not only do many of the observations offered in the following pages, concerned mainly with alternative schools, have clear application to alternative media, but finally the two movements can be seen evolving in a special dynamic relationship, which is central to the Alternative Culture growing piece-by-piece about our ears.

The free school is unique in the history of American education. For one thing it is not simply one more large-scale innovation sweeping the country (progressive education, tracking, flexible scheduling, etc.) but a complete turnabout from the whole trend of bigness. These are small do-it-yourself *non*institutions, brought into being by teachers and parents and sometimes by students themselves out of antipathy for the public schools and the hope of creating for themselves a meaningful learning environment on a people scale. Teachers are often dropouts from the straight system, working for subsistence salaries, with parents and college students volunteering. Classrooms are housed sometimes in storefronts, geodesic domes, or churches, or sometimes float "underground" from one meeting to another; or embark in fleets of VW buses. Sometimes students build their own schools.

"Curriculum" ranges vastly, from cybernetics to hassles with building inspectors, to organizing food co-ops. Junk cars, Zen gardens, goats and occasional VTR portapacks, serve as audiovisual aids. But "audiovisual" is too delimiting a term in this multisensory, "soft" environment. Words like "audiovisual" and "curriculum" imply the alienation which is parcel to the public schools and which the new schools are doing their best to tear out of.

This concern with wholeness and with the senses, along with the absence generally of "classes," places a different stress on media, if we consider that one of the chief uses of educational media traditionally has been to project a message to relatively large groups of people; also when we consider that Bigness in the marketing domain has produced software aimed toward passive children of conservative parents. But before examining these implications, a closer look at free schools is in order.

What is a free school?

Within a movement characterized by mind-boggling diversity there can be no really "typical" model. The term "free school" or "alternative school" has been used to refer to experiments as diverse as schools-without-walls, apprenticeship programs (such as Riverun, which describes itself as "a network of information and contacts with individuals, groups, organizations, and other less essential resources such as space and money"), to ethnic consciousness-raising trips for Blacks and Chicanos), and store-front drop-in centers such as Troutfishing in America, in Cambridge.

Despite this variety, a few characteristics are shared by most free schools. The point of listing them here is not to stereotype the movement but to acquaint the newcomer with some of its rough contours.

Generally, free schools are

—nonauthoritarian, libertarian, even democratic;
— "unstructured" in the sense of imposing minimal formal requirements, and in valuing non-directive behavior;
—concerned with unity of life, aesthetic, ethical, sensory experiences viewed as elements inseparable from the whole learning/life experience;
—politically radical, in the context of the dominant culture.

All the above characteristics are themselves interlocking parts of a whole—one quality implying or leading inevitably to the next. For example at the Sudbury Valley School in Framingham, Massachusetts, all students and staff get one vote each in the School Assembly, and award diplomas after a candidate has defended himself satisfactorily against attack in an open meeting. Presently the school is seeking accreditation to grant B.A. and Ph.D. degrees. Obviously this sort of continuum could not exist except in a nonauthoritarian context; nor can learning be nonauthoritarian where formal requirements are exacted and final judgments are imposed by the few. This commitment to democracy, in turn, is radical compared to those public schools which take pride in their non-authoritarian "atmosphere."

Other characteristics are more peripheral, but should be added. Free schools tend to be

— oriented toward ethical, social, aesthetic and various nonrationalistic concerns (not to be confused here with the "Humanities"), often at the expense of science, foreign languages and mathematics;
— attuned to the Earth—in the sense of land, ecology, cottage crafts, and also in the sense of the global concerns expressed by Buckminster Fuller and Marshall McLuhan and reflected in *The Whole Earth Catalog.*

The list could go on. It could include for instance the growing resolve within the movement to transcend the barriers separating school and community (See Jerry Friedberg's "Beyond Free Schools: Community," which has been reprinted widely); it could include the altruism which is no small part of free school thinking and which translated into cash, means tuitions are typically low and often assigned on a sliding scale according to ability to pay. (Tuitions range from $0-$1000; anything above that is generally considered a rip-off.) An inevitable postscript is that almost every one of these schools is struggling for its economic existence.

How much impact can we expect free schools to have on public education?

The numerical strength of the movement is difficult to assess, given the present ferment. *New Schools Exchange Newsletter* can speak with some authority, having served for nearly two years as the central clearing house for information on alternative schools. Its founder, Harvey Haber, last year estimated the number at 2000. But whether or not a school is "free" leaves obvious room for interpretation. Mike Rossman, also writing for the *Newsletter* (No. 52, "Projections on the New Schools Movement"), last January estimated the number of schools he considered to be "truly free, with no qualifications," at 500. Free schools defined in the broadest sense, including "those schools which would be rated 'progressive and liberative' through those which are radical," Rossman placed at 1,600. He estimates that by 1975 the rate of growth will have leveled off and there will exist some 25-30,000 free schools, comprised of 1,400,000 students.

Rossman's prediction is based, soberly enough, on the straight-line growth of the past two to three years. However, two factors could boost the gain even higher. One is the cumulative effect inherent in introducing choice, where before there was monopoly. The other is the effect of alternative media. Whether or not the actual numbers accelerate beyond the *Newsletter* projection, the leverage is such that the impact on public schools can be expected to exceed by far the numerical growth of the movement.

Implied in this leverage is a tenet which is central to the broader aims of the generation of 30-year-olds engaged in transforming the old culture—a point which is not always obvious to those outside the movement—that the intent is not to produce an experimental model for an educational elite to consider but to provide working "grassroots" alternatives to the existing institutions for individuals to resort to. The principle is profoundly egalitarian, even while favoring the middle class, because it takes responsibility out of the hands of professors and bureaucrats and places it in the hands of people functioning *as people.*

For this reason the alternative school concept can be threatening to those who have predicated their existence on paper. In his proposal to the Borough President of Manhattan, for instituting "Mini-Schools," Paul Goodman cites the objections to be encountered in any plan for decentralizing the schools.

First, the Public School administration does not intend to go largely out of business. Given its mentality, it must see any radical decentralization as impossible to administer and dangerous, for everything cannot be controlled. Some child is bound to break a leg and the insurance companies will not cover; some teenager is bound to be indiscreet and the *Daily News* will explode in headlines.

The United Federation of Teachers will find the proposal to be anathema because it devalues professional prerequisites and floods the schools with the unlicensed. Being mainly broken to the public school harness, most experienced teachers consider free and inventive teaching to be impossible.

Choice implies risk; and choice is the heart of the free school. As Ibsen's characters become real through their choices, so too does the student in the alternative school who is free to come up against his own limits—limits which George Dennison calls "the true edge of necessity," as opposed to the arbitrary rules imposed by an authority-figure. Student and teacher become real, when learning is seen as a continuum involving constant choice and in which "teacher" and "learner" are used to describe often momentary relationships between people, instead of rigid roles which must be filled at the cost of their mutual humanity.

The odds are against widespread public acceptance of an alternative which requires risk-taking on the one hand, and on the other faith in the fundamental goodness of people. Our present society tends to reject both, and nowhere is that rejection more blatant than in the public schools.

Nevertheless, a few responsive chords have been sounded recently within the public systems—in places where one would least expect it. In North Dakota, a large number of the public schools have been revamped along the Leicestershire model. In Vermont, the "Vermont Design for Education" sets forth a student-centered philosophy worthy of any free school. In Philadelphia, a running dialectic between public and private alternatives has generated a renaissance; now Connecticut is borrowing Philadelphia's Parkway program for application in Hartford, while Board of Ed funded "free schools" are springing up in Philadelphia.

The idea of public funds being used to support alternative schools was given impetus last fall at the White House Conference on Children, which entertained the recommendation that school systems hand over some of the schools and some of their budget to groups that want to run competing schools. At present one of the plans being considered at various levels is the so-called "Voucher System," which would allow parents to apply tax money in the form of a voucher toward tuition in a private school of their choice. Yet the racial and religious ramifications of such a plan will take time to be worked out.

Despite these hopeful overtures from the public sector, the preponderance of delays, the hassles of red tape, the dangers of co-option, have kept most founders of free schools clear of the funding arms of Government and foundations alike. (In order to have as little as possible to do with the restrictions laid on nonprofit corporations and schools, Troutfishing in America chose to incorporate as a store.) The strategy remains not to count on solutions from "higher up"; to go it alone.

Independence, however, is purchased only at great cost. Money remains an enormous problem.

Thus when we turn to educational media available commercially, we find severe strictures on what alternative schools can afford. This enforced frugality—in an affluent marketplace—imposes a special clarity in assigning needs, which on one level are simply the needs of schools at large: competently designed individual programs, especially in math and foreign languages; portable language labs with a pricetag people can afford; in science and social studies, materials which make the invisible world visible; accurate overviews. Most important, materials that respect the learner. This last point deserves special comment.

Too many audiovisual materials betray an underlying contempt for the audience. Too many films profane their topic, treating ecology, for example, as a catchword and in their hard-sell arrogance fail to comprehend the possibility that the learner already might feel a mystical connection with the earth, or that the viewer of a science film might tolerate the inclusion of political considerations, or might be aware of beauty *for its own sake* (and untrammeled by some imperious narrator delivering a half-megaton rap about the beauty of nature). Too many Black histories, however good some of them may be, conceal the paucity of people histories which acknowledge the contributions of all peoples in the world continuum and not merely the rise of the technocratic Caucasian. The same film catalogs that are blind to Fascism in Spain and South Africa treat Shakespeare externally, so that what you remember is the beard and the funny pantaloons. Why not a film of snippets of actors simply saying his lines fantastically well? Why not spaces for thought— silences/visuals/music—interspaced with the harder data?

Why not—in the manufacture of software—a little more love?

Other requirements of the new schools cannot be generalized. Because on another level, the alternative school uses media differently, both internally, as a direct learning-aid, and externally to link individual schools with the free school movement at large. This second function, too, differs radically from its counterpart—the traditional dialog between pedagogues contained in scholarly journals and annual professional conferences. The new communications are speeded up, "cooled" down. Conferences are called around a communal pot, often on a couple of months notice, and anybody is welcome. Written communications have seen the quarterly journals, with their one or two-year lag, give way to fast-breaking newsletters which combine the overview of Buckminster Fuller with the pragmatism and verbal alacrity of a floating crap game. Not only has the tempo quickened, but the direction has changed, becoming more reciprocal; a looping information-exchange.

Thus, shut out of the commercial market on economic grounds and at the same time searching for more authentic materials which reflect this faster, cooler, feedback-geared massage, the alternative schools have chosen to grow their own. Basically, this means tape: audio and video. In fact, the one hardware item which will tempt the most backwoods communal school into the cash economy is a portable videotape-recorder. Not only are the portapack VTRs adaptable to the varied terrain of a "soft" environment, but they provide access to the growing number of underground tape banks, and the chance to "loop" into the larger system.

Gene Youngblood, writing in a new magazine called *Print Project Amerika,* describes the excitement which has soared among video freaks during the past year:

In what is being called the Alternate Television Movement, an increasing number of young people around the world are doing just that, teaching themselves television; in Amsterdam, the Video Workshop; in London, TVX Video Co-op; in San Francisco, Ant Farm, Homeskin, the National Center for Experiments in Television, New People's Media Project; in Los Angeles, Nam June Paik's video lab at California Institute of the

Arts. The largest concentration of alternate television groups is in New York City. Recently the New York State Council on the Arts allocated $263,000 to the Jewish Museum to establish a Center for Decentralized Television—with enormous implications for the future of the movement. The funds were to be available to everyone working in alternate video in New York; a substantial portion, however, would be divided amongst the four major groups which constitute practically the whole movement—Raindance Corporation, Videofreex, People's Video Theatre, and Global Village.

Each group approaches decentralized alternate television in its own way, but all share a common technical base—portable half-inch videotape recording systems, of which Sony's AVC-3400 Videocorder popular. [sic] For $1500—that is, for less than a Volkswagen—one can purchase a complete audiovisual information system that is autonomous within itself, unlike film, which is dependent on expensive processing labs. Because of its dependability and versatility, the Sony is preferred over other half-inch systems as produced by, say, Panasonic or Shibaden. With the flick of a switch, the shoulder-slung battery pack becomes a playback deck, and the camera's viewfinder becomes a monitor. Instant replay in the middle of the forest. Or, with an RF adapter, the playback deck plugs into any TV set. Or, for $2500—easily afforded by, say, a group of ten persons—one can purchase a complete "theatrical" information system including camera, 23-inch monitor, shoulder pack, studio playback deck with editing capability, omnidirectional microphone and extension speakers. Put it in your VW bus and you've got a mobile TV station. Tape costs as little as $15 for 30 minutes or $30 for an hour, may be erased and reused dozens of times, and may be played as many as 400 times.

The alternate television groups, cropping up almost wholly in the past year and a half, have not yet tied together in a network for distribution. But even without a broadcast capability as yet, they are moving in that direction. Plans by Videofreex and Raindance Corporation to set up a video counterpart to the already highly successful Underground Press Service are still in the "very early formation stages," according to Ann, of Videofreex. The grant from the New York State Council on the Arts will permit the nine people who comprise Videofreex to outfit a mobile media system and wheel into communities all over the state, turning people on to the human uses of television and to the possiblities of local cable T.V. as a community "information and problem-solving tool."

Cable TV, of course, could make it possible to hook up nothing less than an alternative broadcast grid.

In the meantime, the strategy is clear: to eliminate the existing state of monopoly in broadcasting, by providing people with visible alternatives. This has meant bringing audiences into television theatres, as the People's Video Theatre has done in New York City. And taking television into the street, projecting from within giant inflatables—in effect, creating giant soft television sets—as the Ant Farm and Videofreex have done. Also banking tapes and distributing them by mail. Producing and distributing video magazines, as *Broadside—the Free Video Press* has done on the East Coast, and as *West Coast Video Magazine* is starting to do from San Francisco.

Two print magazines have appeared suddenly, both of them nonlinear in format and exuberant proselytizers of alternative video: *Print Project Amerika* and *Radical Software*. Two others—*Edcentric* and *Media Mix*—keep an exceptionally keen eye posted for media, while being devoted to radical educational reform.

Print media has played an extraordinary role in the rise of the alternative school network. *Vocations for Social Change* was the first of the new generation of newsletters, and still offers access to apprenticeships. *New Schools Exchange Newsletter,* according to Harvey Haber, was "the first grassroots national educational reform tool."

. . . An old hand-crank mimeograph and a typewriter and the New Schools Movement was defined. We were quick to discover that all that is necessary to have a movement is to declare it as such, which we did. So, a couple of dozen new schools with pretensions no greater than wanting to save a couple of hundred kids from the death of public schools found themselves part of a national movement. . . .

Today the *Exchange,* like *Whole Earth Catalog,* channels tremendous energies.

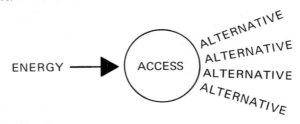

Energy. Access. Alternatives. *Whole Earth Catalog* provides "access to tools." Media Ithaca speaks of "accessing the public broadcast waves." The principle underlying today's radical reform is that—quite simply—information is energy. If people can be provided with access to the alternative media, then the Global Village can *become real.* Once access to cable TV can be obtained, once the alternative educational system can plug into a wealth of programming—so, too, can the public schools—So can we all, plug into the mediasphere.

If this "soft revolution" succeeds, then a lot of flimflam disguised presently as educational media will be consigned quietly to oblivion. But to the manufacturers will fall important new priorities: the production of "hard" instructional materials for video broadcast; development of computerized multisensory and reciprocating learning aids, including trans-sensory programs for the blind and the hearing-impaired; tactile learning kits, on the order of the "soft boxes" developed by Anthony Barton and David Stansfield, and like the Match Units put together by the imaginative people at the Children's Museum in Boston which permit a child to experience a culture through its artifacts by role-playing, actually drilling soapstone with a Nesilik Eskimo bow drill.

What the alternative schools and the alternative media are teaching us is what we have known all along; that education is concerned with providing individuals with access to the world.

The Alternative to Schooling

Ivan Illich

For generations we have tried to make the world a better place by providing more and more schooling, but so far the endeavor has failed. What we have learned instead is that forcing all children to climb an openended education ladder cannot enhance equality but must favor the individual who starts out earlier, healthier, or better prepared; that enforced instruction deadens for most people the will for independent learning; and that knowledge treated as a commodity, delivered in packages, and accepted as private property once it is acquired, must always be scarce.

In response, critics of the educational system are now proposing strong and unorthodox remedies that range from the voucher plan, which would enable each person to buy the education of his choice on an open market, to shifting the responsibility for education from the school to the media and to apprenticeship on the job. Some individuals foresee that the school will have to be disestablished just as the church was disestablished all over the world during the last two centuries. Other reformers propose to replace the universal school with various new systems that would, they claim, better prepare everybody for life in modern society. These proposals for new educational institutions fall into three broad categories: the reformation of the classroom within the school system; the dispersal of free schools throughout society; and the transformation of all society into one huge classroom. But these three approaches—the reformed classroom, the free school, and the worldwide classroom—represent three stages in a proposed escalation of education in which each step threatens more subtle and more pervasive social control than the one it replaces.

I believe that the disestablishment of the school has become inevitable and that this end of an illusion should fill us with hope. But I also believe that the end of the "age of schooling" could usher in the epoch of the

From Ivan Illich, "The Alternative to Schooling," *Saturday Review,* 19 June 1971, pp. 44–48. Reprinted by permission of the author and the publisher. Copyright © 1971 Saturday Review, Inc.

global schoolhouse that would be distinguishable only in name from a global madhouse or global prison in which education, correction, and adjustment become synonymous. I therefore believe that the breakdown of the school forces us to look beyond its imminent demise and to face fundamental alternatives in education. Either we can work for fearsome and potent new educational devices that teach about a world which progressively becomes more opaque and forbidding for man, or we can set the conditions for a new era in which technology would be used to make society more simple and transparent, so that all men can once again know the facts and use the tools that shape their lives. In short, we can disestablish schools or we can deschool culture.

In order to see clearly the alternatives we face, we must first distinguish education from schooling, which means separating the humanistic intent of the teacher from the impact of the invariant structure of the school. This hidden structure constitutes a course of instruction that stays forever beyond the control of the teacher or of his school board. It conveys indelibly the message that only through schooling can an individual prepare himself for adulthood in society, that what is not taught in school is of little value, and that what is learned outside of school is not worth knowing. I call it the hidden curriculum of schooling, because it constitutes the unalterable framework of the system, within which all changes in the curriculum are made.

The hidden curriculum is always the same regardless of school or place. It requires all children of a certain age to assemble in groups of about thirty, under the authority of a certified teacher, for some 500 to 1,000 or more hours each year. It doesn't matter whether the curriculum is designed to teach the principles of fascism, liberalism, Catholicism, or socialism; or whether the purpose of the school is to produce Soviet or United States citizens, mechanics, or doctors. It makes no difference whether the teacher is authoritarian or permissive, whether he imposes his own creed or teaches students to think for themselves. What is important is that students learn that education is valuable when it is acquired in the school through a graded process of consumption; that the degree of success the individual will enjoy in society depends on the amount of learning he consumes; and that learning *about* the world is more valuable than learning *from* the world.

It must be clearly understood that the hidden curriculum translates learning from an activity into a commodity—for which the school monopolizes the market. In all countries knowledge is regarded as the first necessity for survival, but also as a form of currency more liquid than rubles or dollars. We have become accustomed, through Karl Marx's writings, to speak about the alienation of the worker from his work in a class society. We must now recognize the estrangement of man from his learning when it becomes the product of a service profession and he becomes the consumer.

The more learning an individual consumes, the more "knowledge stock" he acquires. The hidden curriculum therefore defines a new class structure for society within which the large consumers of knowledge—

those who have acquired large quantities of knowledge stock—enjoy special privileges, high income, and access to the more powerful tools of production. This kind of knowledge-capitalism has been accepted in all industrialized societies and establishes a rationale for the distribution of jobs and income. (This point is especially important in the light of the lack of correspondence between schooling and occupational competence established in studies such as Ivar Berg's *Education and Jobs: The Great Training Robbery.*)

The endeavor to put all men through successive stages of enlightenment is rooted deeply in alchemy, the great art of the waning Middle Ages. John Amos Comenius, a Moravian bishop, self-styled Pansophist, and pedagogue, is rightly considered one of the founders of the modern schools. He was among the first to propose seven or twelve grades of compulsory learning. In his *Magna Didactica,* he described schools as devices to "teach everybody everything" and outlined a blueprint for the assembly-line production of knowledge, which according to his method would make education cheaper and better and make growth into full humanity possible for all. But Comenius was not only an early efficiency expert, he was an alchemist who adopted the technical language of his craft to describe the art of rearing children. The alchemist sought to refine base elements by leading their distilled spirits through twelve stages of successive enlightenment, so that for their own and all the world's benefit they might be transmuted into gold. Of course, alchemists failed no matter how often they tried, but each time their "science" yielded new reasons for their failure, and they tried again.

Pedagogy opened a new chapter in the history of Ars Magna. Education became the search for an alchemic process that would bring forth a new type of man, who would fit into an environment created by scientific magic. But, no matter now much each generation spent on its schools, it always turned out that the majority of people were unfit for enlightenment by this process and had to be discarded as unprepared for life in a man-made world.

Educational reformers who accept the idea that schools have failed fall into three groups. The most respectable are certainly the great masters of alchemy who promise better schools. The most seductive are popular magicians, who promise to make every kitchen into an alchemic lab. The most sinister are the new Masons of the Universe, who want to transform the entire world into one huge temple of learning. Notable among today's masters of alchemy are certain research directors employed or sponsored by the large foundations who believe that schools, if they could somehow be improved, could also become economically more feasible than those that are now in trouble, and simultaneously could sell a larger package of services. Those who are concerned primarily with the curriculum claim that it is outdated or irrelevant. So the curriculum is filled with new packaged courses on African Culture, North American Imperialism, Women's Lib, Pollution, or the Consumer Society. Passive learning is wrong—it is indeed—so we graciously allow students to decide what and how they want to be taught. Schools are prison houses. Therefore, principals are authorized to approve teachouts, moving the school desks to a roped-off Harlem street. Sensitivity training becomes fashionable. So, we import group therapy into the classroom. School, which was supposed to teach everybody everything, now becomes all things to all children.

Other critics emphasize that schools make inefficient use of modern science. Some would administer drugs to make it easier for the instructor to change the child's behavior. Others would transform school into a stadium for educational gaming. Still others would electrify the classroom. If they are simplistic disciples of McLuhan, they replace blackboards and textbooks with multimedia happenings; if they follow Skinner, they claim to be able to modify behavior more efficiently than old-fashioned classroom practitioners can.

Most of these changes have, of course, some good effects. The experimental schools have fewer truants. Parents do have a greater feeling of participation in a decentralized district. Pupils, assigned by their teacher to an apprenticeship, do often turn out more competent than those who stay in the classroom. Some children do improve their knowledge of Spanish in the language lab because they prefer playing with the knobs of a tape recorder to conversations with their Puerto Rican peers. Yet all these improvements operate within predictably narrow limits, since they leave the hidden curriculum of school intact.

Some reformers would like to shake loose from the hidden curriculum, but they rarely succeed. Free schools that lead to further free schools produce a mirage of freedom, even though the chain of attendance is frequently interrupted by long stretches of loafing. Attendance through seduction inculcates the need for educational treatment more persuasively than the reluctant attendance enforced by a truant officer. Permissive teachers in a padded classroom can easily render their pupils impotent to survive once they leave.

Learning in these schools often remains nothing more than the acquisition of socially valued skills defined, in this instance, by the consensus of a commune rather than by the decree of a school board. New presbyter is but old priest writ large.

Free schools, to be truly free, must meet two conditions: First, they must be run in a way to prevent the reintroduction of the hidden curriculum of graded attendance and certified students studying at the feet of certified teachers. And, more importantly, they must provide a framework in which all participants—staff and pupils—can free themselves from the hidden foundations of a schooled society. The first condition is frequently incorporated in the stated aims of a free school. The second condition is only rarely recognized, and is difficult to state as the goal of a free school.

It is useful to distinguish between the hidden curriculum, which I have described, and the occult foundations of schooling. The hidden curriculum is a ritual that can be considered the official initiation into modern society, institutionally established through the school. It is the purpose of this ritual to hide from its participants the contradictions between the myth of an egalitarian society and the class-conscious reality it certifies.

Once they are recognized as such, rituals lose their power, and this is what is now beginning to happen to schooling. But there are certain fundamental assumptions about growing up—the occult foundations—which now find their expression in the ceremonial of schooling, and which could easily be reinforced by what free schools do.

Among these assumptions is what Peter Schrag calls the "immigration syndrome," which impels us to treat all people as if they were newcomers who must go through a naturalization process. Only certified consumers of knowledge are admitted to citizenship. Men are not born equal, but are made equal through gestation by Alma Mater.

The rhetoric of all schools states that they form a man for the future, but they do not release him for his task before he has developed a high level of tolerance to the ways of his elders: education *for* life rather than *in* everyday life. Few free schools can avoid doing precisely this. Nevertheless they are among the most important centers from which a new life-style radiates, not because of the effect their graduates will have but, rather, because elders who choose to bring up their children without the benefit of properly ordained teachers frequently belong to a radical minority and because their preoccupation with the rearing of their children sustains them in their new style.

The most dangerous category of educational reformer is one who argues that knowledge can be produced and sold much more effectively on an open market than on one controlled by school. These people argue that most skills can be easily acquired from skill-models if the learner is truly interested in their acquisition; that individual entitlements can provide a more equal purchasing power for education. They demand a careful separation of the process by which knowledge is acquired from the process by which it is measured and certified. These seem to me obvious statements. But it would be a fallacy to believe that the establishment of a free market for knowledge would constitute a radical alternative in education.

The establishment of a free market would indeed abolish what I have previously called the hidden curriculum of present schooling—its age-specific attendance at a graded curriculum. Equally, a free market would at first give the appearance of counteracting what I have called the occult foundations of a schooled society: the "immigration syndrome," the institutional monopoly of teaching, and the ritual of linear initiation. But at the same time a free market in education would provide the alchemist with innumerable hidden hands to fit each man into the multiple, tight little niches a more complex technocracy can provide.

Many decades of reliance on schooling has turned knowledge into a commodity, a marketable staple of a special kind. Knowledge is now regarded simultaneously as a first necessity and also as society's most precious currency. (The transformation of knowledge into a commodity is reflected in a corresponding transformation of language. Words that formerly functioned as verbs are becoming nouns that designate possessions. Until recently dwelling and learning and even healing designated activities. They are now usually conceived as commodities or services to be delivered. We talk about the manufacture of housing or the delivery of medical care. Men are no longer regarded fit to house or heal themselves. In such a society people come to believe that professional services are more valuable than personal care. Instead of learning how to nurse grandmother, the teenager learns to picket the hospital that does not admit her.) This attitude could easily survive the disestablishment of school, just as affiliation with a church remained a condition for office long after the adoption of the First Amendment. It is even more evident that test batteries measuring complex knowledge-packages could easily survive the disestablishment of school—and with this would go the compulsion to obligate everybody to acquire a minimum package in the knowledge stock. The scientific measurement of each man's worth and the alchemic dream of each man's "educability to his full humanity" would finally coincide. Under the appearance of a "free" market, the global village would turn into an environmental womb where pedagogic therapists control the complex navel by which each man is nourished.

At present schools limit the teacher's competence to the classroom. They prevent him from claiming man's whole life as his domain. The demise of school will remove this restriction and give a semblance of legitimacy to the life-long pedagogical invasion of everybody's privacy. It will open the way for a scramble for "knowledge" on a free market, which would lead us toward the paradox of a vulgar, albeit seemingly egalitarian, meritocracy. Unless the concept of knowledge is transformed, the disestablishment of school will lead to a wedding between a growing meritocratic system that separates learning from certification and a society committed to provide therapy for each man until he is ripe for the gilded age.

For those who subscribe to the technocratic ethos, whatever is technically possible must be made available at least to a few whether they want it or not. Neither the privation nor the frustration of the majority counts. If cobalt treatment is possible, then the city of Tegucigalpa needs one apparatus in each of its two major hospitals, at a cost that would free an important part of the population of Honduras of parasites. If supersonic speeds are possible, then it must speed the travel of some. If the flight to Mars can be conceived, then a rationale must be found to make it appear a necessity. In the technocratic ethos poverty is modernized: Not only are old alternatives closed off by new monopolies, but the lack of necessities is also compounded by a growing spread between those services that are technologically feasible and those that are in fact available to the majority.

A teacher turns "educator" when he adopts this technocratic ethos. He then acts as if education were a technological enterprise designed to make man fit into whatever environment the "progress" of science creates. He seems blind to the evidence that constant obsolescence of all commodities comes at a high price: the mounting cost of training people to know about them. He seems to forget that the rising cost of tools is purchased at a high price in education: They decrease the labor intensity of the economy, make learning on the job impossible or, at best, a privilege for a few. All over the world the cost of educating men for society rises faster than the productivity of the entire economy, and fewer people have a sense of intelligent participation in the commonweal.

A revolution against those forms of privilege and power, which are based on claims to professional knowledge, must start with a transformation of consciousness about the nature of learning. This means, above all, a shift of responsibility for teaching and learning. Knowledge can be defined as a commodity only as long as it is viewed as the result of institutional enterprise or as the fulfillment of institutional objectives. Only when a man recovers the sense of personal responsibility for what he learns and teaches can this spell be broken and the alienation of learning from living be overcome.

The recovery of the power to learn or to teach means that the teacher who takes the risk of interfering in somebody else's private affairs also assumes responsibility for the results. Similarly, the student who exposes himself to the influence of a teacher must take responsibility for his own education. For such purposes educational institutions—if they are at all needed—ideally take the form of facility centers where one can get a roof of the right size over his head, access to a piano or a kiln, and to records, books, or slides. Schools, TV stations, theaters, and the like are designed primarily for use by professionals. Deschooling society means above all the denial of professional status for the second-oldest profession, namely teaching. The certification of teachers now constitutes an undue restriction of the right to free speech; the corporate structure and professional pretensions of journalism an undue restriction on the right to free press. Compulsory attendance rules interfere with free assembly. The deschooling of society is nothing less than a cultural mutation by which a people recovers the effective use of its Constitutional freedoms: learning and teaching by men who know that they are born free rather than treated to freedom. Most people learn most of the time when they do whatever they enjoy; most people are curious and want to give meaning to whatever they come in contact with; and most people are capable of personal intimate intercourse with others unless they are stupefied by inhuman work or turned off by schooling.

The fact that people in rich countries do not learn much on their own constitutes no proof to the contrary. Rather it is a consequence of life in an environment from which, paradoxically, they cannot learn much, precisely because it is so highly programmed. They are constantly frustrated by the structure of contemporary society in which the facts on which decisions can be made have become elusive. They live in an environment in which tools that can be used for creative purposes have become luxuries, an environment in which channels of communication serve a few to talk to many.

A modern myth would make us believe that the sense of impotence with which most men live today is a consequence of technology that cannot but create huge systems. But it is not technology that makes systems huge, tools immensely powerful, channels of communication one-directional. Quite the contrary: Properly controlled, technology could provide each man with the ability to understand his environment better, to shape it powerfully with his own hands, and to permit him full intercommunication to a degree never before possible. Such an alternative use of technology constitutes the central alternative in education.

If a person is to grow up he needs, first of all, access to things, to places and to processes, to events and to records. He needs to see, to touch, to tinker with, to grasp whatever there is in a meaningful setting. This access is now largely denied. When knowledge became a commodity, it acquired the protections of private property, and thus a principle designed to guard personal intimacy became a rationale for declaring facts off limits for people without the proper credentials. In schools teachers keep knowledge to themselves unless it fits into the day's program. The media inform, but exclude those things they regard as unfit to print. Information is locked into special languages, and specialized teachers live off its retranslation. Patents are protected by corporations, secrets are guarded by bureaucracies, and the power to keep others out of private preserves—be they cockpits, law offices, junkyards, or clinics—is jealously guarded by professions, institutions, and nations. Neither the political nor the professional structure of our societies, East and West, could withstand the elimination of the power to keep entire classes of people from facts that could serve them. The access to facts that I advocate goes far beyond truth in labeling. Access must be built into reality, while all we ask from advertising is a guarantee that it does not mislead. Access to reality constitutes a fundamental alternative in education to a system that only purports to teach *about* it.

Abolishing the right to corporate secrecy—even when professional opinion holds that this secrecy serves the common good—is, as shall presently appear, a much more radical political goal than the traditional demand for public ownership or control of the tools of production. The socialization of tools without the effective socialization of know-how in their use tends to put the knowledge-capitalist into the position formerly held by the financier. The technocrat's only claim to power is the stock he holds in some class of scarce and secret knowledge, and the best means to protect its value is a large and capital-intensive organization that renders access to know-how formidable and forbidding.

It does not take much time for the interested learner to acquire almost any skill that he wants to use. We tend to forget this in a society where professional teachers monopolize entrance into all fields, and thereby stamp teaching by uncertified individuals as quackery. There are few mechanical skills used in industry or research that are as demanding, complex, and dangerous as driving cars, a skill that most people quickly acquire from a peer. Not all people are suited for advanced logic, yet those who are make rapid progress if they are challenged to play mathematical games at an early age. One out of twenty kids in Cuernavaca can beat me at Wiff 'n' Proof after a couple of weeks' training. In four months all but a small percentage of motivated adults at our CIDOC center learn Spanish well enough to conduct academic business in the new language.

A first step toward opening up access to skills would be to provide various incentives for skilled individuals to share their knowledge. Inevitably, this would run counter to the interest of guilds and professions and unions. Yet, multiple apprenticeship is attractive: It provides everybody with an opportunity to learn something about almost anything. There is no reason why a person should not combine the ability to drive a car, repair telephones and toilets, act as a midwife, and function as an architectural draftsman. Special-interest groups and their disciplined consumers would, of course, claim that the public needs the protection of a professional guarantee. But this argument is now steadily being challenged by consumer protection associations. We have to take much more seriously the objection that economists raise to the radical socialization of skills: that "progress" will be impeded if knowledge—patents, skills, and all the rest—is democratized. Their argument can be faced only if we demonstrate to them the growth rate of futile diseconomies generated by any existing educational system.

Access to people willing to share their skills is no guarantee of learning. Such access is restricted not only by the monopoly of educational programs over learning and of unions over licensing but also by a technology of scarcity. The skills that count today are know-how in the use of highly specialized tools that were designed to be scarce. These tools produce goods or render services that everybody wants but only a few can enjoy, and which only a limited number of people know how to use. Only a few privileged individuals out of the total number of people who have a given disease ever benefit from the results of sophisticated medical technology, and even fewer doctors develop the skill to use it.

The same results of medical research have, however, also been employed to create a basic medical tool kit that permits Army and Navy medics, with only a few months of training, to obtain results, under battlefield conditions, that would have been beyond the expectations of full-fledged doctors during World War II. On an even simpler level any peasant girl could learn how to diagnose and treat most infections if medical scientists prepared dosages and instructions specifically for a given geographic area.

All these examples illustrate the fact that educational considerations alone suffice to demand a radical reduction of the professional structure that now impedes the mutual relationship between the scientist and the majority of people who want access to science. If this demand were heeded, all men could learn to use yesterday's tools, rendered more effective and durable by modern science, to create tomorrow's world.

Unfortunately, precisely the contrary trend prevails at present. I know a coastal area in South America where most people support themselves by fishing from small boats. The outboard motor is certainly the tool that has changed most dramatically the lives of these coastal fishermen. But in the area I have surveyed, half of all outboard motors that were purchased between 1945 and 1950 are still kept running by constant tinkering, while half the motors purchased in 1965 no longer run because they were not built to be repaired. Technological progress provides the majority of people with gadgets they cannot afford and deprives them of the simpler tools they need.

Metals, plastics, and ferro cement used in building have greatly improved since the 1940s and ought to provide more people the opportunity to create their own homes. But while in the United States, in 1948, more than 30 percent of all one-family homes were owner-built, by the end of the 1960s the percentage of those who acted as their own contractors had dropped to less than 20 percent.

The lowering of the skill level through so-called economic development becomes even more visible in Latin America. Here most people still build their own homes from floor to roof. Often they use mud, in the form of adobe, and thatchwork of unsurpassed utility in the moist, hot, and windy climate. In other places they make their dwellings out of cardboard, oil drums, and other industrial refuse. Instead of providing people with simple tools and highly standardized, durable, and easily repaired components, all governments have gone in for the mass production of low-cost buildings. It is clear that not one single country can afford to provide satisfactory modern dwelling units for the majority of its people. Yet, everywhere this policy makes it progressively more difficult for the majority to acquire the knowledge and skills they need to build better houses for themselves.

Educational considerations permit us to formulate a second fundamental characteristic that any post-industrial society must possess: a basic tool kit that by its very nature counteracts technocratic control. For educational reasons we must work toward a society in which scientific knowledge is incorporated in tools and components that can be used meaningfully in units small enough to be within the reach of all. Only such tools can socialize access to skills. Only such tools favor temporary associations among those who want to use them for a specific occasion. Only such tools allow specific goals to emerge in the process of their use, as any tinkerer knows. Only the combination of guaranteed access to facts and of limited power in most tools renders it possible to envisage a subsistence economy capable of incorporating the fruits of modern science.

The development of such a scientific subsistence economy is unquestionably to the advantage of the overwhelming majority of all people in poor countries. It is also the only alternative to progressive pollution, exploitation, and opaqueness in rich countries. But, as we have seen, the dethroning of the GNP cannot be achieved without simultaneously subverting GNE (Gross National Education—usually conceived as manpower capitalization). An egalitarian economy cannot exist in a society in which the right to produce is conferred by schools.

The feasibility of a modern subsistence economy does not depend on new scientific inventions. It depends primarily on the ability of a society to agree on fundamental self-chosen antibureaucratic and antitechnocratic restraints.

These restraints can take many forms, but they will not work unless they touch the basic dimensions of life. (The decision of Congress against development of the supersonic transport plane is one of the most encouraging steps in the right direction.) The substance of these voluntary social restraints would be very simple matters that can be fully understood and judged by any prudent man. The issues at stake in the SST controversy provide a good example. All such restraints would be chosen to promote stable and equal enjoyment of scientific know-how. The French say that it takes a thousand years to educate a peasant to deal with a cow. It would not take two generations to help all people in Latin America or Africa to use and repair outboard motors, simple cars, pumps, medicine kits, and ferro cement machines if their design does not change every few years. And since a joyful life is one of constant meaningful intercourse with others in a meaningful environment, equal enjoyment does translate into equal education.

At present a consensus on austerity is difficult to imagine. The reason usually given for the impotence of the majority is stated in terms of political or economic class. What is not usually understood is that the new class structure of a schooled society is even more powerfully controlled by vested interests. No doubt an imperialist and capitalist organization of society provides the social structure within which a minority can have disproportionate influence over the effective opinion of the majority. But in a technocratic society the power of a minority of knowledge capitalists can prevent the formation of true public opinion through control of scientific know-how and the media of communication. Constitutional guarantees of free speech, free press, and free assembly were meant to ensure government by the people. Modern electronics, photo-offset presses, time-sharing computers, and telephones have in principle provided the hardware that could give an entirely new meaning to these freedoms. Unfortunately, these things are used in modern media to increase the power of knowledge-bankers to funnel their program-packages through international chains to more people, instead of being used to increase true networks that provide equal opportunity for encounter among the members of the majority.

Deschooling the culture and social structure requires the use of technology to make participatory politics possible. Only on the basis of a majority coalition can limits to secrecy and growing power be determined without dictatorship. We need a new environment in which growing up can be classless, or we will get a brave new world in which Big Brother educates us all.

QUESTIONS FOR REFLECTION AND DISCUSSION

1. Illich discusses and obviously deplores the "hidden curriculum" of the schools. How valid, from your experience, is his argument? Would the public schools of choice that Fantini advocates be able to escape the charges of a "hidden curriculum"? What, if any, are the hidden curricula in the kind of alternative schools described by Morse?

2. How would you answer the questions with which Hencley and Parsons open their article? Would you argue that there is a need for every child to be educated,

that school-age children ought to go to school? Would your answer differ, do you think, from those of Marland and Illich or from those of Hencley and Parsons?

3. Shane lists some eight "neglected or minimized learnings that a society interested in the survival and in the physical and psychological health of the children and youth should mandate that its schools recognize." Let us assume that the schools did begin to recognize these learnings. What kinds of changes in purpose or in practice or in both would you envision? Could attention to these learnings be better given in the alternative schools described by Morse, in the deschooled society sought by Illich, in the public schools of choice advocated by Fantini, or in the contemporary public schools, given the new impetus sought by Marland?

4. Much of what we think and say about anything stems from our systems of beliefs; our value structure. Based on what they have written in these selections, what similarities and differences do you find among the educational values of Illich, Marland, Fantini, and Hencley and Parsons? How do these values square with your own?

5. Assume you had to rank in order the personal, productive, social, and intellectual goals discussed in the Hencley-Parsons selection. How would you list them? Upon what grounds? Do you agree with Hencley and Parsons that "the present dissatisfaction with the public schools is due to a sense that these goals, though valuable, are not being met in sufficient degree"? Would Shane or Illich agree?

6. Suppose you were suddenly named *philosopher extraordinaire* for American education and were charged with the task of articulating education purposes for the nation's schools. Which of the selections represented in this section would you draw most heavily on as you framed your statement? Why?

Chapter two
Student Unrest

What are the rights of a public school student? Has he the option of protesting if he believes that his education is irrelevant, inhumane, mindless? What limits are there or ought there to be on such protests? What are the debilitating effects on society and on its schools resulting from such protests; the violent ones that involve simple acts of vandalism onward through the bombing of buildings, the nonviolent ones involving students' dropping out of school or becoming apathetic while they stay in? What are the effects on the individual student?

A logician might argue that the importance of a question bears a direct relationship to the difficulty people encounter in trying to answer it. These are questions of that magnitude, important ones yet difficult to answer. Yet society's collective inability to formulate satisfactory responses to these questions in no way absolves the individual of his responsibility to try to answer them. It may be that his answer will be superficial or will fail when translated into practice. But his attempt, his struggle to consider alternative responses, will, in itself, be of significance.

The authors represented in the section have made the attempt to consider student unrest. They have begun with the acceptable premise that the issue is a thorny one and have moved forward from there. What they have said deserves attention.

The first article, by McGhan, presents a number of different, yet common, reactions to student activism: the teacher's, the administrator's, the developmentalists's, the liberal's, the conservative's, and, finally, those of a group McGhan labels "nonchalant." These reactions, though generalized, provide powerful food for thought.

Swift, in the second article, begins by giving some historical perspective to the question of pupil control. He then considers how what has worked in the past (or at least been used in the past) will no longer suffice. A new era raises new questions and requires new answers: past practices must be replaced with new ones that conform to contemporary society.

Hentoff provides compelling—even bizarre—illustrations to support his statement about the constitutional rights of students. Also clear from his article is the fact that the issue has gone well beyond the philosophical; court cases that are sure to have far-reaching ramifications are now pending in several states and more are on the way.

Blankenburg also discusses several court cases as he describes the "newly defined civil rights" of students. He notes the difficult position of the public school—its function as "an extension of the state"—but argues, too, that the constitutional Bill of Rights must be as sacredly adhered to within the schools as without: "If liberty works, it must be made to work at all age levels."

In the final article in this section Wynne describes the causes of student unrest. Importantly, he offers five "practical—but very ambitious—solutions." These would call for significant changes in both educational philosophy and schoolhouse practice, but, as Wynne asserts, the institution of education is too vitally important to attempt any lesser strategies.

Student Movement: Where Do You Stand?

Barry McGhan

The student revolution has been with us long enough so that we can classify certain adult reactions to it. The following analysis of some of these reactions may give you an idea of the complexity of the issues of student activism and student participation in educational decision making.

THE TEACHER REACTION

Students are neither knowledgeable nor experienced enough to make sensible educational decisions.

Many teachers probably have a more gut-level reaction, viewing student power as a capricious threat to their own authority. But it is important to realize that there are different kinds of authority. There is the authority of position in an organization (regardless of competence); the authority of person (charisma); the authority of principle (moral or ethical codes); and the authority of knowledge and skill. While a teacher can exercise any of these types of authority in the right circumstances, it seems clear that the authority which is intrinsic to his work is that which is based on his special knowledge of subject matter and learning theory. This authority has to be protected from the encroachments of nonprofessionals.

In general, we can say that "no item that is recognized on the basis of research and professional expertise as best for the education of pupils" is

From Barry McGhan, "Student Movement: Where Do You Stand?" *The Clearing House* 46 (October 1971): 91–95. Reprinted by permission of *The Clearing House* and the author.

negotiable with students.[1] For instance, this policy might mean that the topic of grades, about which there is considerable lack of agreement, could justifiably be negotiated with students, while the importance of the "discovery method" for teaching mathematics should probably not be the subject of negotiation. (There can be professional debates about the significance of processes and content, but such disagreements must stem from knowledge rather than ignorance; thus students would not participate in these debates.) Even though it seems unreasonable to suggest that students should have any *power* over decisions falling within the educator's realm of expertise, there is no reason why students should not be consulted as much as possible.

In matters where no one is an expert, real student power is possible, although it is not always easily institutionalized. One problem is that the turnover in student personnel gives a formless appearance to issues and people on the student side, and makes it difficult to negotiate conflicts. The impermanency of the individual student's relation to the school also means that the students do not have to live with the consequences of poor decisions. And so there is a temptation to argue that they ought to be limited to participation in short-term policy making.

A final, often ignored, observation is offered here. It is that *student participation* in the decision-making process has to occur in relation to participation by a large number of *other* interested parties. There are only so many dollars to spend, and only so many decisions to be made. Consequently, an increase in student power may mean a decrease in someone else's power. Since teachers have only lately obtained a significant role in decision making, it is unlikely that they will be willing to give up some of their new-found power to students.

THE ADMINISTRATOR REACTION

What can I do to anticipate and prevent disruptive expressions of student power?

Often, people expressing this attitude discuss techniques for dealing with students by according them certain rights and making certain concessions to their demands, while at the same time drawing up contingency plans to deal forcefully with disruption. Clearly, the philosophy that "an ounce of prevention is worth a pound of cure" is sound, and most people would approve of efforts to prevent disruption and violence in the schools. But there are some dangers facing people who feel this way. One danger is that the fear of disruption will cause schoolmen to make changes just to appease students. This could lead to wanton discontinuance of beneficial policies and institution of harmful ones. Also, if changes are not made with honest regard for the rights and needs of students, the administrator's credibility may suffer. Another danger is that the changes may be purely cosmetic, and if so may only postpone disruption until students realize that fact.

There is another possible consequence of dealing with student activists too permissively. It has been found that universities with a strong student influence have become highly politicized, and have generally ceased to be academically distinguished.[2] Secondary schools could suffer a similar adulteration of their academic role. When we talk about student participation in decision making, we have to be very careful that we are talking about the kind and number of decisions that are appropriate to the students' level of maturity.

THE DEVELOPMENTALIST REACTION

This burst of youthful idealism, impatience with the established order, and an urge for action, is typical of this age group. They'll get over it.

It's true that high school and college students are typically at the peak of their mental and physical powers. The passions of life are strong in late adolescence, and students naturally seek to exercise some influence over their lives. But, it is a mistake to assume that student protest stems from nothing more than this.

Our society is far from perfect, and the young see the faults sharply. The pervasiveness of the mass media makes it difficult for them (unlike earlier generations) to hide from the social ills and threats to survival which beset us. Unfortunately, at the same time that their social conscience is stirred up, they find themselves in a virtually powerless position. In fact, things are now worse for teenagers than ever before: puberty occurs, on the average, two years earlier than it did at the turn of the century, and professions and skilled trades have extended their entrance requirements. Considering these changes, it's easy to see that students spend more time in the limbo of adolescence than did past generations. Even when they do reach the point where they can become full-fledged members of society, the system seems to want them to produce and consume goods and services more than it wants them to create the good society.

While they are in this unhappy state "we stuff [them] with vitamins, we stimulate their sexuality with our advertising and our mass fantasies, we encourage them to dream and criticize [until] they are bursting with energy and self-importance."[3] What else can we expect from a generation brought up on instant news, instant technology, and instant cream of wheat than that, driven by their idealism, they expect instant solutions to social problems as well? The consequence of being pushed forward on the one hand and being held back on the other is that they become frustrated, and the frustrations find an outlet in school.

Some people feel that the structure of the schools may also aggravate the students' ambivalent state. They claim that secondary schools are too regimented and the students' role too passive, with few opportunities for important participation. Students react by forming subcultures closed to adults, from which they criticize schools and participate in demonstrations. Suggestions for reform sometimes include calls for a relaxation of the rigid structure of school so that students can take on a greater role as they mature.[4]

THE "LIBERAL" REACTION

The world is going down the drain, and we haven't done anything to stop it. We must heed the cries of the younger generation and give them what they want, for they are our salvation.

People who express this view indulge in two excesses. First, they seem to assume that the older generation has not tried to solve, or succeeded in solving, any critical societal problems. Second, they seem to assume that the younger generation will be able to succeed where the older has failed. These assumptions are unwarranted.

The older generation did not deliberately, through perversity or cowardice, permit the world to develop the problems it has (although such faults always play a part in men's affairs). Rather, the older generation had mixed success in solving the problems it saw, with the means available to it. The younger generation will have to do the same, and because they have the same human frailties, they'll have their share of failures, too. We can *hope* that they will be more successful at problem-solving than the preceding generation (especially in view of the gravity of the problems that need solving), but we succumb to foolish romanticism if we *assume* that they will be more successful.

THE "CONSERVATIVE" REACTION

We are in trouble with this younger generation not because we have failed our country, not because of materialism or stupidity, but simply because we have failed to keep that generation in its place, and failed to put it back there when it got out. We have the power; we do not have the will. We have the right; we have not exercised it.[5]

The hearts of those of us over thirty reach out to people who express this viewpoint. We seem to feel that everything will be all right if we can just return to the values and ways of the "good old days." But, the fact is that society is different now than it was even ten years ago. More people, more pollutants, more complex tensions, more visible acts of violence at home and abroad, and more potentially dangerous political situations exist now than before. New problems often require new solutions. It is comforting, but unrealistic, to think that we can solve these problems by just getting a grip on ourselves.

THE HUMANIST REACTION

> The schools are dull, dreary places, and they treat students in regimented, impersonal, and inhumane ways.

It's true that there are many things wrong with our schools, just as many things are wrong with society at large. In fact, some of the ills of society cause things to go wrong in the schools (e.g., racism). The problem here is partly one of overreaction, for not everything about school is bad. Although the evils are serious, we should still proceed with care in bringing about change (without letting caution be an excuse for inaction).

One of the unstated tenets of people who express this viewpoint seems to be that the individual always deserves more consideration than does society. However, this is an immoderate view; clearly, society has the right to expect certain kinds of behavior from the individuals in it. The balance between the rights of the individual and the rights of society is what democracy and the schools are all about. This means that we can't lash out against "regimentation" without clarifying what we mean. After all, a certain amount of regimentation (e.g., on the highway) is necessary; the important question is, how much is too much?

Another belief that seems to be held by people in this category is that all students are naturally good and have a potential for great growth. They look at the schools and notice that students don't all seem to be turning out to fit *their* image. They also notice that schools have many faults, and they conclude that the schools are to blame for the way people turn out. It apparently does not occur to them that human nature might allow for both bright and dull individuals, regardless of the school's influence.

THE NONCHALANT REACTION

> Don't worry too much about all this student activism. After all, only a tiny fraction of students are involved.

Persons espousing this position go on to point out that the majority of students are well behaved and serious about their studies. They say that the activists only want to be consulted more—that they're not really after more actual power. They point out that most students are too interested in getting an education to be willing to spend the time it takes to guide an educational program. The following kinds of statistics are offered as evidence for this position. A survey showed that 85 percent of 2,000 college students felt that the most important things in life can only be understood through involvement, *but* only a third of them ever took part in regular discussion of national problems, and only 16 percent had participated in a demonstration.[6] The apparent point is that things aren't as as bad as they seem, because most students don't make waves.

Advocates of this view seem unaware that education is a **delicate** proposition, and a little disruption goes a long way. Also, they don't seem to consider the possibility that the visible activism of a few represents the attitudes of a much larger body of students who don't demonstrate, but who support the demonstrator's goals.

In all fairness, it must be added that there is not much evidence that student activists really represent the visible portion of an iceberg of student discontent. Some people go so far as to theorize that the majority of students are passive and conformist because they have a psychological need to believe in the "system"; denial of it would give them a terrific sense of insecurity, frustration, and conflict. Two thirds of the students in one survey, for example, thought that the enforcement of school regulations was about right. The same fraction thought grading was fair. Thus, proponents of this theory say, the myth of institutional paternalism keeps the students from being alienated.[7] If this theory has validity, then we may well want to consider whether we are fostering worthwhile behavior patterns and goals in our schools, or only ones which the students find tolerable.

CONCLUSION

Hopefully, the foregoing discussion has given you an insight into some of the opinions and attitudes about student activism. More importantly, we hope you are convinced that any one viewpoint is likely to have faults which prevent it from encompassing the whole truth.

NOTES

[1] "Secondary School Principals: Up Against the Wall," *Senior Scholastic: The Scholastic Teacher,* 11 April 1969, p. 4.

[2] Stephen Spurr, "The Relative Roles of Faculty and Students in Decision-Making." Address to the Ninth Annual Meeting of the Council of Graduate Schools in the U.S., Washington, D.C., December 4–6 1969.

[3] D. Barr, "Parents Guide to the Age of Revolt," *McCalls* 97 (October 1969).

[4] Newton Fink and Benjamin Cullers, "Student Unrest: Structure of the Public Schools as a Major Factor?" *The Clearing House* 44 (March 1970): 415.

[5] K. Ross Toole, "I'm Tired of the Tyranny of Spoiled Brats," *Reader's Digest* June 1970, p. 129.

[6] "Student Protest: How Far is Too Far?" *Senior Scholastic,* 95, 20 October 1969, p. 6.

[7] Charles Silberman, "Murder in the Schoolroom," *The Atlantic,* June 1970, p. 96.

Changing Patterns of Pupil Control

David W. Swift

Disciplinary methods in American public schools have changed drastically during the past century. Punitive measures of earlier times have been replaced by a concern for the feelings of the child, and corporal punishment has virtually vanished. Although this new approach is generally assumed to be the result of increased public enlightenment this is only part of the story. Gentler discipline emerged not simply for altruistic reasons but also as a matter of expediency: it alleviated urgent custodial problems confronting the school and its personnel. Traditional disciplinary methods had sufficed in the small simple schools of a preindustrial society, but they were no longer satisfactory in large urban systems where, as we shall see, the consequences of disorder became far more serious. A new approach to control was needed, and the progressive ideas of John Dewey and other educators satisfied this need. While humanitarianism played a part it was far from the only factor present.[1]

In a broader context this can be seen as one aspect of the change from simple "folk" *gemeinschaftliche,* "communal" societies to complex *gesellschaftliche,* "associational" societies.[2] Social control in the former is relatively straightforward and effective; in the latter, according to many observers, control is weakened by urbanization, the division of labor, and the rational, impersonal organization of many spheres of human activity.[3]

The first part of this article examines discipline in earlier, traditional times, suggesting reasons why harsh methods were acceptable in the simple village school regardless of their consequences for the student. The second part examines pupil control in the modern, urban era, suggesting problems which required a departure from former methods.[4] The conclusion discusses the possibility that the American experience may be repeated in other industrializing societies.

Two points should be stressed here. First, we are viewing discipline from the perspective of the school rather than the pupil; what is good for one does not necessarily benefit the other. Second, many educators were not aware of the custodial consequences of their acts. They may have supported a particular philosophy for humanitarian or educational reasons rather than for disciplinary purposes. Nevertheless, the implications for control, even if unrecognized, could still be exceedingly important.

From David W. Swift, "Changing Patterns of Pupil Control," *Educational Forum* 36 (January 1972): 199–209. Reprinted by permission of the author and Kappa Delta Pi, an Honor Society in Education, owners of the copyright.

THE TRADITIONAL ERA

The "good old days" were far from idyllic. Misbehavior was a prevalent problem in the traditional American school, and it often attained serious proportions. In 1837, for example, over 300 schools in Massachusetts alone were broken up by rebellious pupils.[5] Disruption of ten percent of the schools in the state[6] during a single year is especially notable in view of the fact that Massachusetts had been a leader in education since earliest colonial times and was still in many respects ahead of the nation. We can assume that conditions in other states were not much better and frequently were considerably worse.[7]

In addition to minor mischief, which undoubtedly went on much of the time, two more serious forms of misbehavior directly challenged the teacher's authority: locking the teacher out of the school and physically assaulting him. At the least, either of these would disrupt the school for several hours, if not the rest of the day. Not infrequently, however, these episodes led to the dismissal of the teacher and the closing of the school until a replacement could be found.

The first of these two types of rebellion was known as "putting out" or "turning out" the teacher; he was removed from the classroom either by subterfuge or by force, and then was prevented from getting back in. This process was discussed by Horace Greeley:

> At the close of the morning session of the first of January, and perhaps on some other day that the big boys chose to consider or make a holiday, the moment the master left the house in quest of his dinner, the little ones were started homeward, the doors and windows suddenly and securely barricaded, and the older pupils, thus fortified against intrusion, proceeded to spend the afternoon in play and hilarity. I have known a master to make a desperate struggle for admission, but the odds were too great. If he appealed to the neighboring fathers, they were apt to advise him to desist, and let matters take their course. I recollect one instance, however, where a [teacher] was shut out who, procuring a piece of board, mounted from a fence to the roof of the schoolhouse and covered the top of the chimney nicely with his board. Ten minutes thereafter, the house was filled with smoke, and its inmates, opening the doors and windows, were glad to make terms with the outsider.[8]

The other serious type of rebellion involved physical interference with, or attacks upon, the teacher. Sometimes these confrontations evolved out of a situation which the rebels felt to be grossly unfair, as in unreasonable punishment administered to a classmate. Mild and just chastisement was not likely to stimulate other pupils to attack the teacher.

If, however, the whipping was continued beyond what was considered by the older boys as reasonable, and the boy happened to be a favorite with his fellows, some protest on the part of the big boys might be made; and if that did not effect the object, forcible, if not indeed armed, intervention might be the result.[9]

Castigation of a big boy was particularly crucial because it ". . . required greater effort, the punishment was usually more severe, and the chances of interference were materially enhanced."[10]

On other occasions, trouble might even grow out of a seemingly innocuous, good-humored contest between teacher and pupils. For example, one nineteenth century account tells of a teacher who lost control over his class after two or three students defeated him in wrestling matches. He subsequently was asked to resign.[11]

For such reasons, the basic task of the traditional teacher was considered to be "schoolkeeping" rather than "school teaching." "The teacher's job was to maintain order—to keep the class intact. In the upper grades, as often as not, this meant that the teacher had to be able physically to subdue the larger members of the class."[12] Severity in a teacher was considered to be a virtue. Unless he made frequent and forceful use of the rod, many parents felt uneasy and doubted that the children could be learning much.[13] The average schoolmaster used extremely primitive methods for controlling his pupils, relying mainly on a three-foot rule, known as a "ferrule," and the "heavy gad," a flexible sapling about five feet in length. These implements were applied "with force and frequency" to boys and girls, to young and old alike.[14] In 1845, for example, the Boston board of education reported that whippings in a "representative" school of 400 pupils averaged 65 per day. The board mentioned "severe injuries" following corporal punishment and stated that, in most cases, the offense was "very trifling."[15] Cubberley aptly summed up the situation when he commented that: "There was little 'soft pedagogy' in the management of either town or rural schools in the days before the Civil War."[16]

Thus, life in the traditional school was often harsh and hectic, for master and pupils alike. It remained this way, with few fundamental changes, for more than 200 years, from the early colonial period to the middle of the nineteenth century. A number of factors contributed to the stability of this traditional pattern: prevailing attitudes regarding public education, the isolation of one-room rural schools, the characteristics of the teacher's job, the homogeneity of the student body, the low economic investment in the schools, and the marginal role of the school in the community.

During the traditional era the public school was not expected to educate everyone. Compulsory education as we know it today did not exist. Before the Civil War only one state had enacted compulsory attendance laws; Massachusetts made schooling mandatory in 1852. In most parts of the country, free public schools were just being established on a broad scale during the 1840s and 1850s. Many districts had only the most rudimentary educational facilities, and other communities, especially in the South, had none at all.[17]

Lack of formal education was not considered a serious handicap in earning a living. As for the more general benefits of universal education, the public was divided, and even members of the school board were sometimes ambivalent, especially when they thought about the expenses involved. Thus, when students dropped out or the school closed down, it was not viewed as a calamity.

Consequently, the traditional public school, when it existed at all, was a selective institution, accomodating only those hardy souls who were able to adapt to its inflexible demands. Those who could not or would not do so dropped out; this was true for teachers as well as pupils. Usually it was the pupils who left, one by one, as punishment or study became unbearable, but occasionally it was the schoolmaster who was compelled to leave. The sporadic disruptions and closings of the school by rebellious pupils did not generate enough pressure to alter the traditional patterns of the school or to encourage critical reappraisals of its methods.

When a school shut down, the teacher was about the only person who suffered any hardship and he was not in a position to do much about it. His duties were simple and it was easy to replace him. Because his pedagogical effectiveness was defined in large part by his capacity to maintain order, his inability to do so was interpreted as evidence that he was incompetent and therefore should not be teaching anyway. He had no colleagues nearby to whom he might turn for support. Most schools before the late nineteenth century were in the country and the majority had only one teacher.

The economic consequences of student revolts were far less serious than they would be today. In fact, school districts actually saved money when the school was closed. The lone teacher was the only paid employee. There were no other personnel—no superintendents, secretaries, principals, custodians, counselors, or coordinators—who would still have to be paid, or laid off, if the teacher left.

In addition, the financial investment in the school plant was small. Most schoolhouses were crude, one-room structures, furnished with a few rough benches and a stove. They were devoid of equipment; there were no free textbooks or supplies, and blackboards did not become common until well into the nineteenth century. Rambunctious students could do little damage and there was nothing worth stealing when the school was closed.

The student body of the traditional school was quite homogeneous by today's standards. In 1850 less than half of the nation's youth between the ages of 5 and 19 were enrolled in public school: for nonwhites the enrollment was under 2 percent.[18] Many poor children were kept out of school by partial tuition fees, charges for books and supplies, and the necessity of working to support the family. The pupils actually in school, therefore, were a relatively select group who were assumed to have some chance of success under the same Spartan conditions that had sufficed in their grandparents' day.

THE MODERN ERA

After the Civil War, traditional patterns of attendance and discipline were shattered by a number of profound changes in American society. These changes, associated to a considerable degree with urbanization, industrialization, and immigration, transformed the character of the student body, increased the school's responsibility toward pupils, made control more urgent, and rendered unusable the orthodox time-honored methods of discipline.

Urbanization drastically altered everyday life. In 1830, 91 percent of the population lived in rural areas, and in 1870 three-fourths of the population was still rural. By the end of the First World War, however, half of the people were living in cities and towns.[19] The large extended family, common in agrarian societies, was broken up as some of its members moved to the cities, leaving behind friends, relatives, and neighbors, and entering an unfamiliar milieu where few others knew them or cared about them.

A new role emerged for the child. In a rural setting he had been a useful member of the family, contributing to its maintenance by working directly in the production of food and marketable goods, or by assisting with household chores. In the city, however, children were no longer assets but became liabilities. Although there was a transitional period during which children could still work in factories or in home industries this opportunity for contributing to family support was eliminated as sentiments against child labor were followed by legislation outlawing the practice.

Consequently the urban youth, in comparison to his rural counterpart, had less productive work to occupy his time and had few adults or older siblings around to supervise his increased leisure. In addition, crowded metropolitan conditions, especially in tenement areas, provided few opportunities for wholesome recreation or for harmless dissipation of youthful energy. Moreover, there were many children in the same situation living within a block or two. The stage was set for juvenile delinquency on a large scale. As early as 1870, the annual report of the Philadelphia schools estimated that " . . . upwards of 20,000 children not attending any school, public, private or parochial, are running the streets in idleness or vagabondism. . . ."[20]

The desire to forestall youthful mischief, concern of working men over competition from cheap child labor, and genuinely altruistic regard forchild welfare probably all contributed to the rising demand for universal compulsory education. This demand forced the schools to change their attitude toward pupils. Teachers could no longer employ a "take it or leave it" approach, eliminating students who were unwilling to cooperate with traditional expectations. Instead, a new system had to be devised which pupils would be willing to tolerate. Of course, many pupils still dropped out before they graduated, but the school now was expected to do all it could to keep them in.

The rapid growth of cities and the obligation to educate all children made urban schools very crowded.[21] This increased tensions among pupils and aggravated problems of control. For several reasons disturbances in large urban schools could be more serious than in small, isolated rural schools. First, there were more pupils who might participate in the disorder. Then, too, there were other personnel, other teachers and administrators whose work might be made more difficult by the outbreak. In addition, disruptions would be noticed immediately by residents and shopkeepers whose homes and businesses adjoined the school. Finally, there was a greater financial investment in the buildings, equipment, supplies, and grounds of the urban school.

To complicate things further, the student body became more heterogeneous and consequently more difficult to handle. Previously minor differences among the earlier settlers from northwestern Europe were dwarfed by the entry of heretofore unfamiliar groups from southern and eastern Europe, not to mention Orientals, Negroes, and Latin Americans. The percentage of nonwhite pupils, infinitesimal during the traditional era, began to rise very rapidly after the Civil War; by 1920 54 percent of the nonwhite school age population was actually enrolled.[22]

As the age of compulsory attendance increased there were more likely to be full grown men and women in school. These older students were less inclined than the younger ones to submit to traditional methods of discipline; if nothing else, their size alone would be a deterrent to the frequent whippings given to smaller students. And, increasingly, there were pupils whose poor scholastic performance was clearly not the simple consequence of laziness. Some of these students came from unsettled or impoverished families, others were handicapped physically or mentally, and still others did not speak English.[23] Of course, there had been pupils with similar handicaps in traditional times, but as their numbers increased toward the end of the nineteenth century, the shortcomings of orthodox methods of instruction and control became more and more obvious. The inadequacy of such time-honored punishments as giving a sharp rap with a ruler for a poorly prepared recitation was more apparent than ever before.

Changes in the composition of the teaching staff also meant that corporal punishment was less practical than it had been. During the eighteenth and early nineteenth centuries most teachers were men, but in later times the majority of American public school teachers have been women. By 1870, the balance had already shifted so that the majority of teachers were women and by 1920, 86 percent of public school teachers were women.[24]

Women usually are less likely than men to rely on brute force. Although there are exceptions, all things considered, feminine assets in the problem of maintaining control consist less of physical strength than of gentler inducements to cooperation. Female capacities and limitations became increasingly important as women assumed a larger share of teaching positions in public schools. This, along with a general softening of public attitudes regarding the treatment of children, rendered traditional reliance on corporal punishment unacceptable and pointed the way to new methods of control, to be discussed in the next pages.

In sum, four major changes made the school's task more difficult after 1870. First, a large part of the responsibility for pupil attendance shifted from the pupil to the school. Second, pupils were more varied than before. Third, traditional methods of control were no longer practical or acceptable. Finally, as schools grew larger and more expensive, the consequences of disorder became more serious.

CUSTODIAL FUNCTIONS OF MILD DISCIPLINE

As a result of these changes public schools in the twentieth century have been confronted with custodial problems quite different from those of the traditional era. The age-old task of maintaining order was still present, but former methods of coping with it could no longer be used. New procedures were necessary. Instead of using force and coercion, public schools now sought the pupils' willing participation. This was done by minimizing academic pressures and, in general, by making school as pleasant as possible. Whatever the pedagogical merits or shortcomings of this approach might have been, it did enable the school to win the cooperation of many pupils who would have resisted a more traditional program.

Relaxing discipline removed much of the sting from education. Harsh punishments of a bygone era have all but disappeared. Some teachers and principals still, on occasion, wield a paddle, give a quick spat with a ruler, twist an ear, or in some other manner inflict momentary pain, but this happens with far less frequency and ferocity than before. Even traditional sanctions not involving physical punishment are used with restraint: ridicule, sarcasm, detention, extra assignments, or suspension for a few days are avoided, and permanent expulsion is rare.

The abandonment of such punishment has eliminated a major source of hostility against the school and the teacher. This is important not only with respect to the individual pupil but also for his classmates, who sometimes intervened in his behalf when they thought his punishment was too severe. In contrast, the mild discipline of today creates few martyrs among students and is less likely to arouse the whole class against the teacher. This danger is reduced still further by concern for the pupil as a worthwhile individual, whose happiness and well being should be encouraged in every possible way. Such an approach enables the teacher to win the affection of many pupils. Students who like their teacher, who receive satisfaction from her, in friendship and praise and encouragement, are less likely to be uncooperative with her or to support rebellion against her.[25]

I am not claiming that control is no longer a problem: I am simply suggesting that, despite the headlines, severe disorders are less likely to occur under the present system than would be the case under a more harsh, traditional regimen. When we consider that there are 40 million pupils in the public elementary and secondary schools of the United States, the percentage of disturbances appears very small indeed. It is certainly far less than the ten percent rate of school closings indicated by Massachusetts' figures of a century and a half ago. Milder discipline may have evolved for other reasons but it also has crucial consequences for control.[26]

CONCLUSION

Mass compulsory education created custodial problems as well as educational ones. The necessity of accommodating a large and varied student body, which could not be controlled by traditional methods of corporal punishment, segregation, failure, or expulsion, forced American public schools to seek new solutions. Milder disciplinary procedures, whatever their educational justification might have been, alleviated urgent problems confronting the schools of a rapidly industrializing society.

Will similar changes occur in other countries? My guess is that they will. Some of these pressures may have been unique to the United States, but others are likely to appear elsewhere. Three steps are involved. First, juvenile delinquency is apt to be a problem in all industrialized nations.[27] Urbanization loosens the primary, kinship constraints of village life, dumping hordes of people into impersonal cities where social controls are weaker. Furthermore, the child becomes an economic liability, no longer contributing directly to the support of his family. He is stripped of most of his former chores, leaving him with few useful functions to perform and many opportunities for mischief; dozens of similarly superfluous youngsters live near by, yet their parents may be working miles away. If the child does seek employment he may be competing against adults for the diminishing number of unskilled jobs available. Eventually laws against child labor are passed, reducing still further the youth's opportunities for productive use of his time. He is not needed at home but he is prohibited from working away from home. Under such conditions trouble seems inevitable.

Second, the agency in an industrial society most likely to be responsible for controlling juveniles is the public school. Located in nearly every neighborhood and processing more young people than any other institution, it is widely viewed as the logical body for regulating youthful behavior. After all, it is already engaged in inculcating other socially desirable skills and attitudes. Some teachers may complain about having to be babysitters or policemen, but the prevailing assumption that the school is responsible for controlling youngsters is seldom seriously challenged. If the urban family does not supervise its children, the school is expected to do it. Consequently, residents protest to the school that adolescents are littering their lawns, businessmen complain that juveniles are annoying customers or shoplifting during the noon hour, and police pick up children playing in the street and ask the principal why they are not in school.

Other alternatives to the school have been suggested: military service, labor camps, detention centers, and so on. Quite apart from humanitarian considerations, however, such harsh measures would lead to other

198693

problems, for industrialization increases not only delinquency but social mobility as well. Many troublemakers today are children of influential, middle-class citizens and therefore cannot be treated in the same heavy-handed way that lower class delinquents might be. Although schools are often criticized, they are generally regarded as altruistic, trying in their bumbling way to help the pupils. As a result, incarceration in a school avoids the repercussions that more obviously custodial instituions might encounter. Many people would object to locking children up in prison for several hours a day, but compulsory attendance in something called a "school" brings forth less opposition.

Third, given the responsibility for controlling large numbers of youngsters, the school's job will be easier if a progressive approach is used. Control by coercion alone requires too much money and manpower, and increases the probability that many pupils will drop out before graduation. The school's task becomes more manageable when pupils comply voluntarily rather than being forced to do so.

Despite ethnic and ideological differences, industrializing nations in many parts of the world are likely to encounter similar problems, including juvenile delinquency. As societies develop, therefore, we can expect that their schools, and perhaps other institutions, too, will relinquish some of their traditional harsh disciplinary methods, not simply for altruism but also for reason of control.

NOTES

[1] For a discussion of discipline in European schools, from medieval to modern times, see Philippe Aries, *Centuries of Childhood* (New York: Random House, 1962), pp. 241–68.

[2] Emile Durkheim, *The Division of Labor in Society*, trans. G. Simpson (New York: Free Press, 1947); Pitirim A. Sorokin, *The Crisis of Our Age* (New York: Dutton, 1941); and Georg Simmel, *Sociology*, trans. Kurt Wolff (New York: Free Press, 1950).

[3] Ely Chinoy, *Society*, 2nd ed. (New York: Random House, 1967).

[4] Although the precise date dividing the two periods is not crucial in a "before" and "after" analysis of this sort, 1870 provides a convenient cutting point. The transition from simple, localized society, still revolving around primary, kinship types of relationships, into more complex, impersonal, national forms of organization, was suggested by a number of events, both in education and in the larger society. The establishment of a U.S. government agency concerned with education, state court decisions permitting taxation for extending education to the secondary level, the proliferation of fulltime school superintendents, and legislation providing for unification of many separate school districts all appeared, or became prominent, around this time. In government, the imposition of federal sovereignty over the defeated southern states, and in commerce, the completion of the transcontinental railroad, also suggest the emergence of organization on a larger scale.

[5] Clifton Johnson, *Old Time Schools and Schoolbooks* (New York: Macmillan, 1904), p. 121.

[6] Ibid., p. 129.

[7] Where not otherwise indicated, the sources for historical details are Ellwood P. Cubberly, *Public Education in the United States,* rev. ed. (Boston: Houghton Mifflin, 1934); and R. Freeman Butts and Lawrence A. Cremin, *A History of Education in American Culture* (New York: Holt, 1953).

[8] Johnson, *Old Time Schools,* p. 126.

[9] Ruth S. Freeman, *Yesterday's Schools* (Watkins Glen, N.Y.: Century House, 1962).

[10] Ibid.

[11] Ibid., pp. 78–79.

[12] Butts and Cremin, *History of Education,* p. 286.

[13] Johnson, *Old Time Schools,* p. 121.

[14] Ibid., pp. 121–22.

[15] Otis W. Caldwell and Stuart A. Courtis, *Then and Now in Education; 1845:1923* (New York: World, 1925).

[16] Cubberly, *Public Education,* p. 328.

[17] Although compulsory education laws had been enacted two centuries earlier, they eventually fell into disuse (Cubberly, *Public Education,* p. 17–18).

[18] U.S. Bureau of the Census, *Historical Statistics of the United States, Colonial Times to 1957* (Washington, D.C.: 1960), p. 213.

[19] Ibid., p. 14.

[20] U.S. Commissioner of Education, *Annual Report of the Commissioner of Education for the Year 1870* (Washington, D.C.: 1870), p. 273.

[21] The reduction of class size to sixty pupils per teacher was often considered an unattainable ideal (Butts and Cremin, *History of Education,* p. 21).

[22] U.S. Bureau of the Census, *Historical Statistics,* p. 207.

[23] By 1909, 58 percent of the pupils in 37 of the nation's largest cities had foreign-born parents (Butts and Cremin, *History of Education,* p. 72).

[24] Ibid., p. 286; N.E.A. statistics quoted by Myron Lieberman, *Education as a Profession* (Englewood Cliffs, N.J.: Prentice-Hall, 1956), p. 242.

[25] For a more detailed analysis of the custodial consequences of "progressive" discipline *see* David W. Swift, *Ideology and Change in the Public Schools* (Columbus, Ohio: Charles E. Merrill Co., 1971), ch. 3.

[26] For example *see* James Herndon's account of an all-Negro junior high school in Oakland, California. About the only pupils who did not participate in the yearly spring riots were in the class of a permissive, "soft" teacher. *The Way it Spozed to Be* (New York: Simon and Schuster, 1968), pp. 165–66.

[27] For an international perspective on delinquency *see* Don Gibbons, *Delinquent Behavior* (Englewood Cliffs, N.J.: Prentice-Hall, 1970), esp. ch 9.

Why Students Want
Their Constitutional Rights

Nat Hentoff

There exists among us a subject population as diverse in ethnic and socioeconomic composition as the nation itself. In increasing numbers, its members are conducting a stubborn, sometimes explosive, struggle for liberation. Their goal, considering the previous history of this group within the United States, is quite revolutionary. They want their constitutional rights.

Nearly thirty years ago, it appeared that this colony, coterminous with the mother country, was about to achieve these rights. The United States Supreme Court proclaimed, in *West Virginia Board of Education v. Barnette,* that "educating the young for citizenship is reason for scrupulous protection of constitutional freedoms of the individual, if we are not to strangle the free mind at its source and teach youth to discount important principles of our government as mere platitudes."

Despite the Court's 1943 pronouncement, there has been little significant change, until recently, in the attitudes of most public school administrators toward their students. The latter, compelled by law to attend these institutions, find their constitutional freedoms routinely violated rather than scrupulously protected by those in charge of the schools. Such basic rights of an American citizen as freedom of speech and assembly, protection from invasion of privacy, and the guarantee of due process of law do not exist for the overwhelming majority of American high school students.

After the first Earth Day, a student at Grady High School, Atlanta, Georgia, observes: "They let us have an assembly on Earth Day, but the principal warned me not to say anything about the war. He says the war is not relevant to high school education."

A student at Central High School, Muncie, Indiana: "They search the lockers anytime they want to. And we're not allowed to be present when they do. They took a bottle of aspirin out of my locker once and sent it down to Indianapolis to have it analyzed. It cost them a lot of money to find out it was really my aspirin. I get migraine headaches, and I really needed it."

In a high school in Sumter, South Carolina, a student running for school office is summarily removed from the ballot by the principal

From Nat Hentoff, "Why Students Want Their Constitutional Rights," *Saturday Review,* 22 May 1971. Reprinted by permission of the author and the publisher. Copyright © 1971 by Saturday Review, Inc. Commissioned by the American Civil Liberties Union, 1970.

because the student has written in the school paper an article critical of the administration.

"But you can't do that!" the boy says. "It's unconstitutional."

"The constitution of this school," the principal informs the student, "takes precedence over the United States Constitution."

In September 1970 in Roseville, Michigan, thirty students are refused entry to the high school because of a provision in the school's dress code that says male students' hair must not touch the ears or shirt collars or fall over the eyebrows.

I have not selected extraordinary illustrations, as nearly any high school student in any part of the country can testify. Put plainly, many administrators and teachers in the public schools honestly believe they are educating their charges for citizenship; but because of the way in which *they* were educated, they have a decidedly limited understanding of the nature of and the necessity for student rights. As Edgar Friedenberg noted in *The Dignity of Youth and Other Atavisms,* "It is idle to talk about civil liberties to adults who were systematically taught in adolescence that they had none; and it is sheer hypocrisy to call such people freedom-loving."

Less harsh is Ed McManus, director of the American Civil Liberties Union affiliate in Milwaukee: "The great majority of schools have a habitual, although not necessarily vicious, disregard for civil liberties. You see, they simply don't perceive them as an issue."

They are recognizing, however, that other people do very much perceive civil liberties in the schools as an issue. In the past decade, a rising number of students and their parents—often in conjunction with affiliates of the ACLU throughout the country—have been bringing, and increasingly winning, suits that make specific the judgment by the Supreme Court in 1967 (*in re: Gault*) that "neither the Fourteenth Amendment nor the Bill of Rights is for adults alone."

This burgeoning revolt by our sequestered youth is rooted in diverse rebellions outside the high schools that began in the early 1960s: the drive for civil rights; the awakenings on college campuses, from the Free Speech Movement to the 1968 Battle of Morningside Heights; and the multidimensional antiwar movement. Out there, all kinds of people were into learning how to be free. But in the secondary schools, as many students have told me, "it was like a prison." But for many of us older survivors, school was always like a prison. (John Holt has observed how often school is the setting for the bad dreams of adults.) We, however, did not have all those enviably venturesome agents of change out there to emulate. And the older generation also did not, as students, grow up during a war that has effectively decimated young people's respect for adult authority—from the president's to the proximate principal's.

There is no discernible chronological pattern with regard to which issues first stirred the thrust by high school students for what Tom Hayden calls "personal legitimacy." In some schools, dress codes were the Battle of Concord. In others, arbitrary suspensions. Or censorship of the school paper. Or a principal's refusal to allow the wearing of armbands or buttons. Although all of it is part of a common cultural pattern, high school constitutionalism has been largely a decentralized phenomenon. But it is becoming more and more powerful as more substantial court battles are won.

The most important of these victories in recent years was the Tinker case. In December 1965, the principals of the Des Moines public schools learned that a group of students planned to wear black armbands during the Christmas season in protest against the war in Vietnam. Meeting in solemn conclave, the educators adopted a policy that any student wearing an armband in school would be asked to remove it. Should he refuse, he would be suspended until he returned without the armband. On December 16, Mary Beth Tinker, age thirteen, and a friend, Christopher Eckhardt, sixteen, went to classes wearing black armbands. John Tinker, fifteen, did the same the next day. The three were suspended.

In February 1968, the Supreme Court decided that the wearing of an armband is "symbolic speech" and is thereby protected under the First Amendment. The Court held that students are indeed "persons" under the Constitution and therefore have fundamental rights, which school authorities must respect. Moreover, the right to self-expression, linked with "personal intercommunication among students," is an "important part of the educational process." Or, as the *Harvard Law Review* distilled the significance of the case, "the Court adopted the view that the process of education in a democracy must be democratic."

Another vital element in *Tinker* was the assertion by the Court that "a student's rights . . . do not embrace merely the classroom hours. When he is in the cafeteria, or on the playing field, or on the campus during the authorized hours, he may express his opinions, even on such controversial subjects as the war in Vietnam, if he does so 'without materially and substantially interfering with appropriate discipline in the operation of the school' and without colliding with the rights of others."

Mere speculation or fear that disruption will follow the exercise of this right does not, the Court made clear, justify the curbing of students' expression of opinion. "In our system," the Court instructed the educators, "undifferentiated fear or apprehension of disturbance is not enough to overcome the right to freedom of expression. Any departure from absolute regimentation may cause trouble. Any variation from the majority's opinion may inspire fear. Any word spoken, in class, in the lunchroom, or on the campus, that deviates from the views of another person may start an argument or cause a disturbance. But our Constitution says we must take this risk . . . and our history says that it is this sort of hazardous freedom—this kind of openness—that is the basis of our national strength and of the independence and vigor of Americans who grow up and live in this relatively permissive, often disputatious, society."

In the *Tinker* decision, the Court referred to an earlier Mississippi case, *Burnside* v. *Byars* (1966), in which the U.S. Court of Appeals for the Fifth Circuit had decided that students could not be suspended for wearing buttons saying "Freedom Now." Approvingly, the Supreme Court cited a point made by Judge Gewin, speaking for the Fifth Circuit, that school officials cannot suppress "expressions of feelings with which they do not wish to contend."

And that includes expressions of feelings that may run abrasively counter to the notion of many school officials that the inculcation of patriotism is one of their primary educative roles. In the *Tinker* case, the Court also referred back to *West Virginia* v. *Barnette*, in which it had already held that the state has no power to compel anyone to pledge allegiance to the flag. The student at issue happened to have been a Jehovah's Witness, but the Court made clear that the issue did not turn on "one's possession of particular religious views. . . . The action of the local authorities in compelling the flag salute and pledge transcends Constitutional limitations on their power and invades the sphere of intellect and spirit, which it is the purpose of the First Amendment to our Constitution to reserve from all official control."

Yet, as clear as that 1943 decision was, schools throughout the country continue to ignore the Constitution and to require the saluting of the flag and the pledging of allegiance. It wasn't until September of last year, for example, that a circuit court judge in Maryland overturned that state's law requiring all students and teachers in Maryland public schools to begin each day with a pledge of allegiance to the flag.

In a number of more "sophisticated" school jurisdictions, officials, grudgingly adhering to the letter of the 1943 decision, nonetheless suspend students who insist on sitting during the pledge of allegiance. In one such case, federal Judge Anthony Travia in New York ruled in July 1970 that a Hicksville youngster could not remain seated because such action *might* lead the boy to become "a conspicuous and distracting force in the classroom."

The weight of Constitutional law is against Judge Travia. In a similar case, in December 1969 a federal judge in the same district, Orrin Judd, held that students do indeed have the Constitutional right to remain seated during the pledge rather than stand silently or leave the room. Citing both the *Barnette* and *Tinker* decisions, Judge Judd noted that "fear of disorder . . . has been ruled out as a ground for limiting peaceful exercise of First Amendment rights." In August 1970, a panel of three federal judges in New Orleans came to the same conclusion, ruling that the Miami school board could not punish students who insist on staying seated during the pledge of allegiance.

In addition to those students who stubbornly hold on to their right to witness against the pledge, there are many more who engage in an "expression of feeling"—and attitude—with which school officials also do not wish to contend, except summarily, their choice of hairstyle and dress. Throughout the country, students are harassed, punished, and even suspended and expelled because of the way they choose to appear. The best brief analysis I have seen of this issue—from both the perspective of constitutional law and that of educating young people to be free citizens—is in a letter to the superintendent and school board of a district in the state of Washington. The writer, Dr. Daniel Larner, president of the local ACLU branch, points out to these school authorities that by banning "unusual" hair and dress, "you tell your students by your actions that it is acceptable to condemn and repress deviations from the norm (whatever they may be). Yet, our Constitution, our Bill of Rights, which protects every one of us, allows us the liberty of our person and the freedom to express ourselves as we choose. The invasion of privacy involved in these regulations not only is unconstitutional but threatens the very maintenance of our democratic institutions. Without any differences, how can there be anything resembling democracy?"

Increasingly, the courts, with some exceptions, are agreeing with Dr. Larner. A focal case—since cited in many other court decisions—is *Breen* v. *Kahl* (1969), in which the expulsion of an eleventh-grade student for violating school hair regulations was held unconstitutional. In affirming that decision, the U.S. Court of Appeals for the Seventh Circuit stated flatly: "The right to wear one's hair at any length or in any desired manner is an ingredient of personal freedom protected by the United States Constitution." There have been parallel court rulings in Illinois, Connecticut, Pennsylvania, Iowa, Indiana, Nebraska, and California, among other states.

Some hair cases, to be sure, have been lost by students. Usually this has happened because of a certain vagueness in part of the *Tinker* decision. The Supreme Court had held that a student may exercise his Constitutional rights if he does so "without materially and substantially interfering with appropriate discipline in the operation of the school." In some cases, school authorities have been able to persuade judges that the wearing of long hair might well lead to the distraction of anti-long-hair students and the disruption of classes. The tide, however, is running strongly the other way. And in August of last year, in a significant decision, the U.S. Court of Appeals for the Seventh Circuit, affirming *Crews* v. *Cloncs* (1969), ruled that a school could not claim that the wearing of long hair was "inherently distracting" to other students unless it had taken clear steps to control or punish those students it claimed would cause disruption because one of their peers chose to wear his hair long. A long-haired student, the court declared, should not be made to forgo his rights "because his neighbors have no self-control."

But even in districts in which the courts have unequivocally declared hair and dress regulations unconstitutional, school authorities often continue to resist the decisions. "Superintendents have actually said they don't care what the courts say," notes Ed McManus of the Milwaukee ACLU. "One of them admitted he knew perfectly well the court would rule against his regulations, but he figured it would be a lengthy and difficult process for the kids and their parents. So the odds were that there would be few challenges, and even those might not go the whole route. He's right. The odds are with him. In one Wisconsin school, for instance, a very bright kid grew a beard and was punished by being removed from an accelerated course. When we went to court, the school backed down but went on harassing him in other ways. We could have won on those harassments, too, but it was a rural school and the parents are just not willing to lay themselves open to that much community criticism.

"No matter what the courts say," McManus adds—and nearly every other ACLU affiliate director agrees—"you have to keep on fighting to get individual principals and school boards to respect the Constitution. And sometimes they're just plain devious. *Tinker* is clear that a student cannot be suspended for wearing an armband, for example, but the school principal may decide that the Supreme Court said nothing about keeping the "offending" student after school. And that's what he'll do."

And although, as I've noted, the *Crews* case is an important decision, the Indiana Civil Liberties Union warns: "Despite *Crews*, and despite the fact that the Indiana State School Board Association agrees with us on the law, . . . school administrators all around Indiana have been lawlessly refusing to admit students because of their hair."

As resistant as many of them are to freedom of student expression as exemplified by long hair, school authorities tend to be even more opposed to freedom of written expression either in school newspapers or in outside material circulated within the school. Yet, in this area too, the courts, with some exceptions, are affirming First Amendment freedoms for students. One of the key cases is *Scoville* v. *Board of Education of Joliet Township* (1970). Two high school students had been expelled for distributing an underground newspaper. The U.S. Court of Appeals for the Second Circuit declared the expulsions unconstitutional, asserting explicitly that "high school students are persons entitled to First and Fourth Amendment protections."

There have been similar decisions in, among other states, Connecticut, Texas, and New York. Again not all cases have been won, but the direction of court opinion is toward broadening high school students' rights to publish and distribute their views. Censorship of school papers and the banning of outside material remain the normative conditions in most schools; but now, when these restrictions are challenged, the burden is increasingly on school authorities to prove that unfettered freedom of expression will lead to substantial disorder in the school or to infringement on the rights of others.

So far, I have focused entirely on what might be termed psychic injuries to high school students' sense of themselves as free citizens or as young men and women learning how to be free. What has astounded me, in the course of preparing this article, is the continued presence in parts of this country of school authorities who still assault children *physically.*

Corporal punishment in the public schools is permitted in 49 states. Although the practice is slowly diminishing, physical punishment is still administered with righteous zeal in many school districts. "Schools," says Carolyn Schumacher of the Committee for the Abolition of Corporal Punishment in Pittsburgh, "are the last place in this country where people can legally be beaten. It has been a hundred years or more since wives and sailors were legally allowed to be flogged. The continuing use of the paddle—and similar weapons—by school administrators and teachers serves to teach violence as a 'solution' to problems."

The most virulent center of corporal punishment among the nation's schools is Dallas. In that city, principals and assistant principals can and do beat children without parental consent, although there are theoretically more stringent "controls" on teachers. In May 1970, a student at Sara Zumwalt Junior High School in Dallas was knocked unconscious by a teacher engaged in enforcing discipline. Dr. William Barris, while medical director for the Dallas Independent School System, cited cases of permanent injury caused by paddling. The leg of one boy, for example, after he had been whipped with a thick, wooden board, atrophied as a result of nerve damage. Dr. Barris is no longer part of the Dallas school system.

A Dallas parent, Marshall Ware, tells of the experience of two of his sons in the Dallas schools: "Our fourteen-year-old—IQ 121—has a minimal brain dysfunction symptomized by visual-motor problems, short attention span, clumsiness, and spelling/writing difficulties. Labeling this as 'not paying attention' and 'laziness' has resulted in spankings from the first grade—plus ridicule and the destruction of his dignity by teachers."

The boy's parents placed him in the Angie Nall School-Hospital for Educational Retraining in Beaumont. But who *really* needed the "educational retraining"?

The Wares' sixteen-year-old son has a high IQ and is characterized by his parents as "sensitive to hypocrisy. He has the problem of being outspoken and can be profiled by the typical undesirable teen-age characteristics as outlined by Gesell, Ilg, and Ames. The school, trying to train him through regular paddling, caused him to become a behavior problem and his grades to drop from Bs to Ds and Fs in all classes. He is now having regular psychiatric sessions. We have doubts that he will ever be interested in high school again—but we do hope he will cease to be uninterested in living."

A Dallas principal, defending corporal punishment, reasons: "It's the only way to get through to them." And School Superintendent Nolan Estes informed the approving majority of the school board last year that he would not want to head a school district that did not allow principals to paddle at their discretion.

So far there have been few court cases on the right of students to be protected from physical punishment. In *Murphy* v. *Kerrigan* (1970), the United States District Court in Massachusetts decreed that the Boston school board and its employees be "permanently enjoined from imposing corporal punishment in any form under any circumstances against any Boston public school students."

That case, however, was settled by stipulation between the parties before trial. What may turn out to be a more influential case has been entered in the U.S. District Court for the Northern District of Texas. Among the plaintiffs are Marshall Ware and his son Douglas. They claim that "the infliction of corporal punishment on its face 'deprives' all public school students as well as Plaintiff . . . of 'liberty without due process of law.'" Also at constitutional issue are charges that corporal punishment constitutes "cruel and unusual punishment" and abridges the "privileges and immunities" of students, including their rights to physical integrity and dignity of personality in violation of the Fourth, Eighth, Ninth, and Fourteenth Amendments.

With specific regard to the due process elements of the case, the suit noted that corporal punishment is routinely inflicted in the Dallas schools, without a hearing for students and parents. Nor is there any advance notice of charges. But due process procedures are absent not only when a student is paddled. Across the board and across the country, as Eleanor Holmes Norton, chairman of the New York City Commission on Human Rights, has underlined, "the schools—which have the primary responsibility for teaching young people the importance of due process in a free society—fail to adhere to the principle of due process more than any other institution except, perhaps, the military."

In many parts of the country, denial of due process is customary in the most severe punishments a school can inflict: suspension and expulsion. In *Breen* v. *Kahl*, the court stated that "when a school board undertakes to expel a public school student"—and suspension, it should be added, is only one step before termination—that board, or a similar authority, "is undertaking to apply the terrible organized force of the state, just as surely as it is applied by the police, the courts, the prison warden, or the militia."

And yet, particularly with regard to suspensions, due process is an alien concept in many school districts. An ACLU lawyer in Indianapolis: "There is no procedure for hearings at any time with the board, or with anyone else, on a suspension case." An ACLU lawyer in Denver: "A principal can suspend for up to five days and can suspend repeatedly. There's no administrative appeal or impartial hearing. There's no notification before the fact. The procedure for expulsion is even more unconstitutional. First it gets under way, and then the parent is told when it's effective. Theoretically, an appeal is possible, but it rarely happens, simply because parents just don't know. If they do find out, the presence of a lawyer is allowed at that hearing; but the way it's set up now the burden of proof is on the parent." Asked about students' procedural rights in Virginia, an ACLU attorney answered: "They just don't exist."

Nearly ten years ago, however, the U.S. Court of Appeals for the Fifth Circuit decided in *Dixon* v. *Alabama State Board of Education* (1961) that students are entitled to notice, an opportunity to be heard, and a chance to present a defense against specific charges in the face of injurious governmental acts. But, as in most other areas of constitutionally protected rights, in suspension and expulsion cases the majority of school administrators persist in excluding their students from the guarantees of the Constitution.

Yet another area in which students' Constitutional rights are ignored is the way pupil records are handled. At issue is chronic invasion of privacy. A Russell Sage Foundation report, *Guidelines for the Collection and Dissemination of Pupil Records*, has observed: "Virtually all school systems maintain extensive pupil records containing, in addition to a pupil's attendance and achievement records, standardized test scores, personality data, information on family background and current status, health data, teacher and counselor observations, anecdotal records, and so on. Despite this fact, very few systems have clearly defined and systematically implemented policies regarding uses of information about pupils, the conditions under which such information is collected, and who may have access to it."

"We found," says Dr. Orville Brim, Jr., president of the foundation, "that there is a lot of release of school-recorded data to unauthorized inquirers—the courts, the police, social welfare agencies—without the parents or the child having the right to know who is getting such information. Furthermore, it is very difficult for the parent to get information about his own child from school files. Typically, parents and students have little, or at best incomplete, knowledge of what's in there."

In many cases, these pupil records include adverse information about a child. Teacher and counselor comments, for instance, are often not checked and are based on hearsay or personality conflict between the student and the person entering the judgment in his record. When made a permanent part of a youngster's file, as often happens, such data can certainly affect college admission or employment prospects.

Among the revelations of a recent New York City Board of Education investigation into the misuse of pupil records was an encounter between a bright student and a teacher who disliked him, in which the teacher promised, "I'll see that you don't get into any college or get a good job." And, indeed, in the pupil's record there was a subsequent notation characterizing him as a "rabble-rouser and troublemaker."

The Russell Sage Foundation report urges that "no information should be collected from students without the prior informed consent of the child and his parents" and that no information be given to anyone outside the school system without "written consent from the student's parents specifying records to be released, and to whom, and with a copy of the records to be released to the student's parents and/or student if desired by the parents"—except in compliance with judicial order. In addition, files containing possibly damaging information about a student should be periodically destroyed.

As with other rights of students under the Constitution, these recommendations are not likely to be widely implemented without persistent pressure on school authorities from students and parents, including, but not limited to, the filing of law suits.

One useful approach to securing student rights, for example, is the planning of Student Bill of Rights proposals. A number of them have been advanced by students, often with the cooperation of ACLU affiliates, in California, Pennsylvania, Washington, Maryland, and other states. These are not simply rhetorical exercises. They are part of an attempt to establish an operative definition of student liberties, rights, and responsibilities—the formulation of which students are to have full participation in—with boards of education and their equivalents through-out the country.

With a clear set of guidelines on paper, it can become much easier for many school administrators to come to terms with the Constitution. Some of them, I suppose, will never be able to admit that a student is indeed protected by that document. But most are men of reasonably good will, who might welcome an agreement on this matter among students, school boards, and themselves. Harried as they are, the removal of at least this weight might be a considerable relief.

So testifies the principal of Ellensburg High School in a small town in the state of Washington. There, after a hair and dress code had been agreed to by students and administrators, the principal observed:

"I didn't like the students coming in with facial hair, but it was getting so that I was spending much of my time hassling with them about it. They were getting mad and I was getting mad. Now we've got the whole thing written down, and although I still don't like it, I recognize that my opinion is different from what I know to be the rightness of the case. It's a relief to be able to get on with the real business of being in school."

A citywide, relatively comprehensive policy statement, "Rights and Responsibilities of Senior High School Students," was adopted by the New York City Board of Education in July 1970. While not flawless from a civil liberties viewpoint, the guidelines do expand the rights and liberties of students with regard to free speech, assembly, publication and distribution of literature, and hair and dress styles.

In Philadelphia, after more than a year of work by a joint committee of administrators, students, parents, faculty, and ACLU staff, the Philadelphia Board of Education last December adopted a "Bill of Rights for High School Students." Among the provisions:

The rights and limits of students respecting freedom of speech, press, and assembly shall be in accord with the First Amendment of the United States Constitution. . . .

Students shall have the right to counsel and due process procedures in the matters of suspension, transfer, and expulsion. . . .

Students shall not be subjected to corporal punishment. . . .

The school systems of Philadelphia, New York, and Ellensburg, however, are still very much the exceptions. For most secondary school students, the battle goes on to win protection under the Constitution. Toward the end of last year, the Center for Research and Education in American Liberties at Teachers College, Columbia University, surveyed the attitudes of nearly 7,000 American students. The center concluded that most of the clashes and tensions in junior and senior high schools are in reaction to the ways in which those institutions are governed.

"The great majority of the students," says Dr. Alan Westin, director of the center, "are angry, frustrated, increasingly alienated by school. They do not believe they receive individual justice or enjoy the rights of dissent or share in critical decision making affecting their lives within the school. Our schools are now educating millions of students who are not forming an allegiance to the democratic political system, simply because they do not experience such a democratic system in their daily lives in school."

A young man at Rufus King High School in Milwaukee speaks for many students, in rural and urban schools, in suburbs, and in ghettos:

"They give us a whole lot of language about responsibility. They punish us for lateness and bad attendance and how we dress and what we say, and we don't have a damn thing to say about any of what they call our education. They claim they're trying to teach us responsibility. But what they're doing has nothing to do with responsibility. It's force. If they really cared about our being responsible, they'd treat us like human beings. They'd listen to us once in a while. The kids here just aren't interested in school, because the whole system is so hypocritical and cynical. It's *got* to be, to treat us this way."

Meanwhile, the battle for student rights intensifies. In March of this year, U.S. District Court Judge Joe Eaton stunned school authorities in Miami by ordering the principal of Douglas MacArthur Junior-Senior High School to reimburse seventeen-year-old Timothy Pyle $182 in court costs and $100 for damages. The principal had expelled Pyle the year before because of the length of his hair. Subsequently, a school admissions committee met in June 1970 and decided that Pyle would not be readmitted for the following academic year. The court declared that both the initial expulsion and the decision by the admissions committee violated the seventeen-year-old's constitutional rights.

Judge Eaton also made "permanent and perpetual" a previous injunction prohibiting the principal or anyone else from using dress codes to "expel, suspend, or impose sanctions" on Pyle and all present and future students at MacArthur "because of the length of their hair." The principal was mandated to reinstate the young man and to help him in "remedying or alleviating lost school time." Moreover, all statements of previous reprimands, suspensions, and expulsions were to be removed from the student's record.

Pyle's suit was in cooperation with the ACLU; and the Florida affiliate believes that the awarding of compensatory damages in this case signals a new breakthrough in student rights. Other students may now decide to sue for damages—just like other American citizens.

SUGGESTED READINGS

Academic Freedom in the Secondary Schools
American Civil Liberties Union, 156 Fifth Avenue, New York, N.Y. 10010

Student Rights Handbook
   Student Rights Project, New York Civil Liberties Union, 84 Fifth Avenue, New York, N.Y. 10011 (This is for New York City but also has national ramifications and is a model of its kind.)
The Reasonable Exercise of Authority
   National Association of Secondary School Principals, 1201 16th Street NW, Washington, D.C. 20036 (Also see the February 1971 Bulletin of the same association: "The Authority Crisis in Our Schools. . . .")
The High School Revolutionaries
   edited by Marc Libarle and Tom Seligson (Vintage)
How Old Will You Be in 1984?
   edited by Diane Divoky (Avon) (See especially "A Study Report on the Montgomery County Public School System: Wanted: A Humane Education.")
Student Power, Participation and Revolution
   edited by John and Susan Erlich (Association Press)
Up Against the Law: The Legal Rights of People Under 21
   by Jean Strouse (Signet/New American Library)

Civil Rights of Public School Students

Richard M. Blankenburg

Lately student protest and activism have raised serious questions concerning the rights of public school students. Because of recent litigation by some students or their parents, the courts have been forced to delineate student rights. Certainly, educators, especially those charged with administrative responsibility, should be well informed of these newly defined civil rights.

Actually, the term "civil rights" has a legal connotation. Civil rights means the rights the individual has under the law. A brief legal definition is: "Civil rights are such that belong to every citizen of the states or the country, or in a wider sense to all its inhabitants." And that includes children. Also civil rights is "A term applied to certain rights secured to citizens by the Fourteenth Amendment and by various acts of Congress"[1] (including the Civil Rights Act of 1964 which has been cited in recent cases dealing with students excluded from school because of long hair).

In looking at the difference between the public schools and the private schools relative to civil rights, it is important to look at the legal relationship between the school and the student. In a public school the relationship is one of government. The public school is an extension of the

From Richard M. Blankenburg, "Civil Rights of Public School Students," *Teachers College Record* 72 (May 1971): 495–504. Reprinted by permission of the author and the publisher.

state. The relationship is one of government and citizen. This is very important in civil rights because the antithesis of civil rights is police power. Police power is defined as "that inherent and plenary power in the state over persons and property which enables the people to prohibit all things inimical to comfort, safety, health, and welfare of society."[2]

Public schools, as an agency of the government, possess police power; this differentiates the relationship between school and student in a public school situation from that in a private school situation. In a legal sense the relationship between the private school and the student is one of contract. It is, however, important to realize a person cannot be deprived of his civil rights by contract; a person cannot contract away his constitutional rights. And, of course, even in a private school, students and administrators are obliged to respect the comfort, safety, health, and welfare of society.

But the public school represents a direct government-citizen relationship. There have been times when the courts have decided on the civil rights of public school students, which many parents and administrators recognize as justified in terms of the legal issues, but question whether the conclusions are in the best interest of the educational operation. For example, for years school teachers have contended, and the courts maintained, in the absence of parents that teachers become a kind of legal parent for the time the student is in school. The legal terminology is *in loco parentis.*

A NEFARIOUS DOCTRINE

A recent decision made by a Wisconsin circuit court shocked many citizens. A male student had been excluded from school because his hair was too long. The judge ruled in this case there was no evidence a male student who allows his hair to grow long is a threat to society. He refused to accept the argument that the school acting *in loco parentis* had a right to determine the length of the student's hair. He stated:

> The argument that school authorities stand *in loco parentis* to the student is a tired, worn out slogan. . . . That nefarious doctrine, *in loco parentis*, has been employed to heap adult abuse against children by judges and courts as well as teachers in the schools. The prejudice and frustrations of people in power cannot be given unbridled license as practiced against children under the hypocritical disguise that the acts committed against them are for the children's own good.[3]

Most parents and educators would have to concede the judge was correct in stating long hair is not a real threat to society or public education. But the same individuals, arguing on educational issues rather than legal ones, would insist that civic pride in their school would be enhanced considerably if all the male students were closely and neatly trimmed. (And some would contend shorn students are better behaved.)

However, those charged with making these final decisions concerning the liberty of the individual citizen must weigh the civil rights of the accused on one side of the scales of justice and the police power of the state on the other side of that scale. In this case the balance swings in favor of civil rights. It is not a matter of majority rule (that would truly be mob rule), but of the unalienable right of the individual.

Most high school classes study civil rights and the Constitution quite thoroughly, and it would be paradoxical for teachers to advocate unalienable rights and then insist that students wait until after graduation to experience them. This seems to be what the judge in Wisconsin was saying—a student is a citizen with all the rights of a citizen under the Constitution. Recently the court trend has been in favor of male students expelled for long hair.[4]

BLACK ARMBANDS

In an important Supreme Court case, *Tinker* v. *Des Moines Independent Community School District*,[5] students of a school district wore black armbands to protest Vietnam war policy. The principals in the district held a meeting, after the initial wearing of the armbands, and enacted a rule prohibiting their use. The Tinker children continued wearing the black armbands, however, and with others were suspended for disobeying the rule. The Court was called upon to rule on the reasonableness of the suspension.

The Court ruled against the school district in this case. In its decision the Court declared that the wearing of an armband was a symbolic act; its purpose was to express certain views. Wearing the armbands, the Court said, was symbolic speech, the kind of free speech protected by the Constitution. (Of course, all speech is not protected by the Constitution. Justice Oliver Wendell Holmes once said shouting "Fire" in a crowded theater would not be a form of free speech protected by the Constitution.) In this case the Court found no evidence that students wearing armbands had created any disruption of classroom activities whatsoever. And because this symbolic display had not caused any disruption, it was judged free speech, of the kind protected by the Constitution.

Secondly, the Court found evidence that the principals' edict against armbands was based upon viewpoints connected with the Vietnam war. The principals simply disagreed with the armband wearers' opinions and reacted by issuing the ban. As a matter of fact, the court found students were allowed to wear other political symbols, such as political badges. Some students were even allowed to wear iron crosses (which the Court felt also had some political symbolism). The Court declared:

The school officials banned and sought to punish petitioners for a silent, passive expression of opinion unaccompanied by any disorder or disturbance on the part of the petitioners. There is, here, no evidence whatever of petitioners' interference, actual or nascent, with the school's work or of collision with the rights of other students to be secure and to be let alone. Accordingly this case does not concern speech or action that intrudes upon the work of the school or the rights of other students.[6]

In another place, the Court said:

In our system undifferentiated fear or apprehension of disturbance is not enough to overcome the right to freedom of expression. Any departure from absolute regimentation may cause trouble. Any variation from the majority's opinion may inspire fear. Any word spoken in class, in the lunchroom, or on the campus that deviates from the views of another person may start an argument or cause a disturbance, but our Constitution says we must take this risk.[7]

The Court further stated: "In our system, state operated schools may not be enclaves of totalitarianism. School officials do not possess absolute authority over their students. Students in school as well as out of school are persons under our Constitution."[8]

FREE SPEECH

Another recent Supreme Court case, *Epperson* v. *State of Arkansas,*[9] also involved free speech. This case deals with the teacher's free speech which, in essence, affects students, since restriction of the teacher's freedom limits the knowledge made available to students. Arkansas had a law that prohibited teaching the theory of evolution. Because the science textbook included this theory, the teacher would be guilty if she taught from it. The teachers brought this case to court to question the constitutionality of the law.

In striking down the Arkansas statute, the Supreme Court for the first time used the term academic freedom in reference to a public elementary or secondary school. The courts previously had talked about academic freedom in regard to universities, where historically there is a precedent for academic freedom; public schools were not organized to do original research as the university was, and consequently, public schools did not warrant traditional academic freedom.

In the *Epperson* case the Court held: "The vigilant protection of Constitutional freedoms is nowhere more vital than in the community of American schools and this Court will be alert against invasions of academic freedom."[10] Apparently, what the Court had in mind was the right of the student to information, stating farther along in its decision: "As this Court said, the First Amendment does not tolerate laws that cast a pall of orthodoxy over the classroom."

IN DEFENSE OF CONSCIENCE

In recent years the Supreme Court has also defended the conscience of public school children by ruling that religious services conducted in public school violated the constitutional guarantee of freedom of religion. It is of interest to note, one hundred thirty years ago, the Fourth Provincial Council of the Catholic Church was pressed to decree:

Since it is evident that in the majority of these provinces a system of public education is being so devised as to be subservient to heresies, by gradually and imperceptibly imbuing the minds of Catholic children with the false principles of sects, we admonish pastors that with all possible zeal they provide for the Christian and Catholic education of Catholic children, and that they diligently watch lest the children use a Protestant version of the Bible, or recite the hymns or prayers of the sects.[11]

Yet it was not until 1963 that the Supreme Court ruled Bible reading (in the form of religious exercises) was an unconstitutional infringement of the children's religious freedom. The Supreme Court in *School District of Abington Township* v. *Schempp*[12] held Bible reading ceremonies in public schools violated two clauses of the Constitution: the guarantee of the free exercise of religion and the prohibition against the governmental establishment of a religion. The Court went on to say, however, "Nothing we have said here indicates that . . . a study of the Bible or religion, when presented objectively as part of a secular program of education, may not be effected consistent with the First Amendment."

An earlier case, *Engel* v. *Vitale,*[13] concerned a prayer which the New York State Board of Regents required be said aloud by each class at the beginning of the school day. The prayer was:

Almighty God, we acknowledge our dependencies upon Thee and we beg thy blessings upon us, our parents, our teachers, and our country.

The U.S. Supreme Court decided this statute had the effect of establishing a state religion and as such violated the First Amendment to the Constitution prohibiting the establishment of a religion by government. Justice Hugo Black, quoting James Madison, commented:

It is proper to take alarm at the first experiment on our liberties . . . Who does not see that the same authority which can establish Christianity, in exclusion of all other religions, may establish with the same ease any particular sect of Christians, in exclusion of all other sects? That the same authority which can force a citizen to contribute three pence only of his property for the support of any one establishment may force him to conform to any other establishment in all cases whatsoever?[14]

LOITERING

In many states the legislatures have been very quick to enact statutes to control the behavior of persons on school grounds, including especially the behavior of students. California, like most other states, enacted a statute which prohibits loitering in the vicinity of the school. In the case of *Huddleson* v. *Hill*,[15] the defendants challenged the constitutionality of the statute claiming the statute was too vague to enforce. To paraphrase the statute, it stated that loitering in the vicinity of the schools would be punishable by six months imprisonment or a $500 fine.

The term "loitering" is defined as to be slow moving, delay, linger, saunter, or lag behind. In the *Huddleson* case, the court decided: (1) If you interpreted the statute in the literal sense, it was too vague to be enforced; (2) when a court can adopt a broad or restricted construction of the statute, and the restricted one would make it a valid statute, then the restricted construction of the statute is the one that the court should adopt and (3) what the statute in its entirety meant, and what the legislatures intended it to mean, was that individuals should be prevented from loitering in the vicinity of schools to commit a crime.

The court specifically defined the meaning of the statute as follows: "As proscribed by the statute, the word loiter obviously connotes lingering in the designated places for the purpose of committing a crime as opportunity may be discovered. . . . Loitering as forbidden includes waiting, but merely waiting for any lawful purpose does not constitute such loitering."[16]

The court then concluded:

> Therefore, as we construe the state statute before us, persons who merely sit on park benches, loll on public beaches, pause in the vicinity of schools, and public areas frequented by children cannot be reasonably considered as loitering within the compass of the statute. It is only when the loitering is of such a nature that from the totality of the person's actions and in the light of the prevailing circumstances, it may be reasonably concluded that it is being engaged in "for the purpose of committing a crime as opportunity may be discovered," such conduct falls within the statute.[17]

It would appear from this wording that if a student is excluded from school, and he returns to wait on the sidewalk for one of his friends, he is not guilty of loitering. The court's definition of the term "loitering" does throw a different light on the statute; the court has provided a more definitive right of a student in cases where the student is "loitering" in the mind of educators, but not within the interpretation of the statutes.

PRIVACY

Another recent case related to the civil rights of students took place in Mount Vernon, New York. The initial case, *People* v. *Overton,*[18] concerned Carlos Overton, a student in the public high school. Detectives from the police force came to the school and informed the vice-principal they had a warrant to search the boy and his locker; the vice-principal opened the locker for the police. Marijuana cigarettes were found there, and the cigarettes were used as evidence to convict the boy. It was later discovered that the search warrant of the police officers was not a valid warrant. The prosecution insisted that the validity of the search warrant was not important because the vice-principal had the authority to open the boy's locker at any time necessary. The highest court in New York supported the prosecution.

Yet in an appeal to the Supreme Court of the United States, the Court in *Overton* v. *New York*[19] overturned the highest court in New York on the basis of more recent Supreme Court decisions. Basically, the Supreme Court held that a person cannot, on the basis of an invalid search warrant, obtain access to the locker of a student after the student has been assigned the locker for his own personal purposes, and obtain evidence from that search to convict the student. The Court did not say a student can grab marijuana cigarettes and run down the hall pursued by the vice-principal and the police department, throw the marijuana in his locker, slam the door, and then demand a search warrant. When there is obvious reason to believe evidence of a crime is concealed in a locker, and there is danger involved in waiting to obtain a search warrant, a school official would be obligated to open a student's locker. What the Supreme Court does say is this: A police officer cannot lie to a student and say he has a valid search warrant when he doesn't, and by these means obtain evidence which can be used to convict the student. The Court also seems to be suggesting that a principal or vice-principal must have good cause to invade the privacy of a locker assigned to a student for personal use.

DUE PROCESS OF LAW

Another aspect of student civil rights, which the courts have been concerned with recently, is the constitutional guarantee that an accused person has "due process of law." The Fifth and Fourteenth Amendments state a person cannot be deprived of life, liberty, or property without "due process of law"; however, due process has not been specifically defined in the Constitution, and the courts have had to determine what actually constitutes due process. A recent case involving students and the due process clause of the Constitution is *In the Matter of Gault.*[20]

In this case, a young man on the basis of his own testimony was declared a juvenile delinquent in a juvenile proceeding and was committed to a state institution. Neither he nor his parents were adequately notified of the charges, nor was he adequately represented by legal counsel. The juvenile authorities contended that cases dealing with juveniles were of such a senstitve nature that some elements of due process cannot always prevail.

The Court held that juvenile proceedings which may lead to commitment to a state institution must be regarded as "criminal proceedings" for purposes of applying the privilege against self-incrimination. Unless a confession meets all the requirements of "due process" (notification of the right to attorney and the consequences of confession), commitment of a juvenile to a state institution cannot be sustained in the absence of sworn testimony and the opportunity for cross-examination.

The Court refused to accept the contention of the authorities that juvenile proceedings, because of their sensitivity, did not require procedure consistent with judicial due process. The Court declared: "Neither the Fourteenth Amendment nor the Bill of Rights is for adults alone. . . . Due process requirements do not interfere with provisions for the processing and treatment of juveniles separately from adults."

A hearing in connection with a juvenile court adjudication of delinquency need not conform to all the requirements of a criminal trial, the Court stated, but it must have all the essentials of due process and fair treatment. The Court declared, "Under the United States Constitution, the condition of being a boy does not justify a kangaroo court."

Madera v. *Board of Education of the City of New York*[21] involved a suspended public school student who was the subject of a school "Guidance Conference." The meeting was attended by the child, the parents, the principal, the superintendent, the assistant superintendent, the guidance counselor, and the school-court coordinator assigned to the district. The conference is not a criminal proceeding, no record is kept, nor is any statement from the conference used in any subsequent criminal proceedings. As a result of such a conference, the student could be reinstated, transferred to another school, or with parents' consent, transferred to a special school for socially maladjusted children. The student contended he had been denied due process because he had been refused the right to be represented by attorney.

The court decided that a "Guidance Conference" did not represent a hearing which required ordinary legal procedure. The purpose of the hearing, the court reasoned, was to consider only educational matters; its consequences, therefore, were not sufficiently serious to require the adversary system ordinarily utilized in court proceedings.

In juvenile hearings which could have serious consequences to the student, it would appear that every care should be taken to guarantee him "due process of law." Boards of education hearings on expulsion would certainly be considered a case of serious consequences to the student. Yet many such hearings do not contain the elements of due process. For example, in many hearings, especially those involving young witnesses, the opportunity for cross-examination is not allowed. Obviously, the effect of an attorney interrogating a young child under the rules of adversary procedure would be difficult to defend. However, there is always the possibility of indirect cross-examination; questions to be directed to the witness could be submitted to the hearing officer by the defense, and then directed to the witness by the less aggressive hearing officer (who could also rule on the relevance of the questions). In this manner the individual could be provided with due process, and the due process could be adapted to juvenile proceedings.

Another aspect of due process relates to how a school handles police investigations of students in the school building. A booklet, *Academic Freedom in the Secondary Schools*, published by the American Civil Liberties Union, outlines the procedure advocated by the ACLU. The booklet states:

Where disciplinary problems involving breaches of law are rampant, schools connot be considered sacrosanct against police and the proper function of law officers cannot be impeded in crime detection. Whenever police are involved in the schools, their activities should not consist of harassment or intimidation. If a student is to be questioned by the police, it is the responsibility of the school administration to see that the interrogation takes place privately in the office of a school official, in the presence of the principal or his representative. Every effort should be made to give a parent the opportunity to be present. All procedural safeguards prescribed by law must be strictly observed. When the interrogation takes place in school, as elsewhere, the student is entitled to be advised of his rights, which should include the right to counsel and the right to remain silent.[22]

SUMMARY

Laws relating to the civil rights of public school students have developed quite rapidly during the past few years, eroding, perhaps even eliminating, the traditional authoritarian stereotype of the public school educator. In addition, a reaction seems to be developing to the compulsory school attendance statutes. Perhaps the trend could be called a democratization of the public schools.

Schools possibly will be called upon to make adjustments to these new decisions by the courts, although some of the adjustment would simply be to provide for constitutional liberty. The best posture for American educators would be to exemplify the constitutional Bill of Rights in their relationships with students. If liberty works, it must be made to work at all age levels. In any real concept of education, this is what schools are for.

NOTES

[1] Henry Campbell Black, *Law Dictionary*, 4th ed. (St. Paul, Minn.: West Publishing Co., 1951.)

[2] Ibid.

[3] *Wisconsin ex rel. Koconis* v. *Fochs,* Circuit Court, Milwaukee County, 372–043 (October 14, 1969).

[4] For a decision favoring the student, in addition to footnote 3, *see Breen* v. *Kahl*, 296 F. Supp. 702 (D.C. Wis. 1969). For contrary decisions, *see Ferrell* v. *Dallas Independent School District*, 392 F. 2d 697 (5 Cir. 1968) and *Davis* v. *Firment*, 269 F. Supp. 524 (D.C. La. 1967).

[5] *Tinker* v. *Des Moines Independent Community School District*, 393 U. S. 503 (1969).

[6] Ibid.

[7] Ibid.

[8] Ibid.

[9] *Epperson v. State of Arkansas*, 393 U. S. 97, 89 S. Ct. 266 (1968).

[10] Ibid.

[11] Sister Mary Salome, "The American Hierarchy and Education" (Doctoral dissertation, Marquette University, Milwaukee, Wisconsin, 1934), p. 165.

[12] *School District of Abington Township, Pa. v. Schempp*, 374 U.S. 203 (1963).

[13] *Engel v. Vitale*, 370 U.S. 421, 82 S. Ct. 1261 (1962).

[14] Ibid.

[15] *Huddleson v. Hill*, 40 Cal. Rep. 581 (1964).

[16] Ibid.

[17] Ibid.

[18] *People v. Overton*, 283 NYS 2d 22 (1967).

[19] *Overton v. New York*, 393 U.S. 85 (1968).

[20] *In the Matter of Gault*, 387 U. S. 1, 87 S. Ct. 1428 (1967).

[21] *Madera v. Board of Education of City of New York*, 386 F. 2d 778 (2 Cir. 1967).

[22] *Academic Freedom in the Secondary Schools* (American Civil Liberties Union, 156 Fifth Avenue, New York, September 1968).

Student Unrest Reexamined

Edward Wynne

In order to understand the phenomenon of student unrest, we must appreciate the history of American education over the past 50 years, how youths achieve maturity in modern America, and how these patterns differ from the past. The chart on the next page shows the remarkable, unprecedented growth in formal or school education in America over the immediate past. It is all the more remarkable when compared with the relatively unchanging curve of formal schooling received by all human society since 10,000 B.C. Never before in human history have such large proportions of youth been kept in school for such long periods. Before the large-scale development of studenthood, most children spent much of their youth working with adults. Many of their tasks were carried out on farms. Such activities helped young people learn how to get along with persons of other ages—and taught adults how to relate to young people. Concurrently, youths learned about the realities of the world of work: that it takes a while to get things done; that not every project succeeds; that give and take is a part of working together to do a job; that all your friends are not your own age, nor all your enemies older. Even when a youth was not

From Edward Wynne, "Student Unrest Reexamined," *Phi Delta Kappan* 53 (October 1971): 102–4, by permission of the author and the publisher.

raised on a farm, interaction of this type frequently occurred in connection with his industrial work. Also, employees on jobs of most types today have far more freedom to exercise their feelings than do students in elementary or high school.

FIGURE 1

How School Attendance in America Compares with International Long-Range Trends

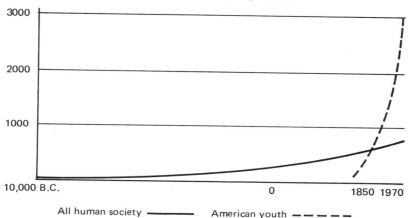

All human society ━━━━━ American youth ━ ━ ━ ━ ━

Average days formal schooling received per youth for all human society, 10,000 B.C.-1970, compared to data on American youths.

Thanks to "modern progress," present-day youths are generally much less likely to work at school age than they were only a few decades ago. When they do work, they are more likely to be relegated to less substantial jobs (thanks to credentialism and the growing complexity of work). As a result, they grow up having relatively little close contact with adults outside of their immediate family. In school their contacts with their teachers are far less intense than those they might have had in traditional work. Typically, a teacher deals with 25 to 30 youths. In many jobs, a supervisor has charge of five to ten workers and is able to give specially concentrated attention to the newer employees; moreover, older employees can help the youth discover the ropes.

Diminishing work experience is one of several modern changes related to youth unrest. Others are:

The increase of suburban living, which reduces intergeneration contacts; in many suburbs, there are only parents and children, not young marrieds or old folks.

The development of shopping centers and modern transportation, which has put homes farther away from work and business, so that children have less of an idea how work is done and become more prone to develop unrealistic ideas about how the real world operates.

The diminishing of the extended family—grandparents, uncles, aunts, cousins, nephews, and nieces. Such families brought children into contact with sympathetic adults with many different perspectives. (Today, they tend to deal only with parents and are less likely to have a chance to come in contact with understanding, diverse adults.)

My analysis is strongly supported by a simple piece of data. Throughout America, only a small percentage of our young people are involved in the more active forms of unrest—sit-ins and violence. Research shows that these activist students come from the families that are more likely to emphasize education, to live in suburbs, and to have parents with jobs which are hard to explain to their children—such as social work, advertising, government administration. While youths from these families may be in rebellion against society, they are not in sharp disagreement with their parents; their parents, in general, agree with many of their criticisms about the war, race and poverty issues, and politics. The parents may not be quite as militant but they do not disagree with the goals of their children. Thus we do not have a conflict between generations but a conflict between two classes in our society with different value systems. The young dissidents are merely the shock troops of their parents.

In other words, both the dissident children and their parents are angry and alienated because of the effect of prolonged school exposure during their youth. On the other hand, college students whose parents have not gone to college are far less likely to be involved in unrest; for example, unrest is far more common on the campuses of better colleges, where the students more frequently come from college-educated parents. Thus better colleges, with more facilities, better faculty-student ratios, and better-off students have more unrest than the colleges where the students might seem to have more palpable grievances. My explanation is that the harm of an excessively school-focused, formalistic education takes about two generations to have an impact.

I call this phenomenon the Buddenbrooks effect, after the Thomas Mann novel. It portrays the gradual decline, over several generations, of a wealthy and vigorous merchant family. It implies that their affluence and increasing aestheticism actually left the successive generations less able to transmit realistic and useful attitudes to their children. At this moment we only have a small number of such families—but the number is growing.

My observations are not a criticism of these dissatisfied families. We have gravely overemphasized the importance of school in maturation. Concurrently, we have undervalued the experiences youths receive from work, living in an intergenerational community, coming in contact with an extended family. Many of the rebellious youths apparently also agree with me—they drop out, travel to seek nonschool experiences, form communes to engage in work without credentials, and even may demonstrate in order to have the vital, emotionally challenging experiences they cannot have sitting in classrooms.

However, my remarks do conflict with many of the theories offered for the current unrest. I claim it is not mainly the product of the war, poor teaching, Maoism, drugs, racism, or poverty. If there should be a millenium where these wrongs were extinguished, I believe the students would still be almost as disturbed—although about some other issue which would still obscure their real frustration. I believe youths are largely dissatisfied because they are deprived of a chance to grow up—to grow up by being given real responsibilities to do real things; by working in close association with seriously concerned adults; by being given real power and responsibilities over real things, not class assignments; by being allowed to laugh, get angry, and cry during the day. The restrictions that schools place on the emotions of youths in school are far harsher than any of the restrictions any boss would dare place on adult workers.

Student militants often inveigh against the supposed unique immorality of our society. We're sometimes puzzled by this conduct, since the actions they condemn are often not so different from the thousands of other wrongs and mistakes that men have committed throughout all history. However, in a strange way, the students can point out one historically new wrong—the way we raise our youth. Our modern maturation system is a new one; it is a kind of wrong that has never been visited on young men and women before in history. It is this new wrong that really triggers the protests.

Let me interject a story illustrating school restrictions. My 12-year-old daughter told my wife and me that she had something she wanted to talk over with her teacher. We said, "Stay awhile after the period and iron it out." Our daughter said she didn't have time. We suggested, "Go to class a little early." Once again, "No time." It sounded strange that there weren't two minutes free, but we dropped it. Later we ran into the principal and raised the question. He said, "Time between classes is tight, since the children are allowed only four minutes to go from one classroom to the next." I said, "Why not be big about it and make it six minutes? It might help things." He said, "With four minutes, half the young people hang around in the halls, since they don't need to walk the full distance. If it was six minutes, they'd hang around for four minutes; there might be crowd-control problems." So my daughter probably couldn't talk to the teacher unless she made the special effort which she was too shy to do.

The principal might have handled it better, but 1,000 12- and 13-year-old children *can* present crowd-control problems. Some unpleasant rules might be necessary. But that's my point! The restrictions that are inevitable when you bring large numbers of children and small numbers of adults together in schools are *dehumanizing.* That's how my daughter felt, dehumanized. After 16 years of such treatment, any person might get angry at the first reasonable excuse. Or he might start taking drugs or rejecting other adult institutions (which in their ignorance young people believe to be like schools). If you grew up in this system, never exploding, because your parents kept telling you the system was good for you, you might give a different signal to your children when they were in school. Unlike your own parents, you would say to your kids, "My parents told me this was right, but I'm not saying that to you. If you want to blow off steam, I won't blame you."

It won't be easy to correct this dangerous situation, since we're concerned with a 150-year-old trend. But we'd better get started. Let me offer some practical—but very ambitious—solutions:

1. Make it easier for youths to start work without credentials; create more opportunities for on-the-job learning. Employers find this expensive, since breaking in young workers takes the time and skills of better workers. And when the breaking-in is over, a youth may exercise his right to seek work elsewhere. Then the employer will lose his training investment. Hence we must offer the employer an incentive for possible loss. I believe we could work out subsidiary or tax forgiveness plans to repay employers their costs of breaking in young workers who have not had lengthy schooling. Such arrangements might cost lots of money, but the money spent would save us the costs we now spend in keeping unhappy students in school.

2. Make it easier for youths to (a) drop out of school and return later to finish; or (b) start college later in life. Today the military draft discourages this. But that will change. Indeed, right now local Selective Service boards can change some of the policies that pressure youths to stay in school where they don't want to be and don't belong. But in any case the draft will end and we will then need school policies that encourage youths to break up their schooling rather than take it all in one dose. The spread-out and postponement policies should especially apply to youths who have had little work experience and have come from homogeneous suburbs. These students often have excellent academic backgrounds, are attractive college material, and are encouraged to go on to college quickly. However, before they go further in school (if they wish to at all), they often should learn a little from life. Today, college and high school policies pressure them to come in quickly and stay as long as possible.

3. Make schools more human while we keep youths in them. This is an enormous subject and can only be mentioned here. However, let me offer one example of an approach. My daughter was a "crowd-control problem" rather than a child, because there were 1,000 students in her junior high school. Why can't we move more quickly toward having 100-student schools? I know there are some efficiencies to be gained by operating large schools (and some important inefficiencies), but can't modern management techniques—computers, TV, telephones, buses—permit us to decentralize and still get some of the facilities of the center out to the fringes? Of course that will take research, but very, very little school money is spent on research, so we just keep building larger prisons to save money.

4. If we think this is a vital problem, we must commit ourselves to treating it like other important issues in our society; we must be prepared to spend money on research. We can now conceive of some immediate directions for change in youth policies. However, in the long run it will be essential for us to have more information on what has been happening, what is happening, what changes in our institutions or practices help or hurt, and how to bring about more useful changes. All these questions require us to collect and analyze information about youth and education. This information is not available today. It is not available for a simple reason: We don't spend much money on educational research. The information we need can't be collected by a committee; people or agencies have to collect and analyze it as a routine matter, just as the weather

bureau, the department of health, and the bureau of labor statistics keep tab on vital developments. No one keeps much data on how youths grow up.

5. While the problem I've described is a national one, all the steps I've described can be started at the local level. In Illinois, for example, tax or subsidiary legislation could be passed. The state university system could analyze and change entrance and readmission requirements to encourage students to seek out-of-school experiences for maturation. School districts, with assistance from the state superintendent of public instruction, could pay greater attention to school humanization themes. The state could appropriate more funds for educational research and ask its universities to accelerate research concerned with these issues. Finally, since a legislative committee may not have time for the in-depth approach that I believe this issue requires, the legislature might recommend that the governor create a nonpartisan citizens committee (with adequate funds for staff assistance) to review the problem and come up with further proposals. Such a review could be coordinated with an intensified research effort.

Let me offer a final caution. School is not an unmitigated blessing. However, it is an essential support for the material wealth of our society and a tool for broadening the opportunities of poorer citizens. A meat-ax approach to higher education costs will not help in solving the problems I have described. The youths who are most likely to get into college, even if budgets are cut, are the ones I have described as most alienated and who most need nonschool experiences. They come from better-off homes; they can pay for college and they have better marks to meet entrance standards. Conversely, the least alienated youths—those from poorer homes, who have less impressive qualifications, who can best use college—are most likely to be kept out by simple budget cutting. Simply saving money will not help. I'm afraid the changes needed will take thought instead of economy.

QUESTIONS FOR REFLECTION AND DISCUSSION

1. In the opening paragraphs of his article, Hentoff cites several examples of violated civil rights. Can you recall any similar violations in your own schooling? If so, what were they and how were they resolved?

2. The title of the McGhan article asks "Where Do You Stand"? Where *do* you stand on the issue of student activism? Do you think all of the authors represented in this section share a common position? If so, what is that position? If not, what are the differences you have uncovered? How do you line up with the position(s) represented here?

3. As Swift notes, patterns of pupil control—most teachers call it discipline—change from time to time. What is your view on such matters as corporal punishment? Student involvement in decision making? More unstructured time for high school youth?

4. Suppose you were a classroom teacher. What rights would you expect your students to want? What ones of these would you be willing to grant? Or is your willingness to grant them or not even germane? Are there some rights a majority of students might want that you would argue against or oppose? If so, what are they?

Chapter three
Teacher Education

In the opening selection in this volume, Marland observes that "more than ever before, the substance of America's future resides in our teachers." The articles in this section strongly echo this sentiment, yet go well beyond it to point out the many and sometimes conflicting difficulties in teacher education.

One problem is basically financial. Colleges and universities have traditionally been responsible for most teacher training, but rarely have these institutions granted to faculties of education the same resources that support training programs in medicine, law, or engineering. Moreover, two trends have made state legislatures chary of increasing their fiscal apportionments to teacher education. First, there is the presently crowded job market. Why, a legislator may argue, should more money be given for teacher training when already we have substantially more teachers in many fields than we have positions for?* Secondly, there is concern about the number of teachers who teach for only a few years and then leave the profession. Legislators quite appropriately may question the wisdom of providing additional funding for a training program that has such a high attrition rate.

Beyond the financial dimension a very practical question exists for the teacher trainer. Ought he try to train teachers for the schools that are or for the schools that ought to be? Boldly stated, as this is, the problem seems more dichotomous than it really is: one should admit that a very good training program can do both jobs. But it is no easy task. For example, a teacher trained to work in open, flexible schools may experience considerable difficulty in the traditional, closed schools Silberman describes in *Crisis in the Classroom.* Yet, to continue to train teachers for a traditional educational environment may be to focus too strongly on the past and the present, too weakly on the future.

A third difficulty is a philosophical-psychological one. Is teaching an art or a skill? Are good teachers born or made? Again, the blunt questions imply more nearly a dichotomy than is really the case, but all teacher educators of even limited experience can identify past students who

---

*This problem of oversupply is, of course, the opposite side of the coin of underdemand. In the early 60s one teacher to thirty students was a viable educational ratio simply because there were not enough teachers to effect a lower ratio. Today there are enough teachers, but the demand has remained essentially the same. If and when school districts choose to try to lower teacher-pupil ratios, then the current oversupply of teachers may rapidly diminish.

seemed to the manor born and others for whom no amount of training would have sufficed. Clearly all prospective teachers can profit from training, can at least acquire knowledge about those skills deemed requisite for successful classroom performance. But, equally clearly, truly effective teachers often exhibit a kind of personal dynamism, a charisma, that no training can produce.

These are but three of the problems confronting teacher educators. The five articles in this section discuss these and numerous others. Denemark begins by indicating some future directions for teacher education. Iannone wonders if the real problem in teacher education centers upon the fact "that the act of teaching is irrelevant for a younger generation born in an Age of Electronics." Lenke extends teacher education beyond the college training center to the schools the new teachers enter and asserts that "a teacher's very employment is a constraint upon true teaching." Swinefords' article discusses ten "critical teaching strategy problem areas" and offers practical suggestions for improvement. The final article, by Shermis and Barth, is future-oriented and is based on two assumptions: "(1) it is desirable for education departments to become more precise and (2) it is entirely possible for such precision to be reached."

Improving Teacher Education: Some Directions

George W. Denemark

The central challenge to teacher education today is the establishment of an appropriate balance among the institutional forces which impinge upon it—schools, the practicing profession, and higher education. Without clarification of the roles appropriate to each and without effecting a balance among them which reflects their unique potential contributions, the future of teacher education is bleak.

Teacher education, while dependent upon schools, colleges, and the profession, is not the principal business of anybody. The major segment of preservice teacher education continues to be provided within colleges and universities. Yet the responsibility has seldom been accepted with the kind of emphasis and enthusiasm that suggests that the institutions view teacher preparation as an important responsibility. "Although the financial survival of many small colleges is dependent upon their programs and enrollments in teacher education, budget allocations seldom reflect this,

From George W. Denemark, "Improving Teacher Education: Some Directions," *Peabody Journal of Education* 49 (October 1971): 4–11. Reprinted by permission of the author and George Peabody College for Teachers, copyright holder.

and priorities for staff and facilities point elsewhere."[1] James C. Stone has referred to teacher education as a "stepchild," unwanted by the colleges,[2] and an increasing number of educators concerned with this neglect have urged a return of teacher education to the public schools, a plan reminiscent of the city teachers colleges of the recent past. School boards frequently view teacher education as peripheral to their responsibilities and even question their cooperation with area colleges when such involvement generates problems of student teacher liability, conduct or dress, added responsibilities for teachers and administrators, etc. And professional organizations, caught up in power struggles with rival organizations and with school boards, too often neglect educational functions in order to build their membership rosters and exert political influence.

THE LIAISON ROLE OF SCHOOLS OF EDUCATION

Schools of education are particularly vulnerable to criticism because by definition they must stand between elementary and secondary schools on the one hand and their academic colleagues in the university on the other. Such a position is of great potential importance in fostering a close liaison between schools and colleges concerned with the education of teachers. It is also one of considerable ambiguity and tension because it is rarely adequately understood or accepted by either quarter. Schools of education are seldom sufficiently practical and reality-oriented to please their public school associates. Neither are they sufficiently academically oriented to attain full status with their university colleagues in the liberal arts disciplines, the segment of higher education which dominates most American universities. Yet, to properly discharge their liaison role between these agencies essential to effective teacher preparation, they must deliberately perpetuate much of this ambiguity. Those that abandon a commitment to the fundamental relationship of teacher education to the basic disciplines and to foundational knowledge will cause teacher education to become preoccupied with technical proficiency rather than the production of teacher-scholars capable of diagnosing learning problems and creating curricular and instructional alternatives to cope with them. On the other hand, those neglectful of the need for teachers who are able to reach and teach young people in today's social milieu will make teacher education largely irrelevant to the world around it.

The current financial crisis of higher education makes the status of college-based teacher education particularly insecure. Reports from many colleges and universities in recent months disclose financial cutbacks of significant proportions at a number of them. Some schools of education have confronted freezes on new faculty appointments even though enrollments have continued to rise. Others have found it necessary to reduce faculty size or to eliminate important services or program facets. While such reductions have, up to this point, been institution-wide rather than directed only toward teacher education, it is possible that the future might be different. In a tight money situation some institutions could conclude that one means of reducing budget demands would be to relinquish pedagogical training to the public schools and divert the resultant savings to the continuation of academic programs. Support for such action might be received from some public school systems where a combination of impatience with the products of teacher education programs and easier access to federal funds for such projects might cause them to feel that they could unilaterally operate the professional training of classroom personnel.

If this were to occur, the pattern of teacher education in the future might become one of a liberal arts content-oriented college education followed by a period of on-the-job training offered by employing school systems and based largely upon an apprenticeship model. Such would seem to be a tragic development for several reasons. The sharp separation of content from method and related pedagogy in teacher education is at odds with what thoughtful scholars have recommended for many years. The apprenticeship mode is more compatible with a concept of teaching as a craft than as a profession. As the responsibilities of the classroom become even more demanding with respect to individualizing instruction and accepting pluralistic cultural patterns, it would seem illogical to settle for an undemanding image of the teacher as a technician rather than as a professional. The movement toward differentiated staffing and the use of a range of paraprofessionals in the school does not invalidate this position but rather lends support to it, for the management, training, and coordination of an expanded instructional team call for greater rather than reduced qualifications in the teachers who assume team leadership roles.

INTEGRATION OF LIBERAL AND PROFESSIONAL STUDIES

Hopefully we are nearing the end of an era when it was thought desirable to tightly segregate liberal and professional studies. In engineering, medicine, and other professional fields there is clearly movement toward an integration of liberal and technical or professional studies throughout the college program instead of continuing the separation of these. Separation of knowledge from the problems and issues to which it applies has too long characterized much of American higher education. There is developing recognition that the career concerns of students can provide important motivation for liberal studies and afford a context within which general knowledge and concepts can be understood. At the same time liberal education can invest professional studies with much needed humanistic qualities. All of these arguments lend support to a continued and expanding cooperative relationship between schools and colleges facilitated by the liaison role of schools of education.

BALANCED INVOLVEMENT OF PRACTITIONERS

An honest analysis of the recent history of teacher education will disclose a serious imbalance in the involvement of elementary and secondary school practitioners in basic decisions relating to professional standards, licensure, accreditation, and other important teacher education matters. Currently, there is a concerted movement to correct this situation. For example, the National Education Association through its Commission on Teacher Education and Professional Standards has proposed a model teacher standards and licensure act for passage in each state. Unfortunately, the proposed model seems in most ways simply to substitute another kind of imbalance for that which presently exists. While recommending standards commissions of thirteen members in each state, the model legislation provides for only two of the thirteen to be representative of higher education. Further, the proposal advocates establishing accreditation at the state level with the possibility of neglect of the important advances made during the last decade in the national accreditation of teacher education. If standards commissions are established in the states without adequate discussion of the need for a more adequate representation of the agencies concerned with schools and teacher preparation and of the central role to be played by colleges and universities in both preservice and in-service education, a giant and perhaps irreversible step will have been taken toward the dissolution of a meaningful partnership involving field and campus personnel. Clearly, more substantial involvement of practitioners must be provided but as a supplement to, not a substitute for, teacher educators in colleges and universities. The need is for a more effective balance rather than for an exchange of one mistake for an earlier one.

HIGHER STANDARDS FOR ADMISSION, RETENTION, AND LICENSURE

Several other directions of development are worthy of mention in considering the future of teacher education. One relates to the changing standards for the admission, retention, and licensure of teachers. Present practices in admission to teacher education and to teacher licensure were developed in an era of teacher scarcity in most fields. A recent report from the Department of Labor, however, has predicted that with a continuation of the present trend in teacher supply and demand there would be between now and 1980 only 2.4 million teaching job openings available to the 4.2 million college graduates prepared for teaching. The United States Office of Education projected an annual surplus of 55,000 persons prepared for teaching over jobs available by the year 1975. For the first time in a quarter of a century young men and women graduating from college may find that teaching jobs will not be readily available to them, particularly in such fields as secondary school English, social studies, and foreign languages.

Both employing school systems and preparing institutions will now be in a position to exercise greater selectivity in personnel admitted to their staffs or training programs. During the period when teachers were in short supply, many colleges operated with minimum standards for admission to and retention in programs of teacher preparation, seldom significantly more demanding than those required of the general student body of the institution. Now, however, with a recurring and growing surplus of teachers in many fields, colleges will need to consider establishing admissions quotas, higher standards, and more meaningful criteria for admission to programs in teacher education.

Recent studies have reaffirmed the impression that graduates of teacher education programs in colleges and universities are much like the graduates of the institution as a whole. If anything, the prospective teachers are sometimes a bit weaker in academic performance. It would seem not only reasonable, however, but necessary that we expect persons to whom we assign significant responsibility for the intellectual, social, and moral development of our children to be capable themselves of better than average performance in these arenas. Whatever excuse we may have had in the past for not expecting more of our teacher candidates clearly cannot hold true in the years immediately ahead.

Evidence of academic excellence should be required for admission and retention in teacher education programs and for recommendation for intitial licensure as a teacher. Obviously, grade point average is not the only factor in judging a candidate's adequacy for a career in teaching, but it does seem reasonable that persons charged with intellectual development responsibilities in others should themselves be skilled in intellectual processes.

A healthy, flexible but stable personality is another important quality to look for in teacher candidates. We have too often avoided making judgments on such matters because of their difficult and controversial nature. The alarming incidence of mental health problems among our population, however, underscores the need for school experiences which represent a constructive influence on the growth of young people in this respect. Psychological screening designed to eliminate those whose own personality needs are so pressing as to interfere with their capacity to focus on the growth of children in their charge is difficult and time-consuming. It appears more urgently needed now than ever before.

Every teacher is fundamentally involved in matters requiring both written and oral communication, yet many have serious deficiencies in these skill areas. The admission and retention process associated with teacher education must in the future place a higher priority on these skills than is presently the case.

Too many persons enroll in teacher education programs viewing them as an *insurance policy* or career substitute for their primary interest. The lack of commitment to a career in teaching generally proves to be wasteful and expensive to the institution providing the training experience.

Possibilities for improvement in the selection process growing out of the changes in supply and demand in teaching should include some measure of a candidate's understanding of career alternatives in teaching and some documentation of his commitment to the demands of such a career. An approach having considerable promise is one which requires students applying to teacher education to present a record of their own initiative and involvement in activities like tutoring, camp counseling, service as a teacher aide or as a community agency worker which can document their commitment to a teaching career. Precollege and lower division experiences designed to provide opportunities for exploring the nature of teaching and developing some commitment to its being developed on some campuses are likely to expand and become regularized in the years ahead.

DIFFERENTIATION OF PREPARATION TO FIT DIFFERENT ROLES

Another direction for development in teacher education for the future is the provision of differentiation between the preparation necessary for beginning teaching and that appropriate to a continuing career in the classroom. We have endured too long a training rationale which assumes the equivalence of the beginning teacher and the seasoned professional with extensive advanced training. As a consequence, we have generally expected too much of the beginner and too little of the experienced teacher. Teacher education programs in the future must be differentiated so that those intended to prepare persons for an intitial license and beginning teaching will be specifically oriented to the fundamental instructional skills needed while other programs will be designed to build upon such fundamental skills and provide the preparation needed by persons assuming instructional leadership posts within the classroom as coordinating or master teachers directing the efforts of instructional teams.

A further differentiation needed in preparation programs relates to the expanding use of instructional teams and differentiated staffs in elementary and secondary schools. An examination of teacher education programs discloses few that are making explicit provision for different levels of responsibility consistent with these concepts gaining increasing acceptance in the schools. Most programs seem to be built upon the model of a self-contained classroom with a single adult working with a standard size group of children. Without experience in working in team relationships and in utilizing support staff effectively, the products of such programs are unlikely to make the contribution they might otherwise make to a school system attempting to modify its mode of instruction. Changing patterns of school staffing, particularly in large urban school systems, make changes imperative in college preparation programs consistent with those developments. Thus the school of education of the future may offer aide, instructional technician, staff teacher, and master teacher training programs.

PROVIDING APPLIED AND CONTEXTUAL KNOWLEDGE

A third promising direction of development in teacher education involves better integration of theoretical and applied study. The current emphasis on performance criteria for teachers is an important one. Taken seriously, it can do much to promote a more realistic assessment of the impact of training programs upon classroom effectiveness. For most teachers, however, and particularly those who will function in team leadership roles, there is interest also in developing diagnostic and analytical abilities which will help them to assess individual learning problems and match instructional resources to learning needs. The role of team leader or coordinator requires a teacher-scholar, not simply a skillful technician. For such a role there is great need for contextual or background knowledge through which teachers can gain the fullest meaning from their experience. The choice need not be an either-or decision between contextual or applied knowledge but rather a matter of selecting the appropriate balance between the two. We must continue to view competence, as James Young put it, " . . . through a prism of doing, being, and knowing."[3] Teachers must develop a sufficient repertoire of instructional skills to use a range of them with confidence and to be freed from some of the survival crises of instruction so as to be able to engage in long-term planning, diagnostic, and assessment activities.

IMPROVED SUPERVISION OF FIELD EXPERIENCES

Still another area for development in teacher education is that of more effective direction and supervision of the laboratory experiences. Existing practices in many colleges seem monumentally ineffective and demand radical change in the future. Student schedules often compel assignment to schools immediately adjacent to the college campus. These schools become so overcrowded with college students that assignments are made to personnel who are inadequately prepared for such significant respon-sibilities. Another difficulty arises from the fact that college supervisors spend a considerable portion of their time in traveling to and from places of student teacher or intern assignment and, as a consequence, relatively little in actual observation and consultation with the student and the cooperating teacher. A change in role for university supervisors of cooperating teachers seems overdue. A promising direction of change would be toward giving greater responsibility for student teacher super-vision to classroom teachers on a purchased time adjunct staff basis with the university supervisory personnel moving toward an in-service training role with these teachers. If outstanding classroom teachers could devote from one-quarter to one-half time to such supervisory duties, the energies of the full-time college personnel could be devoted to working with the instructional staff to improve its effectiveness in that role. Not only can such a plan increase the efficiency of the college teacher education staff, but it is likely to enhance school-college relationships and bring a consistency between the two agents of teacher education that will improve the quality of the teacher preparation experience.

The development of teacher education centers located in school systems at some distance from the college campus is another current development with promise for the future. Cooperative staffing of such centers by several colleges may make some of them feasible in more remote locations where no single institution would have enough students to support a center independently. Each center should contain a corps of well-trained experienced supervisors who were members of the local school staff. Coordination could be provided by a full-time college employee. Some aspects of the professional sequence could be offered at the center either by a joint staff from the cooperating colleges or through a television connection to one or several of the institutions. The use of such centers would permit involvement of personnel located much farther from the campus than is frequently the case and would avoid overuse and overcrowding of certain schools. The outreach of cooperating colleges could be expanded considerably and significant new relationships established with a broader circle of communities beyond those near the campus, a factor of considerable importance for state supported institutions.

CONCLUSION

Space does not permit discussion of other developments of significance to the future of teacher education such as the use of media and simulation techniques, modular program building, cross-cultural experiences, and many more. Central to most of the ideas of promise we have discussed and those simply identified, however, is the relationship established among school systems, colleges, and the practicing profession. If meaningful cooperative relationships can be developed and maintained which provide for appropriate contributions by each partner, the future of American teacher education can be exciting and promising. Without such, the future of teacher education, and with it our schools, is at best uncertain.

NOTES

[1] George W. Denemark, "Teacher Education: Repair, Reform, or Revolution?" *Educational Leadership* 27 (March 1970): 539–43.
[2] *Breakthrough in Teacher Education* (San Francisco: Jossey-Bass, 1968).
[3] "Confusion Is Certification by Performance," *New York State Education* 57 (February 1970): 20–23.

Programmed Unhappiness: When Will Schools of Education Make Teaching a Relevant Act?

Ronald V. Iannone

As a visitor walks through the halls of our schools on a crisp fall day he may hear the following statements from open classroom doors:

> Turn to page . . . List the eight causes . . . What is the answer to number ten . . . Pay attention or go down to the principal's office . . . No talking, the class has begun!

These statements are indicative of what's happening in our schools today. If a person were to follow a student for 6 hours a day, 180 days a year, he would see that the student is spending most of his time just listening or sitting and waiting for something to happen. Usually nothing does happen except the learning of rules for playing the "good student game," which consists of meeting schedules and bells, taking good notes, memorizing irrelevant facts, and passing exams. Today's student either learns these rules or drops out of school psychologically or physically. A pervasive theme of recent educational literature is related to training people to live in a technological world and to free people from boring and menial tasks; in reality, it is the school itself which imposes menial and meaningless tasks upon students. Therefore, it seems to me that today's schools . . . are nothing but programmed unhappiness.

Many of the techniques which cause unhappiness in the schools today are learned by teachers in those meccas of techniques—Schools of Education. Recently, schools of education have done a fairly good job of training prospective teachers to implement such things as the BSCS approach to teaching biology, the PSSC approach to teaching physics, the SMSG approach to teaching mathematics, the linguistics approach to teaching English, the inquiry approach to teaching social studies, etc. In addition, many planners and designers of innovations in education have shown us the advantages of modular scheduling, nongradedness, and computer aided instruction. But what do these new techniques, processes, and innovative models have to do with the needs of our youths? Peter Marin says, "It is always 'materials' and 'techniques'; the chronic American technological vice, the cure that murders as it saves. It is all so smug, so progressively right and yet so useless, so far off the track."[1]

From Ronald V. Iannone, "Programmed Unhappiness: When Will Schools of Education Make Teaching a Relevant Act?" *The Clearing House* 46 (October 1971): 102–5. Reprinted by permission of *The Clearing House* and the author.

There is something missing in our teacher training institutions and we as educators in schools of education know and feel this emptiness but fail to admit our fraudulence to ourselves. We have failed to recognize that our preoccupation with techniques of new innovations masks the real problem; i.e., that the act of teaching is irrelevant for a younger generation born in an Age of Electronics. It has been conservatively estimated that those in our younger generation who have reached the age of 16 have watched over 15,000 hours of T.V. and have only been in school for about 10,000 hours during the same period of time. Marshall McLuhan says that . . . "The sheer quantity of information conveyed by press-magazines-film-T.V.-radio far exceeds the quantity of information conveyed by school instruction and texts."[2] At present, it seems that the young have more access to information than do their teachers. In many cases, the roles could be reversed between teachers and students without any noticeable difference.

Schools of education have failed to examine the effect of this barrage of information on students and how it affects the role of teaching as an information given and cultural transmitter. McLuhan says that a medium is "hot" if it demands very little audience participation and if it only involves the visual sense. It seems that the act of teaching itself meets this criteria for a "hot" medium. Teaching diminishes the student's opportunity to use all of his senses except for the visual sense and to participate in what he is supposed to be learning; whereas new electronic media such as stereophonic equipment and tapes, *because of their structure,* make us do things with our bodies, our senses, our minds. We become involved. This the medium of teaching has failed to accomplish.

The new types of electronic media, says McLuhan, are "cool," for they are restoring some of our sleeping senses and demand participation with the media themselves.[3] To be more specific, we are in the cool age of electronics; for example, the T.V. screen presents to a youth some three million dots of which only a few dozen are selected by him to form his visual image. As a result of these cool media of participation, the electronic-age youths have become interested in participating in politics, in racial issues, in drug issues, in the decision-making process of public school curricula, grading, scheduling, etc.[4] The popularity of the rock festival at Woodstock may seem to bear out the fact that today's electronic oriented youth wants to be involved with his environment: " . . . the electronic age learner is a new breed of cat; he is involved and oriented to involve himself in depth. . . ."[5]

Meanwhile, the schools of education are still training teachers to become carbon copies of textbooks and to ram information into the heads of our young. These schools must realize the importance of the electronic age and why today's youths are seeking total immersion into their environment. In addition, they must ask two important questions: What is the role of the teacher in our Electronic Age? What are the functions of the schools of education in this Electronic Age?

If schools of education realistically evaluate themselves in light of these questions, they would see that the act of teaching maims today's youths. Further, they would see the irrelevancy of the teacher's role, for much of what the teacher teaches can be packaged and programmed and be offered through individualized programs where students could choose whatever they wish to learn.

Therefore, the school of education function is to train each teacher to become more of a human being with a greater awareness of the needs and senses of today's youths. This new teacher doesn't need new skills but qualities such as realness, empathy, openness, warmth, and understanding. These cannot be programmed but only can be achieved through encountering real persons. Only after such encounters will teachers achieve childlike qualities such as spontaneity, natural curiosity, trustworthiness, creativity, and self-realization. Before prejudices are learned, children encounter their parents, teachers, and peers as persons and human beings. They are able to encounter persons without concern about their length of hair, style of dress, color of skin, intelligence level, and social-economic status. They are concerned with individuals as individuals.

It seems to me that many teachers are more childish than childlike. Perhaps, future teachers can become childlike after schools of education recognize that they are like immigrants encountering a new world with a new youth and only by working as partners with their prospective teachers will they be able to train people for our Kaleidoscopic society. Then perhaps schools of education will stop training teachers to educate students only from the neck up and will also educate them from the neck down, which includes emotions and feelings.

The following suggestions should be helpful to schools of education in training teachers to encounter today's youths. (These suggestions are not ranked in order of importance for they are all equally important.)
Schools of education should:

1. Offer many human encounter experiences for prospective teachers so that they may examine themselves as persons and the influence they have on their professors, youngsters, and peers.

2. Create experiences where prospective teachers can examine the concerns and feelings of today's youths in order to find out what they are sensing, feeling, and thinking.

3. Train prospective teachers in individual and group counseling processes so that they may be able to help today's youths solve some of their emotional "hang-ups."

4. Eliminate the traditional lock-step teacher preparation program of courses, credit hours, scheduling, and exams. The prospective teacher should be given the opportunity to progress at different speeds and be given the opportunity to evaluate his own progress through the teacher preparation program.

5. Create opportunities for prospective teachers to examine alternatives in school systems such as the storefront schools in New York City, the schools without walls in Philadelphia, and the open classroom at Berkeley. These experiences may help future teachers to see that

children learn in many different ways and what may work for some youngsters may destroy others.

6. Provide the prospective teachers with opportunities to get all of their senses involved with their environment. Schools of education should create resource areas not only comprised of books but of T.V. cameras, film cameras, still cameras, projectors, records, videotapes, audio tapes, stereophonic equipment and tapes, computers and programs. Each teacher should have his own still camera, 8 mm camera, and tape recorder.

One final note, our youths need to encounter teachers who are real persons who can help them satisfy their quests for active participation in life. Only those professors and administrators in teacher education who are real, who are able to shed the embarrassment of expressing feelings such as love, joy, and anger, and who are able to get "inside the skin and senses" of other persons and see the world from their eyes, will be able to function effectively with today's prospective teachers.

NOTES

[1] Peter Marin, "Children of the Apocalypse," *Saturday Review* 58 (1970): 73.

[2] Marshall McLuhan, *McLuhan, Hot & Cool,* ed. Gerald Emanuel Stearn (New York: Dial Press, 1967), p. 120.

[3] Neil Postman, "The Politics of Reading," *Harvard Educational Review* 40 (May 1970): 240–52.

[4] Robert T. Sidwell, "Cooling Down The Classroom: Some Educational Implications of McLuhan Thesis," *Educational Forum* 32 (March 1968): 356.

[5] Ibid.

Surviving, More or Less

Hal Lenke

When a teacher in school takes as his province the defense and extension of a child's world of learning, he is in danger of losing his job. A teacher's very employment is a constraint upon true teaching. What happens when a teacher sees his work differently from his employer? When his role cannot

From Hal Lenke, "Surviving, More or Less," *Peabody Journal of Education* 49 (January 1972): 126–37, by permission of the author and George Peabody College for Teachers, copyright holder.

be bought and scheduled for him? Then, you and I are faced with a choice in educational—and political—practices: we may either abandon that teacher or defend and support him.

I think we are defaulting on what it means to be an educator; not only are we not supporting teachers, we are not preparing them for survival in schools as they are, and we are not making sufficient efforts to prepare teachers for education as it might be.

My reflections do not follow an orthodox path so far as these things usually go. Precisely because there is so little discussion about the nature of this crisis, I think it is helpful to hear personal—not academic— explorations of the questions that are raised. So this paper is not a survey of existing literature, or a critique of existing programs; if there are any, they have been well camouflaged. It is based, rather, on my own experience and inquiries, conducted without sponsorship or assistance.

I have found that when a teacher in school violates or transcends the role laid out for him by his supervisors and employers, the children to be taught by him feel concomitantly closer to him, and then he has jeopardized his continued employment. In other words, when a teacher comes closest to being a teacher, the school can least tolerate his presence; he becomes a threat to the operation of the school.

That is a nasty seeming paradox since it leads to the conclusion that the school is inimical to true teaching. I have seen the validity of that charge in schools from the elementary through the university level.

The public school teacher's predicament is one of almost abject contradiction. He is an agent of the state, and its victim. When he is out of work, he can't even get unemployment benefits.

How does he come to be out of work? What should we be doing about it? What is the nature of the work he might be doing if he were free to make available those qualities of a teacher that he has?

The school teacher is accountable to everybody and to nobody; he must invent his rewards and impress himself with amorphous achievements. It is a hapless role, fraught with subtle searing delusions and self-justifying deceits.

Teaching was once intimate, prophetic, restorative. We do not think of it that way now. Now it is typically a capture of the imagination, a subservience to all the instrumentation that teachers know are denials of teaching. We talk of how many preparations a day a teacher has. We gear our logistics to the classroom and neglect the person. Teaching is not a vocation—a "calling"—so much as it is a grind. Teaching has been abstracted and systematized into a mundane commodity. True teaching should be full of parable, metaphor, and dilemma, ambiguity, humor and surprise—none of which can be trusted to emerge from certification, tests, grades, and lesson plans.

Robert G. Smith has proposed efficient ways to systematically purge education of its most vital humanity:

Traditionally, the live instructor is an important medium for presenting knowledge; however, research clearly shows that he has no special advantage for this function. The principal advantage to using a live instructor is that he is traditional: students are used to him.

The size of the class is limited by the range of the instructor's voice. With automated techniques, there is practically no limit to the number of students who can be reached.

The principal disadvantage of live instructors is that they are variable. Instructors differ in their ability to speak clearly and distinctly. They differ in the rate at which they speak. Some are more concerned with impressing students with how much they know than with teaching.

The same instructor is also uneven from time to time. He may become bored with teaching the same material over and over again. He may fall behind schedule and attempt to catch up by talking faster.

Excellent guidance is provided the live instructor by Department of the Army Field Manual 21-6, Techniques of Instruction.[1]

Smith is right. Teachers have become professionalized, which is to say standardized, interchangeable, and, therefore, expendable. Smith's new teachers will be cyborgs, specially hybridized, modeled to specifications, outmoded with the advent of new myth, or the vagaries of national priorities.

Teachers are an endangered species—except that, of course, Smith and I don't mean the same thing when we speak of teachers. The profession of teaching has blinded us to the function of teaching. Teaching should be combustible, an encounter with mystery, but it is not. As long as teachers must define their value and success in terms of the approval of their present employers, the best teacher will be the one who is never in danger of losing his job in school. What compromises, what complicity, must a teacher accede to in order to earn such security? What about the ones who can't make it? Why are so many keen, creative, humane people expunged from teaching?

I tried to find out. An anonymous respondent at the U.S. Office of Education wrote, "We have no information on the subject you are requesting. Perhaps you can check with the National Education Association . . ."

The director of the Research Division of the NEA wrote, "We are not aware of a comprehensive study which would show the number of teachers who have been dismissed." He did enclose a reprint of an article on "Teacher Mobility and Loss,"[2] which indicated that 6 percent of teachers now employed "will not be employed in the profession one year from now" and that among the "major reasons for changing location of employment reported by teachers transferring to teach in other schools," 4 percent of the men and 2.3 percent of the women listed "termination of contract." Meanwhile, 9.0 percent of the elementary teachers and 8.7 percent of the secondary teachers said they left their positions because they "disagreed with school policies, administration, etc."

The director of the Department of Research at the American Federation of Teachers, AFL–CIO, in Washington, referred me to the chairman of the Defense Committee of the AFT, in Gary, Indiana, who referred me to the National Organization on Legal Problems in Education, in Topeka, Kansas.

NOLPE's executive secretary wrote, "I know of no source of information concerning teacher firings and nonreappointments." But he suggested, "You might address a letter to each of the 50 state education associations to obtain statistics on this matter, but I would think that these statistics would be largely unreliable because the association would not learn of many of these nonreappointments in question unless the teacher in question filed some kind of formal complaint."

From the Harvard Center for Law and Education came a staff attorney's contribution: "I know of no tabulation of teachers fired or not reappointed."

A woman in the Department of Information of the American Civil Liberties Union replied to my inquiry, "At one time, cases involving dismissed teachers came directly to the ACLU through our Academic Freedom Committee. In the past several years, however, cases of this type are increasingly handled on the affiliate level, and are only sporadically reported to the national office." She suggested that I contact *The Chronicle of Higher Education.*

I went to see that publication's associate editor; he told me that he had no information other than a makeshift file of newspaper clippings, kept in a stack of other things in a corner of his office. He did not know where pertinent information might be found, unless perhaps the AAUP had some.

The annual reports of Committee A of the American Association of University Professors were available to me. So was a chart which showed that as of April 2, 1971, there were 252 cases under study and 250 complaints under staff investigation or mediation.

The NEA's DuShane Emergency Fund recieved 763 individual requests for assistance in their fiscal year 1970-71. As of August 31, 1971, they had funded more than 300 and 350 were still under investigation (the Fund had denied aid to 83 and some 125 cases were otherwise resolved or withdrawn). This is a dramatic increase from the previous year, when 200 teachers received financial support for pursuing redress of their grievances, or the year before when the number was a little more than half that.[3]

The *College Law Bulletin,* published by the National Student Association, carried summaries of selected court cases.

A textbook published in 1970 reported that "There is an estimated 15 percent of a faculty every year who leave the typical school."[4] There was no elaboration.

My point in relating this circuitous research is to amplify my contention that we neglect a great many good teachers. The very fact that we don't know how many we lose is an index of our failing. And I think that we are in a large measure responsible for their vulnerability and for their attrition which is sometimes euphemistically called the turnover rate.

If I can randomly find 20 teachers from across the country who have virtually the same story to tell, think how many more there are whose departure from teaching is going unrecorded. Here are what three women have said to me in letters:

1. There's so little significant change anywhere in public schools and still so much resistance to what seems so obvious, that some sort of revolution seems inevitable. The wrong people are forced out for the right reasons. It's too bad there's no room made for artists-in-residence, or philosophical consultants or the like. Is there any place in schools for true innovation?

2. I . . . decided to try the New York public schools, since originally I felt that the children in these schools were the ones most in need of teachers who cared. I feel pretty battered these days. New York's public school system ought to be bombed one Sunday afternoon. I see myself using techniques to control that are frighteningly similar to those used by all the repressive, child-hating teachers in our school. I don't know if I can do this another year without being sucked in by it. I'm too insecure to believe the ideas I once held about a free classroom atmosphere, and skill development. I'm very white middle class. My children are very poor, black and Spanish. I wonder what . . . I'm doing there, standing up in front of them delivering the Word. So I relax, go with the flow, and the noise becomes unbearable and my supervisor glares at me, and Sra. Alvarado complains that her Javier got hit in the eye by Richard Gonzalez and why can't I keep Order in my room? . . . I may just lay a bomb under the red brick ass of PS———Manh. (the correct way of designating our school) in June after everyone's cleared out and the only ones left inside are the burglar who ransacks my room every weekend and leaves Fuck You written on the door and the mice who creep out to die in my sandbox.

3. . . . there are times when, with my long hair and unstructured classes, I feel like a freak . . . the only enjoyment comes from the kids because that is where it's all at anyway . . . and the kids are the reason why I will not be rehired next year. In a system that prides itself on maintaining a heavy wall of separation between teacher and student and on keeping everyone in line, the type of teacher that I am, who thrives on people relationships and who digs kids, just does not make it . . . I was nearly fired a month ago—for letting two girls into one of my classes (forbidden situation), supposedly out of their study hall. Turns out that the girls lied to me and were actually cutting their French class! (and unfortunately were not cool enough to refrain from mentioning that my room was the room to go to "when you wanted to escape.") I thought the whole administration would stone me . . . We all get into role-playing, myself more than anyone because I play the game for other teachers, except that the kids know I'm playing around . . . Usually, in the middle of "disciplining" I wind up laughing . . . being constantly hassled and frustrated—just not worth the grief. I can't be a friend to kids in this school—I'm just waiting for the day when it blows up. It will happen; kids are already experimenting with blockbusters and fire-crackers in the basement, so it's only a few years away.

Some of the other "forbidden situations" for which teachers are fired include: the general charge of insubordination, lending a student proscribed books or materials, allowing students in the teachers' lounge, informality in class, and allegedly not getting along with colleagues.

I see good teachers getting out of school because they hold a humane, unprogrammed view of education. That is a portentous development. Does it mean that our public comprehensive schools cannot encompass certain views which differ from their own tacit creed? Just how exclusive are these institutions in whose corridors and shadows we toil? Has schooling, for all its claims of universality, effectively left most people outside its reach? And then what delusions are we perpetrating in our rarefied councils?

It is common for a teacher to be offered the opportunity to resign rather than being ousted. (This is done by the superintendent's staff while the school board members are given few if any of the details.) And, as far as I can tell, a large proportion of teachers accepts this option, thereby obscuring the pressures and circumstances behind their departure, their "mobility and loss."

Their decision is understandable; they are under a lot of strain and they seldom have any support. State professional organizations are not always willing to encourage a teacher to make a principled defense. Colleagues want to avoid any unpleasantness that might incriminate them. Those parents who are aware of the matter may prefer to remain quiet, worried about retaliation against their children in school—one of the most revealing and damning observations of our educational system that I've come across.

A teacher is induced to persuade himself that his case is merely a personal outrage; the issues are intramural, esoteric, and difficult to translate into terms of popular causes. Reporters are often not interested unless there is some sensational angle. So a lot of anguish and fury is avoided by submitting an even-tempered letter of resignation, no matter how much it misrepresents the actual situation.

And, of course, that means that the teacher's record is left relatively clean; he has traded a semblance of respectable departure for the termination that would be a certain liability in seeking future jobs.

Administrators might even offer to serve as references in return for the teacher's concession. And administrators then use the teacher's letter as proof to the taxpayers of how congenial an operation they are running.

Some teachers have fought. When they have had the financial resources, they have gone to court. When they do, they feel they surrender their chances of being hired again. They reveal themselves as troublemakers, so that even if they win, they lose. The vindication, coming several years after the event, is truly academic.

There are some efforts to support teachers, the kind who are often a casualty of nervously programmed school bureaucracy. They should all be standard resources of any teacher education course of training, and should be promoted by superintendents, deans, principals, and area chairmen. They include: Change Now! in Fort Wayne, Indiana; the Stowe Caucus in Vermont; the Wisconsin Coalition for Educational Reform; The Teachers,

Inc., project in Chapel Hill, North Carolina; the Bay Area Radical Teachers Organizing Committee in San Francisco; the Teachers Organizing Project in Chicago; Red Pencil in Boston; the Brooklyn Education Task Force; the Children's Foundation in Washington; and the Ontario Institute for Studies in Education.

Meaningful change is up to each community. One real test is whether or not parents believe their children's contention that it is the best teachers who disappear.

But that is not enough. Teachers—those whose identities are conferred by schools—need to make some drastic, and crucial adaptations. Not only must they be enabled to teach in schools, they must learn to teach without schools.

The threats to our well-being are so numerous that we need people who can break out of customary habits of thought and action in order to provide us with ways to deflect and counter those threats, which come from individual and institutional behavior, from purposeful and unintentional acts. We want to learn how to do ourselves and others less harm. People are trying to find places, situations—one might say ecosystems—for learning these strategies of life. It is the practice in this land to wait until children are four or five years old and then gather them from their homes and parents and turn them over to teachers for nine or twelve or eighteen years. These teachers are consigned to schools, where what they effect is called education.

Schools evolved to serve the political economy of the society, but they are oppressive. Schools incapacitate people, children most of all. The more we fortify schools, the more we neglect each other. Teachers are frail—they depend upon kids showing up in their rooms. It is an insecure concubinage. There is an oversupply of teachers, we are told. Schools of education have been impressive in their fecundity. But students do not care. "The average absence rate in Washington, D.C., is 21 percent daily for the senior high schools, 17 percent for junior highs. In the suburbs, the rates seem to be lower but increasing each year as well. New York City reports a 24 percent average absence rate for all senior highs, with some schools reporting rates above 40 percent. Philadelphia has some schools reporting rates of more than 30 percent."[5]

The plight of teachers is not often juxtaposed with that of students, though it should be. They occupy the same nook of civilization; each is the other's burden.

Teachers ought to be provocateurs, disturbers of the peace—but they settle for less:

School personnel are well aware that their basic responsibility in the eyes of the community is to socialize the young. Failures to transmit the formal curriculum are not merely tolerable but accepted as part of the normal set of contradictions we get ourselves into by giving lip-service to cultural and intellectual skills not really very much prized. But a failure to establish adherence to conventional forms of patriotic observance, or uncritical acceptance of authority and dedication to the accumulation of consumer goods, is not tolerable. Indeed, too much success in teaching students to read and to understand the world they live in would in itself constitute prima facie evidence of a failure in socialization, as evidenced by the fact that the sharpest students are nearly always the most unrestful. Consequently, the actions that constitute the most baneful forms of "student unrest" are those that call publicly into question the socialization of the student into acceptance of middle-American norms . . . [6]

We need some revitalized definitions. Education has become a chameleon figure of speech, discussed as if all parties had the same allusion in mind. Education is the 85-billion-dollar-a-year conglomerate enterprise of schools which regularizes thinking and conduct for the convenience of its multifarious goals. Education, as practiced by too many people who are called educators, is the attempt to cull out eccentricities and to penalize those with a different frame of reference from their own.
Goodbye to all that.
Friedenburg states:

The high school, like the university but in far greater degree, is caught in the essential hypocrisy that makes a mass, stratified democracy functional. It must assert what is indeed true—that all men are educable—while it strives to prevent most of them from becoming sufficiently cognizant of either their own intellectual resources or the dynamics of their society to insist on the dignity formally guaranteed them but deadly, should it be invoked, to the institutions that depend on their submission . . . In a mass democracy, institutions of public education may be conceived of as having been installed to occupy the life space in which, if they were not there, education might occur. Rising "student unrest" in high schools suggests that they cannot altogether prevent it from occurring, although they can make life pretty tough for those students who are learning most.[7]

Education is the fundamental political activity of a population. It is the way the population tells itself its story and presents itself to others. Education is a codicil to the population's modal philosophy and the instrument of its economic relations. It is the means by which the society conducts its affairs, arranges its phenomena, and distinguishes its direction.
Education is the way the population chooses to become articulate. It may vary from one population to another; each may specialize in a different intelligibility. The important thing is the way all members of the group are taken into account, how they take part in the articulation, and are mutually comprehended.
What is indispensable for education is learning: mutation, which is the threshold of evolution. But we forbid the liberation of a person

discovering a new self, a new possibility. For we are indentured to schooling, and we become more focused on the overhead involved in the building than we are on the energies in the name of which it was constructed.

We differentiate between public and nonpublic schools in this country. We like to say that nonpublic schools have some ideology or catechism permeating their routines, and that the teachers in such schools are overt conscripts of sectarian creeds.

In the public schools, on the other hand, there is none of that hidden agenda of belief systems insinuated upon the clientele; so we pretend. I think the reverse is true. In an avowedly dogmatic school you know what orthodoxy the teachers are missionaries for, but in a public school you meet every stamp of doctrine with no warning and much disclaimer. The individual teacher's belief system—his precepts about human nature and so on—is the paramount characteristic of his teaching. It governs his roles and limits, his standards, his tolerances, his self-monitoring system, and his resistance to change.

I want to know what the political theology of a teacher is, because when I speak of supporting teachers, I'm in truth interested in supporting only certain kinds of teachers. I am not interested in supporting teachers who disqualify children from exercising the authority of their own lives.

There are a number of proposals for child advocates which, it seems to me, simply corroborate the deficiency of schools and the corruption of the teachers in them.

The proposals for organized advocacy do not see fit to raise the question of whether support should be withdrawn from some of the services and functions that purport to aid children.[8] What if it were not in children's interests for some of these agencies to carry on as they have been allowed to do? It is as if all the facets of agency programs (and schools) were innately benign, and people should make themselves eligible for them, as if the people must be contoured to fit the funded agenda.

Talking in this way may be a necessary buffer against prevailing injustices. But it is a loosely liberal patchwork that reflects the confusion and breakdown of present humanitarian programs. "Child advocacy" is one of the symptoms of the disease of our dominant culture.

Children deserve better than what we concoct for them. Children should be seen as a class belonging to us all, without national allegiance or creedal subscription or any other inheritance of our acquired characteristics. Let children thrive among us while we thrive among them. That is not possible now, for our society doesn't want or need its children. They are obsolete except in calculating the gross national product. As children they are a hindrance to us. We've turned them over to teachers and quarantined them both in schools.

Schools are not permitted to partake of the culture of which they are ostensibly a microcosm. More and more schools are being located in a zoning limbo. Schools are miniaturized simulations of the world beyond, forbidden to become actual. They are prohibited from real touch, real controversy, real exploration.

Teachers can change that only by putting themselves on the line. The issue is whether or not we encourage that or whether we advise them to play it safe.

In schools, teachers might be of some consequence if they didn't ask students to check their lives at the classroom door. An obvious corollary to this is that the teachers also fragment themselves when they enter the school building.

Teachers have been subjected to methods courses, and they have to get through material. (Can you imagine the results if teachers took seriously the homily to individualize instruction?)

Contradictions are the life style of the teacher. He is told he is a client of the parent, but also the employee of the school board, the ward of the state payroll, and the agent of national policy. How are teachers helped to reconcile these oxymorons?

Teachers need only to begin to see themselves as members of the child's staff rather than of the principal's staff and certain things become clearer.

The instructional class period is only one (negligible) part of the child's daily experience. Some teachers elicit from their students a submerged revenge. The kids give back what they get, they act as if the class were the preeminent force in their universe, as if the homework constituted a moral turning point, as if the exams were a religious crisis and grades were sure touchstones on the way to the parole of adulthood.

What we do in the classroom may count somewhat less than breakfast, the basketball team or the weekend excursion, not to mention television. School happens to be the only one of their activities that children and teachers share, so they give it disproportionate attention in their spheres of influence.

Teachers are supposed to accept their roles as pimps for textbooks, the zoos of culture, the domesticated craven artifacts of "right" answers. But teachers need not be the fellow prisoners elevated to warden's stooge.

Is it not the meaning of a teacher to be with the kids, with them and for them even more doggedly than they are for themselves? Is it not redundant then to speak of a teacher as a child advocate, for what else does a teacher advocate if not the childness of the child and the personhood of the person?

Clearly, education happens outside of the school. But while there are people in schools, we should be helping them. We should develop ways for the teacher to survive in his job as an unvanquished human being.

School is where you find out what you are doing there. So the educated teacher—like the educated student—will abandon the building. He will move on in his own life. But while he stays, the teacher should take as his proper bailiwick the institution in all its dimensions.

Teachers should be ombudsmen for the entire milieu of the school. It takes a view of teaching that is not the customary one for it admits the wholeness of lives segmented by classrooms. Principals deny that a school is a community. There are few signals of recognition that all are occupying the same place at the same time and constitute, ipso facto, a civic order.

In school, politics are exercised most often by subterfuge and conspiracy. The students have their connivances, the faculty has its chicanery, and the administration, its covert deals. School is set up so that its political life is one of conflict and exploitation, rather than collaboration and resolution.

Teachers operate in isolation by choice. The classroom is a cove of make-believe freedom. It is said that once the door is closed, you have intoxicating liberty to do what you want with the class; that is a tyranny and a hallucination. It is true only if nobody is ever going to leave the room.

So a teacher could find several colleagues in the building and, without advance planning, they could go into one another's rooms. Periodically take the whole class into another teacher's room. Or they could bring people into their classes—other kids, dropouts, parents, local merchants, clergy, taxi drivers, architects, reporters, gas station mechanics, lawyers, electricians, musicians.

Teachers could have their classes disperse throughout the school and grounds and have students go into the community with which the school should have reciprocal relations anyway.

A teacher who sees himself as an advocate of the child will familiarize himself with the procedures and apparatus of his school. He will know what the students and their parents are subjected to. This means seeing the printed forms that are used, and the letters that go out. It means understanding how to use the public address system, knowing where there is a telephone that can be used in a hurry, knowing where supplies are kept, where records are filed and what the patrolling habits of supervisors are. It means knowing your territory (not just your subject) or you have no business foisting yourself off on kids as their advocate.

Teachers need to go to school board meetings. They need to take pains to understand what students are punished for, what the pattern of enforcement is. A teacher should exemplify what he is teaching his students—how to find out what they need to know, the preparations for discovery, judgments for applying knowledge. That's merely being able to do research in what is the teacher's quintessential field: child advocacy, if that's the name you want to give it. The students can teach the teacher a few things about the school. I have found the most incisive analyses came from those students who are recidivists in detention halls. For a teacher to be of any help to them, he must know the school from their bruised vantage.

A teacher: someone who gives others back to themselves, who unites them with their capabilities. And which of the people is the teacher? The one with the most healthy vision, the one most aware that there is something beyond the classroom. The teacher is the student of his students.

It requires vigilance and some courage to live up to being a teacher in school, because you will find yourself challenging many practices that have become traditional through inertia. There will be disputes over the rights of students—of young people—in many areas. Schools are the institutions which parents think they've contracted with to hold their children's lives in escrow. Schools accept a corrupt guardianship of children. It is corrupt because they serve various, mutually exclusive, masters. Schools have no philosophy of education. They have instead a momentum of discipline.

If a teacher tries to change that, he will be risking his job, it is true, but too much job security is bad for the soul.

The kids know that their teacher is free to leave while they are not. School attendance is, after all, compulsory, which is in violation of the First Amendment freedom of association. Compulsory school attendance is a denial of due process, a violation of the Fourteenth Amendment. Schooling violates the Eighth Amendment, against cruel and unusual punishment, except that it is not unusual. It violates the Fifth Amendment, protecting people from self-incrimination; schools trick, demean, and humiliate children until children get used to it and come to expect it.

I would like to see a lawsuit brought against a school for damaging the brain—the very cell chemistry—of children. For I believe it can be shown that school cripples the energies and synergies of organic processes which would otherwise enhance the learning growth of the child. I think a lawsuit can be brought against a school for being sociopathic, for being the key factor in any number of dysfunctions, from contributing to the delinquency of minors, to drug use, and anomie and other raging malfeasances.

But as we tackle this, we must also learn how to practice a new educational legitimacy without schools.

Perhaps we can develop some strategies to ameliorate the abuses of human lives and relationships. We might encourage one another to devote so much attention to such a pursuit that it would constitute a career, an admittedly precarious lifestyle as free agents amidst the distractions and entanglements of our time. We would occupy a marginal realm, self-employed and yet sustained by others, accustomed to impermanence and uncertainty. We would be, while we could endure it, taking some risks.

There is no particular name for people with that kind of sensibility. I call them teachers-at-large. It is not a safe occupation, but I would like to see more people try it.

Teachers-at-large would be those people who make themselves available as teachers. They would be approached by those whom they could help. Meanwhile, they would cultivate their own gardens. I mean that such teachers would be going about their business as practitioners of real activities, whether carpentry, music making, research, construction, cab driving, sculpting, or any of a myriad of other things.

The teacher would not be guaranteed any customers. He would not carry any weapons, so he could not hurt anyone except by the inflections we all utilize.

Remove certification; remove tenure; remove compulsory attendance; remove the school building. What have we removed? Three snarls of paper work and a load of brick. And what remains? People making their way among one another, ineluctably learning.

It may be argued that this is sketchy and romantic, even anti-intellectual. What you would mean is that you are not ready to make that move yet. To me, it is utterly pragmatic. What is important is the effort a person makes on behalf of the survival and quality of our earthly relations. We need contact with each other, and support, and enlightenment from wherever we can get it.

William Arrowsmith said in "The Future of Teaching,"

> We too lack educators—by which I mean Socratic teachers, visible embodiments of the realized humanity of our aspirations, intelligence, skill, scholarship; men ripened or ripening into realization, as Socrates at the close of the Symposium comes to be, and therefore, personally guarantees, his own definition of love. Our universities and our society need this compelling embodiment, this exemplification of what we are all presumably at, as they have never needed it before. It is men we need, not programs. It is possible for a student to go from kindergarten to graduate school without ever encountering a man—a man who might for the first time give him the only profound motivation for learning, the hope of becoming a better man.[9]

We don't practice, or trust, learning. We seem to have marshalled the very elements against us. Each of us has glimpsed a dire oracle, and yet we resist.

What we need is unprecedented. We might begin by unshackling ourselves from the sterile formulas of our monotonously futile education. We might begin with children. Let us honor them, and our life in them, by not being afraid to go on to a new person in ourself.

NOTES

[1] Robert G. Smith, *Innovations in Teaching and Training* (Detroit: American Data Processing, 1968), p. 31.

[2] *See* National Education Association Research Bulletin (December 1968), pp. 118–26. The questionnaires on which the study is based were distributed March, 1967.

[3] Telephone conversation with Sinowitz, DuShane Fund staff member, Washington, D.C., October 27, 1971.

[4] John F. Ohles, *Introduction to Teaching* (New York: Random House, 1970), p. 32.

[5] "The Class-Cutters," *Washington Post,* 5 June 1971, A-22.

[6] Edgar Z. Friedenberg, "High School as a Focus of Student Unrest," *Annals of the American Academy of Political and Social Science* 395 (May 1971): 125.

[7] Ibid., pp. 125–26.

[8] *See* "The Child Advocate," in *Report to the President: White House Conference on Children* (Washington, D.C., 1970): pp. 387–97.

[9] William Arrowsmith, "The Future of Teaching," in *The Liberal Arts and Teacher Education: A Confrontation,* ed. Donald N. Bigelow (Lincoln: University of Nebraska Press, 1971), p. 40.

Critical Teaching Strategies

Edwin J. Swineford

There are some strategies that are instrumental for successful teaching. These strategies, involving judgment, meaningful experience, and judicious use, have been called "critical teaching strategies" by the author, who has isolated and grouped some of them into ten clusters, each of which is described from an operational level. Spotlighting these critical strategies may alert teacher educators and beginning teachers. The diagnosis of empirically observed teaching ailments may also localize a tender area for in-service and teacher intern growth. In fact, these critical teaching strategies might very well constitute rich curriculum content for interns, since they comprise concepts and skills seldom mastered in the traditional courses of student-teaching experience.

The problems given here were gleaned from a previous study[1] in which over five hundred lessons in English, social studies, mathematics, and science, taught by sixty junior high school student teachers over a four-year period, were observed and immediately reported. An analysis of these reports revealed persistent and recurring problems of teaching strategy. Below is a brief discussion of each of these critical teaching strategy problem areas, with practical, specific suggestions that may be helpful to practitioners, particularly to interns.

1. *Inability To Place the Student in the Center of the Teaching-Learning Process*

    Discussion: This disability appeared frequently with the unsuccessful student teachers; the harder they worked, the more blasé and disinterested the students became. In some cases, the students seemed hypnotized as they watched the busy teachers lecturing, analyzing, writing on the chalkboard, demonstrating, pacing up and down, and assuming entire responsibility and guilt for all the teaching and learning.

    It was impossible to tell what some classes were for; they appeared to be an exhibit of routines and games, the object being to go through the paces without anyone's being hurt or disturbed. This was characterized by a hypocrisy of silence on the part of both students and teacher—if you let us alone, we will not cause any trouble and will play your game. Some students seemed to be especially sensitive to what was coming, and by a series of extremely sophisticated maneuvers, they were able to

From Edwin J. Swineford, "Critical Teaching Strategies" *Journal of Teacher Education* 22 (Spring 1971): 29–36. Reprinted by permission of the author and the publisher.

cop out of the learning situation or to engage in such skillful engineering that the whole class escaped. Teacher and students were engaged in a charade.

Suggestions for improvement:
(1) Be informed of the student's experiental background and start there.
(2) Look critically at the student's learning, not at how hard you worked, how much material you covered, or the dazzling array of educational technology you dragged into the room.
(3) Be zealous about classroom time; set the stage for learning and move the student to it, front and center.
(4) Guide, direct, or turn the flow of experiences so that the student is put into the school teaching-learning frame.
(5) Put on top of the teaching-learning table all the hidden related factors and conditions that may rise up to destroy the teaching-learning process.
(6) Know where you stopped with the class and with individual students, if possible, and start the lesson from this point.
(7) Tell the students your problems in teaching that particular lesson, thus reducing the teaching-learning and student-teacher gap.
(8) Give negative reinforcement to students who "red herring" lessons with calculated deviations and planned distractions.
(9) Plan the lesson for the entire class, not as a reaction to one student's inquiry.
(10) Have a dream; don't settle for cheap, temporary outcomes.
(11) Cause the students to place themselves in the optimum setting for learning.
(12) Hit the students (in terms of teaching and learning) where they live and where a nerve is exposed.
(13) Start preparing a new stage for a new learning while you are polishing off the first one.
(14) Give priority to the immediate teaching-learning setting, placing secondary the bookkeeping and housekeeping duties.

2. *Failure To Establish Clearly the Responsibility for Specific Minimum Learnings for each Member of the Class*

Discussion: This may appear redundant, but it deserves emphasis, particularly in creative and unconventional lessons that fortunately are becoming more numerous. Valuable learnings that might result from creative approaches may be lost because the brilliance of the lesson structure blots out a critical concern—making certain that each student is responsible for specific behavioral outcomes. Even in regular classes, it must be admitted that establishing minimum learnings for each individual is at best a dream, perhaps a myth; as an ideal, it anchors the lesson and facilitates optimum learning.

Suggestions for improvement:
  (1) In creative and unconventional lesson patterns, keep your eye on terminal behavioral changes desired, holding the students to these in spite of the temptation to bask in the glow of a satisfying and glittering presentation.
  (2) Build specific learnings into the lesson, letting these shape the lesson rather than reacting to temporary and superficial student approval.
  (3) Think through your several roles as a teacher, giving priority to being a director of learning.
  (4) In long or complex lessons, use some device, perhaps the chalkboard or overhead projector, to capture the attention of all students at the same time in order to define objectives and expected outcomes clearly.
  (5) Develop a tool to determine the learnings achieved; in many cases, let the students know in advance how and why they will be asked for a feedback.
  (6) Let the most important outcomes come through more strongly than minor outcomes; everything should not sound the same in importance.
  (7) Don't be satisfied with favorable reactions to lessons in which students are not required to do anything except listen.
  (8) Record and document the extent to which individuals achieve the behavioral outcomes.
  (9) Don't undermine student responsibility for learning by taking it all on yourself.
  (10) Use pop tests or quizzes to bring the lesson back to substantive learnings when deviations set in.
  (11) Avoid the use of "I want," or similar expressions, when setting goals.
  (12) Use student names in class to help personalize the lesson.

3. *Tendency to Provide Activity for Its Own Sake and To Work for Narrow Goals*

Discussion: This is a characteristic of lessons that tend to go off in all directions at once; a shotgun is used instead of a rifle. The trick is to capture and retain the teacher drive, while at the same time giving direction and purpose to the random activity.

Suggestions for improvement:
  (1) Be aware when confusion exists and organize it to achieve educational goals.
  (2) Reduce the possibilities for misdirection by paying attention to the freightage of your words and acts.
  (3) Recognize that you have limited time and energy and that you must conserve them for precious activities.
  (4) Use feedback to check on the productivity of the lesson.

(5) Let your activity result in further student activity.

(6) Know when you are doing busy work.

(7) Plan your deviations and how to get back to the mainstream of the lesson.

(8) Work on concepts, principles, and generalizations rather than trivia.

(9) Do those things in class that can be done there only, protecting those precious teaching-learning moments from nonteaching interruptions.

(10) Be lazy; never do something that other available persons, including students, could do better, while they profit from the activity.

4. *Difficulty in Diagnosing Learning Problems of Students*

Discussion: Beginning teachers tend to assume the student's learning slate is wiped clean before they lay on a new lesson. This is compounded by a naive conception of how the student will perceive the prescribed learning. Further complications set in as additional difficulties in learning develop when the lesson is unfolded. This is a prognosis without diagnosis.

Suggestions for improvement:

(1) Assess the total teaching-learning framework before leaping into a lesson.

(2) Get at the why of nonlearning.

(3) Don't assume that the class and individuals will cure themselves of learning disabilities.

(4) Consider whether learning problems are aggravated by your pace, timing, or teaching mixture.

(5) Neutralize environmental factors that might affect the learning situation.

(6) React not only to the questions that are asked but also to why they are being asked and what is really being asked.

(7) Know what to ignore and what to react to as you unfold the lesson.

(8) Avoid reviewing on top of a previous review lesson.

(9) Check on student misconceptions, and don't keep going over solved problems.

(10) Distinguish among lack of ability, laziness, or disinterest.

(11) Get the students' attention before starting a lesson, and continually check on their attention and interest as the lesson unfolds.

(12) If the lesson is vague and loosely organized to you, it will be confused and unorganized to the students.

(13) Monotony and boredom breed learning difficulties.

(14) Students have a right to fail.

(15) Stop when you have finished teaching the lesson; further activity or verbalization may be destructive.

5. *Inability To String Learning Experiences Together Toward Significant Long-Range Outcomes.*

Discussion: The ability to tie together and direct learning experiences so as to achieve significant long-range goals is a top-drawer, master-teacher, operational-level activity; it may be asking too much of a beginning teacher. Actually this can be done only by the learner, but the beginning teacher must recognize his responsibility to facilitate this process by at least offering lessons that point in this direction. Wisdom in this area remains the province of the master teacher.

Suggestions for improvement:
(1) Don't be caught with piecemeal teaching—if what you teach doesn't extend beyond one lesson, it probably isn't worth presenting.
(2) Careful attention to the beginning and ending of a lesson will help give integrity to the total string of lessons.
(3) Systematic overview, review, and homework reinforce the opportunity to achieve long-range goals.
(4) Know when you are on a plateau in the total sweep toward long-range goals.
(5) Be a director of learning, not a reactor to pupil petulance or whim.
(6) Don't compete with the encyclopedia, computer, or teaching machine.
(7) Protect long-range goals, even at the expense of losing a short-range goal.
(8) Watch your lesson deviations and expansion—they may blur the significant goals.
(9) Use subject matter, not as an end in itself but rather as a means of moving toward the goals or purposes.
(10) Work with the students so that they see the relationship of small learnings in the framework of total goals.

6. *Difficulty in Accepting the Student as He Is*

Discussion: One hesitates to bring this up—it is old hat to students. Before teaching, they may have accepted it as a principle; now they are required to put into practice, and this is another matter. This principle is a major hurdle in working with the pupils who are socially and culturally different. Unless it is put into practice, it doesn't matter whether the beginning teacher has had course work in this area or not. The teacher must know who he is before he can accept the student as he is.

Suggestions for improvement:
(1) Assess the student in terms of your concerns in a particular class and stop feeling guilty or responsible for what you find.

(2) Know what the student's experiential background is and start there.

(3) Build interests as well as uncovering them.

(4) Reconcile yourself to living and learning among divergent interests and tensions. You are paid to be disliked.

(5) Simple students like simple procedures. Use uncomplicated approaches with difficult classes.

(6) Don't expect all the students to learn all that you know.

(7) Match your idea of expected class outcomes with the raw material in the class.

(8) Remember that you can't pull or push all the students through the same material at the same time and with the same procedures.

(9) Get behind observable behavior. What are they worrying about? What are they thinking? What are their feelings of concern about themselves?

(10) When you accept the student as he is, you also must accept his image of you as a teacher.

(11) Remember that about half the students are different from you—they are a different sex.

(12) Since they are different, and you are different, the setting for learning must be rich and open, and the strategies varied and creative.

7. *Failure To Translate and Give Meaning to Student Behavior*

Discussion: The initial teacher shock of close contact with youth must be followed by an ability to sort out, classify, and give meaning to apparent random student reactions. Observing student behavior was enough in preteaching situations, now the beginning teacher must interpret it and hypothesize in order to decide what is to be done.

Suggestions for improvement:

(1) The mass of student behavior has meaning, is caused, and is capable of being diagnosed, classified, and understood if the teacher uses intelligence and the right tools.

(2) Be a teacher, not a mediator of boy-girl relationships.

(3) Sift out the voluminous mass of give-and-take in the classroom, which stems from the fact you have young men and young women together.

(4) Act on symptoms, especially when the overt act is predictable.

(5) Decide when to suppress a student and when to support him.

(6) Have your hand on the pulse-beat of the total class; know when to give up and start over, what is reasonable, and when learning is taking place.

(7) Translate student behavior into terms of the total school environment and the student's individual life space.

(8) Ask yourself what the student is doing in terms of the situation he is facing with the tools he has to work with.

(9) Listen to the sounds of the classroom, especially the hidden meanings of student laughter.

(10) Modify negative student behavior in the direction of long-range goals, not as an end in itself.

(11) Be sensitive to the ever-present wall of student apathy and disinterest, accompanied by instant student fatigue.

8. *Failure To Capitalize on Rich Learning Experiences That Emerge As the Lesson Develops*

Discussion: In the formal teacher preparation program, the prospective teacher has been taught the value and techniques of long-range, unit, and daily lesson planning. Many have been harassed into making plans for others to read and approve. The result is that few know how to use plans to liberate themselves for artistic teaching.

Suggestions for improvement:
(1) Plan with goals and purposes clearly understood, but with multiple means in mind to achieve them.

(2) Each teacher makes his own little hell with self-imposed restrictions and blinders that cause him to look at learning through a crack.

(3) Philosophize on what you are doing. Stop regularly and take a long, hard look at yourself as you play your role as a teacher.

(4) Remember the seeds of learning you have previously planted; cultivate them and make room for their flowering in your lesson.

(5) Obstacles to learning may be your opportunity for rich teaching.

(6) Work through a core, an essence, a message, welcoming fresh examples and student-centered experiences that reinforce your means toward the goal.

(7) The wisest teachers prepare for spontaneous student contributions.

(8) Run a string through all your lessons; bead it with student-contributed interests and needs.

(9) Your lesson campus is the student's total experiential background and world of fantasy.

(10) Keep your eye on what is happening to your students as the lesson unfolds, not just on what you thought would or should happen.

9. *Lack of Sensitivity to Timing, Pacing, and Transition*

Discussion: These areas, falling outside the province of the science of teaching and into the area of the art of tuition, are seldom taught to beginning teachers but are caught by them as they grow on the job. Those few who are born teachers may already practice sound timing, pacing, transition; if so they should understand and rationalize what they are doing and consciously utilize these hidden ingredients of master teaching.

Suggestions for improvement:
  (1) The pause, waiting, silence may sound louder to the learner than anything you might say.
  (2) Protect the teachable moment and know when it has arrived.
  (3) Capitalize on immediate visual feedback of the lesson in action.
  (4) Know when to slow down, speed up, stop, repeat, and overview.
  (5) Unload your illustrations, sharp resources, and precious techniques at the time when they can be fully exploited and spent.
  (6) You alone are the expert on timing and pacing concerns for your class; you may have to work against administrative and supervisorial lethargy and ignorance in these critical concerns.
  (7) A sick or lazy teacher seldom experiences concerns in the areas of timing, pacing, and transition.
  (8) Small details of classroom management may wreck timing, pacing, and transition.
  (9) In presenting a lesson, decide when to expand or when to contract on the content.
  (10) A sensitive teacher knows when to start all over again, when to release students for new learnings, when to cover a little more deeply, when to ask and and when to tell, and how long to let the students suffer without answers.
  (11) Present honest lessons—don't try to be too clever. Move directly into the lesson.
  (12) Don't wonder what happened to your lesson; cause things to happen according to plan.
  (13) Plan the transitions from one part of the lesson to another; don't just drift into something new.
  (14) Transitions should be logical and psychological. Logical transitions may satisfy you, but students prefer a transition that is natural to them and gives a feeling of fulfillment.
  (15) By overview and review connect lessons; these should be brief and sharp, not the whole thing over again.

10. *Poor Judgment in Selecting Subject Matter for All the Students in the Class*

Discussion: Curriculum development by the classroom teacher involves among other things the selection of content for the class. This is necessary even when the school has a detailed curriculum guide. Several misconceptions seem to be common among many beginning teachers on content and content selection; one is that subject matter is an end rather than a means to an end. Instead of the teacher's using subject matter, he is manipulated by it. Another idea that hurts is that the teacher must teach all the subject matter in the discipline; this results in a furious attempt to teach all the students all the teacher knows or can extract from available books. The final misconception is the attempt to teach the same thing to all the students at the same time, in the same way, and with uniform results.

Suggestions for improvement:
(1) Determine your purposes and select subject matter to achieve them.
(2) Teach students the structure, essence, or basic concepts of your discipline.
(3) Be generous and creative in the examples or illustrations you use.
(4) Be a scholar in your discipline, possessing a deep pool of knowledge from which you carefully select content in terms of your specific situation.
(5) The subject matter as you know it from college is too rich in most cases for your students. In stepping it down for them, be certain to retain its scholarship.
(6) The critic of your teaching judgments is the best thinking of your profession, not solely the reactions of a group of students.
(7) Don't depend on the class to stumble onto the key concepts. It is poor teaching to base today's lesson on yesterday's omissions.
(8) Aim not at covering all the material for all the students but at building scholarship in varying degrees in each student.
(9) Remember that students can't be perfect—nor can they be poor—in everything.
(10) Take out your frustrations and dissatisfactions on the subject matter, not the students.

NOTES

[1] Swineford, E. J. "An Analysis of Teaching-Improvement Suggestions to Student Teachers." *Journal of Experimental Education 32* (Spring 1964): 299–303.

Precision: The Coming Emphasis in Teacher Education

S. Samuel Shermis and James L. Barth

Teacher education of the future will be considerably more specific about objectives than it is now. The past history of teacher training has seen an emphasis on a vague set of sentiments, as emotionally satisfying to the education professor as they were useless to students. Our position is that (1) it is desirable for education departments to become more precise and (2) it is entirely possible for such precision to be reached.

As any given profession or intellectual discipline matures, it becomes more and more precise. That is, it is able to identify problems more specifically, to gather a greater variety of correct and relevant information, and to apply the answers to concrete situations with more predictability. Another way of saying this is to state that when a profession matures it substitutes precision for intuitive judgment. And while it does this, it automatically raises its standards. What is accepted happily when a discipline or profession is young becomes intolerable when it matures.[1]

Currently, education is in a nether world. It has by no means acquired the maturity of, say, medicine or physics. It is, however, in the process of becoming a genuine profession. Five years ago, Orlich and Shermis wrote that if we use the criteria generally accepted as defining a profession, "... we can characterize teaching either as a nonprofession, as a profession only to a limited degree, or as an occupation striving to become a profession."[2] We believe that in the last ten years education—that quasi profession, that profession in the process of becoming—has invented a variety of strategies for becoming more precise.

In place of telling students to teach for understanding, many teachers have substituted behavioral objectives which detail the meaning of understanding and also provide requirements for judging a particular performance. Understanding can be broken down into major components: identifying, calculating, listing, defending, naming, providing illustrations, and many others. By the same token we have reached that point where it has become possible to identify the components of what has usually been held to be only an intuitive judgment, i.e., *good teaching.* We can say that good teaching involves the use of tested learning theory principles, removing students from the confining classrooms into direct observation of physical and human phenomena, determining where students are at the onset of instruction, and using individually tailored techniques such as assignments, class discussion, grouping practices, and evaluation. There are

From S. Samuel Shermis and James L. Barth, "Precision: The Coming Emphasis in Teacher Education," *Peabody Journal of Education* 49 (October 1971): 20–28. Reprinted by permission of the authors and George Peabody College for Teachers, copyright holder.

other practices which virtually all writers on teaching have identified as desirable for the past fifty years.[3]

What makes precision possible is that we can now get at these components of good teaching. We can individualize by using the audio-tutorial technique. We can use interaction analysis to help students identify specific teaching behaviors and to help them then evaluate such behaviors. Microteaching is a way of verifying that students are learning what they are supposed to learn. Behavioral objectives enable students to translate highly abstract terms into concrete actions.[4]   .

In short, there is now available a variety of techniques that enable professors of education and teachers to decide if they are doing what they believe they are doing. Interaction analysis, audio-tutorial, behavioral objectives, and microteaching are only four techniques that have precision as their essential goal. It may be helpful to see what one division in a department of education at a major university has done to bring about the desired precision.

PURDUE'S SOCIAL STUDIES EDUCATION

Social studies education at Purdue is a division, part of the Department of Education, which is itself part of the School of Humanities, Social Science, and Education. There are three professors and about a half-dozen graduate students at the doctoral level who have been taught the techniques mentioned and who help train undergraduates in their use. Space and facilities are excellent. There is a room used to house seminars and hold class meetings which contains a rich supply of curriculum materials—books, journals, pamphlets, multi-media kits, maps, globes, miniature carrels, texts (both antiquated and new), filmstrips, 8mm film loops, transistorized cameras and TV monitors for microteaching, and a variety of other teaching materials. One room contains a microteaching station and four sophisticated carrels with a variety of self-teaching devices. One room contains curriculum-making equipment of various kinds. Finally, a suite of offices houses the professors and the doctoral candidates who serve as teaching assistants.

MICROTEACHING

Of critical importance to the undergraduate program is microteaching, a technique developed at Stanford University and spread in many variations throughout the country. At Purdue two microteaching stations are involved. Each station contains four microstudents (college seniors), two microteachers (also seniors), and a microsupervisor (a professor or graudate student). The microteacher presents one five-to-seven minute lesson. When he finishes, his peers evaluate him on a rating form. While evaluation takes place, the tape is rewound and then played back on the TV monitor. At this point the microsupervisor, the microteacher, and the four microstudents may stop the tape and make any point or ask any question they wish. These include: Why did he not stop to ask a probing question? That was a confusing sentence. Was he talking only to one person? At this point he seems to be wandering from the topic. Or is it really wandering? In addition, microteaching provides one more opportunity to use interaction analysis in order to show specific teacher-student behaviors.

After the verbal evaluation, the microsupervisor and the microteacher retire to an office where they replan the lesson, taking into account as many criticisms as possible. Replanning may be almost total in that a completely different topic is selected; or it may be minor with changes in emphasis, such as more questions and less lecturing. The microteacher then gives his complete five-to-seven minute lesson before four new microstudents at another station, while the microsupervisor stays to watch what is almost always a greatly improved performance.

Microteaching serves a variety of functions. First, it is a technique through which students practice the all-important skill of posing a real problem. This has to be done almost immediately since students are allotted only five minutes or so for teaching. The microteacher has to *do his thing* immediately or his own peers will become visibly bored. Boredom on a TV screen, as in a classroom, is unmistakable. Second, it is an excellent opportunity for counseling. The microteacher can become aware of his strengths and weaknesses. We have no hard data to support this, but it seems that the problems identified in microteaching are those that appear during student teaching. Students, therefore, have an opportunity to work on problems that could conceivably crop up later in student teaching.

We regard microteaching as a means of isolating *one* teaching technique and practicing it under optimum conditions. As such, microteaching is a means of bringing to the teaching act a high degree of precision.

INTERACTION ANALYSIS

In the bad old days the methods instructor could satisfy himself by cautioning his students not to lecture too much and to *open the classroom to discussion*. Unfortunately, verbal strictures were not and are not very effective. In the last decade and a half interaction analysis has had a greater impact. Interaction analysis is, as the name indicates, a method of identifying and analyzing the verbal interactions that take place between a teacher and students and among students. There are quite a large number of interaction analysis forms now, but at Purdue we use the *Flanders 10 and 30 Category* version. Other interactional analysis schemes provide more useful information than Flanders, but Flanders is simple to learn and relatively easy for seniors to code.

What does interaction analysis do? First, it provides a pattern that students can recognize. Flanders provides enough information so that those who use it can see two important patterns emerging: who asks questions and who does most of the talking. If the teacher asks questions which students answer and then the teacher lectures, the student performing an interaction analysis finds a 4f-8f-5p pattern. This is only Flanders' shorthand: 4f means that the teacher asks a fact question; 8f means that students give a fact answer; and 5p means that the teacher is dispensing personal opinions as information. If students originate the question, a great many 9s appear on the interaction analysis sheet.

Second, with the patterns provided, students can then make inferences. If a 4-8-5 pattern appears with considerable frequency they can decide for themselves that the teacher is originating the questions and the students' only function is to answer them and listen to some more information, none of which they asked for. *Flanders Interaction Scale* also reveals other patterns. It is possible to see what, when, and how a discussion can be *turned off*. The teacher who forces closure too soon or rewards students inappropriately with a "Very good" instead of asking a probing question may stifle discussion. These verbal behaviors form patterns on a Flanders scale. With the sensing of patterns, students may then make inferences, plan alternative patterns, and finally be able to predict student behavior according to specific patterns.

Being able to quantify even gross verbal behavior in a classroom is not the *summum bonum* of the methods class. Ideally, students should discriminate among different kinds of verbal techniques. But Purdue is handicapped by having to compress all education courses in an eight-week block of time, and this militates against more subtle learning. However, interaction analysis, combined with videotapes of actual teaching episodes, is a step in the right direction: the right direction being defined as the ability to discriminate among different kinds of teaching behavior and to classify and then evaluate.

AUDIO-TUTORIAL

Audio-tutorial (AT) refers to a technique by which a student teaches himself using a variety of teaching modes ranging from filmstrips to an instructor. The social studies education section's use of AT was borrowed and modified from the model developed over the last dozen or more years by Professor Samuel Posthelwait of Purdue's biology department. We have found what Posthelwait discovered: students learn more and learn it better when the information is transmitted by ways other than by oral transmission in a conventional classroom.

The primary use made of AT is to individualize instruction. Students can, in fact, take what time they require to perform the varied tasks and do the assigned reading and viewing. Lockstep assignments have vanished. We have also built into our AT units another individualized component: students may read typescripts, listen to lectures on audio tape, or both.

We cannot claim too much for our AT units. It is clear, however, that students *will* read and view rather thoroughly the contents of each AT unit and will perform the tasks assigned. Experience shows that students, without extensive coercion, will *not* read assigned textbooks. Using the simple pragmatic criterion, the AT units work; students learn from them and learn with more enthusiasm than they do from any textbook. We believe the proof is in the student teaching performance; we noted a continuing trend for students who have finished the prescribed AT courses to plan actively, to involve students, and, in general, to be more effective.

We have two basic kinds of AT units, those designed for complex carrels and those planned for simplified ones. In either case, our AT units, like most, require the student to pick up a variety of materials and a guidebook and retire into a cubicle. At the cubicle he opens the guidebook where he sees first the title of the unit. He then reads a table of contents which lists the components of the unit. Following this, he sees a list of behavioral objectives which function to guide his learning by telling specifically what he is expected to *do* or how he is expected to *perform* upon completion of the unit. From then on each guidebook is different.

In social studies education our guidebooks are supplemented with typescripts of lectures which the student hears on tape. Finally, each guidebook contains workpapers, which is our name for specific activities. What kind of activities do students perform? One activity calls for students to compare two different video taped presentations. Another asks students to analyze a lengthy article which advances a particular social studies model. Another task requests that students identify the problems they experienced as student teachers. One workpaper asks the students to break into subunits the process of inquiry. Not only are these workpapers done by individual students, they may also be the basis for later confrontations in the special methods class. That is, a student may say, "I read such and such in AT-II and disagree with a point made there. What about . . . ?" In short, the methods classes are no longer places in which professors *tell* students about good teaching. They are laboratories for analyzing, demonstrating, and practicing good teaching.

A word about the two different kinds of audio-tutorial units. One is done in the simplified carrels in the back of the main social studies room. Usually the AT unit is reduced to written lectures combined with typescripts and illustrations, including possible slides viewed through a miniature hand slide viewer. Some of the units, however, are done in what we call the sophisticated carrels, which contain a TV monitor hooked up to a video-corder and an 8mm projector which can be linked to or kept separate from a tape recorder. Books, journals, posters, reprints, and other reading materials are also stored in each carrel.

In general, we are satisfied with the results of the AT units. They cover basic information more effectively than the older text-lecture-recitation combination. They do in fact what we have talked about for years in theory: they individualize instruction. Students seem to enjoy the experience, and we can detect noticeable improvements in their student teaching. For these and other reasons, we will continue to use audio-tutorial as part of the offering of this section.

BEHAVIORAL OBJECTIVES

Educators have used objectives for decades. For most of the time, they have used them the wrong way. Generally, objectives have been lists (which have been called *atrocious* lists by social studies educator Lawrence Metcalf) of rather high-sounding goals as inspiring as they were unreachable. Most objectives suffered from two irremediable defects: first, they were inconsistent; second, they were pitched at such a high level of abstraction that in no sense could they perform the function attributed to objectives. That is, they could not direct behavior.

In recent years, however, psychologists and educators have done some hard thinking on the entire question of the use of objectives (or goals, ends, and aims, to use the most popular synonyms). What has been seen is that any objective needs refining.

Employing constructs from Robert Mager, Purdue's social studies education division both teaches and uses behavioral objectives. They are used, as we have seen, in the guidebooks that come with each AT lesson. They are also taught and practiced in the classroom.

The heart of a behavioral objective is the naming of a performance or behavior that is expected when a task is completed. Within each behavioral objective, either implicit or explicit, are criteria to determine if, in fact, the objective was reached. An example is needed.

Most history teachers will talk about the need for students to understand or appreciate the impact of the Industrial Revolution. Unfortunately, there is no clear mechanism to tell teachers or students when the desired degree of appreciation or understanding has been reached. Part of the problem is that teachers are most unclear about what an understanding is. They are only dimly aware that an understanding is a seeing of relationships, a subsuming of facts under a general idea, or that it may consist of seeing how something may be used to fulfill some goal, i.e., understanding, as Bigge calls it, "the tool-use of a fact."[5] Another part of the problem is that most objectives are not operational; they do not take into consideration the psychological operations that are required to do the job.[6]

Behavioral objectives attempt to remedy the situation. In place of an understanding of the Industrial Revolution, the teacher keeps in mind that she wants her students to be able to (1) list the inventions that made mass production possible, (2) trace the Enclosure Act to the increased production of wool, (3) relate woolgrowing to the rise of the factory system, (4) relate the factory system to the growth of urban areas in England, and (5) speculate on the meaning of the term revolution, i.e., when does a revolution take place, what does it mean to speak of a revolution?

There is a variety of similar terms that yield the characteristics of a behavioral objective: to calculate, identify, list, and name, for instance. Now, while it is extremely difficult to know if a student has understood the Industrial Revolution, it is clear enough whether he can list, name, identify, defend, explain, or relate. These are behaviors. They are ways of performing whose characteristics can be appraised. One can determine to a fairly precise degree whether one has listed sufficiently the machines that helped generate the Industrial Revolution. One can do more than wishfully hope that a student has identified certain historical characteristics. Either he has or he has not. Or he has to some degree and has failed to some extent. Thus, a term has been qualified precisely, it has been reduced to its components, and its components have been correlated with specific behavior.

THE CLASSROOM

As we have seen, the use of audio-tutorial techniques has changed the quality of classroom teaching. In brief, replacing the classroom as a place for transmission of information is the classroom as a place for confrontation and demonstration.

Confrontation, to employ an overused term, refers to no holds barred discussions of whatever students take to be an issue. Our discussions are not recitations, i.e., hashing over information supposed to have been learned from textbook or lectures. Discussions are attempts to clarify the belief structures of our students. The clarification takes place when our students, disturbed or puzzled by something in an AT lesson, a statement made by a professor, or an attitude expressed by another student, attempt to restructure their cognitive and affective framework. This is easier to write about than it is to do, for in effect we are inviting students to take potshots at our pedagogical theories. It is no good to tell students, "Be critical—except of my position." This clearly suggests either that the professor is a hypocrite or, just as serious, is afflicted with a fragile epidermis. If a professor encourages students to confront one another, texts, or their own students during student teaching, he must be willing to have them confront him. The confrontation is invariably exciting but not always ego-boosting.

First, we find that socialized by 16 years of education-as-transmission, many of our students simply regard our position, in shorthand terms, inquiry, as hopelessly idealistic or as simply weird. Second, associated with the first point, they see discrepancies between an inquiry position and what they know to have been true in their high school and university experience. Asking students to be critical of 16 years of their own experiences is asking them to turn a critical eye on themselves and their own belief structure. The end result is accompanied by not a little hostility as students ask, understandably, "What do you mean I can't tell my students what is right and what is wrong?" or "What do you mean when you say that knowledge without the context that brought it into being is useless?" Our experience has been that after a surprisingly brief time, students generally decide that an inquiry approach is more fruitful than other approaches they have known. But the problem does not end there.

The next step is invariably a vigorous request: "Now how do I translate the pretty theory into something I can use in my classroom, keeping in mind that I will have likely a traditional cooperating teacher and students who have themselves been socialized into accepting education as the transmission of a set of principles, theories, facts, generalizations, and concepts?" We can partly deal with this challenge by demonstrating what we want them to do. We can also deal with it more directly by teaching them to practice effective techniques in microteaching and in presenting brief demonstrations in class. We can also encourage them to use the rich supply of curriculum materials in our classroom not as content to be learned for itself but as evidence to be used in the solution of a problem.

CONCLUSION

The staff of social studies education at Purdue has become increasingly aware of the need to practice what we teach. We have tried to avoid *talking about* desirable teaching techniques and have attempted to demonstrate them.

Audio-tutorial, as we have seen, presents essential information while individualizing the learning process. The questions and problems raised in AT feed into the classroom, causing it to be used as a laboratory for demonstration and confrontation. Since we are interested in getting students to analyze their own behavior, we have employed both interaction analysis and behavioral objectives. The first refines and defines a general objective and keeps students honest about their lesson plans: i.e., their lesson plans now become vehicles for implementing stated objectives. Microteaching gives students a chance to practice before their peers, but more important it allows students to view their own behavior. The goal of microteaching is to permit a student to identify his own teaching behavioral patterns; hence, it is a form of counseling. All of these techniques, taken as a whole, are attempts to bring to teacher training institutions the precision that a mature profession is supposed to require.

NOTES

[1] One of education's more helpful contemporary critics Charles E. Silberman in *Crisis in the Classroom* (New York: Random House, 1970) informs us that "education is not a science or a discipline and cannot be made into one." We are not suggesting that education has become a science but rather that education as a profession is becoming more precise.

[2] Donald C. Orlich and S. Samuel Shermis, "Teaching As a Profession," in *The Pursuit of Excellence: Introductory Readings in Education,* ed. D. C. Orlich and S. S. Shermis (New York: American Book Company,1965), p. 300.

[3] We are conscious of John Dewey's warning that "the real danger is in perpetuating the past under forms that claim to be new but are only disguises of the old." The new techniques as described in this paper are not old tricks revived for a new generation but rather represent a substantial break with the past.

[4] We are not speaking of the old science of education movement. This movement, popular in the 1920s and the 1930s, was borrowed from the Taylor-Mayo-Gilbreth science of administration movement. It was essentially value-free. *See* Raymond Callahan, *Education and the Cult of Efficiency* (Chicago: University of Chicago

Press, 1962). Education as we describe it is not a value-free enterprise but rather a value-based enterprise. We see no inherent conflict between values and precision.

[5] Morris L. Bigge, *Learning Theories for Teachers* (New York: Harper and Row, 1964), pp. 318-23.

[6] Ibid.

QUESTIONS FOR REFLECTION AND DISCUSSION

1. A number of issues in teacher education are identified in the articles in this section. Which one(s) do you regard as the most crucial?

2. Iannone offers six suggestions that "should be helpful to schools of education in training teachers to encounter today's youth." Do you think these, if implemented, would answer the charges Lenke makes? That is, will the survival that Lenke speaks of be enhanced by the kind of teacher education program Iannone advocates? Will the precision teaching Shermis and Barth describe improve chances for survival?

3. In some respects Lenke's article is an indictment of teachers and teaching. In what respects do you agree with his assertions? Disagree?

4. Do the critical teaching strategies Swineford discusses lend themselves to the precision Shermis and Barth argue for?

5. Suppose you were responsible for designing a teacher education program. What ideas included in this section would you accept? Reject? Are there important ideas not included here which you would want to consider? If so, what are they?

Chapter four
The Money Game and Educational Accountability

No one questions that education has both social and moral dimensions. However, it also has a financial dimension, which may override the social and moral. That is, money is a necessary condition for education.

But money is tight. Since the late 1960s each year has witnessed the failure of over 50 percent of the bond issues and tax referenda offered to local voters. Schools across the country have had to face program cutbacks. Some have resorted to double sessions. Others have cut out "nonessential" activities like athletics or music. Still others, notably some schools in Ohio, have simply closed up shop for a period of time to enable the district to effect sufficient economies to keep the doors open the rest of the year.

What seems certain to emerge from the financial crisis education is currently undergoing is a kind of benefit/cost analysis. Those who supply the funding, whether local citizens or state and federal agencies, are now asking not only what the money is to be used for, but also what the results of that use are. When the results are negative or, as is often the case in education, when they are difficult to articulate clearly over the short run, the money-suppliers are likely to withdraw their purses or, at the very least, to want to hold accountable those who spend the monies. Accountability, to appropriate the title of the Morris article in this section, is indeed the "watchword for the 70s."

It is with a look to the future that this section is devoted to accountability. No matter how grave the state of the economy, there will always be some money (but probably never enough, in the minds of many educators) to finance education. Education is simply too vital a national enterprise, too important a societal necessity, to be written off the checkbook entirely. Yet it seems prudent to argue that the money will no longer come forth with "no strings attached." Rather, there will be strings—responsibilities identified, results assessed, future apportionments based on past accomplishments.

Five of the seven articles in this section deal with accountability, those by Lopez, Lessinger, Barro, Bowers, and Morris. Though admittedly there is overlap, each selection is unique, either different in its conception of accountability or different in its author's wishes about the way accountability in education is to be employed. Lopez cites a number of the reasons for failure in the accountability measures so far implemented and

139

suggests specific organizational and personal techniques to ensure a greater likelihood of success. Lessinger describes a number of the movements presently underway and, generally, appears to have a far more sanguine approach to accountability than that held by many educators. Barro, like Lopez, takes a pragmatic look at the problem of accountability in education, asking and attempting to answer some of the very provocative questions the whole issue raises. Bowers addresses himself to the concerns many teachers raise: How can I be held accountable and still avoid the pitfall of doing only the trivial which can be easily measured and on which I can expect my students to demonstrate successful performance? Can I be the humanistic teacher I want to be and still retain my job in an age of accountability? Morris's article links accountability with performance contracting; surely this link, even if only in theory, will be made by school boards confronted with benefit/cost analysis procedures. Performance contracting is more fully explained in Schiller's article, most of it in the form of questions and answers. Finally, Allen provides some needed perspectives on the whole question of school finance.

Accountability in Education
Felix M. Lopez

Accountability refers to the process of expecting each member of an organization to answer to someone for doing specific things according to specific plans and against certain timetables to accomplish tangible performance results. It assumes that everyone who joins an organization does so presumably to help in the achievement of its purposes; it assumes that individual behavior which contributes to these purposes is functional and that which does not is dysfunctional. Accountability is intended, therefore, to insure that the behavior of every member of an organization is largely functional.

Accountability is to be distinguished from responsibility by the fact that the latter is an essential component of authority which cannot be delegated. It is the responsibility of a board of education to insure the effective education of the children in its community. Board members cannot pass this responsibility on to principals and to teachers. But they can hold teachers and principals accountable for the achievement of tangible educational effects *provided* they define clearly what effects they expect and furnish the resources needed to achieve them.

From Felix M. Lopez, "Accountability in Education," *Phi Delta Kappan* 52 (December 1970): 231–35. Reprinted by permission of the author and the publisher.

REASONS FOR FAILURE

A review of accountability programs underlines its uneven, trial-and-error progress and its current inadequacies. Initiated when psychometric theory was largely underdeveloped, embedded early in unrealistic management and legislative mandates, imposed usually from above on an unwilling and uncomprehending supervisor, the program has struggled with the common conception that it is an end rather than a means and with an administrative naiveté that treats it as a student's report card. Personnel textbooks have stressed the idea that an accountability plan must be characterized by simplicity, flexibility, and economy. Ignoring the fact that these qualities are not wholly compatible, administrators have attempted to develop programs along these lines. Their inevitable failures have led to the current disillusionment and distrust and, in some quarters, to the belief that the establishment of an effective program is impossible. Nevertheless, a careful examination of efforts to establish accountability programs suggests some underlying misconceptions that explain the many failures.

1. Most accountability programs have been installed in organizational settings that lack the necessary background and organizational traditions to assimilate them. Insufficient emphasis has been placed on the development of an organizational philosophy and on the determination of accountability policies before the implementation of the program.

2. The administrative procedures governing the program have not been attuned to its purposes. There has been a tendency to make the program accomplish a great deal with an oversimplified procedure. The evidence strongly suggests that despite the ardent wish for economy and simplicity, only a program designed for a specific purpose or involving a multimethod approach is likely to succeed.

3. Accountability systems have not been designed to gain acceptance by those who are covered by them nor by those who have to implement them. For the most part, they have been designed by specialists, approved at the highest levels, and imposed without explanation on those who have to implement them. This occurs because the problem is approached from an organizational rather than an individual perspective.

4. The measures of accountability so far developed have not met even minimum standards of reliability and relevancy. This failure is known as the "criterion problem" and can be summarized briefly as follows:

a. Criteria of effectiveness in a position generally lack clear specifications.

b. Objective measures, when examined closely, are usually found to be either nonobjective or irrelevant.

c. Subjective measures, when examined closely, are usually found to be biased or unreliable.

d. Seemingly adequate criteria can vary over time.

e. Position effectiveness is really multidimensional. Effectiveness in one aspect of a position does not necessarily mean effectiveness in others.

f. When effectiveness in different aspects of a position is measured, there is no sure way to combine these measures into a single index of effectiveness.

g. Different performance patterns achieve the same degree of effectiveness in the same job.

To be successful, therefore, the accountability program must meet the following requirements:

1. It must be an important communications medium in a responsive environment through which members are informed of what is to be accomplished, by whom, and how; wide participation in the obtainment of organization goals must be invited; and the attention of top management must be focused on the accomplishment of individual employees' personal goals.

2. It must reflect an organizational philosophy that inspires confidence and trust in all the members.

3. It must be based on ethical principles and sound policies that can be implemented by a set of dynamic, flexible, and realistic standards, procedures, and practices.

4. It must clearly specify its purposes so that standards, procedures, and practices can be conformed to them.

5. It must be designed primarily to improve the performance of each member in his current job duties. Other effects, such as the acquisition of information on which to base salary and promotion decisions and the personal development of the employees' capacities, may accompany the main effect of improved job performance, but these must be considered merely by-products of the main process.

6. The manner in which the supervisor discusses his evaluation with the subordinate constitutes the core of the process. If this is handled poorly, the program, no matter how well designed and implemented, will fail.

7. To be effective and accepted, both those who use it and those who will be judged by it must participate in the design, installation, administration, and review of the total accountability system.

These principles, then, outline the dimensions of an approach to the establishment of accountability in education. The approach encompasses three broad interventions into the current system, each aimed initially at a distinct level of the organization structure: the top, the middle, and the base, the last named being the teachers themselves. Ultimately, however, all three levels will be involved in all three phases of the accountability program.

INTERVENTION AT THE TOP

Basically, intervention at the top consists of the establishment of organizational goals by the use of a technique referred to in private industry as "Management by Objectives" (MBO) and in government as the

"Planning, Programming, and Budgeting System" (PPBS). Since there are many excellent books describing these techniques in detail, we shall confine ourselves here to a brief summary of the method.[1]

Goal Setting

The underlying concept of the goal-setting approach is· simple: The clearer the idea you have of what you want to accomplish, the greater your chance of accomplishing it. Goal setting, therefore, represents an effort on the part of the management to inhibit the natural tendency of organizational procedures to obscure organizational purposes in the utilization of resources. The central idea is to establish a set of goals for the organization, to integrate individual performance with them, and to relate the rewards system to their accomplishment.

While there is general agreement that this method represents the surest approach to effective management, there is no primrose path to its practical implementation.

In its most commonly accepted form, MBO constitutes an orderly way of goal setting at the top, communication of these goals to lower-unit managers, the development of lower-unit goals that are phased into those set by the higher levels, and comparison of results in terms of goals. The program operates within a network of consultative interviews between supervisor and subordinate in which the subordinate receives ample opportunity to participate in the establishment of his own performance objectives. Thus, the whole concept is oriented to a value system based upon the results achieved; and· the results must be concrete and measurable.

When properly administered, Management by Objectives has much to recommend it:

1. It involves the whole organization in the common purpose.

2. It forces top management to think through its purposes, to review them constantly, to relate the responsibilities of individual units to pre-set goals, and to determine their relative importance.

3. It sets practical work tasks for each individual, holds him accountable for their attainment, and demonstrates clearly how his performance fits into the overall effort.

4. It provides a means of assuring that organization goals are eventually translated into specific work tasks for the individual employee.

It is, therefore, virtually impossible to conceive of an effective accountability program that does not operate within the umbrella of the goal-setting process. When properly designed and implemented, goal setting becomes an ideal basis for other forms of performance evaluation. It insures that subordinate goals and role performances are in support of the goals of the higher levels of the organization and that ultimately the institutional purposes will be achieved.

The Charter of Accountability

One way of implementing the goal-setting process that has been found useful in education is through the development of a charter of accountability. This approach was originally developed by the Ground Systems Group of the Hughes Aircraft Company.[2] The charter is agreed to by two individuals or groups—one in a superordinate and the other in a subordinate capacity—after consultation, discussion, and negotiation. Ultimately, the entire organization is covered by the series of charters beginning at the top with a major organization unit, say, the English department in a local high school. Each teacher's goals are shaped by his unit's charter of accountability. Each unit head is held accountable for the results specified in his charter, which he draws up and which he and his superiors sign. Ultimately, all charters are combined into a system-wide charter that provides the basis of accountability for the board of education and the superintendent of schools.

A charter contains a statement of purposes, goals, and objectives. *Purpose* constitutes the organization's reason for existence and gives meaning and direction to all its activities. Purposes, therefore, are usually stated in broad inspirational terms.

Goals and *objectives* are the tangible expressions of the organization's purposes. Goals are long-range, concrete, end results specified in measurable terms. Objectives are short-range, specific targets to be reached in a period of one year, also specified in measurable terms.

Specifically, a charter of accountability contains the following features:

1. A statement of system-wide purposes or areas of concern and the purposes of the next level above the unit completing the charter of accountability.
2. A statement of the specific purposes of the unit completing the charter.
3. A description of the functional, administrative, and financial accountability necessary to accomplish the unit's purposes.
4. A set of basic assumptions about the future economic, sociopolitical, professional, and technological developments likely to affect the attainment of goals but which are beyond the control of the accountability unit.
5. A listing of the major goals of the unit to be aimed at for the immediate five-year period.
6. A subseries of performance tasks that provide unit supervisors with definitive targets toward which to orient their specialized efforts and with which to define the resources necessary to accomplish them.
7. Statements of the authority and responsibility necessary to complete these tasks.

Space does not permit the full exposition of the process of establishing a charter of accountability. Very broadly, and quite superficially, it would follow this pattern:

    1. A central committee or council composed of representatives of key

members of the system—school administration, local school boards, union, teachers, parent and community groups—would convene to define the broad purposes of the school system. Putting it simply, their job would be to answer these questions: "What is the business of the school system?" What are we trying to accomplish?" While the answers to these questions may seem obvious, in practice they are difficult to articulate. Answering them serves the larger purpose of clarifying thinking about the realistic aims of a school system. In business, the definition of purpose has led to dramatic changes in organization structure, business policies, product mix, and, ultimately, in return on investment.

The purposes delineated by this council are then discussed widely in the community. In particular, they serve to determine the major areas of concern of the school system that have been assigned to it by the community. Both the purposes and the areas of concern, however, must be considered at this point to be tentative and subject to modification by lower levels of the system. They will provide, however, the necessary guidelines for the goal-setting process and the development of charters of accountability by the school districts and other lower level units.

2. Each major subunit—school district, division, or department—meets to define its goals and objectives and to prepare its charter of accountability. Since these goals and objectives can differ substantially according to the needs of specific localities, the criteria of accountability will also differ. This is the important, even crucial point that constitutes the major advantage of the goal-setting process. It provides for multiplicity of measures of accountability that are tailored to the needs and hence the goals of specific operating units. The objectives of a principal of an inner-city school will differ from those of a principal of a suburban school, and so must the measures of accountability. Reading grade equivalents may be an appropriate measure of teacher effectiveness in one school and not in the other.

3. The charters of all units are collated and reviewed by the central council or school board with the advice and assistance of the planning and budgeting unit of the office of the superintendent of schools. Appropriate approvals are granted in accordance with existing policy and legislation. Thus, the combined charters constitute *the* charter of accountability for the board of education and the entire school system. While there will be some uniformity to this charter, it is apparent that it will resemble more a patchwork quilt than a seamless cloak and will, therefore, adhere more closely to the reality it attempts to reflect.

4. As each charter is approved, subcharters are developed in the same way for individual units in each district. Obviously, the heads of these units will have had a voice in the formulation of the district charter so that this will not be a new task for them. But in developing the subunit charters in the schools themselves, all the members of the system will ultimately have a voice.

5. Once the charters have been adopted, they are implemented. In some cases, new inputs will eliminate or change previously stated objectives. In others, objectives will be found to be quite unrealistic. Provisions must be

made, therefore, to amend the charters of accountability as experience dictates. In most cases, however, it is advisable to stick with the original charter until the year-end review and appraisal of results.

6. The evaluation of the .achievement of the period's objectives is made as plans for the next charter are formulated. This is the essence of accountability: results compared to objectives. It is important to note, however, that this evaluation is made not in a punitive, policing climate to check up on people, but rather in a supportive, constructive atmosphere to find out how objectives were achieved and, if they were not, why not. Both parties to this process assume the responsibility for the results and approach the task with the idea of exploring what happened for purposes of problem solving and resetting goals and objectives.

INTERVENTION IN THE MIDDLE

The implementation of an accountability program depends, to a large extent, on the attitudes and the skills of the supervisory force. If it is skeptical, anxious, or hostile to the plan, it will fail no matter how well it is conceived. This has been the bitter experience of many firms that have attempted to install goal-setting and performance-evaluation programs without first preparing their managers and supervisors to implement them.

Thus, a second essential step in introducing accountability into a school system is the establishment of a massive supervisory development program. Such a program must be practical, intensive, and primarily participative in nature. Its purpose is not merely to disseminate information but rather to change attitudes and to impart specific skills, particularly the skill of conducting accountability interviews with subordinates.

This will not be easy. Most supervisors, principals, and teachers have had no experience with such a program to prepare them for the tasks involved. A development program must be tailormade to meet their needs.

The development program must also begin at the top with the superintendent and the assistant superintendents. There is a practical reason for this. When presenting this subject matter to middle managers in other organizations, an almost universal response from them is, "Why can't our bosses take this course? They need it more than we do." Since the program content is likely to be quite strange, even revolutionary, to many of the lower middle-management participants, its credibility can be insured only by its being accepted at the highest levels and applied there first.

The program must enable the top-level people to examine the basic assumptions on which they operate and give them as much time as possible to get these assumptions out in the open. The specific objectives of the program would be:

1. To emphasize the influence process in handling subordinates, managers, and supervisors, as well as teachers, and to de-emphasize the formal authority-power-coercion approach to supervision and administration.

2. To provide a deeper understanding of the communications process itself. Such a program must heighten the awareness of the supervisor as to how he comes across best to others and develop his flexibility in dealing with the broad spectrum of personalities encountered in the fulfillment of his responsibilities. Each supervisor should be given an opportunity to prepare a plan for his self-growth and development.
3. To consider ways of dealing with the more routine aspects of teaching by considering job enrichment techniques.
4. To emphasize the sociopsychological realities that education faces today. The program should make supervisors aware that they simply cannot rely on authoritarianism alone to get results with people.

The format of the program should be primarily participative in nature—that is, it should consist of learning experiences and exercises which require the supervisors to participate actively in the training sessions. Frequent use should be made of audio-visual displays, role playing, conference discussions, and case study techniques. Theoretical ideas and concepts that help develop new ways of thinking and approaching problems can be introduced and amplified through specifically designed case studies. The solutions which result from the systematic examination· of these case studies should be applied directly to specific school system problems. And, finally, attention must be given to problem areas that may be unique to an individual supervisor.

INTERVENTION AT THE BASE

The third phase of the accountability system, and the most pertinent, is the development of specific instruments and techniques to evaluate how individual members of the school system are performing their assigned roles. Since this phase touches the teachers directly, it is the most difficult and also the most delicate. If it is handled properly, it can accelerate the educational development of the community's children. If it is handled poorly, or indifferently, or as just another routine task (as it so often has been in other public agencies), problems of academic retardation will persist.

Description and discussion of the design, development, and installation of individual performance standards and measures for teachers is beyond the scope of this paper.[3] There are a number of approaches to this effort utilizing both objective and subjective measures. But regardless of the measures and procedures employed, there are some general principles that warrant mention here.

Requirements of a Teacher Accountability Program

First, an individual teacher accountability program can function effectively only within the context of a goal-setting program, such as the charter of accountability previously described, and a program of continuous supervisory development in coaching and evaluation interviewing.

Second, it must be quite clear from the outset that the purpose of the accountability program is improvement of present role performance. If the measurements and standards developed are used for other purposes—such as discipline, promotion, and salary increases—the program will fail, positively and absolutely. Of course there must be a relationship between the measures of accountability and these other personnel actions, but the relationship must be indirect and antecedent rather than direct and causal.

Third, the immediate intentions of the instruments developed as part of the accountability program should be to provide the teacher (or other professional worker) with feedback on his efforts and to provide him and his supervisor with material for discussions of ways to strengthen his professional performance.

Instruments of Accountability

The instruments or standards of measurement of performance must be designed to fulfill two purposes:

1. They must be meaningful and acceptable to the person who is evaluated by them.
2. They must permit quantitative consolidation in the form of means, standard scores, and percentiles to serve as criteria with which to evaluate the department, school, and district achievement of objectives.

Such instruments can be of two basic types:

1. *Results-oriented data.* These are hard data geared to the effects of the teacher's performance—attendance, standardized achievement test scores, grade point averages, etc.
2. *Person-oriented data.* These consist of rating completed by peers, superiors, and subordinates describing the *style* of the teacher's performance—that is, his initiative, technical competence, interpersonal competence, etc. It is possible to design the instrument so that the person completing it cannot consciously control the outcome.

None of the information obtained at this level should go beyond the school principal except in a consolidated and hence anonymous form.

To insure the acceptance of these instruments, it is necessary that the teachers themselves and their supervisors actively participate in this research, design, and implementation. This is done in two ways. First, in the initial development of the program, teachers and supervisors should actively assist the professional researchers at every stage.[4] Second, and even more important, in the accountability interview, the teacher takes an active role in what is essentially a problem-solving process.

THE ACCOUNTABILITY INTERVIEW

The entire program described in this paper pivots around the accountability interview between supervisor and teacher. If it is conducted well throughout the school system, then the educational process in that community will thrive. If it is done poorly, the whole accountability program will fail and the school system will be in trouble. Therefore, this encounter is crucial.

To make the interview effective, a number of conditions must exist before, during, and afterward. First, the supervisor must have discussed his own performance with his superior—the principal or the superintendent. He must also have participated in the development of his charter of accountability and that of his school or district. Both the teacher and the supervisor must be familiar with these documents.

They must also be aware of the department's and the school's goals and objectives. The supervisor must have adequate preparation in coaching and interviewing skills. Both the supervisor and the teacher must have met earlier to agree on the dimensions of the teacher's role and on acceptable standards of performance. The teacher must be given adequate time for self-evaluation, and both must have reviewed the data resulting from the accountability instruments referred to above.

During the interview, both discuss the material collected on the teacher's performance. They analyze the teacher's strengths and explore ways of capitalizing on them. They identify areas for improvement, develop an improvement plan, and choose the resources to implement it. The teacher also discusses his professional problems with his supervisor and ways in which the latter can be of greater assistance to him. They establish follow-up schedules with milestones to determine progress. And they put all of this—the plan, the schedule, and the milestones—in writing for subsequent review and follow-up.

This accountability program, sincerely pursued at all these levels, is guaranteed to achieve positive results. There will remain, however, one major obstacle—time. It is obvious that the program will make major demands on a supervisor's time. Consequently, most supervisors will assert that they do not have the time for such a meticulous and detailed approach. In part they will be wrong, and in part they will be right.

They will be wrong, first, because they are not really using the time they now have to maximum advantage. If they are like most managers, they waste a good deal of time in superfluous activities. Secondly, they will be wrong because they are mistaken in their notions of the proper functions of their job. They tend to overemphasize the professional and functional aspects of their responsibilities and to underemphasize the managerial and supervisory concerns that are of paramount importance in the organizational system.

But they will be right because their present school system, like nearly every other organizational system in the United States, requires them to perform many functions that interfere with their basic duties of manager and supervisor.[5]

The answer to this problem, which is one of the chief stumbling blocks to the implementation of an accountability program, seems to lie in a searching examination of the functions performed at each level of supervision. Many of these, upon closer examination, will be found to be delegatable, thus enriching the jobs of their subordinates and freeing them for their real responsibilities of managing one of the most vital enterprises in society—the school system.

NOTES

[1] For example, G. S. Odiorne, *Management by Objectives* (New York: Pitman Publishing Co., 1965); and C. L. Hughes, *Goal Setting: Key to Individual and Organizational Performance* (New York: American Management Association, 1965).

[2] P. N. Scheid, "Charter of Accountability for Executives," *Harvard Business Review*, July-August 1965, pp. 88–98.

[3] Felix M. Lopez, *Evaluating Employee Performance* (Chicago: Public Personnel Association, 1968).

[4] For an expansion of this principle, *see* F. M. Lopez, *Evaluating Employee Performance* pp. 68–69.

[5] *See*, for example, F. M. Lopez, *The Making of a Manager: Guidelines to His Selection and Promotion* (New York: American Management Association, 1970), Chapter 4 ("What Does a Manager Do?").

The Powerful Notion of Accountability in Education

Leon M. Lessinger

Accountability is a policy declaration adopted by a legal body such as a board of education or a state legislature requiring regular outside reports of dollars spent to achieve results. The concept rests on three fundamental bases: *student accomplishment, independent review* of student accomplishment and a *public report,* relating dollars spent to student accomplishment. The grand jury, the congressional hearing, the fiscal audit

From Leon M. Lessinger, "The Powerful Notion of Accountability in Education," *Journal of Secondary Education* 45 (December 1970): 339–47. Reprinted by permission of the author and the publisher.

are powerful and well-tested examples of means for achieving accountability. The absolute requirement of independent replication and communication in establishing scientific phenomena is another example of accountability. Accountability in education shares substance from all these examples. By focusing upon results, on student achievement, it can be a most powerful catalyst in achieving that basic reform and renewal so sorely needed in the school system.

A growing number of influential people are becoming convinced that it is possible to hold the schools—as other important agencies in the public and private sector are held—to account for the results of their activity. In his March 3 Education Message, President Nixon states, "From these considerations we derive another new concept: *Accountability.* School administrators and school teachers alike are responsible for their performance, and it is in their interest as well as in the interest of their pupils that they be held accountable."

The preamble to the agreement between the Board of Education of the City of New York and the United Federation of Teachers for the period September 8, 1969—September 8, 1972, under the title Accountability says,

The Board of Education and the Union recognize that the major problem of our school system is the failure to educate *all* our students and the massive academic retardation which exists especially among minority group students. The Board of the Union therefore agree to join in an effort, in cooperation with universities, community school boards, and parent organizations, to seek solutions to this major problem and to develop objective criteria of professional accountability.

Many more pronouncements, program developments, and policy decisions of a similar sort could be described. A few examples follow:

1. The Oregon State Department of Education has employed a Director of Education Audits and is using an institute of educational engineering to promote its research and development activities.

2. The Virginia State Board of Education has encouraged and authorized the use of Title I E.S.E.A. funds (with U.S.O.E. stimulation) for performance contracting with private enterprise to eliminate deficits in reading and other academic skills among disadvantaged children in Virginia.

3. The guidelines for the federal bilingual and dropout prevention program require an independent educational accomplishment audit.

4. The Louisville, Kentucky school system has an assistant superintendent for accountability.

5. The Colorado Legislature is considering the adoption of an accountability program.

6. The Office of Economic Opportunity is funding 21 school centers to experiment with performance contracts and incentives to achieve accountability.

7. The Dallas, Texas school system is developing a "second generation" Texarkana project to eliminate basic school failure among its disadvantaged children through performance contracts to be checked by an outside audit.

8. The Florida State Legislature has appropriated 1.2 million dollars to establish accountability through development of a variety of student output measures and other programs.

9. The Commission of the States has declared that its central theme along with National Assessment for the 70s is accountability.

10. The President of the National School Boards Association has made accountability the theme of his administration.

The list could be extended to fill the entire presentation. Clearly a new educational movement is under way. The school systems of America are entering what the Washington Post has termed "An Age of Accountability."

Many of the early school laws in America called for accountability. The concept has been rediscovered and elaborated to meet serious conditions in the schools especially those conditions relating to galloping costs, poor student achievement, and the erosion of public authority and confidence in the schools.

Accountability's pointed thrust for a regular public report of an outside review of demonstrated student achievement to arrange for the allocation of resources will fundamentally alter public education. Some of the more important changes are now discussed.

In the first place, successful implementation of an accountability policy will shift the principal focus in the school system from input to output, from teaching to learning. A growing research literature points up the independence of teaching and learning. There can be teaching without learning and learning without teaching. There can, of course, be learning as a result of teaching. So independent is this relationship, that some have called the phenomenon the "teaching/learning paradox." This suggests that the present and traditional methods of requesting resources as well as the principal bases for judging the quality of schools will undergo drastic change. In place of equating quality in terms of resources allocated in the form of inputs e.g., teachers, space, equipment, etc., the important criterion will be results—student learning. This will lead to a second by-product of accountability, a revised educational commitment for the nation.

In principle the American educational commitment has been that every child should have access to an adequate education—this is the familiar, but still unattained, principle of equal educational opportunity. This commitment has been translated into the dollar allocations for the people and the "things" of education. When a child has failed to learn, school personnel have often assigned him a label—"slow," or "unmotivated," or "retarded." Accountability triggers a revised commitment—that every child *shall* learn. Such a revision demands a "Can Do" spirit of enterprise, a willingness to change a system which does not work and find one which does; a seeking of causes of failure as often in the system, its personnel, its organization, its technology, and its knowledge base as is now spent in seeking it solely in students. This revised commitment may come to be called the principle of equity of results. The call for everyman's "Right To Read" clearly foreshadows this tradition.

A third major effect of accountability on schools centers on the notion of better standard practice in America's schoolrooms. Without accountability for results the spread of good practice and the adoption of better technology has moved at a snail's pace. In this connection, it should be remembered that technology is more than equipment, though equipment may be a part of technology. Technology refers to validated practice—the use of tested means to secure demonstrated results. It is the essence of the meaning in the phrase, "what works."

From an organizational, managerial and technological point of view, education is a cottage industry. It is in a backward state, passed by in a time of striking and exciting development in other significant areas of societal activity. As many educators can testify, educational technology is primitive. Teachers and students barely understand the breadth of use to which the household telephone can be used to gather knowledge. And while the telephone is being redesigned to operate in milliseconds under automated commands for slave efforts, education is just beginning to cope with the manual dial.

The example of the equipment portion of technology is not unique. The important part in validated practice played by professional competence in interpersonal behavior is not used in many classrooms. There is a wealth of evidence acquired over the last 30 years about the ways in which people interact, learn from each other, intervene, aid, support, or undermine the work of each other. Yet, there are few teachers who have progressed beyond the classroom methods of several generations ago. In few other fields of any consequence are there patterns of behavior so predictable, so unchanged, so inefficient in terms of the contemporary human organism and how it learns as are commonly found in the classroom.

Accountability is the "hair-shirt" of formal education. It is the response at budget time to the question, "What did you do with that other money? " It is contained in the cry of the outraged parent "If you don't teach my child, I'm going to have you fired."

There is little to be gained by defensiveness or protestation on the part of educators. Nor is a ringing statement of the truly magnificent achievements of the public schools an effective antidote. Handwringing or defensiveness is not the same as problem-solving. Public institutions cannot run on the record of more of the same when conditions and public expectancies have changed. Accountability represents an attractive path for improving support and strengthening the schools. The process of implementing an accountability directive contains elements which can bring new capability and new insights to personnel. These elements are now discussed. The major elements treated here are: developmental capital, modes of proof and education engineering. Built on these foundations, accountability can be welcomed by teachers and administrators—the evidence is accumulating that this is happening. Without them, the concept can be disruptive and even dangerous. There is a history of danger in movements that center on efficiency and effectiveness so ably discussed, for example, in Callahan's *Cult of Efficiency.*

DEVELOPMENTAL CAPITAL AND ACCOUNTABILITY

Money available in a predictable and secure manner for responsible investment via grants management in both school personnel and private enterprise to produce results is the energy of accountability. This is a fourth major aspect of accountability. Developmental capital is the money set aside for investment by school leaders in promising activities, suggested by teachers, students or whomever, which produce results. Added to a good base of solid support plus equalization such monies can act as the "steering" mechanism and the "propeller" to move the "ship" ahead in the desired directions.

Business typically budgets amounts varying from 3 to 15 percent for improved products, service, sales or capability. Until the passage of the Vocational Education Act of 1963 and the Elementary and Secondary Act of 1965 there was virtually no comparable money in education. With the passage of these acts and the subsequent amendments, it is estimated that there is now approximately 1/3 of 1 percent available as developmental capital.

School people need funds around which to bid for the opportunity to show results. The investment of small amounts of venture capital, administered in ways that call out the maximum involvement by staff, together with an outside audit of delivery on the promises to perform has been shown to be very effective. Such an approach needs widespread adoption by states and local education agencies in addition to the federal partner.

School systems today are characterized by archaic budgeting systems; poor use of buildings, staff and equipment; salaries unrelated to performance; inadequate personnel development programs; poorly developed promotion systems; outmoded organization and often repetitious and uninspired instruction. Developmental capital can serve as the incentive to cause movement toward change. It can be the necessary energy to cause the adaption, adoption, installation and successful long-term utilization of better practice and systemwide reform. The experience of the author as a superintendent of schools managing a 1 percent fiscal set-aside in conjunction with teacher hearings as the quality control is an instructive example.

MODES OF PROOF AND ACCOUNTABILITY

The "eye" of accountability lies in the phrase, "modes of proof." Recognition of an expanded notion of assessment of results is a fifth major effect of accountability on school reform. For too long many have confused measurement of results in education with standardized achievement testing of the paper and pencil, normal curve-based variety. Not everything in education can be (or ought to be) quantified in such a manner. But accountability in education, like accountability in other governmental enterprise, can make use of "evidence" from a variety of modes of attaining evidence. The use of hearings, of experts, of certified auditors, of simulations of work situations together with such means of acquiring evidence as video-tape and demonstrated pupil performance selected using small sample statistics come easily to mind. To argue that scientific measurement is limited to narrow so-called objective tests is to display both ignorance of the rich field of assessment, limited experience with science and inability to foresee the rapid development of creative output instruments and strategies which money and attention can promote. The Eight-Year Study and the O.S.S. Assessment of Men activities certainly give cause for optimism in this regard.

The outside review component of accountability is the most vital mode of proof. Science relies for its very existence on qualified, independent review and replication. Nothing is established in science unless and until it can be demonstrated by someone other than he who claims discovery or invention. Scientists are neither better people nor better scholars than educators; they do not pursue more scientifically or intrinsically "better" problems than teachers. They are simply subject to better monitoring by a system that both encourages and mobilizes the criticism of competent peers throughout their lives. Education, on the other hand, substitutes the gaining of a credential or license at a single point in a career for a continuing process of independent review and mandated accomplishment replication.

The accountability process addresses this lack by insisting upon techniques and strategies which promote objectivity, feed back knowledge of results and permit outside replication of demonstrated good practice. The recent inclusion of independent education accomplishment auditors in 86 school systems to verify locally derived objectives in Titles VII and VIII, the bilingual and dropout prevention programs of E.S.E.A., is a practical manifestation of this aspect of accountability.

Outside review tied to a public report probably explains the popularity of the emerging concept of accountability to the public at large. Schools in America serve and are accountable to the citizenry, not the professionals. Since the public served is in reality many "publics," each of whom have legitimate needs for information, accountability can lead to an opening up of the system to bring in new energy and new support.

EDUCATIONAL ENGINEERING AND ACCOUNTABILITY

The process of change in education starts with the design or location of good practice and ends with the installation of that good practice in the classroom and learning centers of the nation where it becomes standard practice. It is known that the change process involves adaptation of good practice and adoption. Educational engineering is the rapidly emerging field designed to produce personnel with competence in this change process. The development of this coherent body of knowledge and procedure represents a sixth powerful concomitant of accountability.

Since World War II several fields have been developed to enable leaders of very complex enterprises to operate effectively and efficiently. These emerging fields include: system design and analysis, management by objectives, contract engineering (including warrantees, performance contracts and incentives), logistics, quality assurance, value engineering and the like. The coordination of these fields around educational concerns for an improved technology of instruction may be conveniently called education engineering. Engineering has traditionally been a problem-solving activity, a profession dedicated to harnessing and creating technology to the accomplishment of desired ends, the resolution of difficulties and the promotion of opportunities.

The heart of the education engineering process is the performance contract. Performance contracts are not new to education. But the concept of holding an educational agency accountable for results is. When a student is able to demonstrate in concrete terms what he has or has not learned, educators will be in a better position to judge where or why a program succeeds or fails and make the necessary changes to achieve success.

In the main, educators have not developed performance criteria for measuring the effectiveness of instructional programs, and many programs are now under way which do not describe what students are expected to gain from their educational experiences.

Instead of vague promises to provide students with an "appreciation of reading," instructional program objectives should be stated as is done in the national assessment program in terms as specific as these in the following example:

Given his state's written driving laws manual, a sample test and sufficient time, the student will be able to correctly answer 90 percent of the questions.

There are and should be larger objectives in education that are difficult to define and impossible to measure as the consequence of any given program. The "training" components of education, illustrated in the basic skills of reading, arithmetic, vocational training, and the like are amenable to performance contracts.

But the fact that many results of education are subjective and not measurable in the "hard," scientific sense should not deter personnel from dealing precisely with those aspects of education that lend themselves to precise definition and assessment. Rather, it demands that maximum use be made of those individual parts that tell what the change in the whole has been.

The Texarkana, Arkansas performance contract of $80 for 80 hours of instruction with rewards for shorter time and penalties for non-achievement together with the Camp Mead use of a micro-society, learning center and achievement motivation are striking examples.

Pursuit of accountability can be expected to cause substantive changes in the schools. A few of the probable changes are listed below. Since it is doubtful that results will be attained without some movement in the listed direction, commitment to accountability in education can be viewed as a commitment to better instructional practice. This is the final major powerful aspect of accountability that can be explored in this presentation.

Here are some of the expected changes in schools as a result of the call for accountability:

1. The teaching role will finally change from information-giving to directing learning. In many classrooms, the person who is active more than a fraction of the time is the teacher, who is generally doing the following:

   a. Preparing and delivering lectures or talks to students whose motivation for paying attention or whose interest in what is being covered may be insufficient.

   b. Preparing, administering, grading and reviewing tests, assignments and homework, and covering the textbook, which, because of the methods applied and the materials generally available, have little value in helping the students to learn or the teachers to judge their own effectiveness.

2. The schools' facilities will become more open, more flexible and less group-oriented.

   Students can learn as individuals or as members of a group. There are no alternatives in any specific learning situation. Group instruction has its values for motivation, for general direction, etc., but is contra-indicated for individual learning. The misuse of time and effort in attempting individual growth through sole or major reliance on group methods is monumental. Facilities encouraging individual instruction are essential in producing results.

3. The curriculum will become more relevant.

   When the emphasis moves from process to results, the whole environment becomes a source for schooling. "School" can then be held in businesses, homes or through "bull" sessions. Teachers can be assisted by students and adults. Since the criterion is results, the process becomes open to a variety of input. Variety is the essence of motivation and can provide the realism so deeply desired by all who seek relevance in their schooling.

4. Outmoded myths and an incomplete educational tradition can be exposed and perhaps eliminated from the schools.

Too much of the behavior towards children in school seems to reflect a "Can't Do" philosophy. Too many seem intent on proving that the bell-shaped curve, with its built-in reflection of failure, ought to be the symbol of education. Accountability for results will prime personnel toward a "Can Do" philosophy. They will be energized to try alternate ways if something isn't working. This change of attitude could be *the* major benefit of the concept of accountability.

Accountability in education may have substantive effects on two of the most pressing educational problems today: student unrest and boredom. Too often today the curriculum is a function of the materials and time. School personnel have the well-established use of textbooks as the chief teaching material and the idea that children have to go to school for approximately eight hours every weekday for roughly ten months a year. For too many, the chief characteristic of school can be listed as time serving, course taking, and credit getting.

Time serving is a basic cause of boredom. For, if time is standardized, one has to fill it up. There is unfortunately, a basic rhythm to time serving—the teacher introduces a topic, "teaches" it, gives an assignment, prepares for the test, gives the test, reviews the test, and then repeats the process until the course is *covered*—even if there is little mastery or great forgetting.

Many people with children in elementary schools, for example, have had their children out of school for extended periods of time for reasons of illness, moving, or vacations. It is not unusual for them to report that their children can miss half of the school year or even skip a year or more and still do the whole program without any difficulty. When time has to be filled, there is a tendency for incredible redundancy and repetition to appear. With over 20 percent mobility in the population, this insight is spreading to many of the patrons of the school system.

Results, criterion performances, striving toward valued and clearly communicated ends can change the climate and place time as a function of outcome. Accountability is not a panacea; it is a change in attitude and perspective. It is precisely the kind of change which many have been seeking.

SUMMARY

The striking picture of the earth itself as a space vehicle, a counterpart of the space capsule from which the television cameras held in the hands of the astronaut beamed the pictures to television sets, gave an enormous segment of the population the lesson that those who live on the earth are stewards of the glorious home God has given. It is clear that we all are managers of precious and limited resources: a planet stocked with life and beauty and opportunity beyond telling; a heritage of freedom as Americans bought so dearly in the sacrifice and work and enterprise of those who went before. In the 1970s we all shall account for that stewardship.

It does not take prophetic vision to know that many of us will discover the very real connection between the lives we lead, the careers we pursue, the institutions we support, the thoughts we think, the values we hold, the priorities we attack, and our future as a people.

The first exercise in accountability must center on the care and nurture of our children. We are stewards of their education and training and the education system we have created consists of more than the schools. Over the years we have gradually dispatched more and more of our personal responsibilities for the young to paraprofessional and professional strangers. The good and bad results of our stewardship are coming home for all to see and feel and experience.

Accountability runs counter to Larry Peter's principle. It jerks us up by the scruff of the neck to answer for our performance.

Perhaps the most fitting summary of the power and potential of accountability in American education can be gotten by considering its relationship to the unsettling change of which we are all so painfully aware.

We live in an age of massive, even shocking change. When men and women are bewildered by such change our efforts *must* speak to their urgent problems—developing and improving an educational system to enable people to cope with and to captain a society in the throes of intellectual, technological and social revolutions far advanced is just such a problem.

Our time is marked as Robert Openheimer once said in a Columbia University speech by, "the dissolution of authority in belief, in ritual and in temporal order." It should not surprise us then that the school is not what is was, that there is great student unrest and patron dissatisfaction and that the issue of relevance is a central issue in our professional life.

Professor Houston Smith, philosopher and teacher at M.I.T. has posed the issue of social change at its most poignant in his recent powerful and wise little book called *Condemned To Meaning.* Let me quote some of his insights.

"We live in a time when history appears to be rushing toward some sort of climax. New knowledge breaks over us with a force and constancy that sweeps us off our feet and keeps us from regaining them. Life's tempo quickens as if to the beat of a conductor crying, 'Faster, faster.'"
With moon travel we're prepared to make a pass at the infinite. With DNA we are thinking of retooling our offspring. What have we not done? What may we yet not do? . . . the future looks dazzling. Or rather, it would were it not for one thing: a growing question as to whether there's any point to the whole affair. For we are witness to one of the great ironies of history. The century which in the West has conquered disease, erased starvation, dispersed affluence, elongated life, and educated everybody has generated in aggregate and average the gloomiest depiction of the human condition ever rendered. An occasional Greek wondered whether it might not have been better never to have been born, but an ingrowing pessimism seems to characterize most

of our writers. Almost unvaryingly they depict a world that is meaningless or absurd. Open nearly any book, enter almost any theater, and "Life is a lie, my sweet. It builds green trees that ease your eyes and draw you under them. Then when you're here in the shade, and you breathe in and say, 'Oh, God, how beautiful,' that's when the bird on the branch lets go his droppings and hits you on the head. Never have men known so much while doubting whether it adds up to anything. Never has life been covertly so empty while overtly so full."

In the face of this void of meaning in our time, in this sustained crises of authority in our time, education must take on different dimensions. Accountability is the public policy declaration that speaks to those different dimensions. Engineering that policy into practical, vital programs is a matter of due urgency. Dr. Peter, bureaucrats, citizens, parents, board members, educators and fellow Americans, take heed!

An Approach to Developing Accountability Measures for the Public Schools

Stephen M. Barro

THE CONCEPT OF ACCOUNTABILITY

Although the term "accountability" is too new in the educational vocabulary to have acquired a standard usage, there is little doubt about its general meaning and import for the schools. The basic idea it conveys is that school systems and schools, or, more precisely, the professional educators who operate them, should be held responsible for educational outcomes—for what children learn. If this can be done, it is maintained, favorable changes in professional performance will occur, and these will be reflected in higher academic achievement, improvement in pupil attitudes, and generally better educational results. This proposition—that higher quality education can be obtained by making the professionals responsible for

From Stephen M. Barro, "An Approach to Developing Accountability Measures for the Public Schools," *Phi Delta Kappan* 52 (December 1970): 196–205. Reprinted by permission of the Rand Corporation and the Publisher.

their product—is what makes accountability an attractive idea and provides the starting point for all discussion of specific accountability systems and their uses in the schools.

The unusual rapidity with which the accountability concept has been assimilated in educational circles and by critics of the schools seems less attributable to its novelty than to its serviceability as a unifying theme. Among its antecedents, one can identify at least four major strands of current thought and action in education: (1) the new, federally stimulated emphasis on evaluation of school systems and their programs; (2) the growing tendency to look at educational enterprises in terms of cost effectiveness; (3) increasing concentration on education for the disadvantaged as a priority area of responsibility for the schools; and (4) the movement to make school systems more directly responsive to their clientele and communities, either by establishing decentralized community control or by introducing consumer choice through a voucher scheme. Under the accountability banner, these diverse programs for educational reform coalesce and reinforce one another, each gaining strength and all, in turn, strengthening already powerful pressures for educational change.

HOW THE SCHOOLS CAN BE MADE ACCOUNTABLE

Accountability in the abstract is a concept to which few would take exception. The doctrine that those employed by the public to provide a service—especially those vested with decision-making power—should be answerable for their product is one that is accepted readily in other spheres and that many would be willing to extend, in principle, to public education. The problems arise in making the concept operational. Then it becomes necessary to deal with a number of sticky questions:

To what extent should each participant in the educational process— teacher, principal, and administrator—be held responsible for results?
To whom should they be responsible?
How are "results" to be defined and measured?
How will each participant's contribution be determined?
What will be the consequences for professional educators of being held responsible?

These are the substantive issues that need to be treated in a discussion of approaches to implementing the accountability concept.

Various proposals for making the schools accountable differ greatly in the degree to which they would require existing structures and practices to be modified. In fact, it is fair to say they range from moderate reform to revolution of the educational system. The following paragraphs summarize the major current ideas that, singly or in combination, have been put forth as approaches to higher quality education through accountability:

Use of improved, output-oriented management methods

What is rapidly becoming a new "establishment" position—though it would have been considered quite revolutionary only a few years ago—is that school district management needs to be transformed if the schools are to become accountable and produce a better product. The focus here is on accountability for effective use of resources. Specific proposals include articulation of goals, introduction of output-oriented management methods (planning-programming-budgeting, systems analysis, etc.), and—most important—regular, comprehensive evaluation of new and ongoing programs. Mainly internal workings of the school system rather than relations between school and community would be affected, except that better information on resource use and educational outcomes would presumably be produced and disseminated.

Institutionalization of external evaluations or educational audits.

Proposals along this line aim at assuring that assessments of educational quality will be objective and comparable among schools and school districts and that appropriate information will be compiled and disseminated to concerned parties. They embody the element of comparative evaluation of school performance and the "carrot" or "stick" associated with public disclosure of relative effectiveness. A prototype for this function may be found in the "external educational audit" now to be required for certain federal programs. However, the need for consistency in examining and comparing school districts suggests that a state or even a federal agency would have to be the evaluator. This would constitute a significant change in the structure of American public education in that it would impose a centralized quality control or "inspectorate" function upon the existing structure of autonomous local school systems.

Performance incentives for school personnel

Perhaps the most direct way to use an accountability system to stimulate improved performance is to relate rewards for educators to measures of effectiveness in advancing learning. One way to do this is to develop pay schedules based on teaching experience and academic training. An alternative approach would be to use differentiated staffing as the framework for determining both pay and promotion. The latter is a more fundamental reform in that it involves changes in school district management and organization as well as changes in the method of rewarding teachers. Professional organizations have tended to oppose such schemes, partly out of fear that performance criteria might be applied subjectively, arbitrarily, or inequitably. Although this may not be the only objection, if a measurement system could be developed that would be widely recognized as "objective" and "fair," the obstacles to acceptance of a system of performance incentives might be substantially reduced.

Performance or incentive contracting

Performance contracting rests on the same philosophy as the proposals for incentives, but applies to organizations outside the school system rather than individual professionals within it. A school district contracts with an outside agency—a private firm or, conceivably, a nonprofit organization—to conduct specified instructional activities leading to specified, measurable educational results. The amount paid to the contractor varies according to how well the agreed-upon objectives are accomplished, thereby providing a very direct incentive for effective instruction. At present, there is too little experience with performance contracting to support conclusions about its potential. However, a large number of experiments and several evaluation efforts are under way.* Should they prove successful, and should this very direct method of making the purveyor of educational services responsible for his product become widely used, there would undoubtedly be substantial and lasting effects on both the technology and organization of American public education.

Decentralization and community control

These are two conceptually distinct approaches to accountability that we lump together under one heading only because they have been so closely linked in recent events. Administrative decentralization, in which decision-making authority is shifted from central administrators to local area administrators or individual school principals, can itself contribute to accountability. The shift of authority should, for example, favor greater professional responsiveness to local conditions and facilitate the exercise of local initiative. Also, it allows responsibility for results to be decentralized and, in so doing, provides the framework within which various performance incentives can be introduced.

The movement for community control of the highly bureaucratized, big city school systems aims at accountability in the sense of making the system more representative of and responsive to its clientele and community. In the context of community control, accountability can be defined very broadly to include not only responsibility for performance in achieving goals, but also for selecting appropriate or "relevant" goals in the first place. Most important, community control provides the means of enforcing accountability by placing decision-making and sanctioning powers over the schools in the hands of those whose lives they affect.

Alternative educational systems

Probably the most radical proposal for achieving better education

*An experiment involving 18 districts and testing several different forms of performance contracting is being carried out in 1970-71 under sponsorship of the Office of Economic Opportunity. Also, the Department of Health, Education and Welfare has contracted with the Rand Corporation to carry out an evaluation of other efforts to plan and implement performance contracts.

through improved accountability is this one, which would allow competing publicly financed school systems to coexist and would permit parents to choose schools for their children. Usually this is coupled with a proposal for financing by means of "educational vouchers,"[1] although this is not the only possible mechanism. The rationale for this "consumer-choice" solution is that there would be direct accountability by the school to the parent. Furthermore, there would be an automatic enforcement mechanism: A dissatisfied parent would move his child—and funds—to another school. Of course, the burden of becoming informed and evaluating the school would be on the individual parent. At present there is very little experience with a system of this kind and little basis for judging how well it would operate or what effect it would have on the quality of education.

THE NEED FOR ACCOUNTABILITY MEASURES

These proposals, though not mutually exclusive, are quite diverse with respect to the kinds of restructuring they would imply and the prospective educational consequences. However, they are alike in one important respect: Each can be carried out only with adequate information on the individual and the collective effectiveness of participants in the educational process. At present, such information does not exist in school systems. Therefore, a major consideration in moving toward accountability must be development of information systems, including the data-gathering and analytical activities needed to support them. This aspect of accountability—the nature of the required effectiveness indicators and the means of obtaining them—will be the principal subject of the remainder of this paper.

Progress in establishing accountability for results within school systems is likely to depend directly on success in developing two specific kinds of effectiveness information: (1) improved, more comprehensive pupil performance measurements; and (2) estimates of contributions to measured pupil performance by individual teachers, administrators, schools, and districts. As will be seen, the two have very different implications. The first calls primarily for expansion and refinement of what is now done in the measurement area. The second requires a kind of analysis that is both highly technical and new to school systems and poses a much greater challenge.

The need for more extensive pupil performance measurement is evident. If teachers, for example, are to be held responsible for what is learned by their pupils, then pupil performance must be measured at least yearly so that gains associated with each teacher can be identified. Also, if the overall effectiveness of educators and schools is to be assessed, measurement will have to be extended to many more dimensions of pupil performance than are covered by instruments in common use. This implies more comprehensive, more frequent testing than is standard practice in most school systems. In the longer run, it will probably require substantial efforts to develop and validate more powerful measurement instruments.

But no program of performance measurement alone, no matter how comprehensive or sophisticated, is sufficient to establish accountability. To do that, we must also be able to attribute results (performance gains) to sources. Only by knowing the contributions of individual professionals or schools would it be possible, for example, for a district to operate an incentive pay or promotion system; for community boards in a decentralized system to evaluate local schools and their staffs; or for parents, under a voucher system, to make informed decisions about schools for their children. To emphasize this point, from now on the term "accountability measures" will be used specifically to refer to estimates of contributions to pupil performance by individual agents in the educational process. These are described as "estimates" advisedly, because, unlike performance, which can be measured directly, *contributions* to performance cannot be measured directly but must be *inferred* from comparative analysis of different classrooms, schools, and districts. The analytical methods for determining individual contributions to pupil performance are the heart of the proposed accountability measurement system.

A PROPOSED APPROACH

In the following pages we describe a specific approach that could be followed by a school system interested in deriving accountability measures, as they have just been defined. First, a general rationale for the proposed approach is presented. Then the analytical methodology to be used is discussed in more detail.

For what results should educators be held responsible?

Ideally, a school system and its constituent parts, as appropriate, should be held responsible for performance in three areas: (1) selecting "correct" objectives and assigning them appropriate priorities, (2) achieving all the stated (or implicit) objectives, and (3) avoiding unintentional adverse effects on pupils. Realistically, much less can even be attempted. The first of the three areas falls entirely outside the realm of objective measurement and analysis, assessment of objectives being an intrinsically subjective, value-laden, and often highly political process. The other two areas can be dealt with in part, subject to the sometimes severe limitations to the current state of the art of educational measurement. The answer to the question posed above must inevitably be a compromise, and not necessarily a favorable one, between what is desirable and what can actually be done.

Any school system aims at affecting many dimensions of pupil performance. In principle, we would like to consider all of them—appropriately weighted—when we assess teacher, school, or district effectiveness. In practice, it is feasible to work with only a subset of educational outcomes, namely, those for which (a) objectives are well defined and (b) we have some ability to measure output. The dimensions of performance that meet these qualifications tend to fall into two groups: first, certain categories of cognitive skills, including reading and mathematics, for which standardized, validated tests are available; second, certain affective dimensions—socialization, attitudes toward the community, self-concept, and the like—for which we have such indicators or proxies as rates of absenteeism, dropout rates, and incidence of vandalism and delinquency. For practical purposes, these are the kinds of educational outcome measures that would be immediately available to a school system setting out today to develop an accountability system.

Because of the limited development of educational measurement, it seems more feasible to pursue this approach to accountability in the elementary grades than at higher levels, at least in the short run. Adequate instruments are available for the basic skill areas—especially reading—which are the targets of most efforts to improve educational quality at the elementary level. They are not generally available—and certainly not as widely used or accepted—for the subject areas taught in the secondary schools. Presumably, this is partly because measurement in those areas is inherently more difficult; it is partly, also, because there is much less agreement about the objectives of secondary education. Whatever the reason, establishing accountability for results at the secondary level is likely to be more difficult. Pending further progress in specifying objectives and measuring output, experiments with accountability measurement systems would probably be more fruitfully carried on in the elementary schools.

Fortunately, existing shortcomings in the measurement area can be overcome in time. Serious efforts to make accountability a reality should, themselves, spur progress in the measurement field. However, for the benefits of progress to be realized, the system must be "open"—not restricted to certain dimensions of performance. For this reason, the methodology described here has been designed to be in no way limiting with respect to the kinds of outcome measures that can be handled or the number of dimensions that can ultimately be included.

Who should be accountable for what?

Once we have determined what kinds of pupil progress to measure, we can turn to the more difficult problem of determining how much teachers, principals, administrators, and others have contributed to the measured results. This is the key element in a methodology for accountability measurement.

The method proposed here rests on the following general principle: *Each participant in the educational process should be held responsible only for those educational outcomes that he can affect by his actions or decisions and only to the extent that he can affect them.* Teachers, for example, should not be deemed "ineffective" because of shortcomings in the curriculum or the way in which instruction is organized, assuming that those matters are determined at the school and district level and not by the individual teacher. The appropriate question is, "How well does the teacher perform, given the environment (possibly adverse) in which she must work and the constraints (possibly overly restrictive) imposed upon her?" Similarly, school principals and other administrators at the school level should be evaluated according to how well they perform within the constraints established by the central administration.

The question then arises of how we know the extent to which teachers or administrators can affect outcomes by actions within their own spheres of responsibility. The answer is that we do not know *a priori;* we must find out from the performance data. This leads to a second principle: *The range over which a teacher, a school principal, or an administrator may be expected to affect outcomes is to be determined empirically from analysis of results obtained by all personnel working in comparable circumstances.* Several implications follow from this statement. First, it clearly establishes that the accountability measures will be relative, involving comparisons among educators at each level of the system. Second, it restricts the applicability of the methodology to systems large enough to have a wide range of professional competence at each level and enough observations to permit reliable estimation of the range of potential teacher and school effects.* Third, it foreshadows several characteristics of the statistical models needed to infer contributions to results. To bring out the meaning of these principles in more detail, we will explore them from the points of view of teachers, school administrators, and district administrators, respectively.

Classroom teachers We know that the educational results obtained in a particular classroom (e.g., pupils' scores on a standard reading test) are determined by many other things besides the skill and effort of the teacher. The analyses in the Coleman report,[2] other analyses of the Coleman survey data,[3] and other statistical studies of the determinants of pupil achievement[4] show that a large fraction of variation in performance levels is accounted for by out-of-school variables, such as the pupils' socioeconomic status and home environment. Another large fraction is attributable to a so-called "peer group" effect; that is, it depends on characteristics of a pupil's classmates rather than on what takes place in the school. Of the fraction of the variation that *is* explained by school variables, only part can be attributed to teachers. Some portion must also be assigned to differences in resource availability at the classroom and school level and differences among schools in the quality of their management and support. Thus, the problem is to separate out the teacher effect from all the others.

To illustrate the implications for the design of an accountability system, consider the problem of comparing teachers who teach very

---

*This does not mean that accountability cannot be established in small school districts. It does mean that the analysis must take place in a broader context, such as a regional or statewide evaluation of performance, which may encompass many districts.

different groups of children. For simplicity, suppose that there are two groups of pupils in a school system, each internally homogeneous, which we may call "middle-class white" and "poor minority." Assume that all nonteacher inputs are identical for the two groups. Then, based on general experience, we would probably expect the whole distribution of results to be higher for the former group than for the latter. In measuring gain in reading performance, we might well find, for example, that even the poorest teacher of middle-class white children obtains higher average gains in her class than the majority of teachers of poor minority children. Moreover, the ranges over which results vary in the two groups might be unequal.

If we have reason to believe that the teachers associated with the poor minority children are about as good, on the average, as those associated with the middle-class white children—that is, if they are drawn from the same manpower pool and assigned to schools and classrooms without bias—then it is apparent that both the difference in average performance of the two groups of pupils and the difference in the range of performance must be taken into account in assessing each teacher's contribution. A teacher whose class registers gains, say, in the upper 10 percent of all poor minority classes should be considered as effective as one whose middle-class white group scores in the upper 10 percent for that category, even though the absolute performance gain in the latter case will probably be much greater.

This illustrates that accountability measures are relative in two senses. First, they are relative in that each teacher's contribution is evaluated by comparing it with the contributions made by other teachers in similar circumstances. In a large city or state school system, it can safely be assumed that the range of teacher capabilities covers the spectrum from poor to excellent. Therefore, the range of observed outcomes, after differences in circumstances have been allowed for, is likely to be representative of the range over which teacher quality can be expected to influence results, given the existing institutional framework. It may be objected that the range of outcomes presently observed understates the potential range of accomplishment because present classroom methods, curricula, teacher training programs, etc., are not optimal. This may be true and important, but it is not relevant in establishing teacher accountability because the authority to change those aspects of the system does not rest with the teacher.

Second, accountability measures are relative in that pupil characteristics and other nonteacher influences on pupil performance must be taken fully into account in measuring each teacher's contribution. Operationally, this means that statistical analyses will have to be conducted of the effects of such variables as ethnicity, socioeconomic status, and prior educational experience on a pupil's progress in a given classroom. Also, the effects of classroom or school variables other than teacher capabilities will have to be taken into account. Performance levels of the pupils assigned to different teachers can be compared only after measured performance has been adjusted for all of these variables. The statistical model for computing these adjustments is, therefore, the most important element in the accountability measurement system.

School administrators Parallel reasoning suggests that school administrators can be held accountable for relative levels of pupil performance in their schools to the extent that the outcomes are not attributable to pupil, teacher, or classroom characteristics or to school variables that they cannot control. The question is, having adjusted for differences in pupil and teacher inputs and having taken account of other characteristics of the schools, are there unexplained differences among schools that can be attributed to differences in the quality of school leadership and administration? Just as for teachers, accountability measures for school administrators are measures of relative pupil performance in a school after adjusting the data for differences in variables outside the administrator's control.

Consideration of the accountability problem at the school level draws attention to one difficulty with the concept of accountability measurement that may also, in some cases, be present at the classroom level. The difficulty is that although we would like to establish accountability for individual professionals, when two or more persons work together to perform an educational task there is no statistical way of separating their effects. This is easy to see at the school level. If a principal and two assistant principals administer a school, we may be able to evaluate their relative proficiency as a team, but since it is not likely that their respective administrative tasks would relate to different pupil performance measures there is no way of judging their individual contributions by analyzing educational outcomes. Similarly, if a classroom teacher works with a teaching assistant, there is no way, strictly speaking, to separate the contributions of the two. It is conventional in these situations to say that the senior person, who has supervisory authority, bears the responsibility for results. However, while this is administratively and perhaps even legally valid, it provides no solution to the problem of assessing the effort and skills of individuals. Therefore, there are definite limits, which must be kept in mind, to the capacity of a statistically based accountability system to aid in assessing individual proficiency.

District administrators Although the same approach applies, in principle, to comparisons among districts (or decentralized components of larger districts), there are problems that may limit its usefulness in establishing accountability at the district level. One, of course, is the problem that has just been alluded to. Even if it were possible to establish the existence of overall district effects, it would be impossible to isolate the contributions of the local district board, the district superintendent, and other members of the district staff. A second problem is that comparisons among districts can easily fail to take account of intangible community characteristics that may affect school performance. For example, such factors as community cohesion, political attitudes, and the existence of racial or other intergroup tensions could strongly influence the whole tone of education. It would be very difficult to separate effects of these factors from effects of direct, district-related variables in trying to assess overal district performance. Third, the concept of responsibility at the district level needs clarifying. In comparing schools, for example, it seems reasonable to adjust for differences in teacher characteristics on the grounds that school administrators should be evaluated according to how well they do, given the personnel assigned to them. However, at the district level, personnel selection itself is one of the functions for which administrators must be held accountable, as are resource allocation, program design, choice of curriculum, and other factors that appear as "givens" to the schools. In other words, in assessing comparative district performance, very little about districts can properly be considered as externally determined except, perhaps, the total level of available resources.* The appropriate policy, then seems to be to include district identity as a variable in comparing schools and teachers so that net district effects, if any, will be taken into account. Districts themselves should be compared on a different basis, allowing only for differences in pupil characteristics, community variables, and overall constraints that are truly outside district control.

A PROPOSED METHODOLOGY

The basic analytical problem in accountability measurement is to develop a technique for estimating the contributions to pupil performance of individual agents in the educational process. A statistical method that may be suitable for that purpose is described here. The basic technique is multiple regression analysis of the relationship between pupil performance and an array of pupil, teacher, and school characteristics. However, the proposed method calls for two or three separate stages of analysis. The strategy is first to estimate the amount of performance variation that exists among classrooms after pupil characteristics have been taken into account, then, in subsequent stages, to attempt to attribute the inter-classroom variables, and school characteristics.[5] This methodology applies both to large school districts, within which it is suitable for estimating the relative effectiveness of individual teachers and schools in advancing pupil performance, and to state school systems, where it can be used, in addition, to obtain estimates of the relative effectiveness of districts. However, as noted above, there are problems that may limit its utility at the interdistrict level.

Pupil performance data

Since we are interested in estimating the contributions of individual teachers and schools, it is appropriate to use a "value-added" concept of output. That is, the appropriate pupil performance magnitudes to associate

---

*In addition, of course, there are constraints imposed by state or federal authorities, but these are likely to be the same across districts.

with a particular teacher are the *gains* in performance made by pupils while in her class. Ideally, the output data would be generated by a program of annual (or more frequent) performance measurement, which would automatically provide before and after measures for pupils at each grade level.

It is assumed that a number of dimensions of pupil performance will be measured, some by standardized tests and some by other indicators or proxy variables. Specific measurement instruments to be used and dimensions of performance to be measured would have to be determined by individual school systems in accordance with their educational objectives. No attempt will be made here to specify what items should be included.* The methodology is intended to apply to any dimension of performance that can be quantified at least on an ordinal scale. Therefore, within a very broad range, it is not affected by the choice of output measures by a potential user.

Data on pupils, teachers, classrooms, and schools

To conform with the model to be described below, the variables entering into the analysis are classified according to the following taxonomy:

1. Individual pupil characteristics (ethnicity, socioeconomic status, home, family, and neighborhood characteristics, age, prior performance, etc.).
2. Teacher and classroom characteristics.
   a. Group characteristics of the pupils (ethnic and socioeconomic composition, distribution of prior performance levels, etc., within the classroom).
   b. Teacher characteristics (age, training, experience, ability and personality measures if available, ethnic and socioeconomic background, etc.).
   c. Other classroom characteristics (measures of resource availability: class size, amount of instructional support, amount of materials, condition of physical facilities, etc.).
3. School characteristics.
   a. Group characteristics of the pupils (same as 2a, but based on the pupil population of the whole school).
   b. Staff characteristics (averages of characteristics in 2b for the school as a whole, turnover and transfer rates; characteristics of administrators—same as 2b).

*Realistically, however, almost every school system will be likely to include reading achievement scores and other scores on standardized tests of cognitive skills among its output variables. Also, it will generally be desirable to include attendance or absenteeism as a variable, both because it may be a proxy for various attitudinal output variables and because it may be an important variable to use in explaining performance. Otherwise, there are innumerable possibilities for dealing with additional dimensions of cognitive and affective performance.

c. Other school characteristics (measures of resource availability: age and condition of building, availability of facilities, amount of administrative and support staff, etc.).¹

No attempt will be made to specify precisely what items should be collected under each of the above headings. Determination of the actual set of variables to be used in a school system would have to follow preliminary experimentation, examination of existing data, and an investigation of the feasibility, difficulty, and cost of obtaining various kinds of information.

Steps in the analysis

The first step is to determine how different pupil performance in each classroom at a given grade level is from mean performance in all classrooms, *after* differences in individual pupil characteristics have been allowed for. The procedure consists of performing a multiple regression analysis with gain in pupil performance as the dependent variable. The independent variables would include (a) the individual pupil characteristics (category 1 of the taxonomy), and (b) a set of "dummy" variables, or identifiers, one for each classroom in the sample. The latter would permit direct estimation of the degree to which pupil performance in each classroom differs from pupil performance in the average classroom. Thus, the product of the first stage of the analysis would be a set of estimates of individual classroom effects, each of which represents the combined effect on pupil performance in a classroom of all the classroom and school variables included in categories 2 and 3 of the taxonomy. At the same time, the procedure would automatically provide measures of the accuracy with which each classroom effect has been estimated. Therefore, it would be possible to say whether average performance gains in a particular classroom are significantly higher or lower than would be expected in a "typical" classroom or not significantly different from the mean.

Heuristically, this procedure compares performance gains by pupils in a classroom with gains that comparable pupils would be likely to achieve in a hypothetical "average" classroom of the system. This can be thought of as comparison of class performance gains against a norm, except that there is, in effect, a particular norm for each classroom based on its unique set of pupil characteristics. It may also be feasible to carry out the same analysis for specific subgroups of pupils in each class so as to determine, for example, whether there are different classroom effects for children from different ethnic or socioeconomic groups.

Estimation of teacher contributions   The second stage of the analysis has two purposes: (1) to separate the effects of the teacher from effects of nonteacher factors that vary among classrooms; and (2) to determine the extent to which pupil performance can be related to specific, measureable teacher attributes. Again, the method to be used is regression analysis, but in this case with a sample of classroom observations rather than individual pupil observations. The dependent variable is now the classroom effect estimated in stage one. The independent variables are the teacher-classroom characteristics and "dummy" variables distinguishing the individual schools.

Two kinds of information can be obtained from the resulting equations. First, it is possible to find out what fraction of the variation in performance gains among classrooms is accounted for by nonteacher characteristics, including group characteristics of the pupils and measures of resource availability in the classroom. The remaining interclassroom differences provide upper-bound estimates of the effects that can be attributed to teachers. If there is sufficient confidence that the important nonteacher variables have been taken into account, then these estimates provide the best teacher accountability measures. They encompass the effects of both measured and unmeasured teacher characteristics on teacher performance. However, there is some danger that such measures also include effects of group and classroom characteristics that were inadvertently neglected in the analysis and that are not properly attributable to teachers. This problem is referred to again below.

Second, we can find out the extent to which differences among classrooms are explained by measured teacher characteristics. Ideally, of course, we would like to be able to attribute the whole "teacher portion" of performance variation to specific teacher attributes and, having done so, we would be much more confident about our overall estimates of teacher effectiveness. But experience to date with achievement determinant studies has shown that the more readily available teacher characteristics—age, training, experience, and the like—account for only a small fraction of the observed variance. It has been shown that more of the variation can be accounted for when a measure of teacher verbal ability is included.[6] Still more, presumably, could be accounted for if a greater variety of teacher ability and personality measurements were available. At present, however, knowledge of what teacher characteristics influence pupil performance is incomplete and satisfactory instruments exist for measuring only a limited range of teacher-related variables. This means that with an accountability information system based on current knowledge, the excluded teacher characteristics could be at least as important as those included in determining teacher effectiveness. For the time being, then, the inter-classroom variation in results that remains after nonteacher effects have been allowed for probably provides the most useful accountability measures, though the danger of bias due to failure to include all relevant nonteacher characteristics must be recognized.

The principal use of these estimates would be in assessing the relative effectiveness of individual teachers in contributing to gains in pupil performance. More precisely, it would be possible to determine whether each teacher's estimated contribution is significantly greater or significantly smaller than that of the average teacher. At least initially, until there is strong confirmation of the validity of the procedure, a rather stringent significance criterion should be used in making these judgments and no attempt should be made to use the results to develop finer gradations of teacher proficiency.

The analysis will also make it possible to determine the extent to which measured teacher characteristics are significantly correlated with teacher effectiveness. Potentially, such information could have important policy implications and impacts on school management, resource allocation, and personnel practices. A number of these potential applications are noted at the end of the paper.

Estimation of contributions by school administrators   The same analytical techniques can be used in estimating the relative effectiveness of different schools in promoting pupil performance. Conceptually, a school accountability index should measure the difference between pupil performance in an individual school and average pupil performance in all schools after all pupil, teacher, and classroom variables have been accounted for. Such measures can be obtained directly if school dummy variables are included in the regression equation, as described earlier. Of course, the results measure *total* school effects, without distinguishing among effects due to school administration, effects of physical attributes of the school, and effects of characteristics of the pupil population. It may be feasible to perform a third-stage analysis in which the results are systematically adjusted for differences in the latter two categories of variables, leaving residual effects that can be attributed to the school administrators. These would constitute the accountability measures to be used in assessing the effectiveness of the principal and his staff. The results may have policy implications with respect to differential allocation of funds or resources among the different schools and, of course, implications with respect to personnel. Also, as would be done for teachers, an attempt could be made to relate measured characteristics of the school administrators to the estimated school effects. By so doing, it might be possible to learn whether administrator training and experience and other attributes are reflected in measured school output. Even negative results could provide important guidance to research on administrator selection and assignment.

Comparisons among districts   For reasons that have already been stated, it would probably be desirable to treat comparisons among districts separately from comparisons among classrooms and schools. This could be done by means of yet another regression analysis, with individual pupil performance gain as the dependent variable and with independent variables consisting of pupil and community characteristics, measures of resource availability, and a dummy variable or identifier for each district being compared. The purpose would be to determine whether there are significant differences in results among districts once the other factors have been allowed for. If there are, the findings could be interpreted as reflections of differences in the quality of district policy making and management. But as pointed out earlier, there would be uncertainty as to the causes of either shortcomings or superior performance. Nevertheless, the results could have some important, policy-related uses, as will be noted shortly.

THE NEED FOR EXPERIMENTAL VERIFICATION
OF THE APPROACH

The methodology described here carries no guarantee. Its success in relating outcomes to sources may depend both on features of the school systems to which it is applied and on the adequacy of the statistical models in mirroring the underlying (and unknown) input-output relationships in education. The validity and usefulness of the results must be determined empirically from field testing in actual school systems. Experimental verification, possibly requiring several cycles of refinement and testing, must precede implementation of a "working" accountability system.

Potential Problems

Three kinds of technical problems can threaten the validity of the system: intercorrelation, omission of variables, and structural limitations of the models. None of these can be discussed in detail without mathematics. However, a brief explanation of each is offered so that the outlook for the proposed approach can be realistically assessed.

Intercorrelation   This is a problem that may arise where there are processes in a school system that create associations (correlations) between supposedly independent variables in the model. An important example is the process—said to exist in many systems—whereby more experienced, better trained, or simply "better" teachers tend to be assigned to transferred to schools with higher socioeconomic status (SES) pupils. Where this occurs, pupil SES will be positively correlated with those teacher characteristics. On the average, high SES children would be taught by one kind of teacher, low SES children by another. This would make it difficult to say whether the higher performance gains likely to be observed for high SES pupils are due to their more advantaged backgrounds or to the superior characteristics of their instructors. There would be ambiguity as to the magnitude of the teacher contribution and a corresponding reduction in the reliability of estimates of individual teacher effectiveness. Thus, the quality of accountability information would be impaired.

This problem can take many forms. There may be strong correlations between characteristics of pupils and characteristics of school staffs, between teacher characteristics and nonteacher attributes of the schools, between classroom-level and district-level variables, and so on. The general effect is the same in each instance: ambiguity resulting in diminished ability to attribute results to sources.[7]

There are several things that can be done to mitigate the effects of intercorrelation. One is to stratify the data. For example, if teacher characteristics were linked to pupil SES, it would be possible to stratify the classrooms by pupil SES and to perform separate analyses for each stratum. This would eliminate some of the ambiguity *within* strata. On the other hand, comparisons of teachers *across* strata would be precluded. Another possible solution would be to take account of interdependence explicitly in the statistical models. Some attempts along this line have been made in studies of determinants of school performance. However, this solution is likely to raise a whole new array of technical problems as well as questions about the feasibility of routine use of the methodology within school systems.

The problem of omitted variables   The validity and fairness of the proposed approach would depend very strongly on inclusion of all major relevant variables that could plausibly be cited by teachers or administrators to "explain" lower-than-average estimated contributions. This means that all variables would have to be included that (a) have significant, independent effects on performance and (b) are likely to be nonuniformly distributed among classrooms and schools.

It will never be possible to demonstrate in a positive sense that all relevant variables have been included. Many intangible, difficult-to-measure variables, such as pupil attitudes, morale, "classroom climate," etc., can always be suggested. What can be done is to determine as well as possible that none of the additional suggested variables is systematically related to the estimated teacher and school contributions. In an experimental setting, administrators could be interviewed for the purpose of identifying alleged special circumstances, and tests could be carried out to see whether they are systematically related to performance differences.

Structural limitations of the models   The models described here may be too simple to take account of some of the important relationships among school inputs and outputs. One such shortcoming has already been noted: The models do not allow for possible interdependencies among the various pupil and school characteristics. Another, which may prove to be more troubling, is that interactions among the various output or performance variables have also not been taken into account.

Researchers have pointed to two distinct kinds of relationships. First, there may be tradeoffs between performance areas.[8] A teacher or school may do well in one area partly at the expense of another by allocating resources or time disproportionately between the two. Second, there may be complementary relationships. Increased performance in one area (reading, for example) may contribute directly to increased performance in others (social studies or mathematics). Therefore, treatment of one dimension of output at a time, without taking the interactions into account, could produce misleading results.

Econometricians have developed "simultaneous" models, consisting of whole sets of equations, specifically to take account of complex, multiple relationships among variables. Some attempts have been made to apply these models to studies of determinants of educational outcomes.[9] It may prove necessary or desirable to use them in an accountability measurement system, despite the complexity they would add, to eliminate biases inherent in simpler models.

Validity

Another important reason for thoroughly testing the accountability measurement system is that its validity needs to be assessed. Some of the procedures mentioned above contribute to this end, but more general demonstration would also be desirable. Two procedures that may be feasible in an experimental situation are as follows:

Replication A strong test of whether the method really gets at differences in effectiveness instead of differences in circumstances would be to apply it to the same teachers and schools during two or more years. Consistency in results from year to year would strongly support the methodology. Lack of consistency would show that major influences on performance remained unmeasured or neglected. Certainly, if the results were to be used in any way in connection with personnel assignment, reward, or promotion, the use of several years' estimates would be an important guarantee of both consistency and fairness.

An external test of validity The most direct way to test the validity of the statistical approach is to compare the results with alternative measures of teacher and school effectiveness. The only measures that are likely to be obtainable are subjective assessments by informed and interested parties. Though such evaluations have many shortcomings, it could be valuable in an experimental situation to see how well they agreed with the statistical results. Two important questions that would have to be answered in making such a comparison are: (1) Who are the appropriate raters—peers, administrators, parents, or even pupils? and (2) What evaluation instruments could be used to assure that subjective assessments apply to the same dimensions of performance as were taken into account in the statistical analysis? It may not be possible to provide satisfactory answers. Nevertheless, the feasibility of a comparison with direct assessments should be considered in connection with any effort to test the proposed accountability measurement system.

POTENTIAL USES OF ACCOUNTABILITY MEASURES

Space does not permit a full review of the potential uses of an accountability measurement system. However, an idea of the range of applications and their utility can be conveyed by listing some of the main possibilities.

Identification of effective schools

The most rudimentary use of the proposed accountability measures is as an identification device. Once relative school effectiveness is known, a variety of actions can follow, even if there is ambiguity about causes. As examples, less formal evaluation efforts can be more precisely targeted once school effectiveness with different kinds of children is known and campaigns can be initiated to discover, disseminate, and emulate good practices of high-performing schools.

Personnel assignment and selection

Accountability measures may help to improve both staff utilization and selection of new personnel. Personnel utilization could be improved by using information on teacher effectiveness in different spheres and with different types of students for guidance in staff assignment. Selection and recruitment could be aided by using information from the models as a guide to performance-related characteristics of applicants and as a basis for revising selection procedures and criteria.

Personnel incentives and compensation

An accountability measurement system can be used to establish a connection between personnel compensation and performance. One use would be in providing evidence to support inclusion of more relevant variables in pay scales than the universally used and widely criticized training and experience factors. Another possibility would be to use accountability measures as inputs in operating incentive pay or promotion systems. The latter, of course, is a controversial proposal, long resisted by professional organizations. Nevertheless, putting aside other arguments pro and con, the availability of objective measures of individual contributions would eliminate a major objection to economic incentives and help to make the idea more acceptable to all concerned.

Improved resource allocation

An accountability measurement system could also contribute to other aspects of resource allocation in school systems. Analytical results from the models could be of value, for example, in setting policies on class size, supporting services, and similar resource variables. More directly, school accountability measures could provide guidance to district administrators in allocating resources differentially among schools according to educational need. Similarly, state-level results could be used in determining appropriate allocations of state aid funds to districts.

Program evaluation and research

Models developed for accountability could prove to be valuable tools for program evaluation and research. They could be readily adapted for comparing alternative ongoing programs simply by including "program" as one of the classroom variables. Also, "norms" provided by the models for specific types of pupils could by used as reference standards in evaluating experimental programs. This would be preferable, in some cases, to using experimental control groups. Viewed as research tools, the models could help to shed light on one of the most basic, policy-related problems in education, the relationship between school inputs and educational output. The process of developing the models could itself be very instructive. The results could add substantially to our knowledge of how teachers and schools make a difference to their pupils.

In sum, there are many potential uses of the proposed measures and models, some going well beyond what is generally understood by "accountability." If the development of a system is undertaken and carried through to completion, the byproducts alone may well prove to be worth the effort.

NOTES

[1] *See, Education Vouchers: A Preliminary Report on Financing Education by Payments to Parents,* Center for the Study of Public Policy (Cambridge, Mass.: March 1970).

[2] James S. Coleman et al., *Equality of Educational Opportunity* (Washington, D.C.: Office of Education, 1966).

[3] George W. Mayeske et al., "A Study of Our Nation's Schools" (a working paper), Office of Education, 1970.

[4] E.G., Eric A. Hanushek, "The Education of Negroes and Whites," Ph.D. dissertation, M.I.T., 1968; and Herbert J. Kiesling, "The Relationship of School Inputs to Public School Performance in New York State" (The Rand Corporation, P-4211, October 1969).

[5] The statistical method described here is essentially the same as that used by Eric A. Hanushek in a study, *The Value of Teachers in Teaching,* published in 1970 by the Rand Corporation.

[6] Hanushek, *The Value of Teachers in Teaching.*

[7] The existence of this type of ambiguity in analyses of the Coleman survey data is one of the principal findings reported in Mayeske, *Study of Our Nation's Schools.*

[8] *See* Henry M. Levin, "A New Model of School Effectiveness," in *Do Teachers Make a Difference?* (Washington, D.C.: Office of Education, 1970), pp. 56-57.

[9] Ibid, pp. 61 ff.

Accountability from a Humanist Point of View

C. A. Bowers

There is increasing reference in the literature and public speeches to the importance of accountability in education. President Nixon, in his Education Message (March 3, 1970), stated that teachers and administrators should be held accountable for their performance. The Superintendent of Public Instruction in Oregon, Dale Parnell, has a commission

From C. A. Bowers, "Accountability from a Humanist Point of View," *Educational Forum* 35 (May 1971): 476–86. Reprinted by permission of the author and Kappa Delta Pi, an Honor Society in Education, owners of the copyright.

working on the task of developing a master plan for the public schools that incorporates the principles of teacher accountability and management by objectives. A writer, commenting on the Texarkana experiment, suggested that perhaps the most far-reaching implication of performance accountability is its potential use in regular classrooms. "In the future," he wrote, "teachers might be required to show measurable evidence that their students are learning at a prescribed level in a prescribed amount of time."[1] At one level of analysis I find myself in general agreement with the concerns which underlie this emphasis on greater accountability in education. I can even see where accountability and management by objectives might have value in upgrading the teaching of such basic skills as reading and arithmetic. But at the risk of seeming to oppose what is becoming another folk value, I would like to argue that when people extend the idea of accountability to all areas of learning in the schools, as is done in the three examples I cited earlier, they are obscuring fundamental questions that are vital to the performance of the competent teacher and to what I conceive to be the purpose of education.

If one examines the literature on accountability in education, he will find that the term is generally used in a highly abstract manner that suggests a hidden political purpose. When the advocates attempt to be specific about what they mean by accountability they invariably identify the quantitative aspects of education: rate of learning, finding the ratio between "inputs" and "outputs," and the unit cost. Later, I shall say more about reducing educational issues to quantitative terms. For now, I would like to analyze the consequences that would result for the student and teacher, if the idea of accountability were actually to be applied in concrete situations.

That the idea of accountability is used in a highly abstract manner can be seen in the fact that the "public" is always identified as the entity to whom the educator is to be held accountable. For example, Leon Lessinger, a former Associate Commissioner in the U.S. Office of Education and a leading advocate of accountability in education, asserts that the "public expects greater relevance in what we teach."[2] Who is this public? Does it have a common point of view, value system, and set of expectations so that everybody represented by the term "public" would agree on what is meant by "relevant education"? Lessinger, like other advocates of accountability, makes the mistake of treating the public as a unitary entity that shares a common set of values and expectations. This is surprising because most knowledgeable teachers, school administrators, and school board members know that their communities are composed of interest groups that have different and often opposing expectations. They also know that these interest groups wield differing amounts of power. When one takes the idea of accountability out of its rhetorical context— where it is often used as a political slogan—and attempts to implement it in a pluralistic community, it becomes obvious that it is not as clear and as workable a concept as its advocates claim.

The principle of accountability, when it is applied in a community composed of diverse interest groups, has the effect of politicizing the educational process. The decisions and performance of the teacher may become a social issue that arouses intense political activity—much of which is directed at the board members and school officials. Even when the issue is not likely to arouse the controversy that results from sex education, or a discussion of whether pacifism is not more consistent with American ideals than militarism, there is still the question of which interest groups are being served by the teacher's actions. By claiming that the teacher must be held accountable to the public the teacher is being placed in the impossible situation where his method of discipline, assigning homework, recommending outside reading, etc. may be approved by some individuals and groups in the community but dissaproved by others.

If we were to follow the principle of accountability to its logical conclusion, the person who believes in prayer in the classroom would have as much right to expect the teacher to conform to his wishes as the person who believes that the teacher should maintain the separation of church and state by omitting religious instruction. Similarly, the trade unionists in the community could legitimately ask that American economic and social history be presented in a light that serves their cause, just as the business group could demand that this same history be interpreted in a way favorable to business interests. The teacher would also be as accountable to minority groups—both economic and racial—as he is to values of the white, Protestant majority. I suspect, however, that the advocates of accountability would not want to have the principle interpreted so literally that every interest group in the community would feel they had a right to control the schools for their own ends.

In addition to serving as an invitation to all individuals and social groups to assess the adequacy of the school's program in terms of their own needs, the current discussion of the virtues of accountability implies that everybody has the right to pass judgment on the teacher's performance regardless of their own competence. For example, the parent who is a school dropout and an anti-intellectual would have the right to pass judgment on the teacher who holds a master's degree in his teaching subject. The idea of accountability is part of the populist ethos to which politicans and educators appeal when they want to win over more supporters. T. S. Eliot identified the limitation of this position when he wrote in *Notes Toward the Definition of Culture,* "A democracy in which everybody has an equal responsibility in everything would be oppressive for the conscientious and licentious for the rest." In view of this problem, it would be useful if the advocates of accountability would clarify whether they really think everybody, regardless of their qualifications and responsibility for the outcome, should be allowed to pass judgment on the teacher's competence.

The academic freedom of the teacher is a related issue that has been totally ignored by the advocates of accountability. Few of us would regard the teacher as competent if he used the classroom for the purpose of indoctrinating students with his own ideas or with the ideas of a powerful special interest group in the community. It can be argued that one of the characteristics of a competent teacher is that he attempts to foster independent and responsible thinking among students by encouraging them to consider conflicting evidence, ideas, and values. This process is essential to developing the student's self-confidence in the power of his own intellect, and to developing his ability to assess the evidence and to formulate his own conclusions. For example, in a social studies class where the settlement of the West is being discussed, unless the viewpoint of the Indian is presented along with the white person's explanation of events, the student would get a distorted interpretation of this period in American history. A presentation of the Indian's side of the story would undoubtedly include the long list of broken treaties, the Trail of Tears, and the battle of Wounded Knee where Indians were senselessly massacred. According to the principle of accountability, a parent could intervene in the classroom if he felt that the teacher in presenting the Indian's interpretation of these events was being unpatriotic in teaching about the settlement of the West. Such intervention would jeopardize the teacher's academic freedom, just as it would be threatened by the parent who thinks that the teacher should be accountable to his point of view by not teaching the theory of evolution. In both examples the freedom that must exist in the classroom if we are to avoid having the truth determined on the basis of which social group can exert the greatest pressure on the school board is being sacrificed for a political slogan.

No matter how the issue is argued, the idea of holding teachers directly accountable to individuals in the community is incompatible with academic freedom. It is ironic that those individuals who are advocating greater teaching accountability, presumably out of a genuine concern for improving public education, have not realized that they are threatening the very thing that is necessary for the teacher to function properly and to keep the classroom free of partisan politics.

There are some other pertinent questions about how the idea of accountability will be interpreted and applied to education. Will the teacher be held accountable for teaching students, in addition to the basic tools of communication, to raise their own questions, to make their own synthesis of ideas, to trust their own insights, and to understand their culture so they will no longer be influenced by its unexamined premises? These intellectual qualities are the ones usually associated with the mature and responsible citizen. Yet, I suspect that teachers will not be held accountable for fostering these traits. This approach to education would involve an intellectual treatment of the subject matter, as well as academic freedom for the teacher. That the advocates of accountability have been silent on this aspect of education suggests that either they have overlooked its importance—which indicates that they do not really understand the mental traits of a mature and responsible person—or they have been unable to reconcile the intellectual process which academic freedom is designed to protect with their populist interpretation of accountability.

I suspect that another reason the advocates of accountability have not talked about education as an intellectual experience is that they have committed themselves to a quantitative system of measurement. There is some usefulness in knowing the rate at which a person can perform a skill.

But I am not sure that we can measure objectively and quantitatively what a student learns in the social sciences and humanities unless they are rendered lifeless by being reduced to names, dates, and places. The true-false and the fill-in examinations—which provide the quantitative score—necessitate transforming the complexities of the phenomena being studied into an overly simplified view of reality where it can more easily be labeled as true or false. Educational measurement encourages teachers to offer a simplistic view of life, conditions students to look for the right or wrong answer without doing the hard work of thinking and wrestling with ambiguities, and allows the educator to maintain the illusion that he is conducting his enterprise on a scientific basis. Perhaps this is the only approach to education that our present system of accountability in education will tolerate. Here I am referring to control of education by local boards that must be responsive to diverse and often conflicting interest groups.

In reading the literature on accountability, especially such documents as the recent report of the Society of Educational Engineers, a group in Oregon composed mainly of superintendents, one has the feeling that history indeed repeats itself. The values of efficiency, scientific measurement, and accountability, which seem so new and full of promise to some of these educational reformers, have been tried before, and, it must be added, without the great success that was hoped for. In the early nineteen hundreds attempts were being made to measure and increase the efficiency within the schools. In his book, *Education and the Cult of Efficiency,* Raymond Callahan reports that by 1915 there were special "efficiency bureaus" set up in major cities where "educational efficiency experts" worked full time developing rating procedures to measure the teachers' performance, and to apply the principles of scientific management to public education. Then, as now, the ideas came from the areas of business and industrial engineering. Perhaps if we were better aware of the history of American education we would be able to place the following statement by Leon Lessinger, which he made to the Society of Educational Engineers, in its proper context. Lessinger told his audience that

Clearly, a new educational movement is under way. We seem to be entering the age of accountability in education. This is a most radical departure from present-day practice. It attempts to put us in a position to tell the public and ourselves what we accomplished by the expenditure of a given amount of the funds. It permits us to judge our system of instruction by the results we produce. There is hope that it will lead to cost-benefit data and insight.[3]

The principles and techniques that are being heralded as new are the same ones that dominated public education between 1900 and the Depression, although the labels have been updated. Callahan summed up the consequences of applying business-industrial procedures and values to that period of education by noting:

that educational questions were subordinated to business considerations, that administrators were produced who were not, in any true sense, educators; that a scientific label was put on some very unscientific and dubious methods and practices; and that an anti-intellectual climate already prevalent, was strengthened.[4]

There is a certain tragic irony in the fact that while many educators are attempting to transform education into a technology that will make the control of students more efficient, the students themselves are turning against the technological view of reality because of its dehumanizing effects. Theodore Roszak, the author of *The Making of a Counter Culture: Reflections on the Technocratic Society and Its Youthful Opposition,* found that many of the youth are seriously addressing themselves to the question of "how shall we live?"[5] They are asking questions about what constitutes personally and socially meaningful work, whether excessive reliance on technology and the world view it promotes are partly the source of our alienation, whether our social priorities are morally sound, and what constitutes an adequate sense of personal and social responsibility. If the student looks to the educator for help in clarifying the assumptions and values that underlie these pressing issues, he will find that the "efficiency" oriented educator can only respond by talking about systems analysis, management by objectives, accountability, performance contracting, and the technology of modifying behavior. It should not be a great surprise to anybody when the students reject the educators for attempting to turn them into technologists, rather than assisting them in clarifying the assumptions they wish to live by. I am afraid, however, that as the students increasingly rebel against the spiritual emptiness of their technologically oriented educators, the efficiency hungry educators will respond by calling for more and better techniques for controlling behavior rather than examining their own assumptions and goals.

I should like to suggest that we begin to think of accountability in terms of what the student needs in order to realize his fullest potential as a person, rather than what it is the public wants—which is often defined in self-serving economic and social terms. The problem can be stated in a way that makes clearer the danger of looking to the public for the answers to the purpose of education. Determining the purpose of education is the same as determining the potential and purpose of man. It is an important philosophic question, and thus it cannot be answered by finding out what the consensus is in the community or state nor can the answer come from individuals and interest groups who attempt to settle educational questions by using economic, social, or religious criteria without considering their implications for education.

One way to answer the question is to determine those characteristics that are associated with maturity, and I think we know enough to identify some of these characteristics. We would all agree, I believe, that the mature person is one who is aware of his own freedom and has a well developed sense of values that enables him to use it in a personally and socially responsible manner. Moreover, he has a positive self-concept that is derived from a feeling of self-mastery of his own rational and physical abilities, rather than from the crowd that gives approval in exchange for blind conformity. He would certainly be proficient in using the symbolic and communication skills of his culture, and he would be knowledgeable about his culture and its underlying assumptions. While he would not represent the final answer to the question of man's potential, his lifestyle and creativeness might cause those interested in the question to see new potentials that were not seen before.

The educator has to make a decision about whether he is going to use his talents and energies to help each student develop in the direction of his own maturity or whether he sees himself as being accountable to interest groups who may want the classroom to be used for such varied ends as maintaining the community's status system, providing a compliant work force, or indoctrinating students with the beliefs and values held by the dominant interest groups in the community. Those educators who think they can serve both the needs of the students—and I am not talking only about the needs the students themselves can identify—and the interests of local groups are engaged in a game of self-deception. For in order to limit the student's understanding and abilities to what can be tolerated by interest groups it is often necessary to manipulate the student's self-identity so that he feels confident about himself only when his behavior conforms to the norms of the interest groups. The teacher would also have to condition him into believing that the range of his freedom is circumscribed by the expectations of others. This is really what socialization is all about, but when it is carried on in the unexamined manner demanded by many interest groups, it becomes debilitating for the person undergoing the process.

If, on the other hand, the teacher feels himself accountable to the long-range needs of the students, he will attempt to create an atmosphere of trust in the classroom where genuine inquiry can take place. In this atmosphere the student does not have to earn a positive self-image by meeting somebody else's terms. He can begin to develop a positive self regard as he learns to trust his own intellectual and emotional responses as he encounters different aspects of his culture. The teacher must also have the ability to teach him the information gathering skills without turning off his interest in learning by using fear and guilt as a means of controlling his behavior. Equally important to the student's future development is the teacher's knowledge of the culture and his awareness that he cannot know what, among all the ideas, assumptions, and values he teaches, will prove dysfunctional at some future point in time. When the teacher is sensitive to the risks the student faces in learning from others, he will discourage the students from uncritically accepting as real what are actually the notions, imaginings, and longings of a particular people at a particular point in history. For when the student unquestionably accepts the truths of other people he may be trapped into reliving the problems connected with their form of cultural blindness.

We are reminded almost daily that some of our most basic cultural assumptions about the environment, meaningful work, the nature of scientific technology, our view of progress, and our Protestant attitude toward the nature of time, need to be rethought as we face a deepening crisis with our environment, and in our relations with each other in urban centers. These inescapable facts should make educators more conscious of being accountable to students for insuring that their education does not become simply a matter of training for a job that may shortly be eliminated by advances in technology. The students need to learn about their culture, particularly about those assumptions and values that are at the root of current social and ecological problems. They also need to learn how to deal with social issues at an intellectual rather than an emotional and fearful level—as many adults now do. If the current advocates of accountability were genuinely concerned with this form of education, they would be talking about the importance of academic freedom, the problems of recruiting more intellectually mature and socially representative people into the field of teaching, the kind of education that teachers need in order to be culturally literate, and the kind of education that adminis-trators need in order to understand the educational process and their role in protecting it from fearful and anti-intellectual elements in the community. Instead, we hear them talking about input-output indicators, auditing the teacher's performance, applying systems analysis and design to education, and the need for establishing a Educational Engineering Institute in Oregon so that all the schools may be controlled more efficiently.

The language of the educational engineer has a great power for mesmerizing people, but it does not tell us anything about the vital issues in education. Before we can talk about accountability we must first clarify the issues that relate to the purpose of education. Otherwise, the technological aspects of education will become ends in themselves.

NOTES

[1] Dale Bratten, Corline Gillin and Robert E. Rousch, "Performance Contracting: How It Works in Texarkana," *School Management,* August 1970, p. 10.

[2] Leon Lessinger "Evaluation and Accountability in Educational Management," *Academy of Educational Engineers* (published by the Society of Educational Engineers, 1970), pp. 7–8.

[3] Ibid.

[4] Raymond Callahan, *Education and the Cult Efficiency* (Chicago: The University of Chicago Press, 1962), p. 246.

[5] Theodore Roszak, *The Making of a Counter Culture* (New York: Anchor Books, 1969), p. 233.

Accountability:
Watchword for the 70s

John E. Morris

To think about education in terms of decades seems to be the "in" thing. Great emphases have been placed on *Schools for the Sixties* and *Schools for the Seventies* and in each decade much ado is made about educational problems and reforms. Most of the sixties were devoted to curriculum reforms resulting in a proliferation of NEWS—new math, new social studies, new English, new science—which were to contribute to the solution of many problems relating to student achievement. If the sentiment of certain educators, government, business, and lay leaders is an indication of what this decade holds, it is certainly the dawning of the age of accountability wrapped in the self-governance package of the educational profession and bound by performance contracts.

As yet, there seems to be no definition which can be considered an accurate index into the scope and meaning of accountability. Yet, the focus is certainly upon the achievement or lack of achievement of students who enter our public schools in relation to constantly increasing school budgets. The crux of the issue, in greatly simplified form, seems to be that if teachers cannot teach pupils to read; solve mathematical problems; speak and write correctly; memorize principles, laws, and formulas in science; and regurgitate names of people, places, things, and dates found in social studies texts; then some business concern will guarantee to do so at a predetermined level of performance and cost.

Accountability is not new to teachers and schools (although the use of the term in connection with teacher performance did not appear in the *Education Index* until June, 1970), for we have always been accountable to some one or some constituted authority. One of the most revered teachers, Socrates, was accountable unto his death for his teaching. The sophists were accountable to their students, for herein lay their means of livelihood. The first universities were, to a great extent, accountable to the student body and the local community. Today, the classroom teacher is legally accountable to the local school board and morally accountable to self, profession, community, and nation.

The form of accountability has varied from time-to-time, but the end product—performance—has remained relatively constant. Since the family was the first educational institution, parents were accountable for the instruction of their children in the form of skills necessary for survival. With the development of clans, tribes, and states, the functions of education became more formalized and the fortunes of the clans, tribes,

From John E. Morris, "Accountability: Watchword for the 70s," *The Clearing House* 45 (February 1971): 323–28. Reprinted by permission of *The Clearing House* and the author.

and states were more or less determined by the performance of the educational system. In western education accountability has often taken the form of examinations administered at prescribed levels of the educational ladder. It was not uncommon for teachers to be retained, dismissed, or promoted on the basis of pupil performance on these examinations. A school whose students did not consistently score high on examinations might cease to attract sufficient students to make possible its continued existence. Merit pay, compensation of students for scholastic achievement as in the Martin Luther King Junior High School in Portland, Oregon,[1] and other "third factors" are means proposed or applied in an effort to insure accountability. The current emphasis for accountability has grown out of the movement for national assessment of education and President Nixon's "Message on Higher Education" which stressed the *wrongs* in education and the necessity for accountability.

In any country at any given time there exist critics, both in and outside the profession, who complain about declining standards, failure of students to learn basic fundamentals, teacher incompetencies, parental unconcern, over permissiveness of administrators, decline of student morals, excessive expenditure of public funds, and a host of other real or imagined shortcomings. This was particularly characteristic of the immediate post-sputnik period when Russian education was considered by some, especially Rickover, to be superior to ours. It would indeed be interesting to know what public reaction would have been had the United States launched the first satellite. One can only assume that the opposite reaction would have been the rule. Now that our astronauts have walked on the moon on more than one occasion, it seems as though our schools are producing students who are capable of not only maintaining but advancing the technological and scientific progress so necessary to our well-being. If one reads "The Schools Behind Masters of the Moon,"[2] Polley's "What's Right with American Education,"[3] and Rickover's "A Comparison: European Vs. American Secondary Schools,"[4] one is confronted with the contradictions which are so characteristic of American society. It may be that the current emphasis on accountability is another such contradiction.

REASONS FOR ACCOUNTABILITY MOVEMENT

There are several interesting generalizations which can be made about the reasons for the current emphasis on accountability. First, criticism and reform movements seem to wax and wane in relation to the current social milieu. The "roaring twenties" resulted in rapid changes in economic, societal, and personal values. Then came the depression and the frantic search for explanations as to the causes for such upheavals. The criticisms of this era are reflected by Professor Thomas H. Briggs when he stated that education should be a

" . . . long-term investment by the state to make itself a better place in which to live and in which to make a living, to perpetuate itself, and promote its own interests . . . . authorities have made no serious efforts to formulate for secondary schools a curriculum which promises maximum good to the supporting state . . . . there has been no respectable achievement, even in the subjects offered in secondary school curricula . . . . no effort has been made sufficient to establish in students appreciation of the values of the subjects in the curricula such as to insure continued study either in higher schools or independently after compulsory classes . . . . a state's attorney might conceivable present against an educational authority an indictment for malfeasance in office and misappropriation of public funds.[5]

The thirties witnessed rapid expansion of the progressive education movement aimed at eliminating many of these deficiencies.

Second, criticism and reform movements follow a shocking event in which we tend to come out second best. This is illustrated in the writings of Rickover, Bestor, and Conant in the post-sputnik era.

Third, since the schools are considered to be second only to the family in terms of safeguarding and extending traditional values, they are especially susceptible to attacks during times when these values are disappearing and new values to fill the vacuum have not been born. Such periods are characterized by mounting uncertainties, confusion, contradictions, and search, especially by youth, for identity. Jan Smithers, one of 775 youth included in a nationwide opinion poll, seems to express these conditions when she said: "Sometimes when I'm sitting in my room I just feel like screaming and pounding my pillow. I'm so confused about this whole world and everything that's happening."[6]

Fourth, schools are supposed to prepare leaders who are able to solve many of the pressing social, political, and economic problems which confront a nation. Today the magnitude and hopelessness of the military entanglements in Indochina and the Middle East, poverty, race relations, the drug problem, and violence on our campuses and in our streets is, to a very great extent, directed toward the educational institutions and accountability is the battle cry.

Fifth, the general state of the economy, coupled with the social factors already mentioned, is a major cause of the current emphasis on accountability. There is widespread and increasing militance on the part of voters toward inflation and tax increases. A record defeat rate of school bond issues and millage increases does not necessarily mean that voters are antieducation. Instead, there is resistance to all tax increases and it so happens that those involving school finance are about the only increases voters directly control. This resentment has certainly increased as a result of action taken by various militant groups, violence on the campuses of junior highs, high schools and colleges, and by creation of unitary school districts in the South and massive busing of students in some areas outside the South.

Sixth, there is widespread agreement that something is basically wrong with public education. Too many students cannot read, are deficient in basic communication skills, quit before completing the twelfth grade, and seem to be unpatriotic.

Seventh, today more parents are better educated because they have attended high school and college. They judge the progress of their children on the basis of their experiences and the widely publicized advancements in educational technology. They see the realities of the educational dilemma and are becoming more critical of and less willing to believe educational authorities. They are demanding that administrators and teachers be more accountable for the progress of students.

WHAT WILL ACCOUNTABILITY REQUIRE?

It is too early to envision all that will be required in terms of knowledge, skills, attitudes, personnel, money, and technology to put public education on an accountability basis as envisioned, for example, by Lessinger.[7] However, a number of requirements are already evident.

First, Davies states that accountability will require ". . . changing people . . . and changing the institutions that control education."[8] Lessinger believes that ". . . educational accountability can be implemented successfully only if educational objectives are clearly stated before the instruction starts."[9] Since accountability implies predetermined levels of performance by students, an educational performance contract[10] would have to be initiated prior to the beginning of a prescribed program of instruction.

Second, accountability will most certainly require application of principles involved in differentiated staffing similar to those advocated by Olivero[11] and Barbee.[12] Perhaps a more fundamental requirement, and one which may be more difficult to secure, is self-determination of the teaching profession. Bain states that self-goverance will have to become a reality before accountability is possible.[13]

Third, there must be more involvement of the community and teachers in determining policies, programs, performance levels, and incentive criteria.

Fourth, teacher education programs which are highly individualized, predicated on the basis of performance criteria, and providing more contact with the "real world" of teaching throughout the entire program instead of the limited experiences of present programs, will have to be inaugurated.

Fifth, there must be far more extensive and sophisticated use of educational technology than teacher education programs and public schools to have been willing and/or able to use.

Sixth, a financial base to replace our present outdated and inequitable system of financing public education will have to be initiated.

Seventh, education must become, not only in theory but in fact, child centered. We will be forced to write programs for each child based on extensive results of highly sophisticated diagnostic instruments.

Eighth, the efficiency and effectiveness of the organization and administration of schools must be improved. The self-contained classrooms and principals who spend much of their time collecting lunch money and filling vending machines will have to go.

Ninth, instruments which are more reliable, individualized, and valid for measuring ability and performance in the cognitive and affective domains must be developed. Lessinger conceives of "... a process designed to ensure that any individual can determine for himself if the schools are producing the results promised. The most public aspect of accountability would be independent accomplishment audits that report educational results in factual, understandable, and meaningful terms."[14]

Tenth, new teacher-student roles and responsibilities will have to be defined and implemented. It is not certain what these would be, but the present ones of dispenser and container would either disappear or become more widespread.

SOME VITAL QUESTIONS

Accountability has already raised vital questions which must be considered before and *if* this concept advances beyond the experimental stages. The most serious questions center around accountability and the affective domain. We have long been aware of the vital role of such factors as attitudes, values, creativity, and self-concept, but have never come to grips with them. We, as teachers and parents, have long observed that it is not always the "most intelligent" student who is "successful." *Who* is to determine what values, attitudes, creative abilities, etc., are to be taught? *Who* will write the performance contract? *Who* will perform the "independent accomplishments audits?" *Who* will determine what influences education is to have on the shaping of American democracy and the quality of life of the American people and *how* will these influences be measured? In short, how can we "... gauge behavior modifications that schooling is supposed to effect?"[15] Similar, although not as controversial, questions are in order for the knowledge and skills for which we are to be accountable.

Accountability also raises the issue of further dehumanization of education. There is already much discontent with the dehumanizing effects of teaching machines; computer assisted instruction; the "do not fold, staple, or multilate" system of identification, scheduling, and reporting; the lack of a humanizing curriculum; and the bureaucratic, impersonal school organization.

Would accountability virtually force teachers to "teach the test?" There is evidence that this has already happened in the Texarkana project.[16] The same practice has occurred in the United States and other countries when educational performance, teacher retention, and school finances were, to a greater or lesser degree, determined by examination scores.

Further questions are asked by Davies:

> How do we move from a mass approach to teaching and learning to a highly individualized approach?
> How do we go about the "simple" task of treating each child as an individual human being?
> How do we substitute a vigorous, enjoyable classroom atmosphere for one that has too often been marked by competition, pain, fear, and failure?
> ... how do we build into ourselves the capacity for continuing self-renewal, for meeting increasing demands for adapting to new roles?[17]

FUTURE PROSPECTS

It would be presumptuous to try to assess the possible impact of accountability on public education at this time. There are few certainties in those areas involving human beings. But one thing is certain—Pandora's Box has been opened and education will never be the same.

Approximately 200 school districts in various parts of the nation are trying accountability in some form. In Gary, Indiana, an elementary school has been completely turned over to Behavioral Research Laboratories for a three-year period. Dr. Alfonso Holliday II, president of the Gary school board, is quoted as saying: "With education costs rising 15 to 20 percent a year, we didn't feel we could keep asking for more money when our children were learning below their grade levels. . . . We are at rock bottom and must try new approaches. . . . We must be willing to be pioneers, and no longer say our children lack ability to learn."[18] John Gardner is quoted as saying that accountability offers ". . . a well-tested way out of the dizzying atmosphere of talk and emotion . . ."[19] and Martin Filogamo of the Texarkana project believes that: "If it succeeds, it could well lead the way to the direct involvement of private industry in the education of the nation's school children."[20] The 70s promise to be interesting and challenging years in education, and *accountability* may be the most interesting, challenging, disruptive, and, in the end, productive issue of all.

NOTES

[1] *Phi Delta Kappan*, June 1970, p. 510.

[2] "The Schools Behind Masters of the Moon," *Phi Delta Kappan,* September 1969, pp. 2–7.

[3] Ira Polley, "What's Right with American Education," *Phi Delta Kappan,* September 1969, pp. 13–15.

[4] H. G. Rickover, "A Comparison: European Vs. American Secondary Schools," *Phi Delta Kappan,* November 1958, pp. 60–64.

[5] Ellwood P. Cubberley, *Readings in Public Education in the United States* (Boston: Riverside Press, 1934), p. 468.

[6] "The Teenager," *Newsweek,* 21 March 1966, p. 66.

[7] Leon Lessinger, "Accountability in Public Education," *Today's Education,* May 1970, pp. 52–53.

[8] Don Davies, "The Relevance of Accountability," *Journal of Teacher Education,* Spring 1970, p. 128.

[9] Lessinger, *Accountability,* p. 52.

[10] Ibid.

[11] James L. Olivero, "The Meaning and Application of Differentiated Staffing in Teaching," *Phi Delta Kappan,* September 1970, pp. 36–40.

[12] Don Barbee, "Differentiated Staffing: Expectations and Pitfalls," *TEPS Write-in Paper No. 1 on Flexible Staffing Patterns* (Washington, D.C.: National Commission on Teacher Education and Professional Standards, March 1969).

[13] Helen Bain, "Self-Governance Must Come First, Then Accountability," *Phi Delta Kappan,* April 1970, p. 413.

[14] Lessinger, *Accountability,* p. 52.

[15] C. Grieder, "Educators Should Welcome Pressure for Accountability," *Nations Schools,* May 1970, p. 14.

[16] Stan Elam, "The Chameleon's Dish," *Phi Delta Kappan,* September 1970, pp. 71–72.

[17] Davies, *Relevance of Accountability,* p. 129.

[18] "Where Private Firm Runs Public School," *U. S. News and World Report,* 12 October 1970, p. 41.

[19] Lessinger, *Accountability,* p. 52.

[20] Martin J. Filogamo, "New Angle on Accountability," *Today's Education,* May 1970, p. 53.

Performance Contracting: Some Questions and Answers

Jeffery Schiller

The concept behind performance contracting is deceptively simple: You pay for what you get and only what you get. You aren't concerned with the cost to the supplier to produce what you're buying; you don't care how he produces it, as long as the product meets your quality specifications.

From Jeffry Schiller, "Performance Contracting: Some Questions and Answers," *American Education* 7 (May 1971): 3–5. Reprinted by permission of the author and the U.S. Office of Education.

The idea has tremendous inherent appeal to logic. But when the concept is applied to education, it becomes not so simple. Its potential for helping poor children, however, convinced the Office of Economic Opportunity (OEO) to mount an experiment to test its capabilities.

Performance contracting in education first gained national attention when preliminary reports from a project in Texarkana indicated that a private firm was improving the reading and math skills of poor, underachieving students and that the students were staying in school. But the Texarkana experience was not set up as an experiment; it did not include the evaluation design or administrative controls necessary to assess the capabilities of performance contracting in any reliable fashion. Furthermore, the Texarkana experience, even had it included a rigorous evaluation design, would not have indicated whether any results achieved there could be replicated elsewhere.

Thus, the OEO mounted a nationwide test of performance contracting in education in the fall of 1970. The OEO has awarded grants to 18 school districts from Maine to California, and the districts have, in turn, contracted with six private firms to teach their underachieving students reading and math. The contractors' pay is determined solely by their success in improving the students' skills in these two areas. The contractors are not even reimbursed for expenses until the students' skill levels improve by an average of one grade level in both subjects. The students' skill levels will have to improve by about 1.6 grade levels (nearly four times the improvement they had been making during a school year) before the contractors will begin to make a profit.

The American Federation of Teachers has strongly opposed both the experiment and the concept itself. The National Education Association initially agreed with the AFT, but it recently modified its stance. It now argues only that no performance contract should be approved unless it includes conditions to protect the teachers' involvement in the education process and their bargaining rights.

There is no question that teachers and school administrators throughout the country are concerned about performance contracting, as is the OEO. To clarify its position and the intent of the experiment, OEO officials have discussed performance contracting with hundreds of educators. Here are some of the questions most frequently asked by the educators, with answers based on the most current information gathered by OEO.

Q. You said your interest in performance contracting was sparked by preliminary reports from Texarkana. Yet, weren't the achievement test results there seriously contaminated?

A. At this point, no one can say with any certainty just what effects the Texarkana project did have on achievement. A review alleges that the contractor included the same questions in the classroom material that later appeared on the tests. The contractor has threatened to file a suit against the school district claiming that he did not teach to the tests. So we really don't know what happened there in terms of skill improvement. We do know, however, that only 6.5 percent of those in the project dropped out of school during the year, while 17.8 percent of a comparison group dropped out during the same period.

We feel that the uncertainty surrounding the Texarkana experience, if anything, underscores the need for a carefully designed national test of performance contracting. It's apparent that performance contracting may become an educational fad, and we feel strongly that school districts should have an indication of the concept's capabilities—and its potential pitfalls—before they leap onto the performance contracting bandwagon.

Q. What about teaching to the test? Since contractors' pay and, in some instances, even teachers' pay is dependent upon their students' performance on tests, how can the temptation to teach to the tests be overcome?

A. We don't know that it can be. That's one of the major reasons for this experiment. We do have an evaluation design that we hope will preclude any possibility of teaching to the tests.

For example, we're not basing pay on the standardized tests alone. We're also using criterion-referenced tests designed to determine how well the student has mastered the particular subject matter to which he has been exposed. The contractors won't begin to make a profit until the students show significant improvement on both the standardized and the criterion-referenced tests.

Second, students are selected on a random basis for one of three standardized tests, and those three were chosen from among eight different tests. Because neither school personnel nor the contractors' staffs are involved in administering or scoring the standardized tests, it would be difficult for them to learn which of the eight tests are being used.

Third, a random sampling of curriculum items from all companies will be run through a computer match with all of the questions on the tests to ensure that the curriculum items and test questions do coincide.

There are a number of other safeguards, but these, I think will give you an idea of the lengths to which we have gone to prevent teaching to the tests. But as I said earlier, we can't say now whether they will work. Equally important, we don't know whether they can or will be replicated by an individual school district entering into a performance contract on its own or whether it would be possible for districts to develop the relatively sohpisticated criterion-referenced test.

Q. I'm concerned, too, about the fairness of using tests standardized to the performance of white, middle-class children to judge the performance of minority children from poor socioeconomic backgrounds. How do you get around this problem?

A. We certainly agree that it's a problem, but I would like to point out that these children are going to be competing against essentially white, middle-class norms all their lives.

Q. Okay, but is it fair to base a teacher's pay, as some of your contractors are, on the performance of her students? After all, the children come from a variety of backgrounds, and some are just more likely to be able to succeed than others.

A. We've tried to address those issues in the experiment, too. Let me first clarify one thing. In no instance are contractors or teachers rewarded for bringing all students to one certain level—up to grade level, for example. Rather the rewards are based on improvement. The contractor will earn just as much by bringing a ninth-grader from a second-grade to a fourth grade reading level as he would from bringing another from seventh to ninth.

We have done our best, though, to be sure that there isn't great disparity in ability among the students in the experiment. After retarded and emotionally disturbed children were excluded, the lowest-achieving students in each site were chosen from among all students performing below grade level. Most are at least two grade levels below norm, so one teacher isn't struggling to bring a seventh-grader from fifth-grade to seventh-grade achievement levels while another is being rewarded for increasing a seventh-grader's level from eighth to tenth grade for example. Further, virtually all the students in the experiment are from the same socioeconomic background; that is, most are poor by the official Federal definition.

Q. In some neighborhoods with high family mobility, a teacher may have a completely different class at the end of the year than she had at the beginning. It doesn't seem right to judge her performance on the same standard as you would a teacher who had no transfers in or out.

A. You're right. It wouldn't be. So we have a formula to adjust payment according to the length of time the student is in class.

Q. Aside from all this, I really question whether it's appropriate to base a teacher's pay, or a private firm's pay for that matter, on the children's performance in just the two areas of reading and math. There's so much more to education than those two skills.

A. Certainly we realize that reading and math are just part of a total education. But without reading and math skills, there aren't very many subjects a student can master, are there? It's painfully evident that these students can't gain from their years in school what you and I consider other important aspects of an education until they have mastered these basic skills.

At the same time, I would like to go into another aspect of this question. One of the things that excites us most about performance contracting is the possibility for talk between teachers, administrators, and school boards while they are drawing up the contract. As the National Education Association has pointed out, learning objectives must be developed with community and professional involvement. I think the process of sorting all this out— deciding just what it is that should be done, how it should be done, how to measure the results—quite probably will be fascinating. The potential is even greater when you consider that all those concerned with education—the teachers, the administrators, the school board, and the parents—will be discussing these problems together.

Q. Is it true that you have two sites where there is no private firm involved, where the school boards have contracted with their own teachers?

A. That's right. In Stockton, Calif., and Mesa, Ariz., the teachers will be paid bonuses in addition to their base pay at the end of the year if their students show at least eight-tenths of a grade level improvement during the program. We've made 80 percent of the maximum funds that the teachers could earn available to them now. The teachers can use these funds in any way they see fit: They may pocket the extra money, or they may use it to purchase incentive rewards for the children or additional instructional materials.

These two sites, however, really aren't a part of the performance contracting experiment, because they were started too late in the school year for any results they achieve to be comparable to the performance of the private firms. The Stockton and Mesa projects are being viewed as a completely separate and independent demonstration.

Q. What is performance contracting really going to mean for me, the teacher? If it works, am I going to find myself replaced by representatives of private firms, teaching machines, and paraprofessionals?

A. Let me emphasize first that I do not see a massive nationwide implementation of performance contracting in the immediate future. We are currently advising educators to wait until after we've seen the results of retention tests in the 1971-72 school year before initiating a performance contract. While we will have some pretty solid indications of the results by the end of the summer, the most crucial aspect of the system, the retention of any gains, won't be evident until the retention tests are analyzed.

Furthermore, before school districts individually begin to undertake performance contracts, they'll need to develop a whole new expertise in the fields of procurement, contract negotiation, and monitoring.

Then there's the turnkey phase, which is the transfer of the programs to the school systems when the contract expires. Quite honestly our office hasn't given a great deal of thought to this. School districts will have open a number of options: Should private firms be brought in only to conduct special training sessions for teachers? Should the firms be asked only to prepare new curriculum packages? In other words, just what sort of turnkey effort should take place after the initial pilot period? How should turnkey contracts be written? and what should the performance criteria be? What role will teachers' organizations play in future performance contracting projects? These are all questions that will have to be dealt with after we learn whether the concept itself works.

What will happen, I think, is that new instructional systems employing audiovisual devices and paraprofessionals supervised by a teacher will be able to free certified teachers from many of the routine, secretarial duties that now take up so much of a classroom teacher's time. Even more exciting, I think, is the possibility that teachers in inner-city schools may, for the first time, be able to work with an entire class of children who are performing at grade level in reading and math. Can you imagine what you, as a teacher, could do with these youngsters if you didn't have to spend the year on remedial efforts?

I might also add that each of the private firms in the experiment are relying heavily on certified teachers.

Q. Since the experiment is more than half finished, do you have any initial indications of whether performance contracting is, indeed, successful?

A. Obviously nothing that we sense at this time is anything more than an unsupported feeling, since we won't have any data for several more months. But it does seem that, at the elementary level especially, performance contracting is turning youngsters on to learning. There's an unmistakable excitement in the first-, second-, and third-grade classes as the children learn that school can be fun, that they can learn to read and to work their math problems. As some solid indication of this, we are finding a number of students who have been habitual truants or absentees coming regularly to school for the first time. Sometimes they come only for their performance contracting classes, but even at that, they're coming for two class periods a day.

We've also learned a great deal about the administrative complexities of performance contracting. We've had some problems, as any outsider would, mounting a major project in such a short period of time. And, as I implied earlier, the school boards have recognized that they have a great deal yet to learn about administering a performance contract.

On the whole, the OEO is optimistic about the potential of performance contracting to help poor children learn. And, we hope that if we can find a way that is successful in reaching these youngsters, we'll have the key to providing them with the skills and the credentials they need to become self-supporting members of our society. If performance contracting doesn't work, the OEO will continue to seek new alternatives to improving the education of poor children.

Perspectives on School Finance

James E. Allen, Jr.

Anyone who today accepts a request to write for a journal devoted to *Perspectives on Education* takes on a hazardous assignment. Indeed, whatever the field, trying to maintain perspective in thinking about social purposes, values and procedures is perhaps the most difficult task in these times of widespread uncertainty, unrest and confusion.

Perspective is defined as "the relative importance of facts and matters from any special point of view." At a time when we are trying to meet the needs of the disadvantaged, to eliminate segregation, to extend the range of opportunities to include wider provision for the early childhood as well as for the postsecondary years, to bring into being a concept of education that goes beyond the classroom, the "facts and matters" of education have achieved new levels of complexity and urgency which in turn are generating unprecedented pressure.

Pressure is, of course, in many ways good—a necessary ingredient of the motivating force that urges us forward. In these recent fast-moving times in education, pressures—practical, philosophical and moral—have forced us not only to take care of newly emerging needs but to act on matters that should have been faced up to long before.

The pressure of the current "facts and matters" of education is giving compelling emphasis to the further extension of the definition of perspective which prescribes the "presentation" of facts and matters "with just regard to their proportional importance."

In seeking solutions to pressing problems of education it has become increasingly clear that a just regard for proportional importance demands immediate attention to the development of major new approaches to school finance.

The form and adequacy of the financial provisions for education have always determined in large measure our success in meeting educational needs. But now when more support and greater flexibility are essential, finance is more than ever a controlling factor.

In terms of present and future needs the general pattern of school support is more often restrictive than supportive. It is primarily geared to a system of local school organization and control that no longer accurately reflects, and cannot respond to, the sweeping social and economic changes now taking place.

Most attempts thus far to modernize our system of school finance have been of a piecemeal and patchwork variety. Fortunately, the call is now growing for a major overhaul.

President Nixon's Commission on School Finance (Dr. John H. Fischer,

President of TC, is a member) is now at work on a study, and it is to be hoped that the report of this review will soon be ready and that it will reflect the character and scope of the needs of education today. Many states are also seeking to update their own financial patterns and practices.

If the needed overhaul is to achieve its objective, two major principles must obtain.

First, *provision must be made for the direct and speedy application of funds to special educational needs whenever and wherever they exist.*

Second, *the responsibility for raising and allocating funds should be placed at those levels of government most capable of achieving adequacy of funds and equity of opportunity.*

Obviously, the application of these principles will entail drastic changes. In many states, constitutional revisions will be required; outmoded and restrictive statutes will have to be discarded or amended; agencies for the governance of education, both state and local, will have to be streamlined and strengthened; new tax programs will need to be devised. It is not my intention to deal here with the specifics of needed changes but rather to discuss two suggested approaches that seem likely to shape the framework of a revamped program of school support.

The first of these is the proposal that the states should assume substantially all of the local costs of elementary and secondary education. This proposal, at first considered very radical, has been gaining support as localities, particularly the cities, have encountered increasing financial difficulties and as educational inequities have become more apparent.

The principal objection often raised to such a move is that it would constitute a threat to local control. While there is room for reasonable concern, there are many circumstances and aspects relating to local control as it now operates which would point to the possibility of breaking the tie between it and local financing, not only without detriment either to the exercise of true local control or the equality of the education being provided, but, indeed, with a strengthening of both.

The value of local control can be measured only in terms of its effectiveness in operation. In the total educational enterprise of today, there are many limits upon this effectiveness.

School districts inadequate in size (either in population or geography, or in the nature of the area encompassed, or both), variations among districts in the amount of taxable property, and the existence of outmoded tax and debt limits are so impeditive as to reduce local control to merely a control of unduly limited opportunities and restricted choices.

Pertinent also is the question of *how local* is local in terms of today. The separation which once gave to localities their special identity and peculiar needs and problems has virtually disappeared with the mobility, the close communication and the interdependence which now shape the structure of society and characterize our modes of living.

But of greatest significance in assessing the effect of breaking the tie between local control and local finance is the question of the real meaning of local control. The true interest of thoughtful citizens and concerned parents is in the quality of education that is provided for the children of their locality. It is to the character and quality of the instruction provided in the schools—the selection and deployment of the administrative and teaching staffs and the determination of the program required to meet local needs—that local control should be most significantly directed.

As the public school system now operates, however, so much of the energy and time of local boards of education and superintendents must be devoted to financing the budget, negotiating staff salaries and dealing with bond issues, that there is too little time left for concentration upon this central purpose.

This proposed plan of abolishing local taxation for schools would greatly help to free local school authorities for dealing with education itself and enable them to make decisions solely on the basis of educational merit.

It is obvious, of course, that total state financing would pose dangers of undue state control and that safeguards would have to be provided. These safeguards should deal with such essentials as the maintenance and encouragement of local initiative, the stimulation of innovation and experimentation, the provision of more accurate measures of educational need so that state financing could recognize special situations such as disproportionately large numbers of disadvantaged children, etc.

In other words, in eliminating certain barriers to educational improvement by cutting the ties between local control and local financing, the utmost care must be exercised to avoid similar barriers that could result if total state financing were to be accompanied by excessive state prescription.

What would be the further advantages of state assumption of local school costs?

A primary advantage is that it would be easier for the state, which by law and tradition is responsible for the provision of education, to ensure in all of its communities those conditions necessary for good education.

One of the greatest barriers in many states to the general establishment of such conditions is the rigidity of present school district organization.

At present many school districts are too small to offer a good comprehensive program operated efficiently and economically, while others are so huge and so removed from community influence and concern that the schools operate almost in a vacuum.

Many small districts could be eliminated and larger ones made more effective by consolidation or reorganization, but these possibilities are impeded because the financing of the schools is in large measure a function of local action.

With existing variations among districts in tax rates, property values per pupil, school debt obligations, and constitutional tax and debt limits, the redrawing of lines is made extremely difficult, if not impossible. If all funds for salaries and other current expense needs and for construction came from the state, the desirable reshaping of school districts would be greatly facilitated.

If the local community were relieved of the requirement of levying local school taxes, the strong educational arguments in favor of district reorganization would be much better received. In other words, the educational system in a state could be much more efficiently and economically organized, with resultant educational gains, if only educational and sociological considerations were involved in drawing district boundaries.

The flexibility in school district reorganization that would be made possible by shifting local financing of education to the state would substantially assist the achievement of school integration and the allocation of resources to urban centers and other areas of special need.

Another gain would be in the rapidly growing area of collective bargaining between school employees and school boards. As long as the bargaining takes place at the local level, involving hundreds of districts, the situation is bound to be uncertain and confused. In many cities it is complicated by the fact that the power to tax for school needs rests with the city government, not with the board of education. In any case, the local district is not the source of a considerable part of the money involved because state aid enters the picture.

If the state were the only source of money, the bargaining would take place at the state level. This would eliminate the possibility of maneuvering by school boards to hold salaries at a given level as well as by teachers to used a higher level of salary in one district as a kind of whipsaw to effect increases in others. There would be each year a greater likelihood of a reasonable and fair settlement of the demands of teachers.

Fixing salaries on a statewide basis would provide an additional incentive to teachers to remain in the cities or in the rural areas rather than to migrate to the wealthier suburban communities for the higher salaries paid there. Inasmuch as the suburbs have other incentives to offer, this would not be expected to be a serious deterrent to the quality of education there. It could be expected to increase the quality in rural areas and in the cities.

There are still further advantages. Take, for example, the question of providing equality of opportunity among all school districts. It is impossible to be complacent about the present wide variations in provisions which affect the quality of education offered to children within a state. Removing considerations of financing from the local level would make it possible to eliminate these wide variations and to bring about greater equity.

Possible also would be increased emphasis on regional planning for the provision of services which can be best performed at the regional level as, for example, the provision of special education. Improved practices and methods could be more rapidly and efficiently disseminated throughout the state. Better and wider use of educational technology could be achieved.

Finally, the increasing strength of the state unit should enable the states to deal more effectively with the federal government in providing for the use of federal funds. There would be less excuse for the federal government to be directly involved in the state-local relationship.

From my experience in dealing with problems of education as Commissioner of Education at both the state and federal levels, I am convinced that the advantages of state assumption of local school costs far outweigh the disadvantages and that this is the direction in which states should be moving in future financial planning.

The second approach shaping the framework of a revamped program of school support is federal revenue sharing. It is possible that this approach may soon be a reality with the attention and momentum created by President Nixon's plan now before the Congress and by the energetic demands coming from many governors and mayors of large cities. Whatever the outcome may be with respect to current proposals for revenue sharing, some type of revenue sharing plan is inevitable, and it is essential that the whole idea be examined from the special point of view of education.

If a revenue sharing plan is to be of benefit to education, the proposals relating to this function must be appraised in terms of their relationship to the broader question of achieving a proper balance of power, support and responsibility among the three levels of government.

The achievement of a proper and productive balance depends upon the suitability of the role assigned to each level. It is my opinion that the states must continue to occupy the central position which by law and practice they have always held. But such a position for the states does not preclude a strong role for the federal government.

Participation by the federal government in education has increased many fold in recent years. There are those who would argue that this increase is a result of the failure of the states and localities to carry out their responsibilities, and to some degree this is an accurate view. In the main, however, the growing federal participation has been in response to conditions and needs that are national in character and concern, and, on this basis, will increase rather than diminish.

In defining the role of the federal government in education, it is obvious that the nature of our society today and the kinds of educational needs being generated are giving new emphasis to the leadership role at the federal level, calling for a reappraisal of the place and the power of education in the federal structure. While granting the utmost importance to this aspect of the federal role, I am here concerned primarily with financial aspects.

In this area I believe the federal role should encompass three objectives: to equalize educational opportunity by an equalization of resources among the states; to provide for special or short-term nationally recognized needs; and to encourage and support research and development.

Simply returning money to the states—and this is true also of the localities—through revenue sharing or any other method will not necessarily ensure greater strength. I have long supported the principle of general federal aid, believing that some funding should be available to encourage state initiative, with freedom for the states to determine how the money should be spent in relation to state identified needs and purposes. But I also believe that the obligation of the federal government to strengthen the states mandates that general aid be accompanied by incentives and requirements for reform.

This is not a popular idea and, if adopted, would be considered by many to be an infringement of states' rights. I too am concerned for the rights of states but I do not believe that these rights include the right to allow poor education to continue within their borders.

Too many state structures for education are anachronistic, and to allow federal funds to be used merely to perpetuate inefficiency and mediocrity would be a gross waste of money and an abdication of one of the most important obligations and opportunities of the federal government for the nationwide improvement of education.

The subject of the financing of education is not an exciting or particularly interesting one, except perhaps to those who specialize in it or to taxpayers indignant over rising costs. Other matters relating to education are much more appealing, and this is especially true now when there is so strong a trend toward change and innovation, with the attractive challenges of early childhood education, open schools, technological developments, external degrees, etc.

But finance should be the interest of anyone, layman or professional, concerned for the future of education. Without adequate financing, the possibilities and hopes for improvement have little chance of being realized.

The current attention to finance is tremendously encouraging, but many studies and reports made in the past have resulted in little but bulky additions to already crowded files labeled "plans for educational improvement." At a time when the need for a major overhaul of the financing of education is so painfully illustrated by the desperate situation in so many of our cities, such a "copout" must not be allowed to happen again.

Support for the modernization of educational financing, both in form and adequacy, must be widespread and insistent, and certainly the profession should lead the way in supplying this support.

If we can accomplish a major overhaul that reflects the two basic principles of provision for meeting special needs and of assignment of fiscal response to the proper levels of government, the "just proportional importance" of finance in the reform and improvement of education will have been recognized and one of the most important requirements of prudent perspective will have been met.

The first objective of equalization underscores a need that only the federal government can meet. The disparity among the states in fiscal capacity to support education produces wide variations in quality and substantially hinders the realization of the goal of equality of opportunity. Only through federal action can these disparities be reduced, and thus an obligation for equalization is central in the role of the federal government. Whatever form federal aid to education takes in addition to a continuing program of categorical aids—whether it be general aid, revenue sharing, or a combination of these two—some provision must be made for equalization.

The second objective of the federal role, to provide for special or short-term nationally recognized needs, implies a continuing program of categorical aids. The federal government has an obligation to provide financial assistance in meeting special needs and this function must still be a major feature of federal participation.

But the federal government is unique in its opportunity to exert leverage in raising the educational performance of states and localities, and I believe this opportunity can be more fully realized by a modification of the categorical approach. Many of the present categorical programs, such as Title I of ESEA, are shaped primarily in terms of economic conditions, seeking to compensate for the disadvantages of poverty. It is my belief that this goal can be more effectively met by shaping these programs more directly on a basis of performance, using them as leverage for the maintenance of nationally determined minimum standards of performance in the basic skills of reading and math and in vocational competence. Funds should be channeled as incentives and operational support for communities not exerting sufficient effort or not making sufficient progress toward these standards.

The third objective of the federal role, the encouragement and support of research and development, recognizes both the vital importance of increased capability in this area and the necessary contribution of the federal government to this endeavor through coordination of effort and marshaling of resources. The proposed National Institute of Education is intended to carry out this objective. The establishment of the NIE should be accomplished without delay so that this essential function of the federal role can be more effectively performed.

These three objectives define, in the main, the financial role in education of the federal government. But underlying this role as well as the broader one of leadership is the obligation of the federal government for strengthening the capability of the states so that their central role in the three-way partnership can be carried out with the full effectiveness necessary to maintain a proper and productive balance among the three levels of government.

QUESTIONS FOR REFLECTION AND DISCUSSION

1. The first five articles in this section deal with accountability. Yet not all the authors define accountability, either broadly or as it relates to education, in the same way. What are the differences? Are these substantial enough to make differences in implementation? Which definition do you find most satisfactory? Why?

2. Lessinger cites four "expected changes in the schools as a result of the call for accountability." Does Bowers, do you believe, anticipate these same changes? How might a discussion between Bowers and Lessinger about educational accountability go?

3. Barro identified, as a potential use of accountability measures, the "connection between personnel compensation and performance." Suppose you were a teacher. Would you be willing to have your salary dependent upon your accomplishment? If so, would you want particular kinds of students or particular kinds of nonhuman resources? Is·it fair to hold all the teachers in, say, an English department or an entire

school or school district accountable for the same level and degree of accomplishment?

4. Traditionally education has received much of its support from local school districts. As a result schools in wealthy, generous districts had greater financial resources than schools in impoverished or penurious districts. Allen discusses total state financing of education. What are some of the implications of such a proposal? How, for example, might the arguments of parents who had undergone an expensive move from the cities to the suburbs for their children's education be countered? Would statewide financing have any effect on differences between very rich states like New York or California and very poor ones like Mississippi or Arkansas?

Chapter five
Urban Education

Urban education, to borrow an apt cliché, is a can of worms. The schooling of youth in our cities has and is posing problems for which there appear to be no ready solutions. Some societal problems, like certain aspects of pollution, can be solved if society is willing to commit the requisite human and monetary resources. But other problems—and urban education, like cancer, is one of these—seem to require more than mere manpower, more than simply money.

The complexity of the problems and their various interfaces renders solutions almost imponderable. It seems a bit like the child trying to plug the hole in the dike with his finger. When he plugs the first hole, another one erupts. He plugs it, but then there is another, and so on. And he has only ten fingers.

One significant aspect of urban education is the sheer weight of the numbers of people involved. In New York City, for example, the student population is roughly equal to the total population of St. Louis; the teaching corps equals a city the size of Peoria, Illinois. Books must be purchased by the tens of thousands. Paper for duplicating machines runs into tons and tons, not simply of sheets, but of reams. Other examples are equally enormous and attest equally to the insurmountable problems of bigness and its attendant bureaucracy.

But bigness is not the only culprit. Now, for the first time in America's history, most United States citizens live in the suburbs of the nation's large cities, those generally affluent and manageably-sized urban structures that ring every major city. The rate of suburban growth, it is true, has lessened somewhat, but this is a numerical slowdown, not a status one. For the fact remains that more and more middle-class white city dwellers are leaving the city for the suburbs, escaping what they believe to be schoolhouse chaos in order to find what they hope will be better educational opportunities for their children in the more orderly suburban districts. City schools thus receive an ever greater number of socially deprived, ethnic minority children. More and more of their students are on welfare. Fewer and fewer have educational aspirations that reach beyond high school, if indeed that far. In some cities one-half of the present fifth graders will have dropped out of school before high school graduation. Teachers too often leave the city slums and ghettos at their earliest chance or else stay on resignedly, simply trying to muddle through somehow.

Certainly a one-sided picture like the above ought to be at least dotted with a few of the successes—schools like the Bronx High School of Science, for example. But these exceptions do little more than prove the rule: urban education remains a can of worms. Perhaps hope ought not to be extinguished entirely, however. The authors represented in this section, for instance, all hold out some optimism for a better time ahead. They offer no unqualified panaceas, hold out no universal solutions, but they do remain confident that something can be done to improve urban education. Let us hope they are correct.

Some may question the placement of the first article in the section. Ornstein has written about the disadvantaged, who are by no means limited to the nation's urban areas. Yet certainly two facts can go without serious challenge: (1) many of the children in urban schools are disadvantaged and (2) most of the nation's disadvantaged do reside in the cities. Hence, Ornstein's thorough and careful review of recent research is aptly placed in this section and deserves the thoughtful consideration of all who are interested in urban education.

Passow, in the second article, initially notes the enormous numbers game in urban education. But he also offers some strategies for improvement in urban education, some 21 specific proposals that, if implemented, can make a difference.

Wayson, in the third article, discusses the need for "involvement, problem solving, accountability, and continual growth" in the establishment of responsible education in urban schools. His recounting of the program at a specific school provides a model for educational reform.

Finally, Ornstein's second article in this section argues for decentralization in urban areas.

Recent Historical Perspectives for Educating the Disadvantaged

Allan C. Ornstein

By the 1940's, the concern for color and caste was evident in the academic community. A few of the classic studies are worth mentioning. The relationship between social class and education and the ways in which the lower class was penalized' in schools, were shown by Davis (1948), Hollingshead (1949), and Warner et al. (1944). The social, economical, and political problems of blacks, and the ways in which racial discrimination and segregation were related to these problems, were shown by Davis and Dollard (1940), Drake and Cayton (1945), and Myrdal (1944).

THE PROBLEM OF RACE AND POVERTY

It was not until the early 1960s that there was interest on a national level in the poor, especially the black poor, as a result of the civil rights movement and the subsequent War on Poverty. The fact that racism accommodates the nation's needs, that it is a contradiction of the American slogan of "liberty, justice, and equality," and that it contradicts the melting-pot concept had caused white America to avoid the reality of and direct dealing with the social process. Also, the fact that poverty—such an obvious, crushing contradiction in American life—escaped widespread public concern, surfaced, suddenly, in the ardent reaches of the American consciousness.

The civil rights movement, spearheaded by Rev. Martin Luther King, Jr., exposed white prejudices and discrimination. It was nonviolence—not black power or race riots—that brought forth white anxiety and white violence. The peaceful civil rights movement preceded Stokeley Carmichael and Watts. Today, however, white racism, and the directly related rise of black racism among a small group, confront each other and threaten the social fabric of the country.

"Recent Historical Perspectives for Educating the Disadvantaged" by Allan C. Ornstein is reprinted from *Urban Education,* Volume 5, Number 4 (January 1971) pp. 378–99, by permission of the Publisher, Sage Publications, Inc.

Harrington (1963) was essential in sparking the War on Poverty and subsequently related federal programs for the education of poor and minority-group children. Not since Dickens had someone dramatically captured the problems and life styles of the poor—but this time the poor that were being described were Americans. Harrington estimated that there were between 40 and 50 million Americans who lived in poverty, and their poverty was hereditary or structural. The number of poor was challenged by numerous authorities and councils—including the government, which contended there were between 30 and 35 million poor Americans. However, Harrington's point was that a piecemeal, individual-case approach could not solve the problem; massive funds and a full-scale program were needed. The problem was not only blacks and other racial minorities, but poor whites; poor whites were just as much a minority group. Because they were white they were "invisible," and nobody paid much attention to them. Harrington directly struck at the American conscience by declaring that the poor were the victims of our affluent, industrial society; moreover, he charged for the first time that a society had the material ability to end poverty but lacked the will to do so.

In the meantime, educators began to reflect the nation's concern over the twin problems of race and poverty—fear of a possible conflict between the "haves" and the "have nots," especially between whites and blacks. Educators focused on the children of the poor, blacks, and other minorities with such euphemisms as the disadvantaged, deprived, and underprivileged. The classification of "cultural deprivation" was added to the *Educational Index,* beginning with 21 entries in Volume 13, July 1961-June 1963; by Volume 15, July 1964-June 1965, the number had increased to 122 entries; by Volume 19, July 1968-June 1969, the most recently completed volume at the time of this writing, the number of entries was 370, with several other similar headings such as city schools, cultural difference, poverty, Negro, and so forth. It is with this period, from the beginning of the 1960s to the present, that the rest of the paper will be concerned, and an attempt will be made to synthesize the literature.

THE LITERATURE

Beginnings

Perhaps the three books that presaged the field and had the greatest impact were Conant (1961), Riessman (1962), and Sexton (1964).

Conant, in rather cursory and nondocumented form, compared the slum schools and the slum students with their respective counterparts in suburbia. He coined the term "social dynamite" and warned that conditions were reaching an intolerable and explosive point in the ghettos of the cities. Conant's prestige and influence were a major factor in awakening educators and other responsible citizens to the plight of the slum school.

Reissman, at that time a relatively unknown psychologist at Bard College, became the "expert" in the field as a result of his book: upon publication, the book became a "sleeper," reaching the market at the so-called right time—when society was becoming more sensitive to the problems of the disadvantaged. Riessman helped people understand the problems of educating these children and youth. Although he tended to romanticize the disadvantaged, even to the point of comparing their mental styles to that of true genius, he clearly showed that the disadvantaged had their own culture and that this culture was in conflict with the schools' middle-class values. He went on to list several suggestions for classroom teachers, which were fundamental but practical. Until the end of the decade, almost all subsequent books on the subject referred to or cited the book; at this time, the book has gone through twelve printings.

Sexton statistically showed the lack of equal educational opportunity for low-income youth and the numerous discriminatory characteristics of the low-income schools' physical plant, staff, and resources in comparison with higher-income schools. For nearly every school characteristic, Sexton showed that advantage was positively correlated with the median income of the students' parents. Actually, the results were not earthshaking but a confirmation of sociological "wisdom," which dated back at least to the Lynd and Lynd study of Middletown in 1929. What Sexton did, however, was to show how income related to educational opportunity with the use of simple statistics accompanied by a readable discussion, so that the "average" reader could understand the implications of the study. Another intangible variable was contemporary history. This time (as with Riessman), educators, government officials, and citizens were willing to listen. Therefore, by the end of the decade most of the low-income schools, at least in the northern cities, equalized or more than equalized most of the characteristics described in the study through extra money and special programs. However, one important characteristic which probably has not been equalized are the teacher's attitudes, behaviors, and morale—all of which are extremely difficult to change and have very little to do with the amount of money a school spends on programs for educating its students.

By the mid-sixties, interest in the disadvantaged had reached the "bandwagon" status. Several of the educational journals had already published or were soon to publish feature issues on the disadvantaged. The increasing amount of research in the field led the *Review of Educational Research* to devote its October 1965 issue to the subject. The same year, one of nineteen ERIC clearinghouses funded by the U.S. Office of Education was dedicated to the disadvantaged—to collect and disseminate the rapidly proliferating reports and studies on the subject. The ERIC file accumulated several thousand reports and studies in their 1956-1965 *Office of Educational Reports,* and in 1965 *Research in Education,* a monthly index, was published and still continues their monthly listings.

Training programs for teachers of the disadvantaged, and related courses and advanced degrees in the field, began to appear across the country. Corresponding with the increased concern for educating teachers for the disadvantaged, was a surge of conferences, position papers, and books on the subject, not to mention the growth of journals, articles, and research studies in the field—most of which repeated nearly the same "wisdom" and tired statements of what was wrong, coupled with suggested solutions based on hunches, sentiment, and unverified or subjective data.

Reiteration also pervaded among most of the "experts." They merely lifted whole sections or major portions of one manuscript and transformed them to another manuscript, revised or updated the same discussion and organized it under different titles. Because of space limitations, only a few examples will be given here.

Edmond Gordon reviewed basically the same compensatory programs under different subheadings in at least four different publications.[1] Robert Havighurst repeated the same theme about the characteristics of the disadvantaged in three manuscripts.[2] Irwin Katz mainly reviewed psychological problems of black children and youth in four studies.[3] Frank Riessman discussed the disadvantaged child's mental styles and physical and hidden verbal ability in at least nine different sources.[4] J. M. Hunt repeated the same discussion about the different views of intelligence and the need for environmental stimulation in at least three different sources.[5]

Controversial Studies

From the period of the mid-sixties to the closing of the decade, six reports or studies were considered controversial: Moynihan (1965) *The Negro Family;* Coleman et al. (1966) *Equality of Educational Opportunity;* Bereiter and Englemann (1966) *Teaching Disadvantaged Children in Preschool* and (1967) *Reconnection for Learning;* Rosenthal and Jacobson (1968) *Pygmalion in the Classroom;* and Jensen's article "How Much Can We Boost IQ and Scholastic Achievement," which was published in the Winter 1969 issue of the *Harvard Educational Review.*

The Negro Family, The Case for National Action, better known as the Moynihan Report, was written in an effort to justify federal intervention in civil rights and poverty. Moynihan focused on the problems and deficiencies of the black family. His conclusions largely coincided with Frazier (1939), the black sociologist's view of the matriarchal nature of the black family. However, the social and political conditions of the period, and the fact that Moynihan was white, caused considerable discontent, especially within the black community. He was criticized for emphasizing the negative characteristics of black life and for indirectly blaming blacks for their disadvantaged condition, which actually was caused mainly by society.

J. S. Coleman and other social scientists were commissioned by the federal government to conduct the study, *Equality of Educational Opportunity.* The study took approximately two years, included a sample of schools by regions across the country, and comprised over 1,500 pages—mainly statistical in nature—making it perhaps the largest study in the history of education. Because of its sheer size, and although there are several ill-defined conclusions that can substantiate different and conflicting opinions, the report is continuously referred to in subsequent writings by other authors.

The report set out to show that school facilities of minority children were unequal and this inequality was related to student achievement; the implications would then coincide with the Johnson Administration's attempt to foster school integration. Although there are several interpretations to the report, according to Moynihan (1968) and Stodolsky and Lesser (1967), the outcomes did not support either intention.

The major findings were: (1) the schools are similar in the effect they have on student achievement, (2) student achievement is mainly related to family characteristics, and (3) minority children are more affected by the schools' characteristics—teachers, resources, facilities, and so on—than are white, middle-class children. Just one example how the findings can be interpreted in two different ways: it can be argued that integration, compensatory education, or, for that matter, whatever the school does, are premature, since student achievement is generally unrelated to what the school does but a function of the home environment. Not until the child's family characteristics improve will the student have an equal educational opportunity. On the other hand, it can be argued that since minority children are more affected by the characteristics of the school, integration is necessary because white middle-class schools usually have better teachers, resources, facilities, and the like.

The Winter 1968 issue of the *Harvard Educational Review* summarized most of the major criticisms of the Coleman Report.[6]

The survey was on a districtwide basis, inapplicable to particular schools (Dyer).

There was a high percentage (50 percent or more) of nonresponses in many categories, which tended to invalidate the results (Dyer).

The responses reveal several elements of distortion and defensiveness among the respondents (Katz), and the responses suffer from an unevenness, since the questions were filled out by students, teachers, and administrators of various levels of understanding and honesty.

The school correlates were defined as having a +2 correlation, which is a lenient figure (Dyer).

The criterion for school achievement was verbal ability, more a product of the student's home than of the school, and verbal-ability tests discriminate against ghetto students (Dyer, Wilson); therefore, the criterion is biased, and it should not have been used to compare achievement gains of middle-class whites.

It is likely that middle-class black and minority families tend to place their children in integrated schools and influence their children's academic achievement in ways not mentioned by the report whereas low-income families live in ghettos and send their children to segregated schools (Pettigrew, Wilson). The statistical analysis did not take into account many of the effects of these variables (Wilson), nor did it distinguish among the overlapping variables of family background, attitudes, school resources, and so on (Bowles).

In particular, the schools' resources and teachers' morale and performance represent a downward bias of the estimates between student achievement and school integration (Bowles).

The social conditions toward race prevented analysis of several student characteristics which might have correlated with student achievement (Moynihan).

Bereiter and Englemann presented an innovative program for counteracting the disadvantaged child's deprivation, to enable him to start the first grade on an equal basis with his middle-class counterpart. For purposes of educating the disadvantaged child, the authors challenged many of our entrenched values and ideas: Piaget's theory of cognitive development and the concepts of the whole child, student motivation, personalized teacher-student interaction, and play-oreinted nursery schools. Rather, they concentrated on old-fashioned, repetitious drill, in logical sequence and at a rapid pace—which coincided with a computer; it was supposed to produce tension, moderate competition, and anxiety among the children. Students were encouraged to be quiet and restrained so the most could be made of the limited time. Classroom discipline involved "a slap, or a good gentle shaking," and, if the misconduct continued, it was recommended that the child be placed in the "isolation room," which was, in effect, "a small poorly lighted closet with a single chair." The key to learning was considered to be linked with language. A detailed curriculum, with emphasis on language development, was outlined in "cookbook" fashion.

The book aroused vigorous criticism. Hymes (1967) raised the possibility of detrimental side effects. He pointed out that the program was based mainly upon the success of one experiment involving only fifteen children and the data from one test, the Illinois Test of Psycholinguistic Abilities, which has, as do most tests, questionable validity. Friedlander (1968) and Hymes both pointed out the regimentation of school and the definition of punishment as an administrative act. Friedlander noted the lack of concern for personal and affective needs of children and of personal interaction between the teacher and the students, and that some teachers might not know when to stop disciplining a child or be able to distinguish between guidance and discipline. Moskovitz (1968) questioned the lack of distinction between language and thought, and the assumptions that lower-class children lack a structured dialect and that the teaching of language fosters sensory and cognitive development.

The Bundy Report

In 1967, the New York Mayor's Advisory Panel on Decentralization was organized and subsequently presented the document, *Reconnection for Learning—A Community School System for New York City,* commonly known as the Bundy Report, after McGeorge Bundy, who served as chairman of the panel. Bearing in mind that school controversies that start in New York City often spread to other cities, the basic ideas of the report have spread across the country. The basic recommendations could be summed as reorganizing New York City's schools into thirty to sixty local districts, ranging in size from about 12,000 to 40,000 pupils. The community districts would be governed by a local board elected in part by the community and in part by the mayor from a list of citywide candidates. The local boards would have power over personnel, curriculum, and the budget. The purpose of the report was to increase community awareness and participation in the educational process, make the schools more responsive to the diverse needs and problems of the city's diversified population, and provide flexibility and innovation at the local level.

The major criticisms of the plan were synthesized by the positions of the United Federation of Teachers (which also stated repeatedly that it was in favor of a different decentralization plan), the Supervisory Association, and the central board of education. They were: The plan did little to improve education, rather, it was a political tactic which would increase the power of the mayor's office and local pressure groups which were militant and vocal but did not necessarily have the support of the community; the city would be further balkanized; segregated schooling would be reinforced; it would increase black-white racism; it would be possible for "vigilante" groups to harass the school personnel; the merit system would be eliminated; and it would reduce the power and professional integrity of teachers and supervisors.

There were additional questions and objections. Thelen (1967) suggested the possibility of additional red tape and replication, that school systems might lack contact and be out of step with each other, and that changing the school system would not necessarily change old attitudes or lead to quality education. Baratta (1969) suggested that the plan would lead to poor intracommunication and increased institutionalization of local "wisdom." Sizer (1968) suggested that the plan was a tactic to lower the pressure of the black community, and that it was questionable whether parents had the expertise to run the schools. Sizer and Shanker (1969) argued that the responsibility for educating poor and black children would be shifted away from the school and the whole society to the poor and black community. Shanker argued that the plan would cause many integrationists to be resigned to segregated schools, or even become active supporters of racial separation, and restrict the rights of unions which have two million members.

The plan led to the creation of the three experimental districts, which included the controversial Oceanhill-Brownsville District in New York City, and, in this respect, was indirectly one of the sparks that ignited the New York City ten-week-long teachers' strike in 1968—the strike that morally and psychologically demoralized the city, teachers, and children, and racially polarized the black community and predominantly white teachers' union.

Teachers of the Disadvantaged

In their study, *Pygmalion in the Classroom,* Rosenthal and Jacobson showed that the teachers' expectations influence the achievement gains of elementary school students, and that this influence is greatest in the first two grades. (The greater teacher effect at the early grades coincides with prevailing theories of cognitive development and importance of early years.) At the beginning of the school year, eighteen teachers of grades one through six were given the names of randomly selected children who were supposed to show dramatic intellectual growth. As many as 65 students (about twenty percent) were falsely labeled as "late bloomers" or failed to show this intellectual growth. The difference between the experimental children and the rest of the children existed only in the minds of the teachers. Pre- and posttests showed that the experimental group had a mean gain of 3.8 more than the control (ordinary) group, significant at the .02 level. Thus, the study statistically confirmed the self-fulfilling prophecy that was first expounded by Merton and has since appeared in the literature about teachers of the disadvantaged.

Besides the authors indirectly criticizing the weaknesses of their own study, the problems of the experimenter bias, Hawthorne effect, placebo effect, "halo effect," and the demand characteristics of the subjects, Gephart and Antonoplos (1969) elaborated upon these biases.

Closely related to the problem of demand characteristics, the teachers believed in the treatment and did not seem to question that the selected students were late bloomers, partially because of the status attached to Rosenthal's affiliation with Harvard University. Their attitudes and behaviors were probably more extreme in this case than if a colleague or supervisor had told them of a student who was a late bloomer. The fact that the teachers cooperated indicated, in part, that they wanted the experiment to succeed, and therefore, they tried harder than usual—thus trapping themselves into proving the author's hypothesis.

Gephart and Antonoplos (1969) indicated that the analysis should have compared class means, not individual students' gain scores, since the teachers received the experimental treatment; moreover, the assumptions inherent in their statistical tests were violated. Barber et al. (1969) were unable to replicate the original study on five separate occasions. Thorndike (1968) pointed out statistical defects with the levels of significance, and the few numbers of subjects in the first and second grade (t=19); their scores provided the principal effect.

Snow (1968) pointed out that the authors tested the children four times but only compared the pretest with the third test. There was no mention that results of the other posttests were markedly different from the scores on the third test. All four tests were equally as important and should have been analyzed. Also, there was no mention of the effects of subject loss (20 percent) as the study progressed.

Snow showed that the test administered to the children lacked adequate norms for the younger children. For example, the pretest reasoning IQ means for all first-grade children was 58. Were the children morons? More likely, the test did not function at this grade level; in fact, the test did not have norms below an average of 60. Yet the reasoning subscores in grades one and two provided the principal effect, and it is these scores that were most dubious.

Snow also showed that many other IQ scores were equally as questionable. Three examples suffice: One subject with a pretest reasoning IQ of 17 had posttest scores of 148, 110, and 112. Another obtained reasoning IQs of 18, 44, 122, and 98. On the other side of the coin, one subject had verbal scores of 183, 166, 221, and 168, yet the test did not have norms above 160. Was this child a genius? Many students, over a two-year period, also showed IQ gains of more than 100 points—making the test, test procedures, sample, or statistics suspect.

In short, the actual study has so many flaws that it is doubtful whether it would have been accepted in a professional journal. The study is an excellent example of "how to lie with statistics"; furthermore, the average reader lacks knowledge and insight into research and statistical procedures, and therefore, is unaware of the lie. He does not analyze the figures; often, he merely reads the summary. Naively, the reader perpetuates the "wisdom" of teachers' expectations and refers to the study as "hard data."

The Jensen Controversy

Jensen's (1969) 123-page article (to this author's knowledge, the longest one published by the *Harvard Educational Review*) entitled, "How Much Can We Boost IQ and Scholastic Achievement," rekindled the emotional issues of race, intelligence, and heredity. Based largely on a review of a large body of research, as well as on his own recent studies, he concluded that heredity was the major factor for determining intelligence—a direct counter-argument to the prevailing environmentalists. It was his conclusion that about eighty percent of the difference in IQ was related to heredity, and that blacks lagged about fifteen points behind the white average in IQ. Jensen also contended that blacks and disadvantaged children in general tended to have difficulty in abstract reasoning, and unfortunately, the schools have assumed that all children can master higher cognitive skills. Compensatory education had failed because it was trying to compensate children of limited intellectual talents with learning processes that were really geared for students of superior talent.

The article aroused a bulk of publications, reviews, rejoinders, and debates—largely because of the facts that Harvard had published the article, the prominence of the author himself, and the tense racial situation. The article became (and still is) required reading for several white supremacy organizations, and it has been duplicated without Harvard's permission[7] and forwarded by these organizations to teacher groups in several parts of the country. It has been introduced as evidence in court cases by opponents of school integration, and it has had the possible effect of weakening support for compensatory education.

Although hundreds of social scientists have criticized Jensen's findings, the most comprehensive analysis is perhaps by seven social scientists invited by the *Review* to respond. The group was largely composed of environmentalists; their conclusions are summarized:[8]

1. Throughout the manuscript there are misstatements and errors (at least 17 errors—e.g., as 68 percent being reversed to 86 percent on the next page), maximizing differences between blacks and whites and maximizing the possibility that such differences are attributed to heredity (Cronbach).

2. Much of Jensen's research is based on relatively small samples, therefore, the parameter estimates are suspect. The reality of the assumptions implicit in the analysis of variance models also are doubtful (Crow).

3. Hereditary-environment interaction is impossible to distinguish (Cronbach, Crow, Hunt) and "mesh" with many uncontrollable and unidentifiable variables.

4. The direction and extent of genetic race differences are unable to be accurately assessed (Cronbach, Crow).

5. IQ outcomes are affected by such variables as malnutrition, inadequate prenatal care, as well as early childhood stimulation—which are difficult to accurately measure (Bereiter, Elkind, Hunt).

6. Race prejudice could account for any differences in IQ that might exist between whites and blacks; the difference of racial group experiences limits the validity of group comparisons (Crow).

7. Different IQ scores might reflect different learning styles of blacks and whites; these differences have cultural and social origins (Brazziel).

8. It is impossible to determine which genes—black or white—make a difference between the two races because more than ninety percent of blacks have white genes (Brazziel).

9. Jensen overlooked much research among infants and identical twins which suggested the importance of environment (Kagan, Hunt).

10. One criterion for a test's validity is that it assumes that the distribution of scores is normally distributed. Since the black subjects' scores are not normally distributed in comparison to the white scores (but skewed below the mean), the results for and comparisons of black subjects are invalid (Elkind, Hunt).

11. The assumption that the disadvantaged can only be taught rote skills or low cognitive processes is detrimental to an egalitarian society (Cronbach).

12. Granted, billions of dollars have been spent on compensatory education and the results have not been impressive. It is possible that we have not reached the threshold where amount of money per child makes an impact. Also, it is too early to determine the long-range effect on achievement and IQ (Bereiter, Elkind, Kagan).

The period of the mid- and late sixties also saw a superabundance of overgeneralized, highly emotional exposés of ghetto teachers and schools. A few examples suffice: Greene and Ryan (1965), Kozol (1967), Kohl (1967), Herndon (1968), Haskins (1969). These books were written by teachers who coupled an appeal to emotionalism with an exposé, which readers fancy, and were able to convince their readers about the racism, indifference, and general wickedness among ghetto teachers and school systems. Not only do angry, emotional, and so-called sensitive and socially concerned authors usually distort reality, but those ingredients usually sell books.

The books had a diary format, and like most diaries they were extremely selective—merely a filtration of what the respective authors wanted to see and report—a bias that probably had developed before the beginning of the school year. Because the writings were nonscientific, based on preconceived hunches, the authors had wide latitude to focus on any subject, for an entire year, that coincided with and reinforced their preconceived notions, and which also made good (not necessarily honest) reading. Indeed, the books were a series of angry half truths; the whole teaching equation was never reported, for surely given a year in any school there is some good besides what the authors tell about themselves. Given a staff of 50 or 100 teachers, the law of averages provides enough racists and incompetents in a particular school so that an author could have a large field for reporting on these few teachers, thus blowing the negative side of the equation up out of proportion.

The only dedicated and committed teachers (excepting Herndon who admitted that he grew to dislike his students) were seemingly the respective authors—trying to overcome heavy odds. Because the authors were personalizing their own stories, and often ego-involved about their own successes, the books tend to lack intellectual honesty, but this generally went unnoticed because the writings coincided with many readers' own feelings about criticizing teachers and the establishment. Young prospective teachers, especially blacks, were thrilled to see teachers, in effect caretakers of the establishment, being vilified. The students were construed as the helpless underdogs for readers to root for. Certainly, each book was not representative of ghetto teachers or schools but was a tirade about one school (with the exception of the Greene and Ryan book, which was about two schools). Yet the readers were trapped by their own biases and assumed the accounts were true and generalized to a larger teacher and school pupulation (Ornstein, 1970).

Viewing the entire decade as an entity, the literature centered around 12 general themes:

1. Descriptions and characteristics of the disadvantaged—mainly in sociopsychological and racial terms, with a prevailing negative image.

2. Analysis of racial and ethnic differences between and among groups as a basis for school achievement and intelligence.

3. Concern over achievement, reading, and intelligence tests, with general agreement that they discriminated against the disadvantaged.

4. Descriptions and evaluations of compensatory programs, with special emphasis on both extremes of the educational continuum—prekindergarten and college. Most of the programs were considered ineffective.

5. Descriptions and characteristics of teachers of the disadvantaged, mainly in terms of negative attitudes and behaviors and limited experience.

6. Concern over instructional techniques for the disadvantaged, which could be lumped under "good" teaching for all children, but more necessary for the disadvantaged.

7. Descriptions and evaluations of teacher-training programs, most of which were judged to emphasize theory and deemphasize practice. Training of local residents as paraprofessionals and eventually as teachers of the disadvantaged.

8. Methods for recruiting teachers of the disadvantaged, with emphasis on assigning qualified teachers to ghetto schools.

9. The growth of teacher unions in city schools, and especially in the ghetto areas, where teacher morale is often low.

10. Concern over curriculum reform, with emphasis on "relevant" materials, developing language and cognitive skills, improving the image of minorities in textbooks and quality of integrated primers, and revising the content so that it portrays a more realistic role of minorities.

11. Descriptions of the schools serving the disadvantaged, negatively portrayed—and the effects of segregated and integrated schools on black students.

12. Concern over school reorganization and providing alternative schemes for educating the disadvantaged—including state and federal subsities (vouchers) for students.

At the time of this writing, the direction and problems of the 1970s also seem to be:

1. Teacher accountability and teacher-behavior models and learning theories applicable for working with the disadvantaged.

2. Possible elimination of merit pay and promotion based on formal examinations and increased preferential hiring and promoting of minority group-school personnel in black and other minority group schools.

3. Increased use of sensitivity training for school personnel.

4. Concern over reduced governmental and school-system spending on all

educational programs, with a ripple effect for educating the disadvantaged.

5. Renewed interest in behavioral objectives for teaching the disadvantaged.

6. Community-action-related educational and health programs.

7. Increased open enrollment at the college level (mainly city and state institutions) and special educational and financial assistance for the disadvantaged.

8. Increased black-white racism in schools and communities, with special emphasis for local control by a vocal minority of blacks, and special concern by whites to maintain "neighborhood" schools.

9. A subsystems approach to educating the disadvantaged, including governmental, business, scientific, and cultural agencies.

10. Interest in contract purchasing by business companies, many whose initial teaching and evaluative procedures have been criticized as unethical.

11. Institutes to combat racism.

12. The role of the social scientist, and the merits of reporting research that negatively depicts an ethnic or racial group and the right for free inquiry in such sensitive areas.

Reflecting upon the last decade, educators have come to realize that they lack answers. Little has been definite and consistent, excepting the obvious—e.g., poor students have lower achievement grades than middle-class students. The lack of our knowledge seems to be partially due to the fact that variables and subsequent results vary because they are functional to varied situations. As the complexities of the problem have become evident, the old truism has become applicable to the field—we are only at the first stage of wisdom: humble confession of how little we know. Rather than formulate ideas and programs that are based on hunches, we now have come to the realization that we first have to find what can work, with whom, to what extent, under which conditions.

NOTES

[1] In 1965, "A Review of Programs of Compensatory Education," *American Journal of Orthopsychiatry* 35: 644–51; with Doxey A. Wilkerson (1966) Compensatory Education for the Disadvantaged (New York: College Entrance Examination Board); in 1968, "Programs of Compensatory Education," in M. Deutsch et al., eds., *Social Class, Race, and Psychological Development* (New York: Holt, Rinehart & Winston), pp. 381–410; and with Adelaide Jabolonsky (1968) "Compensatory Education in the Equalization of Educational Opportunity." *Journal of Negro Education* 37: 268–79.

[2] In 1964, "Who are the Disadvantaged?" *Journal of Negro Education* 33: 210–17; in

1970, "Social Backgrounds: Their Impact on School Children," pp. 11–20 in T. D. Horn, ed., *Reading for the Disadvantaged* (New York: Harcourt, Brace & World); and also in 1970, "Minority Subcultures and the Law of Effect," *American Psychologist* 25: 313–22.

[3] In 1964, "Review of Evidence Relating to Effects of Desegregation on the Intellectual Performance of Negroes" *American Psychologist* 19: 381–99; in 1967-1968, "Desegregation or Integration in Public Schools? The Policy Implications of Research." Integrated Education 5: 15–27; in 1968, "Factors Influencing Negro Performance in the Desegregated School," pp. 254–89 in M. Deutsch et al., eds., *Social Class, Race, and Psychological Development* (New York: Holt, Rinehart & Winston); and in 1969, "A Critique of Personality Approaches to Negro Performance, With Research Suggestions" *Journal of Social Issues* 25: 13–27.

[4] In 1962, *The Culturally Deprived Child* (New York: Harper & Row); in 1963, "Culturally Deprived Child: A New View" School Life 45: 5–7; in 1964, "Overlooked Positives of Disadvantaged Groups" *Journal of Negro Education* 33: 225–31 and "The Strategy of Style" Teachers College Record 65: 484–89; in 1965, "Low Income Culture, the Adolescent, and the School" *National Association of Secondary School Principals* 49: 45–49; in 1966, "Styles of Learning" *NEA Journal* 55: 15–17 and *Helping the Disadvantaged Pupil to Learn More Easily* (Englewood Cliffs, N.J.: Prentice-Hall); in 1967, "Teachers of the Poor: a Five Point Plan" *Journal of Teacher Education* 18: 326–36; and in 1967 also, "Further Thoughts on Educating the Disadvantaged," in A. H. Passow, ed., *Developing Programs for the Educationally Disadvantaged* (New York: Teachers College, Columbia University).

[5] In 1961, *Intelligence and Experience* (New York: Ronald Press); in 1964, "Pre-school Enrichment as an Antidote for Cultural Deprivation" *Merrill-Palmer Quarterly* 10: 209–48, and also in 1964, "How Children Develop Intellectually." *Children* 11: 83–91. (To be correct, the author, although no "expert," is also guilty as charged.)

[6] The social scientists invited by the *Review* to analyze the Coleman Report were: Henry S. Dyer, Irwin Katz, Thomas F. Pettigrew, and Alan B. Wilson. The discussion also includes criticisms raised in two supplementary articles which appeared in the same issue by Daniel P. Moynihan and Samuel S. Bowles.

[7] It should be noted that the article was published in the May 1969 issue of the *Congressional Record,* and it has become public domain.

[8] The social scientists invited by the *Review* to analyze the Jensen study were: Jerome S. Kagan, J. M. Hunt, James F. Crow, Carl Bereiter, David Elkind, Lee J. Cronbach, and William F. Brazziel. Additional responses and letters to the editors were published in the summer issue—involving a host of other political, technical, and theoretical factors.

REFERENCES

Baratta, A. N. "School Decentralization: Impetus or Dilemma for Learning and Teaching," pp. 311–26 in A. C. Ornstein and P. D. Vario (eds.), *How To Teach Disadvantaged Youth.* New York: David McKay, 1969.

Barber, T. X. et al. "Five attempts To Replicate the 'Experimenter Bias' effect." *Journal of Consulting and Clinical Psychology* 33 (1969): 1–14.

Bereiter, C. and S. Englemann. *Teaching Disadvantaged Children in Preschool.* Englewood Cliffs, N.J.: Prentice-Hall, 1966.

Coleman, J. S. et al.*Equality of Educational Opportunity.* Washington, D.C.: Government Printing Office, 1966.

Conant, J. B. *Slums and Suburbs.* New York: McGraw-Hill, 1961.

Davis, A. *Social Class Influences Upon Learning.* Cambridge, Mass.: Harvard University Press, 1948.

———and J. Dollard. *Children of Bondage.* Washington, D.C.: American Council on Education, 1940.

Deutsch, M. "Organizational and conceptual barriers to social change." *Journal of Social Issues* 25 (1969): 5–18.

Drake, S. C. and H. R. Cayton. *Black Metropolis.* New York: Harper, 1945.

Frazier, E. F. *The Negro in the United States.* New York: Macmillan, 1939.

Friedlander, B. Z. "The Bereiter-Englemann Approach." *Educational Forum* 32 (1968): 359–62.

Gephart, W. J. and D. P. Antonoplos. "The Effects of Expectancy and Other Research-Biasing Factors." *Phi Delta Kappan* 50 (1969): 579–83.

Glazer, N. "Ethnic Groups and Education: Towards the Tolerance of Difference," *Journal of Negro Education* 38 (1969): 187–95.

Greene, M. F. and O. Ryan. *The Schoolchildren.* New York: Pantheon, 1969.

Harrington, M. *The Other America.* New York: Macmillan, 1963.

Harvard Educational Review. "Research Issues on Equality of Educational Opportunity." 38 (1968): 37–84.

Haskins, J. *Diary of a Harlem Schoolteacher.* New York: Grove, 1969.

Herndon, J. *The Way It Spozed To Be.* New York: Simon & Schuster, 1968.

Hollingshead, A. B. *Elmtown's Youth.* New York: John Wiley, 1949.

Hymes, J. L., Jr. "Review of Teaching Disadvantaged Children in the Preschool." *Educational Leadership* 24 (1967): 463ff.

Jensen, A. R. "How Much Can We Boost IQ and Scholastic Achievement?" *Harvard Educational Review* 39 (1969): 1–123.

———"Meaningfulness and Concepts; Concepts and Meaningfulness," pp. 65–68 in H. J. Klausmeier and C. W. Harris (eds.), *Analysis of Concept Learning.* New York: Academic Press, 1966.

Katz, I. "A Critique of Personality Approaches to Negro Performance, with Research Suggestions." *Journal of Social Issues* 25 (1969): 13–27.

——— "Review of Evidence Relating to Effects of Desegregation on the Intellectual Performance of Negroes." *American Psychologist* 19 (1964): 381–99.

Kohl, H. *Thirty-Six Children.* New York: New American Library, 1967.

Kozol, J. *Death at an Early Age.* Boston: Houghton-Mifflin, 1967.

Lesser, G. et al. "Mental Abilities of Children From Different Social Class and Cultural Groups." Monographs of the Society for Research in Child Development. Serial 102, 30 (4). Chicago: University of Chicago, 1965.

Lynd, R. and H. M. Lynd. *Middletown.* New York: Harcourt, Brace & World, 1929.

Mayeske, G. W. et al. *A Study of Our Nation's Schools.* Washington, D.C.: Government Printing Office, 1970.

Mayor's Advisory Panel on Decentralization of the New York City Schools. *Reconnection for Learning: A Community School System for New York City.* New York, 1967.

Moskovitz, S. T. "Some Assumptions Underlying the Bereiter Approach." *Young Children* 24 (1968): 24–31.

Moynihan, D. P. "Sources of Resistance to the Coleman Report." *Harvard Educational Review* 38 (1968): 23–36.

——— *The Negro Family, The Case for National Action.* Washington, D.C.: Government Printing Office, 1964.

Myrdal, G. *The American Dilemma.* New York: Harper & Row, 1944.

Ornstein, A. C. "Review of Teaching and Learning in City Schools." *Harvard Educational Review* 40 (1970): 336–38.

Passow, A. H. *Toward Creating a Model Urban School System: A Study of the Washington, D.C. Public Schools.* New York: Teachers College, Columbia University, 1967.

Pettigrew, T. E. *A Profile of the Negro American.* Princeton, N.J.: D. Van Nostrand, 1964.

"Racial and Social Class Isolation in the Schools: Summary Report." *Report to the Board of Regents of the University of the State of New York.* Albany, N.Y.: State Education Department, Division of Research, 1970.

Riessman, F. *The Culturally Deprived Child.* New York: Harper & Row, 1962.

Rosenthal, R. and L. Jacobson. *Pygmalion in the Classroom.* New York: Holt, Rinehart & Winston, 1968.

Sexton, P. C. *Education and Income.* New York: Viking, 1964.

Shanker, A. "The Real Meaning of the New York City Teachers' Strike." *Phi Delta Kappan* 50: 434–441.

Sizer, T. R. "Report analysis, reconnection for learning: a community school system for New York City." *Harvard Educational Review* 38 (1968): 176–84.

Snow, R. E. "Unfinished Pygmalion." *Contemporary Psychology* 14 (1968): 197–99.

Stodolsky, S. S. and G. Lesser. "Learning Patterns in the Disadvantaged." *Harvard Educational Review* 37 (1967).

Thelen, H. A. "Urban School Systems (A Response to Mr. Katz)." *Phi Delta Kappan* 48 (1967): 327–28.

Thorndike, R. "Review of Pygmalion in the Classroom" *American Educational Research Journal* 5 (1968): 708–11.

Warner, L., R. J. Havighurst, and M. Loeb. *Who Shall Be Educated?* New York: Harper & Row, 1944.

Wilson, A. B. "Educational Consequences of Segregation in a California Community." pp. 165–206 in *Racial Isolation in the Public Schools,* Part 2. Washington, D.C.: Government Printing Office, 1967.

———"Social Stratification and Academic Achievement," pp. 217–35 in A. H. Passow (ed.), *Education in Depressed Areas.* New York: Teachers College, Columbia University, 1963.

Urban Education in the 1970s

A. Harry Passow

Having, in the past decade, spent billions of dollars on compensatory education, initiated thousands of projects, completed hundreds of studies, entered numerous judicial decisions and rulings, experienced dozens of riots and disorders, and generated whole new agencies and educational institutions, the nation's urban schools continue to operate in a vortex of segregation, alienation, and declining achievement. Various strategies and programs have been proposed for achieving equality of educational opportunity. The crisis in urban education has stimulated total rethinking about the educative process—the goals, the means, the resources, the strategies, the relationships—for all individuals, the advantaged and the disadvantaged, the majority and the minority. No panaceas exist but comprehensive planning based on the reservoir of experience, research, and theory can provide for effective learning in which the entire community becomes the site for education of urban populations.

What is ahead for urban education in the 1970s? What will be the

Reprinted by Permission of the Publisher and the author from A. Harry Passow, *Urban Education in the 1970s.* (New York: Teachers College Press, 1971; Copyright 1971 by Teachers College, Columbia University). A longer version of this paper appeared in *Urban Education in the 1970s,* a collection of ten lectures published by Teachers College Press in January 1971, edited by A. Harry Passow.

future of the ghetto and the slum in American cities and how will it affect and be affected by education? In what ways will education for urban populations—particularly the increasing portion designated as the "disadvantaged"—be reshaped, and will changes result in substantial opening of opportunities for individuals from these groups? These are hard questions about which to speculate, especially in the light of events of the past decade.

In the early 1960s, as the civil rights movement and the war on poverty gathered momentum and as the post-Sputnik concern for skilled manpower highlighted the inadequate development of talent among minority groups, Congress was on the threshold of new social legislation and one could be optimistic, despite the apparent complexities of the problems. A summer 1962 conference concerned with education in depressed areas concluded on this note: "The outlook is hopeful in the forces which are being mobilized to dissect and resolve this wasteful, destructive problem of displaced citizens in a rejecting and ignoring homeland."[1]

Since then, having spent billions of dollars on compensatory education, initiated thousands of projects (each with its own clever acronym title), completed hundreds of studies of uneven significance and even more disparate quality, entered numerous judicial decisions and rulings, experienced dozens of riots and disorders, and generated whole new agencies and educational institutions, the nation's urban schools continue to operate in a vortex of segregation, alienation, and declining achievement.

Despite a considerable amount of rhetoric and numerous studies and reports, what has been called the "urban crisis" grows more intense in all its dimensions. The Kerner Commission, probing for the causes of civil disorders, pointed to the interactions of a variety of factors—economic, political, health, welfare, education, justice, security—and warned: "None of us can escape the consequences of the continuing economic and social decay of the central city and the closely related problem of rural poverty."[2] The Commission saw a continued movement toward two societies—one essentially white in the suburbs, small cities, and outlying districts, and the other largely nonwhite, located in the central cities—and declared that "we are well on the way to just such a divided nation."

While the concentration of the poor and the nonwhite populations continues in central cities, Downs asserts that "not one single significant program of any federal, state, or local government is aimed at altering this tendency or is likely to have the unintended effect of doing so."[3] Preliminary data from the 1970 national census indicates that the greatest population growth has been in suburbia with the segregation of the poor and minority groups becoming even more intense in central cities. Black and other nonwhite migration to suburbia does appear to be increasing at a rate that seems to be exceeding earlier projections. An analysis by Birch noted that the consequences of these population shifts "on the inner suburbs and, eventually, on the outer suburbs, may be quite dramatic. Already inner suburb densities are approaching those of central cities, and increasingly this density growth is attributable to the poor and the Blacks."[4]

The American city faces a fourfold dilemma: fewer tax dollars available as middle-income taxpayers move out and property values, business, and commerce decline; more tax dollars needed for essential public services and facilities and for meeting the basic needs of low-income groups; increasing costs of goods and services resulting in dwindling tax dollars buying less; and increasing dissatisfactions with services provided as needs, expectations, and living standards increase.[5] While it is possible to cite improvements in many aspects of urban life and development, the imperative needs call for far greater investments of our intellectual and financial resources. In the current crisis, education is part of the problem as well as part of the solution. Aside from the role of schools in developing "brainpower" and all that is entailed in those endeavors, education represents the means for creating the commitments and attitudes needed to grapple with the problems as well as the promise of our urban centers.

Urban Education in Trouble

Surveys of large-city school systems continue to document the failures of the inner-city schools, confirming that they are, as the situation in Washington, D.C. was characterized, "in deep and probably worsening trouble." The District of Columbia schools report, noting that the same findings would undoubtedly obtain in most large-city systems, observed:

> Applying the usual criteria of scholastic achievement as measured by holding power of the school, by college-going and further education, by post secondary school employment status, by performance on Armed Forced induction tests, the District schools do not measure up well. Like most school systems, the District has no measures on the extent to which schools are helping students attain other educational objectives, for there are no data on self-concepts, ego-development, values, attitudes, aspirations, citizenship and other 'nonacademic' but important aspects of personal growth. However, the inability of large numbers of children to reverse the spiral of futility and break out of the poverty-stricken ghettos suggests that the schools are no more successful in attaining these goals than they are in the more traditional objectives.[6]

The HEW Urban Education Task Force cited as indicators of the challenge facing urban schools such facts as student unrest on secondary school and college campuses, groups seeking community control of neighborhood schools, teacher strikes, voter rejection of bond issues, court suits, lack of priority for education evidenced by state and local governments, and a sharp increase in alternative plans for schooling. Most important, however, is the conviction of large numbers of minority ethnic and racial groups that "they have been short-changed by their fellow American citizens—the white majority—who largely control the social, economic, political and educational institutions of our nation."[7]

After presenting "evidence which indicates the enormity of the failure of the urban public schools to educate the poor in the past and the present," Pressman argued that those concerned with educating the urban poor "cannot realistically rely on the public schools to do more than a disappointingly small fraction of the job at hand."[8] And gloomy observers, such as Kozol, warned: "An ominous cloud hangs over the major cities of America: It is the danger that our ghetto schools, having long ceased to educate children entrusted to their care, will shortly cease to function altogether."[9]

The Kerner Commission pointed to the failure of the ghetto schools to provide the kind and quality of education that would help overcome the effects of discrimination and deprivation as one of the festering sources of resentment and grievance in Black communities, contributing to increasing conflict and disruption. Moreover, the "bleak record of public education for ghetto children is growing worse. In the critical skills—verbal and reading ability—Negro students fall farther behind whites with each year of school completed."[10]

Assessing the nation's response to the Kerner Commission Report one year later, the staffs of Urban America and the Urban Coalition concluded that "the indictment of failure passed on education in the slums and ghettos is just as valid and even more familiar."[11] However, the staffs felt that the ferment begun by the so-called Coleman report[12] and the Commission on Civil Rights study[13] and accelerated by the Kerner Commission report had "increased to the point where it is rocking—in some instances, even toppling—the educational establishment."

The massive Coleman report, 737 pages plus a 548-page supplemental appendix, represented the U.S. Commissioner of Education's compliance with the Civil Rights Act of 1964 provision for a survey on the "lack of availability of equal educational opportunities for individuals by reason of race, color, religion, or national origin in public educational institutions at all levels."[14] The report yielded a rather bleak picture of widespread segregation of both students and staffs, of scholastic attainment of Black students substantially below that of white students, and with achievement disparities becoming progressively greater with each year of schooling.

The "companion report" by the U.S. Commission on Civil Rights, involved some further analyses of Coleman's data, some special studies for the Commission, and assessments of the effectiveness of a number of compensatory education programs in large cities. The Commission reported that in the metropolitan areas where two-thirds of the Black and white populations now live, school segregation was even more severe than for the nation as a whole: "In 15 large metropolitan areas in 1960, 79 percent of the nonwhite public school enrollment was in central city schools, while 68 percent of the white enrollment was suburban."[15]

The Commission on Civil Rights rejected "number of years of schooling" as a meaningful measure of educational attainment. Coleman's data on verbal ability and reading achievement indicated that "by the time twelfth grade is reached, the average white student performs at or slightly below the twelfth-grade level, but the average Negro student performs below the 9th-grade level. Thus years of school completed has an entirely different meaning for Negroes and whites."[16] Moreover, while acknowledging that the 1950s had brought some economic progress to the Black population in absolute terms (i.e., higher income levels, greater college-going rate, increased entrance to the professions, and more skilled jobs) the relative change with respect either to whites or to more affluent Blacks was small. Most Blacks, the Commission concluded, are still have-not Americans: "The closer the promise of equality seems to come, the further it slips away. In every American city today, most Negroes inhabit a world largely isolated from the affluence and mobility of mainstream America."[17] With some exception for the Oriental population, much the same picture could be detailed for other minority groups—the Puerto Ricans, the Mexican-Americans, the American Indinas—and all poor groups, including whites. Socioeconomic differences in scholastic performance have been consnstently significant. In 1968, it was estimated that twice as many whites were below the poverty level as nonwhites—17.4 million as compared to 8.0 million.[18] Income level alone does not take into account discriminatory practices. Consequently, "poverty" takes on different meanings for different populations; to be poor and a member of a nonwhite group can have different consequences from being poor and white.

Schools and the educational delivery systems are part and parcel of the urban crisis—both a consequence and a contributing factor. The HEW Urban Education Task Force pointed out that the problems facing urban schools are not entirely new and have actually existed for a considerable period of time. What is different now is the surfacing nationally of these problems and the recognition of their complexities and severity, including "the steadily dwindling financial resources; the persistence of racism; the rising expectations of impoverished urban residents; and the interrelatedness of *all* the problems to poverty."[19]

QUALITY AND EQUALITY

The increasingly active and militant demands for schools to upgrade the achievement levels of inner-city pupils and prepare them more adequately for life in an urban technical society has been expressed in the calls for "quality education" and "equality of educational opportunities." Neither phrase has been clearly defined but discussions have served a useful function in highlighting existing ambiguities and resulting conflicts in educational practice. *Quality education* is defined by some groups as "the kind of education provided the white middle-class suburban child" and measured by standardized tests of achievement and admissions gained to colleges and universities. Others see such a goal as too limited and describe quality in terms of "maximization of human potential," maintaining that the kind of education presently provided even the majority child is totally inadequate and inappropriate.

Conceptions of the meaning of *equality of educational opportunity* are equally varied, ranging from equality with respect to various school and community inputs to equal educational outcomes. The mandate to assess "the lack of equality of educational opportunity" among racial and other minority groups required that Coleman and his staff define equality and inequality. He has observed:

> The original concept could be examined by determining the degree to which all children in a locality had access to the same schools and the same curriculum, free of charge. The existence of diverse secondary curricula appropriate to different futures could be assessed relatively easily. But the very assignment of a child to a specific curriculum implies acceptance of the concept of equality which takes futures as given. And the introduction of the new interpretations, equality as measured by results of schooling and equality defined by racial integration, confounded the issue even further.[20]

In a memorandum to his staff, which determined the design of the survey, Coleman set forth five "types of inequality" defined in terms of: (1) differences in *community inputs* to the school (e.g., per-pupil expenditures, facilities, teacher quality); (2) *racial compositon* of the school on the basis of the 1954 Supreme Court decision that segregated schooling was inherently inferior; (3) differences in *various intangible characteristics* of the school and the other factors related to community inputs to the school (e.g., teachers' expectations, level of student interest in learning, teacher morale); (4) educational outcomes for students with equal backgrounds and abilities (i.e., equal results given similar inputs); and (5) educational consequences for individuals with unequal backgrounds and abilities (i.e., equal results given different individual inputs). The Coleman study focused primarily on the fourth definition on the basis that the findings might best be translated into policies that could inprove the effects of schooling—that is, the determination of those elements that are effective for learning.[21]

Among the controversial findings from his survey was one stressing the significance of the social context in determining achievement in contrast to school services and resources. The survey reported that differences in majority Black and majority white school characteristics that had been considered significant—e.g., per-pupil expenditures, physical facilities, teacher preparation expressed as years of training—were not nearly as large as had been expected.

In fact, regional differences were much greater than majority-minority differences. Because the school service variables explained only a small part of the pupil performance variances, Coleman concluded:

> Taking all these results together, one implication stands above all: That schools bring little influence to bear upon a child's achievement that is independent of his background and general social context; and that this very lack of independent effect means that the inequalities imposed on

children by their home, neighborhood, and peer environment are carried along to become the inequalities with which they confront adult life at the end of school. For equality of educational opportunity through the schools must imply a strong effect of schools that is independent of the child's immediate social environment, and that strong independent effect is not present in American schools.[22]

The Coleman study did find differences among ethnic groups in their apparent sensitivity to the effect of some school factors such as the quality of teachers and the availability of enriched programs. Generally, school factors appeared to be strongest for Black schools in the South. In addition, a pupil attitude factor that appeared to have a particularly strong relationship to achievement—stronger than all "school" factors—was the extent to which the individual pupil felt he had some control over his own destiny. While minority pupils tended to have far less conviction than whites that they could affect their own environments and futures, when they did have such a belief, their achievement was higher than that of whites who lacked it. Furthermore, for Black students, the environmental control variable appeared to be related to the proportion of whites in the school—the Blacks in schools with a higher proportion of whites had a greater sense of control. What the origins are of strong feelings of fate and environmental control is quite unclear, whether the conviction is a cause or consequence and how the school influences it.

The Coleman report raised many questions for policy-makers and program-planners. For example, Guthrie has pointed out that since the publication of the Coleman report,

> the belief has become increasingly pervasive that patterns of academic performance are immutably molded by social and economic conditions outside the school. If incorrect, and if allowed to persist unexamined and unchallenged, this belief could have wildly disabling consequences. It is not at all difficult to foresee how it could become self-fulfilling; administrators and teachers believing that their school and schoolroom actions make no difference might begin to behave accordingly. Conversely, if the assertion is correct but allowed to pass unheeded, the prospect of pouring even more billions of local, State, and Federal dollars down an ineffective rathole labeled 'schools' is equally unsettling.[23]

A reanalysis of the Coleman data by the Office of Education has tempered somewhat the flat assertion in the original report, suggesting that the influence of the school on achievement cannot be separated from that of the student's social background and vice versa: "In conclusion, it may be stated that the overwhelming impression received from these data is that the schools are indeed important. It is equally clear, however, that their influence is bound up with that of the student's social background."[24] On the basis of a review of 19 studies, Guthrie reported that he was "impressed with the amount and consistency of evidence supporting the effectiveness of school services in influencing the academic performance of pupils."[25] While expressing the hope that the time would come when it would be possible to determine which school service components have greatest impact and in what proportion, he concluded, "there can be little doubt that schools do make a difference."

The U.S. Commission on Civil Rights interprets the Coleman findings as supporting school desegregation—both racial and socioeconomic—since there is a strong relationship between the family economic and educational background of the child and his achievement and attitudes: "Regardless of his own family background, an individual student achieves better in schools where most of his fellow students are from advantaged backgrounds than in schools where most of his fellow students are from disadvantaged backgrounds."[26] However, some analysts accept the Coleman findings on the extent of segregation and academic retardation while questioning the causal relationships between segregation and retardation.

The then U.S. Commissioner of Education James E. Allen viewed "opportunities for learning" as encompassing much more than school buildings and specially trained qualified teachers:

'Opportunity for learning' means, to me, a community where fathers are employed and where children can learn through their fathers about the dignity of man. It means a community where the population of rats does not exceed the population of children, and where children can learn the values of a healthy society. It means a community of clean streets, of playgrounds, of uncrowded homes, where children can learn the value of living in a free country and the importance of keeping it free. And finally, it means a community free of fear, where children can learn to love life and their fellow man.[27]

The policy implications of the Coleman and Commission on Civil Rights reports point to the interaction of family, neighborhood, and school on the academic and affective growth of children and the need to improve these environments. But, the questions concerning equality and inequality in educational process inputs and outcomes are now being more intelligently examined.

RESEARCH AND DEVELOPMENT

Poor scholastic performance of disadvantaged populations has been so amply documented that few challenge the accuracy of such reports. The past decade has witnessed an outpouring of research and experimentation and the initiation of a vast array of programs and projects. Most of this research, Gordon notes, can be divided into two broad classifications—one encompassing studies of the performance characteristics of disadvantaged groups and the other containing descriptions and superficial assessments of programs presumably designed to provide for the disadvantaged. Much of the research tends to focus on "deficits" or "differences" of disadvantaged from more advantaged populations with such deviations "used to account for the observed dysfunctions in educational performance among members" of the former group.[28]

There is a rich and growing body of literature on cognitive and affective development differences among various racial, ethnic, and socioeconomic groups; on family structure, life styles, and childrearing patterns as these affect educational processes; on language development and linguistic differences; and on other behavioral characteristics of individuals and groups. While many studies focus on social and cultural factors affecting educational achievement, there is increasing attention to the health of the disadvantaged child as a contributing factor to scholastic failure. Reviewing a variety of studies, Birch concluded that "a serious consideration of available health information leaves little doubt that children who are economically and socially disadvantaged and in an ethnic group exposed to discrimination, are exposed to massively excessive risks for maldevelopment."[29] Social class and the socialization processes have been widely studied with respect to behavioral correlates, especially of young children.[30] A variety of studies have focused on the effects of segregation and the consequences of desegregation on minority group performance.[31] Research has also shed some light on the effects of organizational and grouping practices, teacher expectations, curricular options, instructional materials, and neighborhood setting, and similar factors on achievement of disadvantaged students.

Some research and experimentation have stimulated new treatment programs and intervention strategies—e.g., the mushrooming of preschool and early childhood programs—but the relation of program to theory and research has been somewhat tenuous. Gordon has observed that,

> treatments tended to emerge from special biases or dominant models in the field, with either the fact of intervention or the magnitude of interventions receiving more attention than the specific nature or quality of interventions. This tendency may account for the fact that much of the research referable to treatment and programs is characterized by superficial description of program or practice and general evaluation of impact.[32]

Most program proposals, almost by necessity, contain some implicit, if not explicit, indication of the hypotheses or theoretical bases underlying the proposed intervention or treatment. For example, if experiential differentials and deprivations in infancy are perceived as accounting for minority group youngsters entering classrooms ill-prepared to cope with the demands of the school, then early childhood programs should be designed to compensate for such deficiencies. If language development impedes transition from concrete to abstract modes of thought, then programs should provide appropriate linguistic experiences that will nurture such growth. If childrearing patterns and maternal teaching styles affect cognitive growth, then parent education programs should develop different skills and behaviors. But even research that does provide the kinds of analyses that contribute to building theory and understanding behavior often reports equivocal findings that open debate rather than provide guidelines for the practitioner. Consequently, there are several "theories" or explanations or models set forth to explain inferior scholastic attainment and intellectual functioning of poor children—none of which is completely satisfying. Nor is it likely that a theory will emerge although hopefully theoretical models will provide better guidance for program planners and decision-makers. However, the cafeteria-eclectic approach that presently prevails leaves much to be desired.

Some of the ambiguities for the program-planner and practitioner are illustrated by an analysis of early childhood research by the Baratzes. In a review of "the interventionist literature with particular emphasis on the role of social pathology in interpreting the behavior of the ghetto mother," Baratz and Baratz conclude that much of the research represents "the predominant ethnocentric view of the Negro community by social science [which] produces a distorted image of the life patterns of that community."[33] They contend that intervention programs that aim at changing the child's home environment, altering the childrearing patterns of Black families, and improving his language and cognitive skills "are, at best, unrealistic in terms of current linguistic and anthropological data and, at worst, ethnocentric and racist." The Baratzes reject interpretations of research that support either the social pathology or genetic inferiority models and set forth instead a cultural difference model based on the assumption "that the behavior of Negroes is not pathological but can be explained within a coherent, distinct, American Negro culture which represents a synthesis of African culture in contact with American European culture from the time of slavery to the present day."[34] Thus, they argue that intervention programs are needed but that these should deal with the materials and processes of the school rather than with the children being served in such programs. They also point out that interpretations of research are often subject to the sociopolitical convictions of the person doing the research.

Gordon has observed that "in contrast to the rather well-designed and detailed research into the characteristics of disadvantaged groups, the description and evaluation of educational programs and practices for these children have generally been superficial."[35] He suggests that such research can be grouped into four categories: (1) studies of large-scale projects such as Head Start, Elementary and Secondary Education Act (ESEA) Title I, and Upward Bound; (2) studies of specific projects and services in schools such as curricular innovations, remedial reading programs, and tutoring groups; (3) studies of administrative and organizational changes such as desegregation, flexible grouping, pupil-teacher ratios; and (4) studies of attitudinal and skill changes in school personnel, focusing on teacher expectations and role models.[36]

Evaluation of various kinds of programs, from preschool through college, compensatory and remedial, have not indicated uniform or considerable "success." On the basis of its comprehensive review of compensatory programs, the U.S. Commission on Civil Rights concluded that such efforts had not produced lasting effects in improving student achievement probably "because they have attempted to solve problems that stem, in large part, from racial and social class isolation in schools which themselves are isolated by race and social class."[37]

A study of Title I ESEA programs at the end of the second year in 39 cities indicated that concentrated remedial help could raise the level of pupil achievement but that such programs were extremely costly in terms of teachers, space, specialists, and materials—resources that tend to be particularly scarce in the central cities. However, the costs per student were often almost prohibitive.[38] The Fourth Annual Report of the National Advisory Council on the Education of Disadvantaged Children observed:

It has long been clear that the mere addition of people, equipment, and special services does not by itself constitute compensatory education; success in making up for the educational deprivation which stems from poverty requires a strategy for blending these resources in an integrated program that strikes at both roots and consequences of disadvantage. The details of this strategy, however, have by no means been clear.[39]

Despite the fact that all Title I ESEA proposals require an evaluation component, in the view of the Advisory Council, the combination of insufficient experience with compensatory programs and the wide variation in the kind and quality of evaluative data collected has prevented any overall nationwide evaluation of such efforts and made it difficult to identify elements that contribute to any successes. The Advisory Council observes, rather ambiguously: "What is clear is that among the thousands of different programs and approaches labeled as compensatory education, some efforts are paying off and others are not."[40] The Council's report includes details concerning 21 programs (screened from 1,000 of the more than 20,000 ESEA programs) that the American Institute for Research found to have produced significant achievement gains in language and numerical skills. The successful programs were compared by AIR with unsuccessful ones to ascertain what distinguished the two. AIR identified two requirements: establish clear goals and specific academic objectives, and concentrate attention and resources on these objectives.

A different kind of assessment of Title I ESEA was prepared by the Washington Research Project and the NAACP, two organizations whose concern is with the rights of the poor. Their report focused on how Title I is administered and the money spent and the consequences for poor children. They did not attempt to study the educational value or impact of specific programs of compensatory education. The review found that in school systems across the country, Title I:

"—has not reached eligible children in many instances;

—has not been concentrated on those most in need so that there is reasonable promise of success;

—has purchased hardware at the expense of instructional programs;

—has not been used to meet the most serious educational needs of school children; and

—has not been used in a manner that involves parents and communities in carrying out Title I projects."[41]

This review of the administration of Title I funds at the local, state, and federal levels, raised serious questions about whether the pessimistic evaluations of compensatory programs resulted from mismanagement and misapplication of the funds rather than from the nature of the programs themselves. The report reinforced observations made earlier that compensatory education had not failed—rather, it had never really been tried as yet.

Even studies of nationwide programs such as Head Start have been rather restricted in scope or results. The Westinghouse-Ohio University National Evaluation of Head Start reported that: summer programs alone produced neither cognitive nor affective gains that persisted through the early elementary grades; year-round programs had marginal effects on cognitive development that persisted in the early grades but had little influence on affective development; programs appeared to be most effective in mainly Black centers in scattered central cities; Head Start children seem still to be below norms on achievement and psycholinguistic tests but approached norms on readiness tests; and parents approved and participated in Head Start activities.[42]

The Westinghouse-Ohio University evaluation was not the first of Head Start but the timing and the nature of the release of the findings resulted in a widespread impression that such programs were of very limited value and such efforts were generally futile. Smith and Bissell[43] reanalyzed some of the data and indicated that findings were far more positive. However, the Westinghouse-Ohio University researchers rejected most of the reanalysis and defended their own procedures and findings.[44]

Evaluative and research studies of such nationwide projects as Upward Bound (to help underachieving low-income students prepare for higher education) and the Neighborhood Youth Corps (to prevent and assist high school dropouts) have provided insights into the nature of the populations served as well as some of the consequences of the program activities.[45]

In general, project evaluations consist of pre- and post-treatment testing, usually of reading, mathematics, and general intelligence. Few efforts have been made to assess affective growth. Few compensatory projects have been designed with sufficient sophistication to provide insights as to what aspects of the treatment or program produced a change, if any. The vast majority of evaluation efforts have simply attempted to determine whether there has been an "improvement" in basic skills and intellectual ability after a period of time. Most school-based projects are primarily interested in program development—providing what it is hoped will be more appropriate experiences—and not in research to determine what inputs account for change. The fact that it is in the area of preschool and early childhood education that the best designed research is taking place may be the result, in part, of such programs functioning outside the ongoing school framework and the feasibility of controlled experimentation.

Discussing the complexities in assessing compensatory education, McDill, McDill, and Sprehe point to three general problems: (1) difficulties in determining program effectiveness because the critical variables are either unknown or cannot be measured adequately—for example, are changes the result of treatment or maturational effects or both and to what extent; (2) difficulties in separating the effects of interaction of various socializing agencies, since learning takes place in a variety of settings in and out of the school; and (3) technical difficulties resulting from the shortage of rigorous measuring instruments even when the criterion and predictor variables are known. Along with these general problems, compensatory program evaluators face recurring problems such as: pressures for immediate as opposed to long-term, carefully planned evaluation; vagueness of criteria and the setting of objectives that are politically sound but operationally impossible; altering treatment before adequate evaluation; scarcity of such resources as money and skills that mitigate against replicability; and difficulties in initiating and maintaining treatment and nontreatment populations.[46] Underlying all of these is the fact that "in compensatory programs, we are still trying to diagnose the problems and their causes while simultaneously applying remedies. The society insists that we be receptive to the possibility of finding a workable solution even before we understand the mechanism by which the solution works."[47]

STRATEGIES AND MODELS
FOR URBAN PROGRAMS

A continuum of six basic strategies for reforming urban schools has been set forth by Fantini and Young: (1) *compensatory education*— attempts to overcome shortcomings in learners and to raise their achievement levels; (2) *desegregation*—designed to improve educational achievement and human relationships through a better racial and socio-economic mix; (3) *model subsystems*—development of experimental units to improve staff-training, curriculum, methodologies, and school-community relations and have such units serve as demonstration and dissemination bases for the rest of the system; (4) *parallel systems*— establishment of private schools, often operated by nonprofit companies, which presumably would be free of public school bureaucracies and be more responsive to ghetto educational needs; (5) *total system reform*— aimed at providing new leadership and structural changes and increasing efficiency of the existing system; and (6) *new systems development*—

conceptualization of an educational system for a new community or a newly designated area autonomous from the rest of the system.[48]

A somewhat different analysis of alternative models for transforming the institutional structure of inner-city schools has been set forth by Janowitz: (1) the *mental health model* assumes that slum family resources are so limited and the values so different from those of the school that the school itself must intervene to insure that the needs and services required by each child are made available, becoming responsible for the total social space of the child even if this means becoming a residential institution; (2) the *early education model* assumes that if the school is unable to become a residential institution then it can intervene during the critical years of infancy and early childhood; (3) the *specialization model* involves the introduction on a piecemeal basis of new techniques, programs, specialists, administrative procedures—each of which may appear valid—so that the teaching process is broken up into more and more specialized roles performed by specialists and resource personnel; and (4) the *aggregation model* stresses the need for maintaining and strengthening the teacher's role as central manager of a classroom that is essentially a social system and involving other personnel and resources as needed.[49] Each of these models has different implications for such aspects as "classroom management; the use of the new media; teacher education and career lines; authority and decentralization; pupil composition; school-community relations."[50]

Miller and Roby believe that the various strategies for improving educational performance of poor and minority group children can be subsumed into four categories: (1) *changing the student and his family*—aiming at " 'compensatory socialization' in which the deficiencies of the educational environment provided by low-income family life would be made up later"; (2) *changing the school*—aiming at bringing about changes in the teachers, administrators, curriculum, materials, services, etc., rather than focusing on the deficiencies of the learners; (3) *increasing resources and changing their distribution*—increasing the level of funding and also altering the integration; (4) *changing control of the schools*—decentralizing administrative arrangements for schools and providing for greater community control and involvement in decision making. Miller and Roby contend that our limited understandings of how to bring about changes at the micro-level of education (teaching of reading or teachers' attitudes, for example) result in efforts at alteration at the macro-level: "Hopefully, when we have accomplished change at the macro-level—change in the organizational context, changes across urban-suburban lines in student composition, changes in the distribution of educational and economic resources, and the development of alternatives to education for economic self-improvement—we will be able to function at the micro-level."[51] However, it can be argued that many programs are simply projects at a micro-level with no basic conceptual model involved.

A U.S. Office of Education publication titled *Profiles in Quality Education,* typical of program description literature, contains information on "150 outstanding Title I projects . . . designated by State Title I Coordinators as worth emulating." No data are provided to support the introductory statement that each of these programs "provides valuable assistance to the low-income children it serves."[52] The projects cover a wide variety of foci and include examples of "work-study programs, health services, remedial programs, English as a second language activities, college preparatory classes, teacher training . . . programs that concentrate on early childhood education, the dropout, the vocational student."[53] The various projects encompass all aspects of the educational process, most restricted to some facet of the problem and only a few designed to be comprehensive and inclusive.

Most such programs, particularly those at the secondary school level, are aimed at upgrading academic achievement in standard subjects. A comprehensive study of student objectives of compensatory programs for adolescents by Harrison involved gleaning stated or implied goals from 432 documents. Harrison identified 689 distinct, operational objectives that could be cataloged by behavior (cognitive or affective) and by referent (specific school subject, general academic achievement, social development or career development) and found that primary emphasis (75% of all objectives) was on academic achievement with little or no concern for social or career development. This stress on academic achievement at the expense of the development of other behaviors was essentially the same emphasis for the more advantaged youth and represented a rigidity in school structure, requiring "all students to adapt to the system of expectations, rather than changing the system and its expectations to adapt to the contemporaneous need of the students."[54]

To reverse present trends and to move toward the provision of full equality of educational opportunity, the Kerner Commission recommended the pursuit of four "basic strategies," and provided suggested programs for each:

Increasing efforts to eliminate de facto segregation—increased financial aid to school systems seeking to eliminate segregation within the system itself or in cooperation with neighborhood systems; establishment of major educational magnet schools to draw racially and socioeconomically mixed populations and provide special curricula and specialized educational programs; establishment of supplemental education centers to provide racially integrated educational experiences for white and Black students.

Improving the quality of teaching in ghetto schools—year-round education for disadvantaged students; establishment of early childhood programs designed to overcome effects of disadvantaged environment, involving parents and the home as well as the child; provision of extra incentives for highly qualified teachers in ghetto schools; reduction in maximum class size; curricular recognition of the history, culture and contribution of minority groups; individualized instruction; intensive concentration on basic verbal skills; and development of new patterns of education for students who do not fit into traditional forms.

Improving community-school relations—elimination of obstacles to community participation in the educational process; opening schools for a variety of community service functions; use of local residents as teacher aides and tutors; increasing the accountability of schools to the community.

Expanding opportunities for higher and vocational education—expansion of Upward Bound Program; removal of financial barriers to higher education; emphasis on part-time cooperative education and work-study programs through use of release time; elimination of barriers to full participation in vocational education programs; increased training to meet the critical need for more workers in professional, semiprofessional and technical fields.[55]

The Kerner Commission suggests no priorities for these four "strategies." It could well be that education in the ghetto is in such a state that any of the suggested programs has some potential payoff. In fact, examples of each of these suggested "strategies" can already be found in operation in many urban school systems. In a critique of functioning compensatory programs, Gordon and Wilkerson observed:

For all their variety of means, the programs have generally suffered from one fundamental difficulty—they are based on sentiment rather than fact. . . . The great majority of the programs are simply an attempt to 'do something' about these problems. Their stated aims are usually couched in unarguable generalities. . . . The urge to do something has been so compelling that many of the programs have been designed without grounding in any systematic study of ways and means.[56]

What is needed, Gordon and Wilkerson argue, is not a filling in of gaps so that disadvantaged children can be reached by existing practices, but rather an inquiry of a different kind: "What kind of educational experience is most appropriate to what these children need and to what our society is becoming?"[57]

The many urban education programs and projects can be characterized and cataloged in a variety of ways: by *target population* (e.g., preschool, elementary, higher education, adult, teacher); by *nature of treatment* (e.g., therapeutic, compensatory, remedial, enrichment); by *nature of services* (e.g., instructional, counseling, community development, health); by *locus of activities* (i.e., in school, family, community, industry, nonschool agency); by *basic intent of strategy* (e.g., reform of system, changing child or family, integration, reallocation of resources); by *focus of diagnosis and prescriptive activities* (e.g., learners, professionals, the educational system, society); and by *source of funding* (e.g., Office of Education, Office of Economic Opportunity, state, local, governmental agency, foundation, industry). These catalog sets are not mutually exclusive, of course. Some efforts are limited and restricted (e.g., a Head Start class for 12 four-year-olds), while others are more global and comprehensive (e.g., an "open" high school or a model subsystem). Most school programs tend to be additive rather than designed for fundamental reform. Some proposals deal with personnel changes, some with organizational changes, and others with affecting the relationships and interactions among various components of the educational enterprise.

Any listing of urban education projects would be quite lengthy, as indicated by the publications issued by the U.S. Office of Education and the ERIC Information Retrieval Center on the Disadvantaged at Teachers College, Columbia University. The general patterns of strategies and programs that follow simply provide an overview of the range and diversity of activities attacking some aspect of the urban education problem.

1. *Infant education and intervention in family life*—various efforts aimed at changing childrearing relationships between parent (usually the mother) and the infant, often involving the mother as a direct teacher.

2. *Early childhood education*—preschool programs ranging from traditional nursery and kindergarten practices through highly structured, academic oriented programs designed to develop specific skills for learning; largest number of such programs included in Head Start.

3. *Reading, language, and basic skills development*—new curricula, methodologies, materials, personnel deployment, and "systems" designed to improve the reading and basic skills performance of disadvantaged children.

4. *Bilingual education*—programs designed for pupils whose mother tongue is other than English or whose dialect and speech are so divergent as to be considered nonstandard; instruction in the mother tongue and teaching of English as a second language.

5. *Curriculum relevance*—modifications of existing courses and introduction of new courses that have a more direct relationship "to the world the student knows outside school or to the roles he plays now or will later play in his adult life";[58] addition of programs dealing with racial and ethnic minority group experiences and heritage; introduction of courses dealing with significant current social, political, economic, and personal problems.

6. *Compensatory and remedial programs*—programs aimed at presumed or real deficiencies in disadvantaged learners; remedial activities designed to overcome poor performance in basic areas; cultural enrichment programs aimed at broadening horizons of inner-city pupils.

7. *Guidance and counseling*—guidance, psychological, and therapeutic services adapted to the needs of disadvantaged pupils and their parents; addition of social workers and community agents to bridge gap between school and family.

8. *Tutoring programs*—individual and small-group tutoring by professionals, paraprofessionals, and volunteers, adults and youth, based in school or nonschool agency or institution.

9. *Testing, measurement, and evaluation*—efforts made to develop more effective diagnostic and evaluative procedures that serve instructional rather than selective functions; reappraisal of grouping and tracking procedures; development of more appropriate grading procedures; sensi-

tization of staff members to the consequences of expectations from grading and testing procedures.

10. *School organization*—extended school days, extended school years, year-round schools, team teaching, ungraded programs, open classrooms, modular scheduling, flexible grouping to replace rigid tracking systems.

11. *Instructional materials and resources*—production of new multi-media instructional resources aimed at central-city students; increase in the availability of multiracial, multiethnic, multisocial-class, multilevel, urban-oriented materials; development of resources dealing with the racial and ethnic experience in America.

12. *Vocational education, dropout prevention, and return programs*—compensatory and remedial programs, additional counseling and guidance, addition of social and community workers, vocational preparation in and out of school, work experience, work-study programs, and revised vocational-technical programs specifically designed for the 16- to-21-year-old group.

13. *Urban school staffing*—programs aimed at recruitment, training, induction, retention, and continuing education of all professional personnel at pre- and in-service levels; development of new relationships and programs between colleges and school systems, between industries and schools; attention to attitudes and expectations; new staffing patterns; addition of various kinds of "specialists" in schools.

14. *Auxiliary school personnel*—programs aimed at recruiting, training, and involving paraprofessionals, volunteers, and aides in a variety of educational and supportive services; building of new careers and career ladders in the realm of public service; involvement of parents and volunteers in teaching programs.

15. *Post-secondary and higher education*—high school programs aimed at motivating and preparing disadvantaged youth for college; development of new selection and admissions procedures; provision of services to smooth transition from school to college and increase success chances; modification of college curriculum to increase relevance for minority groups; expanding opportunities for higher education through new institutions.

16. *Community school and community development*—development of schools as educational, neighborhood and community services, and community development centers; programs involving joint school and community agencies in attacking urban problems.

17. *Desegregation and integration*—programs designed to correct racial and ethnic imbalance, de jure and de facto, and to provide for a more integrated, pluralistic school society; counter-drive for separatism and for local control of schools, sometimes as an end and sometimes as an interim step toward pluralism.

18. *Decentralization and community control*—programs designed to bring decision making closer to the community and redistribute power and control; efforts to establish accountability for effectiveness of teaching and schools.

19. *Alternative schools and school systems*—proposals for establishing

competitive systems, private and public; provisions for "education by voucher"; establishment of alternative schools within public and nonpublic sectors; initiation of performance contracts with nonpublic school companies and agencies.

20. *Federally supported or assisted programs*—programs authorized by federal legislation, such as ESEA (particularly Titles I and III) and programs such as Job Corps, Neighborhood Youth Corps, Upward Bound, National Teacher Corps, Head Start, Manpower Development and Training Programs; various programs of categorical aid and assistance with desegregation.

21. *Allocation of educational resources*—efforts through court litigation and pressures for new legislation to correct intrastate and intradistrict inequalities in allocation of educational resources; substantial additional funding for some ghetto schools (e.g., More Effective Schools program).

IN THE DECADE AHEAD

Almost every aspect of the educational process is being modified and adapted through projects, programs, and "innovations," each aimed at improving the quality of urban education and opening educational opportunities. Most of these efforts represent changes intended to increase the effectiveness in attaining the traditional educational objectives of public schools—at a minimum, the attainment of basic literacy. Few projects aim at fundamental reappraisal of urban education, propose major reforms, or suggest new goals or delivery systems. Some programs could result in significant reform but, generally, schools have been responsive to immediate crises, to the availability of funds, or to pressure from groups.

The Washington, D.C. schools represent a prototype for what America's central-city schools have become. Since 1947, the District of Columbia schools pupil population has changed from 46 percent Black to more than 93 percent Black. Scholastic achievement on standardized tests has fallen below national means. A 1965 bulletin entitled *Innovation in Instruction* listed almost 100 separate programs and projects each aimed at improving instruction. As funds became available through ESEA and other legislation in 1965, the number of programs and projects increased further. Since 1967, the District Board of Education has been presented with four documents, each containing recommendations, proposals, and plans for changing the school system or a part thereof. The so-called Passow report (*Toward Creating a Model Urban School System*) resulted from a comprehensive study of all aspects of education and schooling in the District and contained scores of recommendations regarding the total school system and its functioning in the community.[59] The Anacostia Community School Project proposal emerged from a month-long summer workshop and consisted of 25 programs ranging from total community participation to updating equipment in the ten schools in the area, which contains about half of Washington's public housing.[60] The Fort Lincoln New Town proposal represented a case study in the development of an educational program for a new town to be built on a 335-acre site in northeast Washington.[61] The so-called Clark report (*A Possible Reality*) proposed focusing on the improvement of reading achievement, calling for a Reading Mobilization Year, assigning a Reading Mobilization Team in each school, and providing differentiated staffing and salaries based on teacher accountability.[62] These four reports represent a range of proposals for confronting the educational crisis in the schools of the nation's capital.

The HEW Urban Education Task Force urged "that the problem of urban areas should be considered as the major priority of the Administration's domestic program in the 1970s. Within this priority, education—broadly conceived and with new constituencies involved—should become a first consideration."[63] Recognizing a need for long-term comprehensive planning, the Task Force concluded that the urgency of the situation required proposals for immediate action as well. The report called for:

1. Money—significantly increased levels of funding far exceeding current appropriations and authorizations.
2. Concept of urban education—expansion of the concept of the educative process to deal with the whole individual, "his health, his emotional well-being, his intellectual capacities, his future employment, his self-realization. . . ."
3. Master plan for urban education—development and implementation of master plans for education, each tailored to particular urban areas, dealing with causes and symptoms "within a framework of overall urban problem solving rather than education per se. . . ."
4. Institutional changes—deliberate sequencing of plans and steps leading to institutional changes, fundamental changes within the system itself.
5. Community determination—active participation in decision making by community residents and students, including priorities for using funds, designing curriculum and program components, and employing and evaluating personnel.
6. Performance standards—clear statements of specific knowledges, attitudes, and skills that students are expected to demonstrate and that can serve for personnel and school accountability.
7. Assessment—continuous assessment of all aspects of the educational program with regular feedback enabling immediate adjustments and modifications.
8. Racial and ethnic integration—integration should be a major element for all planning; separatism, local control, and a demand for a recognized identity are viewed not as antithetical to integration but rather as alternative channels to the ultimate aim of integration.[64]

The major recommendation of the Urban Education Task Force was for development of an Urban Education Act "designed to fund the planning, development, and implementation of a comprehensive master plan to meet the specific, long-range broadly conceived educational needs of inner-city areas."[65] If enacted, such legislation would simply set in motion preparation of guidelines and criteria for potential grantees to develop such local master plans. No model master plan for urban education is provided but rather the report calls attention to the need for comprehensive consideration of education in the urban setting instead of the present fragmented, piecemeal, project approach that presently exists.

What the crisis in urban education has done is to stimulate total rethinking about the educative process—the goals, the means, the resources, the strategies, the relationships. The "tinkering approach" having proved less than adequate, we may now be ready for more comprehensive reforms based on research and theory. We have already been reminded that education is taking place in many places other than the classroom and that much learning consists of behavior about which the school has given little consideration. As one looks at the dilemmas the nation faces, one must ask to what extent adequate and appropriate education is being provided any group or set of individuals, advantaged or disadvantaged, majority or minority. Reform in education, in the same way as reform in society of which schools are a part, does not come easily for there are constant struggles for power and prerogatives among individuals, groups, and agencies.

A master plan for urban education will necessarily deal with urban schooling in the broadest sense, with many components of the educative process at many different levels. These are not, nor can there be, panaceas in urban education; no single programs or practices will resolve the problems of urban systems. Poverty, discrimination, racism, and other problems of our society have deep roots. Full and equal employment opportunities, sound housing, political power, safety and security, adequate health and sanitation, cultural satisfactions are part and parcel of the solution to urban educational problems just as they are, in part, a consequence of good education. The school represents one element in the educative process in the community. It cannot remain isolated from the other elements nor can it do the educative job alone. In some instances, the school may be the catalyst for other agencies to plan jointly their educative efforts; in other instances, the school has prime responsibility.

There is no blueprint for urban education in the decade ahead, but a considerable reservoir of experience and research that, when combined with serious intent and fundamental commitment to build a better society for all, can provide the basis for a more effective nurturing of human potential. What is needed now is a reassessment of the total educational process—programs, personnel, facilities, resources, relationships, delivery systems—to ascertain where and how effective learning opportunities can be arranged. The entire community, not the location we now call "school," must become the site for education of future urban populations.

A decade ago, educators were pressed by events to drop their defensive stances and face up to their responsibilities for educating all the members of society. Even then the directions were well marked and the goals quite clear. Comprehensive planning for education rather than fragmented proposals for schooling is needed if public schools are to fulfill their responsibility for helping to build a richer urban society in which all individuals can "do their thing."

NOTES

[1] A. H. Passow, *Education in Depressed Areas* (New York: Teachers College Press, 1963), p. 351.

[2] National Advisory Commission on Civil Disorders (NACCD), Report of the National Advisory Commission on Civil Disorders (New York: Bantam Books, 1968), p. 410.

[3] A. Downs, "Alternative Futures for the American Ghetto," *Daedalus* 97 (1968): 1333.

[4] D. L. Birch, *The Economic Future of City and Suburbs* (New York: Committee for Economic Development, 1970), p. 36.

[5] NAACD, *Report,* p. 399.

[6] A. H. Passow, *Toward Creating a Model Urban School System: A Study of the Washington, D.C. Schools* (New York: Teachers College, Columbia University, 1967), p. 2.

[7] HEW Urban Education Task Force, *Urban School Crisis: The Problem and Solutions* (Washington, D.C.: National School Public Relations Association, 1970), p. 5.

[8] H. Pressman, "The Failure of the Public Schools," *Urban Education* 2 (1966): p. 62.

[9] J. Kozol, "In Roxbury, Way Out of a Fortress," *Think* 36 (1970): 28.

[10] NACCD, *Report,* p. 425.

[11] Urban America and the Urban Coalition, *One Year Later: An Assessment of the Nation's Response to the Crisis Described by the National Advisory Commission on Civil Disorders* (Washington, D.C.: Urban America and the Urban Coalition, 1969), p. 33.

[12] J. S. Coleman et al., *Equality of Educational Opportunity* (Washington, D.C.: Office of Education, 1966).

[13] U.S. Commission on Civil Rights, *Racial Isolation in the Public Schools* (Washington, D.C.: Government Printing Office, 1967).

[14] Coleman et al., *Equality of Educational Opportunity,* p. iii.

[15] U.S. Commission on Civil Rights, *Racial Isolation,* p. 3.

[16] Coleman et al., *Equality of Educational Opportunity,* p. 14.

[17] Ibid, p. 15.

[18] U.S. Bureau of the Census, *Current Population Reports* (Washington, D.C.: The Bureau, 1969).

[19] HEW, *Urban School Crisis,* p. 5.

[20] J. S. Coleman, "The Concept of Equality of Educational Opportunity," in *Equal Educational Opportunity* (Cambridge, Mass.: Harvard University Press, 1969), p. 18.

[21] Ibid., p. 18–19.

[22] Coleman et al., *Equality of Educational Opportunity,* p. 325.

[23] J. W. Guthrie, "A Survey of School Effectiveness," in *Do Teachers Make a Difference?* (Washington, D.C.: Government Printing Office, 1970), p. 25.

[24] U.S. Office of Education, A Study of Our Nation's Schools (Washington, D.C.: Government Printing Office, 1970), p. xiv.

[25] Guthrie, "School Effectiveness Studies," p. 46.

[26] U.S. Commission on Civil Rights, *Racial Isolation,* p. 203.

[27] J. E. Allen, Jr., "Educational Problems of the Handicapped in the Inner City," background paper for the Conference on Problems of Education of Children in the Inner City, President's Committee on Mental Retardation, Washington, D.C., 1969, p. 81.

[28] E. W. Gordon, "Education for Socially Disadvantaged Children: Introduction," *Review of Educational Research* 40 (1970): 1–2.

[29] H. G. Birch, "Health and the Education of Socially Disadvantaged Children," paper presented at Conference on Bio-Social Factors in the Development and Learning of Disadvantaged Children, Syracuse University, 1967, p. 30–31.

[30] E. Zigler, "Social Class and the Socialization Process," *Review of Educational Research* 40 (1970): 87–110.

[31] M. Weinberg, *Desegregation Research: An Appraisal,* rev. ed. (Bloomington, Indiana: Phi Delta Kappa, 1970).

[32] Gordon, "Education for Disadvantaged Children," p. 8.

[33] S. S. Baratz and J. C. Baratz, "Early Childhood Intervention: The Social Science Base of Institutional Racism," *Harvard Educational Review* 40 (1970): 30.

[34] Ibid., p. 45.

[35] E. W. Gordon, *Significant Trends in the Education of the Disadvantaged* (New York: Eric—IRCD, Teachers College, Columbia University, 1970), p. 8.

[36] Ibid., pp. 8–12.

[37] U.S. Commission on Civil Rights, *Racial Isolation,* p. 205.

[38] U.S. Office of Education, Title I/Year II (Washington, D.C.: Government Printing Office, 1968).

[39] National Advisory Council on the Education of Disadvantaged Children, *Title I ESEA—A Review and a Forward Look* (Washington, D.C.: Government Printing Office, 1969), p. 3.

[40] Ibid.

[41] Washington Research Project and NAACP Legal Defense and Educational Fund, *Title I of ESEA: Is it Helping Poor Children?* (Washington, D.C.: Washington Research Project, 1969) pp. i–ii.

[42] N. S. Smith and J. S. Bissell, "Report Analysis: The Impact of Head Start," *Harvard Educational Review* 40 (1970): 51–52.

[43] Ibid.

[44] U. G. Cicirelli, J. W. Evans, and J. S. Schiller, "The Impact of Head Start: A Reply to the Report Analysis," *Harvard Educational Review* 40 (1970): 105–29.

[45] Office of Economic Opportunity, *Findings and Conclusions: An Evaluation of Upward Bound* (Washington, D.C.: Office of Economic Opportunity, 1970), and U.S. Department of Labor, *The Neighborhood Youth Corps: A Review of Research,* Manpower Research Monograph no. 13 (Washington, D.C.: Government Printing Office, 1970).

[46] E. L. McDill, M. S. McDill, and J. T. Sprehe, *Strategies for Success in Compensatory Education* (Baltimore: Johns Hopkins, 1969), pp. 9–13.

[47] Ibid., p. 66.

[48] M. D. Fantini and M. A. Young, *Designing Education for Tomorrow's Cities* (New York: Holt, Rinehart & Winston, 1970), pp. 13–20.

[49] M. Janowitz, *Institution Building in Urban Education* (New York: Russell Sage Foundation, 1969), pp. 35–60.

[50] Ibid., p. 60.

[51] S. M. Miller and P. Roby, "Educational Strategies and the Disadvantaged: An Overview," paper presented at the Seventh Annual Work Conference on Urban Education, Teachers College, Columbia University, June 1969, p. 29.

[52] U.S. Office of Education, *Profiles in Quality Education* (Washington, D.C.: Government Printing Office, 1968), p. iv.

[53] Ibid.

[54] F. I. Harrison, *Objectives and Instruments for Evaluation of Compensatory Education* (Washington, D.C.: Office of Education, Bureau of Research, 1969), p. 13.

[55] NAACD, *Report,* pp. 438–55.

[56] E. W. Gordon and D. A. Wilkerson, *Compensatory Education for the Disadvantaged* (New York: College Entrance Examination Board, 1966), p. 158.

[57] Ibid., p. 159.

[58] Fantini and Young, *Designing Education for Tomorrow's Cities,* p. 50.

[59] Passow, *Creating a Model Urban School System.*

[60] Anacostia Community Planning Council, *The Anacostia Community School Project* (Washington, D.C.: The Council 1968).

[61] Fantini and Young, *Designing Education for Tomorrow's Cities.*

[62] K. B. Clark et al., *A Possible Reality* (New York: Metropolitan Applied Research Center, 1970).

[63] HEW, *School Crisis,* p. 6.

[64] Ibid., pp. 6–7.

[65] Ibid., p. 44.

REFERENCES

Bowman, G. W., & Klopf, G. J. Auxiliary Personnel in Educational Programs for the Disadvantaged. In A. H. Passow ed., *Reaching the Disadvantaged Learner.* New York: Teachers College Press, 1970. Pp. 337–60.

Busing is Opposed by 8-1 margin, Gallop Poll Finds. *New York Times,* April 5, 1970, p. 49.

Carr, R. A., & Hayward, G. G. Education by Chit: An Examination of Voucher Proposals. *Education and Urban Society* 2 (1970) pp. 179–91.

Cohen, S. *Teach Them All To Read: Theory, Methods, and Materials for Teaching the Disadvantaged.* New York: Random House, 1969.

Coleman, J. S. Toward Open Schools. *Public Interest* 9 (1967): 20–27.

Congreve, W. J. Collaborating for Urban Education in Chicago. The Woodlawn Development Project. *Education and Urban Society* 1 (1969): 177–91.

Day, N. A. The Case for all-Black Schools. In *Equal Educational Opportunity.* Cambridge: Harvard University Press, 1969. Pp. 205–12.

District of Columbia Schools. *Innovation in Instruction.* Washington, D.C.: District of Columbia Public Schools, 1965.

Gittel, M. Community Control of Education. In M. Gittell & A. G. Hevesi eds., *The Politics of Urban Education.* New York: Praeger, 1969. Pp. 363–77.

Gordon, E. W. Higher Education and the Challenge of Universal Access to Post-Secondary Education. *IRCD Bulletin* 5 (1969): 1–2, 10–11.

Grotberg, E., ed. *Critical Issues in Research Related to Disadvantaged Children.* Princeton: Educational Testing Service, 1969.

Horn, T. D., ed., *Reading for the Disadvantaged: Problems of Linguistically Different Learners.* New York: Harcourt, Brace & World, 1970.

Jencks, C. Private Schools for Black Children. *New York Times Magazine,* November 3, 1968, pp. 30, 132–39.

Kendrick, S. A., & Thomas, C. L. Transition from School to College. *Review of Educational Research* 40 (1970): 151–79.

Passow, A. H. Diminishing Teacher Prejudice. In R. D. Strom, ed., *The Inner-City Classroom: Teachers' Behaviors.* Columbus: Merrill, 1966. Pp. 93–109.

Passow, A. H. *Statement for the Ad Hoc Subcommittee on De Facto Segregation of the Committee on Education and Labor of the U.S. House of Representatives.* Washington, D.C.: Government Printing Office, 1966. Pp. 244–47.

Passow, A. H. The Gifted and the Advantaged. In *Notes and Working Papers Concerning the Administration of Title III Programs.* Washington, D.C.: Government Printing Office, 1967. Pp. 215–29.

Rist, R. C. Student Social Class and Teacher Expectations: The Self-Fulfilling Prophecy in Ghetto Education. *Harvard Educational Review* 40 (1970): 411–51.

Rosenthal, R., & Jacobson, L. *Pygmalion in the Classroom.* New York: Holt, Rinehart & Winston, 1968.

St. John, N. H. Desegregation and Minority Group Performance. *Review of Educational Research* 40 (1970): 111–33.

Silard, J., & White, S. Intrastate Inequalities in Public Education: The Case for Judicial Relief under the Equal Protection Clause. *Wisconsin Law Review* 7 (1970): 7–34.

Smith, B. O., Cohen, S. B., & Pearl, A. *Teachers for the Real World.* Washington, D.C.: American Association of Colleges for Teacher Education, 1969.

Three-man Panel Scores Education for Spanish-Speaking Students. *New York Times,* August 19, 1970, p. 24.

Twyman, C. R. The Community School in New Haven. In A. H. Passow, ed., *Reaching the Disadvantaged Learner.* New York: Teachers College Press, 1970. Pp. 203–18.

Venn, G. Vocational-Technical Education Needs and Programs for Urban Schools. Paper presented at Seventh Work Conference on Urban Education, Teachers College, Columbia University, June 1969.

Organizing Urban Schools for Responsible Education

William W. Wayson

This school is failing every child in it. That is your responsibility. The usual excuses—bad kids, poor parents, lousy administrator, bad curriculum—will not be acceptable. You are the only people in the world who can solve the problem. You have all the knowledge and skills to find ways to meet the problem, but it will require that we learn them together. If the principal is bad, get rid of him; if the curriculum is bad, throw it out the window and develop something that you think will work. The job of the administrator is to create conditions in which you can help kids learn and to protect you from pressures to do the same old things.[1]

From William W. Wayson, "Organizing Urban Schools for Responsible Education," *Phi Delta Kappan* 52 (February 1971): 344–47. Reprinted by permission of the author and the publisher.

With this address to the faculty, the principal set the stage upon which a school staff demonstrated what responsible educators could accomplish in a large inner-city school.

The shortcomings of the American school system are inherent in the network of interactions and the styles of thinking that are fostered throughout the system. Professionals have been chained in Plato's cave so long that they themselves have merged with the shadows. The Dr. Martin Luther King School was established in Syracuse, N.Y., in 1967 and demonstrated during the next three years that it could perform more effectively when bureaucratic restraints were removed, when personnel concerned themselves more with ends than with means, and when responsibility and authority were centered in the school building.

The key concepts for developing the school were: *involvement, problem solving, accountability,* and *continual growth.* It is doubtful whether any significant or lasting advancement can be made in public schools without attending to these fundamental dynamic qualities of organizations.

INVOLVEMENT

Involvement in an educational enterprise depends upon having school staffs share a sense of common purpose which lifts them above daily crises and interpersonal squabblings. They also must feel that their contribution is important to the enterprise—a feeling that inadvertently but continually is beaten down in large cities. Teachers and principals are treated as machine parts who are incapable of making effective decisions about the educational process; consequently, through the exercise of hundreds of subtle cues (mostly unintended), staff members are reminded that the enterprise and its efforts are out of their ken and touch. They begin to behave as expected and psychologically withdraw their efforts to produce, though for survival they will defend the school if they feel personally attacked.

Lack of purpose and being denied involvement in "really important" decisions combine to prevent full participation in the school. "My room is my responsibility—all else can go hang" is the teacher's definition of his role. Everyone else—the principal, secretaries, custodians, parents, and children respond the same way. The school becomes a conglomeration of strangers drawn into one place at best to stay out of one anothers' inferred purposes.

The staff at Dr. King School worked together to find ways to make the school more effective by reducing the causes of ineffectiveness. Belonging-ness was reinforced by pointing out the teachers' (and the custodians' and the secretaries') key roles in teaching the children, by reinforcing the cruciality of their decisions, and by having them choose methods and materials, group children, schedule and organize time and space, and answer questions about what was happening in the school. Participation was forced (though at varying degrees) by the organization of the school and by removing all possible organizational crutches.

PROBLEM SOLVING

People get excited about solving problems in their world. In Dr. King School the staff agreed that they should not try to hide problems, but should try to solve them. Anytime a person says that the solution of a problem absolutely depends upon forces beyond his control, he is copping out. Most school problems may be defined so that there is a way over, under, around, or through any obstacle. Most of the staff in the school accepted the challenge and responsibility of surmounting obstacles.

It was pleasing to find that about 80 percent of the staff were eager to get on with the new functions. Unhappily, many staff members lacked the elementary skills for problem solving. Almost all in-service programs were therefore designed to teach skills for working effectively in groups to solve problems and make decisions.

The school was organized in a way that enhanced problem solving.[2] The staff worked in decision teams of six to eight teachers, an aide, perhaps one specialist (who was considered a resource and not a superior), and any volunteers they could co-opt. Each team was assigned a group of children of about 25 times the number of regular classroom teachers in the team and a number of rooms equal to the number of teachers. The team was charged with making all decisions about grouping children, choosing materials for instruction, and deciding upon the use of time, space, and personnel. Each team could operate differently from other teams consistent with the philosophy and general policies of the building.

School policies were made by the school cabinet, a legislative body made up of a representative elected from each team, the administrators, and three parents elected by the parent-teacher organization. This group could make any policy that it could enforce and it had full power to veto decisions of the principal.[3]

Problem solving proceeded at a hectic pace, with some teams acting more effectively than others, but with all freed from waiting for the others to move. The entire school took on a different character. Parents and other community leaders gave it respect and love. Other educators gave it respect but not love.

FIXING RESPONSIBILITY

Most organizations fear the consequences of bad decisions and prohibit all members from making any decisions. As a result, vital decisions do not get made. Basic decisions should be made close to the problem, and the *natural consequences* of the decision must be readily apparent to the person who made it. Schools support a dependent and nonresponsible role for all personnel. At present, a teacher who wishes not to perform responsibly can get succor and solace from colleagues and superiors. Excuses are protected. But one does not have to be deterred from developing more effective schools because a few do not accept independence and responsibility. Effective practices tend to be contagious and they carry great satisfaction. A school building may move forward rapidly with fewer than a third of the staff committed to change if the administrator rewards action and if someone in the building can mobilize feedback that will not permit problems to be buried.

Fixed responsibility obviously depends upon having goals to which one is committed and which are understood widely enough so that failure to achieve them will be apparent to everyone. The staff of Dr. King School recognized that they had no clear goals and that much of the frustration and failure in the school arose from the children's not knowing what was expected of them and from teachers' not knowing what success was.

The ordeal of sitting for hours and days and years in a classroom where we do not know what is expected leaves us totally dependent upon others for evidence of progress and success. This dependence leaves us no way of judging ourselves or our abilities. Since achievement is founded upon confidence in one's own ability to change the world (self-esteem, self-actualization, or a sense of control over one's environment), the staff of the school felt it imperative to build that confidence as a prerequisite to achievement in the school. They wrote a proposal and received funds under Title III, ESEA, to educate themselves to produce a curriculum designed to give children a sense of control over the environment.[4] As part of the effort to build the students' confidence, the staff devoted three full weeks during a six-week institute to learning how to write clearly stated behavioral goals. The difficulty of writing such goals and the educators' unpreparedness for thinking about goals slowed progress, so three years passed before the staff prepared even the most rudimentary statement of academic goals for the classes.[5] Nevertheless, progress was evident and it was clear that the statement of goals in itself was a highly effective teaching device. If we ever succeed in communicating our goals clearly, we will run out of things to do about 10:00 each morning as we eliminate the uncertainty surrounding present procedures.

The school gained in other ways from learning to state goals clearly. Staff members could question one another and communicate suggestions much more effectively once vagueness and subjectively evaluative overtones gave way to behavioral and objective observations. Even when teachers sat with the principal for end-of-the-year "evaluations," the teacher often asked, "Won't you be more behavioral about that?" Clarifying goals and stating them to others also strengthened requests to the central office or other sources because others gained confidence from the staff's "knowing what it was doing."

Responsibility also results from having poeple who will ask for an occasional accounting, especially if their interests are not served. The school typically assigns evaluation and supervision to levels that have no vested interest in the actions that they are assigned to assess. For example, a central office supervisor has no vested interest and feels no sense of personal loss if children in a classroom are mistreated or do not learn to read, and a principal feels no gut-level hostility if a teacher has abused a child. Responsibility cannot be a driving force in any setting unless two conditions prevail: First, the important decisions are made as close to the client as possible; second, the client (or his representative) can go *directly* to the decision maker to learn about the decision and to register praise, complaints, or suggestions. In a school the person closest to the client is the teacher, and the client is the child; his representative usually is a parent, but it could be any figure who accepts responsibility for his welfare. An accountable system must open up every decision maker at every level to direct feedback from the persons affected by the decision. The resultant feedback is the most productive and least expensive of all supervisory and in-service techniques that we can devise.

At Dr. King School the process employed was to open the system and to teach skills for upward communications from all possible levels. The only barriers to communication arose from the reluctance, dependence, and insecurity which developed in pupils, parents, teachers, and administrators through previous experience and training. Children were taught how to deal with authority figures to obtain better instruction. They learned to speak with their teachers and the principal without either subservience or hostility. They learned a variety of techniques, from conversing about their concerns to writing petitions and picketing. They learned to state their purposes and analyze their own responsibilities. They operated in the school under a bill of rights,[6] and although the procedures were never codified, they learned legitimate grievance procedures similar to those in the Martin Luther King School in Sausalito, California.[7] On one occasion, students used the grievance procedure to call the superintendent to ask his opinion about the enforcement of the goals program. Teachers and the school earned much respect from these procedures as they developed confidence from being able to accept responsibility for their actions.

Other "feedback loops" were built into the organization. Among them was a policy that any parent or visitor should go directly to the person whose procedures they wanted to discuss. There was none of the usual "get permission from the principal," which treats both teachers and parents as irresponsible children. Visitors had to "obey" one authority—the teacher responsible for the classroom. They came in large numbers, and they generally left highly impressed with the openness of the teachers in the school. Parents or other volunteers often worked for hours in the classroom. Even the most fearful teachers on the staff soon found it difficult to accept the opposition to "outsiders" that they saw in other schools.

CONTINUAL GROWTH

An organization that survives and functions effectively must be continually learning. It learns by adapting to its environment; it must be open to its environment. Problem solving, utilizing the processes of the school as a curriculum for life, and fixing responsibility in themselves help teachers to develop their skills and to advance their sense of worth in the performance of a useful life work. The processes built into the school's operation constitute a "life curriculum for in-service" and these processes were the most effective in-service that could be provided.

However, high levels of teacher turnover are a part of life in most areas today. In Dr. King School, it seemed to be so much a part of life that the administrator gave very low priority to trying to stem turnover. Though turnover was about 25 percent, many of these left because their husbands left the area or to learn new skills and to see new situations. Consequently, the solution was to provide a true staff development program for new staff members so that they could move easily into the new roles and functions required in the school.

Every school is a teacher training institution and must give explicit attention to making the training relate to educational purposes. Most of the training should be consciously built into ongoing operations in the school; some of it should be provided in more formalized experiences designed by and for the staff as a part of its problem solving, but great care must be exercised to prevent those experiences from becoming the useless waste of time and human resources that typify many, if not most, in-service programs. The problems of educating are so great that we must see the development of teachers as *more important* than having children in school, for until the school can be made educational, children and teachers alike are deprived of the chance to learn what schools are supposed to help them learn. One can easily guarantee that children will learn more if we send them home at noon every day and use the remainder of the teachers' day (say, until four or five o'clock) for personal and group in-service development, home visits, individual appointments with children and parents, resource gathering, materials development, and—something without which teachers try to operate now—reading.

Such experiences must be developed in the school building. With few exceptions, in-service programs designed by larger units (such as the teachers' association or the curriculum department) can have small influence on what goes on in a school or classroom. The Dr. King staff never really had sufficient time for staff development, but some time was gained by closing the school 20 minutes early each day, by closing an hour early every Thursday, by closing the school for half a day every month, and by using all faculty meetings as in-service time. When the school board found out about these invasions upon the child's day (a year later), it permitted other schools to get time off because the school staff had demonstrated that production came from using school time differently. The King teachers' departure from usual practice *rested solely upon responsible use of time* and demonstrated willingness to give out-of-school time to the effort. The staff had discovered that attacking and resolving important problems lessened petty concerns about working hours and the soul-destroying mediocrity of worrying about what everyone else is doing.

FUNCTIONS OF EFFECTIVE TEACHERS

It will be said that "none of the practices described in this paper have anything to do with teaching; they involve the teacher in a lot of things outside the classroom." That is correct. These things have little to do with teaching and the classroom *as we know them.* But we do know that teaching and classrooms as we know them have little to do with education. These new functions in reality have everything to do with what we want from teaching and the classroom, because they mean that the teacher will be a fully functioning adult, working more with adults than with children. A childish teacher cannot help a child acquire the traits required to become an effective adult.

Adult teachers cannot develop, survive, or grow in the school as it exists today. Experience in Dr. King School indicates that it is possible to step confidently toward a new system that may produce adult teachers. The most potent opposition to such a system is within the present one; the procedures and attitudes presently employed simply do not support the new functions. Unless leadership emerges within the system,[8] pressure will be required to bring about improved practices.[9] Teachers educated for the new functions could provide much of this pressure.

NOTES ON EDUCATIONAL REFORMATION

Learning is not always neat and orderly and it cannot be made so. It is motivated best by a sense of constructive tension in the learner, and that tension derives from some feeling of discontent about the existing state of things. Learning involves the risk of meeting new ideas, new practices, unknown forces, unanticipated and unanticipatable consequences—all of which promise failure, uncertainty, ambiguity, and insecurity as well as success. Learning in social settings involves unavoidable conflicts (can you imagine learning to recognize and analyze one's prejudice without any emotional upsets?). Indeed the conflict through which one goes may be considered the best and possibly the only effective teacher. Helping people learn new functions and processes necessarily requires conflicts, tensions, and uncertainties. He who hopes to move forward without them not only must fail, but will waste his talents trying to eliminate the most essential parts of the process of growing and learning, much as if a cook spent his life trying to eliminate the flavors from a steak dinner.

No organization can ever get 100 percent cooperation and support from all the people who contribute to it. One cannot expect that all pupils, teachers, parents, administrators, and others will move together or with equal fervor. If one wants to create a learning organization, he must work with fallible people. One can never get everyone "with it," but one does not need more than a fraction of the total to make measurable progress; focusing on those who won't move means that no one ever starts.

Educational reforms are never "over." One cannot work to produce the perfect system and then spend his life exporting it—packaged with a guarantee of success. Each school building, each teacher, and each child has a peculiar personality, and all changes must be screened through that maze of individual differences. If education is life and life is the best educator, the school must be alive; it must be an institution in which the only thing that is institutionalized is the individual's responsible pursuit of new experiences, new challenges, new responses. The processes of that pursuit are all that a formal education enterprise can transfer to its students. They promote the only learning that has the guarantee that the learner will learn for learning's sake.

NOTES

[1] An address to the staff published in William Wayson, "The Curriculum in the Inner-City School," *Integrated Education,* January-February 1968.

[2] The organization, complete with roles and functions for the principal, teams, teachers, aides, and the cabinet, is presented in *Organizing Schools for Responsible Urban Education,* a handbook for teachers at Dr. Martin Luther King, Jr., Elementary School, prepared by teachers under the direction of Lynn Sullivan, under a grant from Title III, ESEA, to promote self-esteem among students, 1969-1970.

[3] Arthur Blumberg, William Wayson, and Will Weber, "The Elementary School Cabinet: Report of an Experience in Participative Decision Making," *Educational Administration Quarterly,* Fall 1969, pp. 39–52.

[4] The staff of Dr. King Elementary School, Syracuse, N.Y., "A Proposal to Prepare a Curriculum to Promote a Sense of Control Over Environment Among Disadvantaged Children," submitted to Title III, ESEA, 1968. The institute resulted in "Teaching a Sense of Control Over Environment in Inner-City Schools: A Handbook of Learning Experiences," Dr. King School, Syracuse, 1968, mimeographed.

[5] Dr. Martin Luther King, Jr., Elementary School, "Minimal Goals for Instruction: Stated in Behavioral Terms with Policies Governing Their Application," 1970, mimeographed.

[6] "Student Role and Functions," in *Organizing Schools for Responsible Urban Education.*

[7] Mimeographed handout from Sidney Walton, principal, Martin Luther King School, Sausalito, California.

[8] William Wayson, "The Emerging New Breed of Educational Leadership," commissioned by Croft Publications, 1970.

[9] *See* articles in *Saturday Review,* 19 September 1970.

Decentralizing Urban Schools

Allan C. Ornstein

I will admit that when integration was the "liberal" thing, I believed in it and advocated it. Now it is becoming fashionable to call for school decentralization, and perhaps I have been misled and seduced by the literature, or perhaps I am reflecting my "liberal" guilt or the current rhetoric, for I, too, now call for decentralization.[1] In advocating school decentralization, I realize that I may, unwittingly, become an ally of the white and black racists who make it difficult to unite America. Having thus cautioned the reader about my biases, I will proceed with the discussion, namely (1) a brief sociohistorical introduction and (2) the arguments for and against decentralization.

SOCIOHISTORICAL INTRODUCTION

Although most surveys show that blacks still prefer integration, investigators fail to recognize that blacks do not seek integration per se, but wish to send their children to white schools because they are "better" or wish to live in white communities because life in the ghetto is often painful and ugly. Most black people, especially in our northern ghettoes, have repudiated the ideology of integration as a farce, a honkie hoax. One hundred fifty years of slavery and one hundred years of being second-class citizens have taught blacks that the methods used by Dr. George Washington Carver and Dr. Martin Luther King are impractical. Rather than work within the system, many blacks seek to create their own system.

Black power advocates that black children be educated in black schools with black teachers and administrators, that teachers and administrators be accountable to the black community. Black power demands that the school curriculum not only include black history and culture, but that history be reinterpreted so that students realize that George Washington, the father of white America, used to tell lies and that he owned slaves; that the Constitution of white America considered a black as three-fifths of a person, etc. Rather than black students learning about the "contributions" of Negroes and seeing the Negro as part of American history, there is a demand for the study of the germinal heritage of black culture—Nat Turner, E.W. Dubois, Marcus Garvey, Franz Fanon, etc. Rather than the black students having to seek self-realization through defensive polemics

From Allan C. Ornstein, "Decentralizing Urban Schools," *Journal of Secondary Education* 46 (February 1971): 83–91. Reprinted by permission of the author and the publisher.

and discussion of Negro heroes that are "acceptable" to whites, the students are given the opportunity to assert their own identity and shift discussion to the offensive, or to what is valid according to blacks. They are given the opportunity to view not themselves, but the white power system as a source of their problems, and they discuss possibilities of rectifying the situation.

Traditionally the schools have been responsive only to the dominant white power structure. Subordinate groups that were once considered apolitical or indifferent are now demanding that the schools be responsive to them, too. The pending crisis is keenly described in the Report of the National Advisory Commission on Civil Disorders:

Ghetto schools often appear to be unresponsive to the community . . . and parents are distrustful of officials responsible for formulating education policy.

The consequences for the education of students attending these schools are serious. Parental hostility to the school is reflected in the attitudes of their children. Since the needs and concerns of the ghetto community are rarely reflected in educational policy formulated on a citywide basis, the schools are often seen by ghetto youth as being irrelevant . . .

In the schools, as in the large society, the isolation of ghetto residents from policy-making institutions of local government is adding to the polarization of the community and depriving the system of its self-rectifying potential.

Black teachers welcome school decentralization; they envision it as an opportunity to bolster local black power, as well as their own green power through administrative promotions which they have generally been denied. Indeed, it is legally and morally justified for black controlled school boards to hire or promote qualified principals or superintendents on the basis that the individual is black, BLACK.

Our laws have permitted other groups a degree of separatism, permitting them to establish their own schools in order to maintain their customs and religious beliefs. The white "liberals" who belong to the NAACP and move to suburbia are often seeking "better" schools for their children. In effect, they establish their own school systems, and tend to favor individuals of their own ethnic groups in their employment and reward practices.

Much of the present demand for local control must be viewed in the context of the present unrest in the ghettoes which is partially due to frustration arising from the fact that blacks have not been permitted to shake loose the albatross of dependency which has historically hung around their necks.

The urban school systems are viewed as part of the white power structure, and the white power structure has often been viewed by blacks as the enemy. Now the pendulum is beginning to swing the other way; blacks are beginning to get their way too. For most whites, local control of the schools by the black community is construed as a black victory and white defeat. But most whites cannot accept the feeling of being outnumbered or outvoted by blacks. The exodus of whites from the inner cities and their bewildered statements such as "They want everything their way," "What do they expect from us?," "Will they ever be satisfied?," illustrate the whites' discomfort and their desire to maintain the luxury of supremacy.

While some blacks consider that the ultimate reforms will justify the immediate trauma, others recognize that they are trapped by their own rhetoric, and that each successful demand breeds more demands which eventually may foster white extremism—in quest and in defense of law and order—as a virtue. Although collective force is instrumental now in accomplishing black objectives, it also invites massive counter force. Even among "liberals" and among those whites who advocate decentralization and community control in print or in speeches, this author sometimes senses an underlying uneasiness, a sense of doubt, alarm, fear, even racism at certain times, in conversation with such "good" people. Behind closed doors and among white friends, people who often profess to be the friends of the black community renege on their "principles," and blacks surely realize this and do not trust well-intentioned whites.

The most noted and controversial schemes for decentralization began in New York City in 1967. Three experimental school sites—I.S. 201 school complex, Two Bridges, and Ocean-Hill Brownsville School Districts—were decentralized, indicative, during the initial periods, of subsystem reform. However, the subsystems became susceptible to and transformed under a wide range of inputs and influences. The result was that the three subsystems changed to multisubsystems; that is, they deviated from the "mother" system's intended objectives and their behaviors were "dysfunctional" in nature, an unanticipated consequence of subsystem reform. In particular, the Ocean-Hill Brownsville multisubsystem threatened the "mother" system and its line-staff members, to the extent, in fact, that the supervisors and teachers cemented an uncommon alliance and plunged New York City into a ten-week teacher strike in 1968.

The most comprehensive and controversial proposal for school decentralization and community control is the Bundy Report, endorsed by the Ford Foundation and presented to the Mayor of New York City in 1967. The plan suggested that:

1. New York City schools be reorganized into 30 to 60 community school districts, ranging from 12,000 to 40,000 students.
2. A central board of education—either nominated by the Mayor or in part by the Mayor and the community school boards, and a superintendent of schools—have responsibility for determining city-wide school policies and adhering to state regulations.
3. The community school districts be governed by a local board of education, selected in part by the Mayor from a city-wide list of candidates and selected in part by the community.
4. The local board of education have control of all elementary and

secondary education within its boundaries; they would have control over the budget, curriculum, and personnel, including the right to hire, fire, and promote personnel but all policies and personnel would have to meet state standards. In the meantime, all tenure rights of teachers and supervisors would be retained.

The effects of the Bundy Report, compounded by racial tension in New York City, especially between the black community and the predominantly white teacher's union and supervisory association as well as political pressure from the Mayor and community groups, led to the New York Decentralization Act of 1969. Thus New York has become the first big city that has decentralized the entire school system.[2] In part, the three experimental decentralized subsystems had transformed into successful multisubsystems—to the extent that the entire system was reformed, at least on paper. Also, the influence of the Bundy Report is clearly observed in the regulations of the Decentralization Act; the law can be summarized as follows:

1. District school lines should be established so as to create between 30 and 33 local school districts, each with its own community board of education.
2. The central board of education should consist of seven members, five of whom are to be elected from each borough and two to be elected by the Mayor.[3]
3. Local school boards may be elected by registered voters and parents of students enrolled in schools of each district.
4. Local school boards may hire their own superintendent so long as he meets state education requirements. Principals may be hired, too, from city-wide qualifying lists. For those schools whose students fall within the lower 45 percentile in reading, local school boards may hire their own teachers from various qualifying lists—based on the Board of Examiners' tests or a passing score on the National Teacher Examinations.[4] The local school boards may control the curriculum, but the central board will retain control over the budget.[5]

THE ARGUMENTS FOR AND AGAINST DECENTRALIZATION

The arguments for and against decentralization tend to focus around 12 themes:[6]

1. *Decentralization will impede integration.* Those who make this claim—the white power structure of the city and schools and the "average" white parent—have often tried to maintain the status quo. This meant being against integration when blacks demanded it and now keeping them from gaining control over their own communities and schools. Integration demanded that blacks be admitted into the system; they were never really

allowed entry, so now they seek to change the system. Whites no longer have to decide what to do with those "niggers"; those "niggers" have decided that integration is no longer feasible or in their best interests. Integration connotes assimilation into the WASP system, being processed by an environment and a school that the black child has little control over. The majority of blacks now demand an open and free society which recognizes their identity.

In any event, the northern schools are more segregated today than they were prior to the Supreme Court decision in 1954. Most educators contend that schools cannot be integrated unless the communities are integrated, and it is unrealistic in the foreseeable future to expect white communities to welcome blacks in large numbers. Most whites never really wanted to integrate; most blacks no longer want it, and its doesn't seem feasible—with or without decentralization.

2. *Decentralization will balkanize the cities.* The myth of the melting pot no longer exists. The cities are already balkanized, especially among racial patterns. In reality, the concept of twentieth century America is a nation of many nations, a nation of many races, a place where different cultural and ethnic groups can exist together with justice and equality. This being the case, the nation has no right to mouth democratic slogans unless it is willing to accept cultural and ethnic differences, unless it is willing to allow such groups to have power—at least control over their own destinies, in their communities and schools. Decentralization does not necessarily have to lead to isolation; it can mean that minorities find new ways to work with the larger community on a more equal basis so they become a part of the total system, without losing their identity or surrendering their culture.

3. *Decentralization is the return to the myth of "separate but equal."* Most blacks have always wanted better schools for their children. This meant trying to attend integrated schools (especially in the south, where the white power structure puts the most money and best equipment into schools attended by white students). However, this did not mean integration for the sole purpose of integration. If the black schools were made superior, or at least as good as the white schools, the black community, even Messrs. Clark, Carter, and Rustin, would probably be satisfied.

Most black people recognized long ago that integration in the north, due to the racial attitudes and demographical trends, was fast becoming infeasible. They demanded integration partially because they were trapped by their own rhetoric and partially because it pressured school systems to try to improve ghetto schools. Decentralization is based on the belief that blacks can improve their own schools better than the system can—or will under normal circumstances.

Also, the Brown decision claimed that *de jure* segregation facilities were unequal, not *de facto* segregation or self-imposed segregation. The latter type of segregation, in fact, is common in American society; it should not be misconstrued as unequal or nihilistic; it merely reveals that different culture and ethnic groups prefer to live together and send their children to the same school. This is the basis of an open and free society, as well as the neighborhood school.

4. *Decentralization is a scheme for alleviating the pressure from the black community.* Decentralization connotes community involvement, thereby a possible reduction of alienation between the schools and community. No matter how well-chosen and how well-intentioned the members of the school board in a large city, they cannot possibly be as adequately informed about the interest and needs of the schools in each neighborhood as a local school board—with its own ethnic and cultural differences and with its own administrator-teacher-student problems.

In the past city schools have excluded the poor from policy making. This is smug contempt toward nonwhites and poor; it is contradictory to participatory democracy. The middle-class suburbanite would not tolerate a school system run by an outside agency, especially one that failed to educate or recognize the needs of his children. In effect, we permit whites who can afford to move to suburbia to set up and run their own schools, while we exclude poor minorities from controlling their own city schools.

5. *Ghetto parents, with little formal education, are unable to effectively run public schools.* There is no proof that the poor are unable to run their schools, since schools, in the city, suburbs or rural areas, have been customarily controlled by the middle and upper classes. Past experience reveals that the "experts," whether they come from Harvard Univeristy or school headquarters or the nation's capital, are unable to solve the educational ills of the ghetto. Professional educators—teachers, adminis-trators, etc.—have failed to educate the black poor, too. Decentralization is an attempt to cope with this failure; it is an attempt to increase parental participation in educational decision making. Since they should be more aware of their own problems and the problems of their children, they should be able to make good use of their new power.

At any rate, the parents will not run the schools but rather vote for a local school board that will hire teachers and administrators to make the professional decisions and run the school on a daily basis; the school personnel will also be accountable to the local school board—not to a remote city school board which is usually unable to grasp local problems and which usually seeks to maintain the status quo. To question the feasibility of giving the poor and/or ghetto residents the right to elect their own school board is analogous to questioning the fundamental concept of democracy—the right of the people to elect their own representatives to city hall and Congress.

6. *Decentralization will enhance black racism.* Charges of racism are exaggerated and in most cases connote white fear of and racism toward different racial groups, a twin enigma which is rooted in American history. In the few cases where blacks are teaching white hate, this enmity is better for the students than the customary process of learning to hate themselves—a "civilized" racism, subtle but inherent in our texts and curricula, as well as indicated by adult feelings and gestures which are

communicated to the students—and over a period of time is more destructive to the students' selfhood than is the "uncivilized" rhetoric of "pigs," "honkiedom," "whitey," etc.

The schools are a product of society—WASP society—which has injured black children. If charges of racism are justified, they also should be directed at white society and their schools which have defined blacks, at best, as inferior or "invisible" second-class citizens. Black parents want to control their own schools to stop this injury to their children. Their children need an education that will help them cope with frequent white discrimination and racism. Indeed, there is justice in the demand for black pride to replace white mythology; however, it should be noted that there may be a tipping point—where black pride begins to duplicate the errors of racist white and racial narcissism. Blacks, rather than becoming infatuated by slogans and myths, hopefully, will seek to reinterpret history.

7. *Decentralization will foster "vigilante" groups which will harass white teachers and supervisors.* Middle-class whites do not have to resort to such groups because they do not experience the same intense frustration; moreover, they have enough influence so that dissatisfaction with the schools and staff is minimal. So long as blacks are discriminated against and refused the right to control their own schools, self-appointed groups or black power groups will try to change the system—and most white teachers and administrators are part of the system, or at least help perpetuate it. Once blacks gain control of their own schools and once the rhetoric ceases, there will be no need for black groups to harass white school personnel; moreover, the parents can be trusted to stop this harassment because their children's education is at stake. The group that probably cannot be trusted is the school personnel—black or white—whose major interests are to themselves, and not their students—and this is possibly one reason for the need for professional accountability.

8. *Decentralization will reject white participation.* Blacks recognize that decentralization largely depends upon the white taxpayer paying for it and the white power structure permitting it. They are a minority group and can go only as far in improving their schools as whites allow. Granted, there is talk about only black teachers and administrators being qualified to work with black children, but blacks recognize the need for and help of capable and concerned white professionals. Nevertheless, it behooves the white teacher to answer these false pronouncements. Most white teachers refuse, however, to speak out because it invites confrontations and charges of racism. Yet not to deal with these pronouncements is to invite future confrontations and the loss of many competent ghetto teachers.

Presently, the black community is ruled by white businessmen; the black schools are run by white educators. Black pride and power rejects white domination, but not white participation. White controlled schools have failed to educate black youth. Decentralization permits blacks to control their own schools, to decide who they want to hire to teach their children. Most blacks are not saying they do not want to have anything to do with white teachers and supervisors; they are saying they should have a voice in the affairs of educating their own children.

9. *Decentralization means the professional standards, especially the merit system, will be lowered.* Although the merit system has helped reduce corruption and patronage in city schools, it has unwittingly created inbreeding and has discriminated against ethnic groups different from those in control of the system. For example, in Boston the teachers, administrators, and headquarter barons are predominantly Irish. In New York City, they are predominantly Jewish. In Milwaukee, they are predominantly German and Scandinavian.

The merit system is also designed to discriminate against professionals from outside the "mother" system. Participating in a supervisory examination usually involves traveling to specific test centers on several occasions over a six month to one year period. Answers to questions are largely based on local "wisdom," not state or nationwide professionalism or philosophy. Rigorous test procedures make test candidates study for years and memorize monographs on index cards. Those who pass these tests prove they are good test takers and have facility with the English language; there seems to be no correlation between high scores and "effective" leaders.

The present merit system needs to be abolished and replaced by one that is more flexible and allows for diversity and outside leadership. State standards permit such freedom, and decentralization plans in most cities adhere to state regulations.

10. *Decentralization will weaken the teachers' and supervisors' organizations.* Large city school systems breed and perpetuate administrative bureaucrats—school personnel who seek to maintain the status quo. The only group to successfully challenge the bureaucrats' control has been the teachers' union, and their major concern has been to improve teacher salaries and conditions—and rightfully so, since the function of a union is to further the interests of its members.

Decentralization means a loss of teacher and administrator power, at best a sharing of power with the community but at worst, complete professional accountability to the community. The growing threat to the teachers' and supervisors' organizations was reflected in the fact that during the 1968 New York City teacher strike the three experimental school areas remained open and 85 percent of its staff crossed the picket lines. Also, black teacher and supervisory organizations are growing across the country—a potential threat to the present AFT and supervisory associations.

For the community to demand control of their own schools means they must challenge those who are now in power. Conflict should be expected because those who have power are rarely willing to surrender it, and those who seek it, if continuously frustrated, will often resort to force.

11. *Decentralization is inefficient and creates duplication and extra costs.* The battle against school bigness in government, industry, universities, churches, etc. Bigness makes the system unresponsive to the needs of the community and schools; pilot programs and special reports are implemented at a great cost; they are generally ineffective but formulated to maintain the status quo and to imply that the system is responsive to

the schools. Bigness alienates the average citizen and ignores "grass roots," which is tantamount to ignoring participatory democracy; this conflict with citizen participation reduces school morale and often causes overt conflict which cannot be measured in dollars but has a detrimental impact on teaching and learning. Any cost of duplication should be offset by the cost of school bigness.

12. *Decentralization does not change the system; it merely changes the size.* Decentralization is also part of a social process of change in the cities. Redistribution of power is in itself an aspect of change. Passing the responsibility of education from the bureaucrats to the people is a change, and considering how very far from their promise and potential the schools have come to educating the poor, they should get better with community participation. School decentralization and local control connote a change in the curriculum and simultaneous motivation for publishers to print more objective materials, as well as to reinterpret literature and history—which is beneficial so long as it does not lead to systematic distortion.

Decentralization means the schools belong to the people, making it possible for the schools to relate to the parents and their children. The community-controlled school is certainly more aware of the needs and interest of local residents—including the adult population, thereby serving as an innovative force in meeting their recreational, cultural, and educational needs. The closer bond between school and community permits the school to become a center for coordinating community policies related to urban problems—including housing, welfare, employment and legal aid.

CONCLUSION

The schools have always been controlled by the middle- and upper-middle class society. This went unnoticed because the gap between the poor and affluent was not always so wide and the black-white conflict had not yet surfaced. There was more hope, too, among the poor for entering the mainstream and among blacks for experiencing the promises of integration.

The schools have always failed to educate most of the poor, for the great majority dropped out of school or graduated as functional illiterates. This also went unnoticed in the past because the labor market absorbed these educational waste products; moreover, these school failures were white and did not face job discrimination; they were able to assimilate in one or two generations whereas the new poor—mainly nonwhites—no matter how many generations are considered, find assimilation difficult, if not impossible.

If it were not for the school systems' monopoly on the education of the poor, most schools would have gone bankrupt long ago. As of now the population that can afford to send their children to private or parochial schools or flee to the suburbs do just that—and in doing so forsake the city public schools.

Decentralization is an attempt to remedy the present educational crisis in the ghetto; it is a crisis that has been growing since blacks began their exodus to the "Promised Land" across the Mason-Dixon line. Since the civil rights movement and the War on Poverty, the crisis has become more evident. Most blacks are now claiming that their children can receive an equal or superior education in their own communities, rather than in a white school that doesn't really want them. Decentralization is linked to the black power movement; both trends seek to expose the system and create a new one—viable, innovative, and related to the needs and interest of black youth. It has more potential for good than for evil. We should at least give it a try.

NOTES

[1] For purposes of this discussion, the author contends that the issues of decentralization and local control are theoretically comingled and should not be separated. Granted the schools can be decentralized without providing community control; however, in order for the community to gain control on a large scale the schools will probably have to be decentralized.

[2] In 1970 Los Angeles (the second largest school system) and Detroit (the fourth largest school system) decentralized their respective school systems. Los Angeles divided the system into twelve administrative areas and Detroit divided the system into eight regions.

[3] Since the populace of Manhattan and the Bronx is predominantly black and Puerto Rican, it is not unlikely that with a liberal or black Mayor the central board would consist of a majority of blacks and/or Puerto Ricans, two elected and two appointed, and rightfully so since the majority of the public school students consists of these two racial groups.

[4] It should be noted that the NTE does not require a written essay, which some educators claim discriminates against most minorities whose education is perhaps inferior.

[5] This last point is critical. For the community to gain real control of the schools, it is essential that it acquire control of the purse strings. Economic power is related to political power. As long as the local community is dependent on the goodwill of the central board, the local community does not have complete independence or authority; in fact, the larger system is still in a position to sabotage the local board's operation.

[6] See Mario D. Fantini, "Decentralizing Urban School Systems," in Alvin Toffler, ed., *The Schoolhouse in the City* (New York: Praeger, 1968), pp. 110–135.

QUESTIONS FOR REFLECTION AND DISCUSSION

1. Ornstein's opening article cites much of the recent research relating to the education of the urban disadvantaged. Which of these research studies, as Ornstein reports them, would provide support for the proposals called for by Passow? Would any of the research studies run counter to what Passow is proposing? If so, which ones and why?

2. Syracuse, New York, the city in which is located the Martin Luther King School that Wayson reports on, is vastly smaller than, say, New York or Detroit. Would the kind of program implemented at King work in a much larger area? Would it have

greater likelihood for success if it were accompanied by the decentralization program Ornstein writes of in the final article?

3. Ornstein, in his second article, notes that "the arguments for and against decentralization tend to focus around 12 themes." How do you react to each of these positions? Suppose you were a teacher in a ghetto school in a large city? Might you react differently? How do these 12 arguments relate to the proposals Passow advocates?

Chapter six
Racism and American Education

Claims that American society is racist date back a number of years, but the recent increase in what might be called minority militancy in recent years has made them more pronounced. Moreover, no longer are those who make such assertions talking only of individuals, taken either singly or collectively. They are now speaking of the institutions of society—its governmental structures, its churches, its military units, its schools. Indeed, the attacks on the schools may be the most severe of all.

The issue of racism and American education is far deeper than the question of integration and segregation, though a discussion of it must start there. For years the South practiced *de jure* separation of the races, the North *de facto*. In the former, schools were segregated by law: blacks and whites could not legally attend the same schools. Some southern districts, responding to the Supreme Courts "separate schools are inherently unequal" decision of 1954, modified their positions in the early 1960s, going to what was called a "freedom of choice" plan. Theoretically students were free to attend any school in their district; in practice only a few blacks integrated the previously all-white schools and there was virtually no movement in the other direction. Supreme Court rulings during the late 1960s abolished many of the laws governing segregation and demanded integration of both faculties and student bodies. To effect this integration, massive busing became the order of the day.*

The *de facto* segregation of the North was based not on legal foundations but on neighborhood housing patterns. Schools served their immediate neighborhoods. The busing required to effect large scale integration would have to cut across neighborhood and even school district boundaries. Given the moratorium on new busing to achieve racial balance declared by President Nixon in the spring of 1972, it seems likely that *de facto* segregation will remain in effect for some time yet.

Even though one can predict with some certainty that integration will ultimately become common in all public schools, that black and white

---

*It is well worth mentioning that, despite the hue and cry about busing in the South, the amount of busing necessary to achieve racial integration is only slightly more than that required in the preintegration days to preserve segregation.

(and Chicano and Indian and Puerto Rican) will all eventually go to school together, those schools already integrated attest to the fact that the problems are not completely removed simply by a lowering of the racial barriers for entrance. Many newly integrated schools have had riots among their students over racial matters, discord among the faculty, distrust among the parents. Financial resources have worn thin in some districts which have discovered that they now must buy more school buses, hire consultants to conduct sensitivity sessions among members of different groups, spend greater sums on riot and vandalism prevention. Differing educational aspirations and varied past academic accomplishments assume new importance when neighborhoods of vastly different socioeconomic structures are merged into single schools. Grouping practices in some schools must be gauged carefully lest they uniwttingly implement an integration-in-the-school-but-segregation-in-the-classroom pattern.

The four articles in this section treat these and other problems surrounding the issue of racism and American education. Record's article opens with a recounting of the failures of whites to enter into minority education in a meaningful and relevant way, then concludes with five suggestions for improvement. Green addresses himself to these significant questions: What is the damage (to members of all races) caused by racial isolation? What can be done to raise the quality of teachers from minority groups, who themselves were victims of inferior education in a time of segregation? How may facilities be improved, especially in the ghetto areas? Can tracking (grouping) be continued? Banks, in the third article, defends the often-overlooked position that the problems are as acute for the white majority as for the ethnic minority. Yet, because the whites typically hold the balance of power, they must overcome their resistance to change. Vacca focuses on "the classroom teacher as a dimension of public school desegregation" and considers some of the court cases arising out of faculty integration.

The White Professional Educators and the Black Ghetto Schools

Wilson Record

Social change, however beneficial it may be to society in the long run, frequently has a very harmful and enduring effect on some groups. For example, changes in the educational system during the past quarter century have greatly benefitted middle-class urban whites. But Negroes, Mexicans, Puerto Ricans, and rural poor whites continue to be denied entry into the mainstream via the educational channel. Had they been given such access they might not have chosen the militant and sometimes violent roads which an increasing number are taking as the only appropriate alternative. Blocking of that passage early produced a Martin Luther King; continued denial has contributed to the emergence of a Stokeley Carmichael; one cannot view hopefully the consequences of the continued closure of educational opportunity.

We have a long and strong tradition of equating change with progress, of believing that things are getting better, however annoying, even critical, some of the dislocations may be. And not without reason. As members of a white, middle-class society we find our optimism sustained by experience and reinforced by our reasonable hope of still better things to come. It has been we who could best cushion the impact of change and grasp the new and promising alternatives. We could, for example, best capitalize chances to attend free public universities and best prepare our children to enter them. In contrast, few members of our major racial and ethnic minorities have ever been able to link change and opportunity and "take advantage" of it. For them, social, and specific educational, change did not mean progress. On the contrary, a frequent outcome was frustration, alienation, anger, and violence.

For professional educators, in Maryland and elsewhere, social change during the past quarter century has produced some striking advances: growing public interest, more financial resources, a vast array of new hardware, ever expanding plants and facilities, differently trained per-

From Wilson Record, "The White Professional Educators and the Black Ghetto Schools," *Journal of Negro Education* 39 (Winter 1970): 44-49. Reprinted by permission of the author.

sonnel, and more specialization and sophisticated organization. For the career teacher, counselor, and administrator, it has meant greater prestige, higher income, (although surely not enough), professional recognition, and stronger voice in school, community, and society. Indeed, we seem to have almost an embarrassment of riches. We have most, if not all, of those things we thought were essential for doing an effective educational job and for having rewarding personal involvement in the process.

But we are far from happy. Underneath our public confidence and enthusiasm lie serious misgivings about our ability to diagnose educational issues, develop new ideas, and realize those personal changes essential to applying new knowledge to the increasingly complex problem of educating minority pupils. Negroes, Mexicans, Puerto Ricans, and Indians have subcultures far removed from that of the white middle-class to whose needs the public schools have been almost exclusively geared. We ought to be disturbed and professionally embarrassed as we look at the hard facts of our failure to reach effectively more than a small percentage of pupils in these groups.

True, an outstanding Negro man such as the Reverend Walter Fauntroy was not destroyed by Washington's segregated and inferior Grimke, Patterson, and Dunbar schools. Moreover, he completed college and went on for graduate study at Yale. But for every Fauntroy there were a hundred young Negroes—in Washington, Atlanta, Chicago, and Portland— whose "death at an early age" was guaranteed by the educational system to which we belong and whose shortcomings each of us shares. Of course, other institutions too failed these minorities. But the schools, I think, were the most crucial. They might have provided the basic tools with which the shortcomings of the others might have been challenged. How much better to have had twenty Fauntroys who were no doubt there to be discovered and educated and whose loss we cannot now retrieve.

We can no longer postpone confrontation of our failure and of its victims. The Negro high school dropout (or is it shoveout, or counselout?) will no longer drop unprotestingly into the common labor market. That market is rapidly shrinking. But even if it were expanding, he feels that he deserves a better break from the society to which his forbears contributed much and which has such generous rewards for those of the right skin color. He is prepared to make forceful demands on that society, and his ranks grow rapidly. Organizations such as the Black United Front articulate in violent language frequently, and in violent action on occasion, the bitterness that grips young Negroes who experience school and school people not as friends, not as neutral custodians, but as enemies. Nor will Negro parents, or the older, moderate leaders in Negro communities, countenance continued neglect. They never approved. Now they can and will do something about it.

Social change has not meant social progress for major racial and ethnic minorities. And some of them have already given up on those processes through which it might have been realized. This has disturbing consequences for the whole American society and the process of relatively nonviolent resolution of conflict which is minimal for a pluralist, democratic order. The fate of moderate minority leaders is in the balance in the education arena. They have not been able to produce enough results. They need help from us and they need a lot of it. And it is required at every level of education.

As schoolmen we have a great many things in common. However, if you are an elementary or high school teacher, or administrator or counselor, you may well resent strange college professors harranguing you about failure to educate the black pupils in Montgomery County, Maryland. But recently the people in academe have had some forceful reminders of *their* failure to deal effectively with disadvantaged minorities. They find themselves now in a position similar to yours and no less distressed by their halting responses and ambiguities. Their research has not resolved critical questions; their teaching has proved to be inadequate; their counseling has frequently been irrelevant; their inability to adapt has underscored their conservatism. (Where did the idea of radical academicians come from anyway?) Whether one is teaching in a graduate school or prekindergarten program he faces the problem of developing meaningful educational services for groups heretofore largely excluded. Few college professors these days are unaware of the demands of black students for a "black curriculum and a black faculty." This is a strong reminder, however disturbing its implications, that college teachers' critical skills are frequently unworkable and perhaps irrelevant where minorities are concerned. The limited success of some compensatory elementary programs, for example, is paralleled by limited success of "high risk" programs under which many Negroes have been recently enrolled in colleges. Experienced public school people may take some perverse satisfaction at the deep discomfort of college "experts" who for so long have been telling you how to put your house in order while acting as if all was well in the groves of academe.

Regardless of the level at which one chooses to work, the white educator confronts both a professional and personal crisis in making himself relevant to the education of Negroes. Is one really resourceful and imaginative enough to teach reading to colored slum children, particularly when the model on which he has been trained is the white, middle-class youngster? And if he is, can he dedicate himself to the task which must be undertaken in far from ideal circumstances? Can one develop the skills to teach college math or western civilization or introductory sociology to "high-risk" Negro college students? And if he has the skills and techniques, will he apply them there, or take the easier route with already well-prepared white upperclassmen and graduate students? Are school boards sufficiently skillful and bold to develop and support new and effective but perhaps unpopular programs? Are college faculties willing to do more than simply talk about bold, new, "innovative" programs that will bring disadvantaged but bright black students into their classrooms, and keep them there? The answers to these and other questions will be a telling measure of both our professional competence and personal commitment in educating the uneducated and righting a long-standing wrong.

Given the complexity and emotional depth of race and education, it is not surprising that some schoolmen have given up, have been afraid, and have sought safe retreats in schools and grades where the problems are neat, clean, and white. A number of my colleagues, for example, have relinquished race relations courses because of new racial tensions in and outside the classrooms. Others have refused to make changes in instructional techniques for "high-risk" black students even though they are highly skeptical of tests and high school records as measures of these students. There is probably no administrator here who does not realistically anticipate receiving a large number of transfer requests from white teachers when disadvantaged students are admitted in any significant numbers to schools under his jurisdiction. And one could go on. The giving up and the running away take many forms and avenues. We must remember that education involves a commitment to knowledge and to the people to whom it is to be transmitted. Heretofore we have assumed that our ideas and techniques were fairly adequate at worst and superb at best, even in the face of a great deal of public criticism and adverse scientific evaluation. We held, as do most conservative professionals, that little was basically wrong. Whatever flaws there were, even in the schooling of minorities, could be remedied by a new committee, an administrative review, a reorganization of special services, a summer workshop, or a new course at the local school of education. Had ours remained a static society, had change not been so rapid, had technology not been so dynamic, had Negroes been willing to wait another hundred years, this easy-going, pragmatic approach might have worked. But change did not stop, its rate did not decrease, and it affected in many unexpected ways all of our institutions, perhaps most of all the public schools.

Even when we had sharp reminders that we were not effectively changing with social change, we had some easy outs, or so we thought. The colleges blamed the high schools; the high schools blamed the elementary schools; the elementary schools blamed the community, the Negro family and other targets of opportunity. But no more. We all share a responsibility not easily evaded. Let's face it: the college professor, the high school science teacher, and the elementary reading teacher are in the same boat: we really aren't teaching disadvantaged Negroes. We haven't been able to do so. We don't seem to be making any giant strides to close the gaps. So marked has been our failure and so meager our response that we now face demands that the schools be removed from established professional control and placed in the hands of minority peoples themselves, or that we even abandon the public schools altogether since they are thought to be hopelessly rigid and their personnel self-satisfied beyond measure.

The subject of race and education has been so thoroughly explored that one is almost overwhelmed by the volume of published material. New research is under way and we can anticipate a continuing stream of books, reports, surveys, and projects. Perhaps new findings will be more helpful than those accumulated during the past fifteen years. But that may not be the critical factor at all. We need to remember that ideas without action and data without application help us little. And knowledge without moral commitment is sterile. However limited our knowledge, we can't now very well argue that we did not know or that we had no personal responsibility. And if the education of Negroes is not accomplished in the framework of the free public school, we are in no position, on the record to date, to resist its being transferred to other agencies.

What we require, I believe, is not more data. After all, we do have the Coleman Report, the Kerner Report, and before that the Myrdal Study, and a hundred others developed over the past quarter century. What we need most is a strategy for the application of what we know and enough professional courage and personal insight to actively shape the structure of and techniques for educating Negroes.

Social changes which have led to the problems and opportunities now before us are going to continue. Demands upon us are going to increase, not diminish. In these circumstances what alternatives are open to us? What, briefly, ought we to do? I wish I had some clear-cut and easily applied recommendations. I don't, but will conclude with some suggestions.

First, we must learn more about the issues and the feelings of people when it comes to race and education. This is usually on the agenda and evokes few exceptions. But I mean a particular kind of learning, that is, by doing, by first-hand involvement, by encounter with disadvantaged peoples, and by confrontation in day-to-day situations in the schools, in the home, in the streets. In this process, and perhaps in this process only, one learns something about the other world of minorities from which he is separated by a much greater distance than it is comfortable to admit. Probably just as important, he learns something about himself and begins to recognize the depth of his own racial antipathies and the narrowness of his vaunted professional skills. He may discover, too, that, in spite of the pervasive racism which affects both Negro and white, he can be sensitive, warm and responsive toward people who need desperately the education into which he can guide them.

Second, I suggest that you scrutinize carefully the educational establishment of which you are a part and determine the resources it has or might obtain for adaptation to the needs of disadvantaged groups. Bureaucracies are rigid and they change only reluctantly, but they can be modified. But how? Many of us, while critical of the educational establishment and its rules and rigidities, are nevertheless glad that it changes so slowly and resists innovation. We can pose as one of its victims when we face moral ambiguities and make tough personal decisions. The educational bureaucracy can be changed from within if people want to change it. But something else is also required; namely, some ideas about how it should be changed and the direction in which it should move. This means becoming knowledgeable not only about minority peoples and educational techniques, but also about the structure and patterns of power and influence in the educational system. It could well mean active cooperation with community groups whose desire to make the system relevant to the needs of minorities you may share. Such groups are usually defined as uninformed intruders; they may be viewed as sources of new ideas and as supports for good, new ventures in educating the disadvantaged.

My third suggestion is that you actively involve yourselves in the selection of new personnel whose basic philosophies and personalities enable them to be most effective in reaching disadvantaged groups. We are all recruiters to the teaching profession. By simply being in it we affirm its importance. But we do much more. We are concerned with its expansion and improvement and its contining relevance to the changing society. We have neglected recruiting people capable of carrying education to ghetto people. Even worse, we have through outlandish requirements and "mickey mouse" courses, turned off sensitive, dedicated and bright people keenly concerned with educating poor Negroes, Mexicans, and other minorities. We ought to insist that schools of education modify drastically not only the curriculum, but their selection and certification procedures. We should make clear that courses in educational methods must be reduced and that those in basic subjects increased. We should insist that basic subjects emphasize the social, psychological and cultural diversity of pupil and parent groups. Along with this, we should demand that practice teaching be drastically modified so that the recruit serves a real apprenticeship in realistic ghetto and minority schools and thus learns something of what life and work there are like. In this way he may learn not to be afraid, may find positive values in the ghetto school and community, and may regard assignment there as a challenge and not as a purgatory through which he must pass before entering the heaven of a white middle-class school.

Fourth, I believe that each of us in his own particular role can draw upon and contribute to resources of the minority community. This we have been very reluctant to do, in part, because we have meaningful relations with few Negroes or other minority people. In part because we have misgivings about administrators or fellow teachers or our own students, fearing adverse reactions or some difficult incidents. But I think we will find that Negroes and Mexicans and others are eager to be heard and will have something to say and something to be in confrontation. One should not restrict his encounters to safe and conservative spokesmen. There aren't many left these days. In the same context, we can make ourselves available and encounter minorities on their own grounds. Not all Negroes by any means hate whites with such a passion that they can communicate only through violence. And certainly the diversity of white response to the Negro revolution suggests that some whites, including many school people, are still capable of sensitivity, compassion and acceptance where Negroes are concerned. This reciprocity can be extended. Organized minority groups should be assisted rather than fought as challenges to the school operations and personnel. They need and want technical knowledge required to constructively influence educational change. As specialists—teachers, administrators, counselors—we can provide it without attempting to direct the way it is used or usurp their legitimate participation in public school policy-making.

One other suggestion and I am through. There are none so holy as the recently converted, and none who are likely to fall from grace so soon. I applaud those whose moral indignation leads them to active involvement in the race relations scene, but I have reservations about those people who suddenly discover Négroes, or poor people, or Puerto Ricans, and become immersed in their causes. Negroes and poor people share those reservations. They are not looking for saviors; and however messianic you are, the chances of their accepting you are something less than a hundred to one. What you in one way or another can bring is understanding as a fellow human being and some skills as a teacher or administrator or staff specialist. And if there is suspicion, mistrust, ignorance, and apathy among them you may also find warmth, hope, intelligence, and acceptance. After all, you didn't become an educator to preside over collections of highly enlightened people, but to spread knowledge, regardless of the race, creed, or color of those who sought knowledge.

Racism in American Education
Robert L. Green

For many years, whites in Northern communities and the liberal white press have been basking in self-righteousness, condemning Southern whites for "mistreating black Americans." Yet as they raised their voices in protest over the attitudes of Southern whites toward school desegregation, they refused to look at the conditions in their own communities—segregated housing, discrimination in employment, and, most importantly, segregated inferior schools for blacks. Before whites had time to reflect on racial injustice "Northern style," they were suddenly faced with urban unrest, school boycotts, and cries for integration, separatism, and community control.

Even today the North is not responding to the legitimate concerns of its black citizens. In 1971 the major confrontations over school desegregation in the U.S. occurred in a Michigan community, not in the Deep South. Several buses were blown up the day before they were to be used to cross-bus black and white pupils in Pontiac, Michigan. The only major violent incident in 1971 that led to the arrest of Ku Klux Klan leaders was also in Pontiac. Clearly, Southern whites do not have a monopoly on racism and educational inequities.

From Robert L. Green, "Racism in American Education," *Phi Delta Kappan* 53 (January 1972): 274–76. Reprinted by permission of the author and the publisher.

Throughout its history, the American educational system in all regions has perpetrated the subordination of racial minorities and the poor. It has failed to provide all children with relevant education of high quality. The schools have reflected, reinforced, and sometimes promoted the same discrepant treatment of children on the basis of race and social class that exists in the larger society. As the National Advisory Commission on Civil Disorders (Kerner Commission) reported, "The schools have failed to provide the educational experience which could help overcome the effects of discrimination and deprivation."[1]

White middle-class school administrators and government officials are responsible for the inequities in public education. They have deliberately established school boundaries along racial and class lines. In Detroit, Michigan, U.S. District Judge Stephen J. Roth recently ruled that the city's schools are illegally segregated and that government action was responsible for the residential segregation in the city. Judge Roth also said that the school board, attempting to relieve overcrowding, had admitted that black students were bused past or away from nearby white schools with available classroom space to black schools that were overcrowded. In Benton Harbor, Michigan, evidence was presented in a suit against the school district which showed that black youngsters were being bused from black neighborhoods to white schools, isolated in all-black classrooms for the day, and then returned to the black neighborhoods in the afternoon.

DAMAGE CAUSED BY RACIAL ISOLATION

Racial isolation in the schools is damaging to black children because they are denied the resources that are often available to white pupils. It is also detrimental to white children because they develop a false sense of superiority. "Whites who attend racially isolated schools develop unrealistic self-concepts, hate, fear, suspicions, and other attitudes that alienate them from minorities," Preston Wilcox has written.[2] Although American public education has encouraged patriotism, it has neglected to develop respect for humanity and people of diverse backgrounds. White children learn at a very early age at home, and are often reinforced by teachers and textbooks, not to respect people of color; whites have been socialized to feel superior to blacks and browns. As Wilcox noted, "The myth of white supremacy remains a myth perpetrated to foster the privileges of white skin."[3]

The public schools are not providing minority and poor children with the knowledge and skills they will need to earn a decent living and to participate in the social and political life of the community. More ethnic minority students than white students drop out of school and "many of those who do graduate are not equipped to enter the normal job market, and have great difficulty securing employment," the Kerner Commission reported.[4] School administrators, teachers, parents, and students all tend to regard urban schools as inferior.

LESS QUALIFIED TEACHERS

The quality of teachers and administrators in inner-city schools is a major factor which often makes the school experience for the ethnic minority child unsuccessful. Most teachers in urban schools have inferior credentials and often have fewer years of teaching experience. It was documented in the Benton Harbor, Michigan, case that teachers with inferior credentials were assigned to black schools and that teachers were also assigned by race. When faced with desegregation suits, school districts often place their best qualified black teachers in predominantly white schools. Robert Havighurst reported in 1967 that 36 percent of the teachers in the Chicago public schools with large minority enrollments were full-time substitutes. No other Chicago schools averaged more than 14 percent in this category. Eighty-two percent of all substitutes in the system were assigned to minority schools. The median years of teaching experience in those schools was four years, while in other Chicago schools it was no less than nine years and usually more.[5]

A 1963 study of the Chicago public schools showed that only 63.2 percent of all teachers in the 10 schools ranking lowest in socioeconomic status were fully certified.[6] Seven of the 10 schools had black enrollments exceeding 90 percent. Of the 10 highest ranking schools, eight were almost totally white, and of the teachers in the highest ranking schools, 90.3 percent were fully certified.

A major problem in inner-city schools results from the large number of permanent substitutes and individuals teaching out of their fields of specialization. To be effective, a teacher must have a strong command of his discipline. In 1968, Chicago public school officials announced that for the first time in many years they had a waiting list of teachers for their inner-city schools. The reason was that draft deferments were promised to college students who taught in low-income schools. The prospective teachers said thay they would not have accepted the positions if the war in Vietnam were over; only a small percent of them planned to remain in teaching.

LESS THAN ADEQUATE FACILITIES

Inner-city schools are overcrowded and tend to be the oldest and most ill-equipped schools in the nation. In 1967, 30 of the occupied school buildings in Detroit had been dedicated during President Grant's Administration. The Coleman Report stated that "Negro pupils have fewer of some of the facilities that seem most related to achievement." Curricula and materials used in urban schools are often not relevant to the experiences of the students; they are intended to serve a middle-class population.

Although some progress has been made and there are notable exceptions, most white middle-class teachers have little understanding or appreciation of minority cultures and do not instill an appreciation of different cultures in minority students. Immigrants to this country in the mid-nineteenth century faced a similar problem. Many teachers and principals viewed immigrant parents as "ignorant, prejudiced, and highly excitable people." Children of immigrants were taught to be ashamed of their parents. Although these immigrants were minorities, they were eventually able to fit into the American "mainstream." They were able to develop what the majority considered appropriate behavior. In American life, being part of the mainstream means dressing, looking, and thinking like the ideal middle-class white American. The interesting aspect of this concept of becoming a part of the American heritage is that it means feeling guilty about being Jewish, Polish, Chicano, or black.

The real barrier to the concept of equal educational opportunity and the development of democratic attitudes is related to the set of values instilled in young children. The mainstream is a myth; otherwise it would include all people. Instead, the dominant culture forces upon minority and majority children subjects that are not at all relevant to their lives. Students are often bored with sixteenth-century approaches to European literature and history. This is one reason why many children of all races drop out of school. Teachers often convince the ethnic minority child that his culture and life-style do not merit study in school. When working with ethnic children educators often violate the sound educational principle that the school experience should reflect the life-styles and interests of their pupils.

TRACKING

Minority youngsters are often placed in tracks on the basis of their performance on intelligence tests, and tracking is often a manifestation of racism. In Benton Harbor, Michigan, for example, black students were given reading tests; those doing poorly were assigned to "lower academic" tracks, no matter how proficient they were in other subjects. Court testimony showed that teachers of youngsters in lower tracks viewed them as nonachievers, and expected little from them academically. When students are provided inferior educational training in the early grades and are not positively reinforced and helped to develop adequate self-concepts, they cannot be expected to perform well on standardized aptitude tests. Beyond this, the validity of many tests used to predict the academic success of ethnic minority students has been seriously questioned by black psychologists and educators. They argue that test constructors usually exclude ethnic students when establishing group norms. Consequently, standardized test results often reinforce the negative self-images of minority youths and are frequently used to deny them equal educational opportunities.

ALTERNATIVES TO RACISM IN EDUCATION

All of the factors discussed above indicate that racism exists in the public schools. Six areas in which changes could help to mitigate racism in education are: (1) the development of multiracial schools early in the child's career, (2) improving teacher training, (3) establishing units on antiracist behavior, (4) retraining teacher trainers, (5) leadership, and (6) ongoing in-service training.

One method to achieve multiracial schools is two-way busing. Practiced in the South for many years as a means of assuring segregated schools, busing was then advocated by blacks in the North to enable black students to attend better equipped schools in white communities. But "integration" did not work as harmoniously as had been anticipated. Black children were bused miles away to white schools, while white students were not bused. Some perceived this one-way busing as punishment for blacks pursuing integration. As the Citizens Committee on Equal Educational Opportunities in Richmond, California, said, "The only real way to solve segregation problems is by two-way busing."[7]

It is not clear why parents are so opposed to busing to achieve desegregation. Many white children are bused daily to private schools with parental approval. Neither do most people object to busing a child who has a physical handicap to a school where he can get a good education. The purpose of busing should be to improve the quality of education. The arguments that center around busing today are highly racially motivated. Other issues are merely attempts to evade the main problem.

Segregated schools foster a sense of superiority in whites and also hate, fear, and suspicion of minorities. Minorities, in turn, develop a sense of inferiority along with feelings of hostility, resentment, and resignation. Consequently, neither group is able to function properly in a multiracial setting. It is a vicious circle, but the circle must be broken. Multiracial settings contribute to improving minority self-perception; improvement of the minority youngster's self-image can lead to greater academic achievement.

Another way to achieve multiracial schools is by developing magnet schools or high-caliber schools attractive to all, with interdistrict busing. This provides for alteration of school districts and the creation of wider metropolitan school boundary lines.

Educational leaders must also apply pressure to metropolitan governments to end racism in housing. President Nixon's recent negative stand on expanded housing opportunities was a blow to those striving for multiracial communities; the federal government has not assumed an active role in creating racial harmony in America.

IMPROVED TEACHER TRAINING

Teacher training institutions must develop programs that reflect and promote ethnic diversity. How do we do this? We must begin to desegregate teaching staffs systematically at every level in teacher training programs within colleges of education in large universities. The largest colleges of education throughout the U.S. have essentially all-white staffs.

We cannot realistically expect to help students develop nonracist attitudes when teaching staffs are selected from a population that has been trained to be biased. A complete sequence of curriculum development and in-service training should be planned and initiated, and minority members must be included in this planning and used in teaching roles.

The first two years of teacher training might parallel the VISTA or Peace Corps experience. Students should spend less time in the classroom and more time in field projects with racial minorities and the poor. Internships with such individuals as Cesar Chavez and the Reverend Jesse Jackson, with groups like the black poor in Green County, Alabama, and with institutions such as the Martin Luther King, Jr., Memorial Center and the Institute of the Black World should be structured for students early in their training programs. Two years of academic course work in the classroom could well be enough. Students should spend more time learning about people from diverse backgrounds and becoming more humanistic by actually participating in work projects with urban and rural residents from all walks of life and from diverse racial backgrounds.

UNITS TO COMBAT RACISM

There should be lesson plans and units in the public schools that teach children how to develop nonracist attitudes. Units on democracy, living with people who are different, and units teaching respect for the life-style of the poor would help children to develop more positive racial feelings.

TRAINING AND LEADERSHIP

Ongoing in-service training for all teachers should be established, focused on eradicating biased attitudes toward the poor and racial minorities. Individuals who have demonstrated that they are very sensitive to the plight of the poor and racial minorities should be selected to head these workshops.

The National Education Association and local education groups must speak out against injustice. Educators cannot purport to be neutral when minorities are discriminated against in housing, employment, and education. Poor people have always been suspicious of teachers and administrators, not only because they have failed to educate their children but because organized educational bodies have seldom spoken out against racial injustice. Teachers' unions, unfortunately, often parallel other unions such as the electrical workers' union and the carpenters' union, in that they struggle mainly for higher salaries rather than for human or civil rights. They can no longer remain neutral on race-related issues. They cannot remain neutral when quality education is at stake. They cannot remain neutral when the rights of minorities are threatened.

Replying to the attorney for the Detroit Board of Education who stated that the school board could not be held responsible for the acts of other governmental bodies, Judge Stephen Roth countered that ". . . the actions or the failures to act by responsible school authorities . . . were linked to actions of . . . other governmental units."[8] Therefore, if the educational system is to serve all of the nation's children, it must change its direction and pace. Unless it changes its posture toward ethnic minorities and the poor, our schools will continue to be the sources of conflict and turmoil in the community.

NOTES

[1] *Report of the National Advisory Commission on Civil Disorders* (New York: E. P. Dutton and Co., 1968), p. 425.

[2] Preston Wilcox, "Education for Black Humanism: A Way of Approaching It," in N. Wright, Jr., ed., *What Black Educators Are Saying* (New York: Hawthorn Books, Inc., 1970), p. 7.

[3] Ibid., p. 12.

[4] *Report of the National Advisory Commission,* pp. 425–26.

[5] Robert I. Havighurst, *Education in Metropolitan Areas* (Boston: Allyn and Bacon, 1967).

[6] *Report of the National Advisory Commission,* p. 428.

[7] James E. Allen, Jr., "Integration Is Better Education," *Integrated Education,* September-October, 1969, p. 30.

[8] William Grant, "Suit Unraveled Long History of Race Segregation in City," *Detroit Free Press,* 11 October 1971, p. 4B.

Imperatives in Ethnic Minority Education

James A. Banks

As we approach the threshold of the twenty-first century, our nation is witnessing technological progress which has been unparalleled in human history, yet is plagued with social problems of such magnitude that they pose a serious threat to the ideals of American democracy and to man's very survival. Environmental pollution, poverty, war, deteriorating cities, and ethnic conflict are the intractable social problems which Americans must resolve if we are to survive and create a just, humane society. Our society is becoming increasingly polarized and dehumanized, largely

From James A. Banks, "Imperatives in Ethnic Minority Education," *Phi Delta Kappan* 53 (January 1972): 266–69. Reprinted by permission of the author and the publisher.

because of institutional racism and ethnic hostility. The elimination of conflicts between the races must be our top priority.

One of the founding principles of this nation was that oppressed peoples from other lands would find in America tolerance and acceptance, if not a utopia for the full development of their potential. People who were denied religious, economic, and political freedom flocked to the New World in search of a better life. Perhaps more than any nation in human history, the United States has succeeded in culturally assimilating its immigrants and providing them with the opportunity to attain the "good life." The elimination of differences among peoples of diverse nationalities was the essence of the "melting pot" concept.

While the United States has successfully assimilated ethnic groups which shared a set of values and behavior patterns of European origin, it has blatantly denied its black, brown, red, and yellow citizens the opportunity to share fully in the American Dream because they possess physical and cultural characteristics which are non-European. Ethnic minority groups have been the victims of institutional racism in America primarily because of their unique physical traits and the myths which emerged extolling the intrinsic virtues of European civilization and describing non-European peoples as ruthless savages. European and white ancestry have been the primary requisites for full realization of the American Dream. For most colored peoples in the United States, the dream has been deferred. The shattered dream and the denial of equal opportunities to ethnic minority groups have been the sources of acute ethnic conflict within America; it has now reached crisis proportions. The flames that burned in Watts, the blood that ran in Detroit, and now the Attica massacre are alarming manifestations of our inability to resolve conflicts between the majority and ethnic minority groups in America.

No sensitive and perceptive student of American society can deny the seriousness of our current racial problems. In recent years they have intensified as blacks and other powerless ethnic groups have taken aggressive actions to liberate themselves from oppression. Reactions of the white community to the new ethnic militancy have been intense and persisting. A "law and order" cult has emerged to eradicate ethnic revolts. To many white Americans, the plea for law and order is a call for an end to protests by ethnic groups and alienated youths. The fact that many law and order advocates demanded that Lt. Calley go free for killing numbers of civilian colored peoples in Asia indicates that many "middle" Americans do not consistently value law, order, or human life. The law and order movement is directed primarily toward the poor, the colored, and the powerless. One example is the "no-knock" law in Washington, D.C. Although promises to bring law and order to the street often ensure victory in public elections, the most costly and destructive crimes in America are committed by powerful syndicates, corrupted government officials, and industries that pollute our environment, not by the ghetto looter and the petty thief. Also, few constructive actions have been taken by local and national leaders to eliminate the hopelessness, alienation, and poverty which often cause the ghetto dweller to violate laws in order to survive. As our nation becomes increasingly polarized, we are rapidly becoming two separate and unequal societies.[1]

Because the public school is an integral part of our social system, it has been a partner in the denial of equal opportunities to America's ethnic minorities; it has served mainly to perpetuate the status quo and to reinforce social class and racial stratification. Sensitive and perceptive writers such as Kozol and Kohl, and researchers like Pettigrew and Coleman, have extensively documented the ways in which the public schools make the ethnic child feel "invisible," while at the same time teaching the American Dream. Such contradictory behavior on the part of educators makes the ethnic minority child, as Baldwin has insightfully stated, run "the risk of becoming schizophrenic."[2]

Despite the school's reluctance to initiate social change, despite its tendency to reinforce and perpetuate the status quo, whenever our nation faces a crisis we call upon the school to help resolve it. Obviously, this is not because schools have historically responded creatively and imaginatively to social problems. It is because many Americans retain an unshaken faith in the school's *potential* for improving society. *I* share that faith. The school does have potential to promote and lead constructive social change. In fact, it may be the only institution within our society which can spearhead the changes essential to prevent racial wars and chaos in America. I would now like to propose a number of changes which must take place in the school if it is going to exercise a leadership role in eliminating ethnic hostility and conflict in America.

Because the teacher is the most important variable in the child's learning environment, classroom teachers must develop more positive attitudes toward ethnic minorities and their cultures and must develop higher academic expectations for ethnic youths. Teacher attitudes and expectations have a profound impact on students' perceptions, academic behavior, self-concepts, and beliefs. Many teachers do not accept and respect the diverse cultures of ethnic youths, hence ethnic students often find the school's culture alien. The "cultural clash" in the classroom is by now a cliché. Studies by scholars such as Becker, Gottlieb, and Clark indicate that teachers typically have negative attitudes and low academic expectations for their black, brown, red, and poor pupils. Other research suggests that teachers, next to parents, are the most "significant others" in children's lives, and that teachers play an important role in the formation of children's racial attitudes and beliefs. A study by Davidson and Lang indicates that the assessment a child makes of himself is significantly related to the evaluation that "significant" people, such as teachers, make of him.[3]

It is necessary for *all* teachers to view ethnic groups and their cultures more positively, whether they teach in suburbia or in the inner city. The problems in the ghetto are deeply implicated in the larger society. Our future presidents, senators, mayors, policemen, and absentee landlords are taught in suburban classrooms. Unless teachers can succeed in helping these future leaders to develop more humane attitudes toward ethnic minorities, the ghetto will continue to thrive and destroy human lives.

The research on changing teacher attitudes is both sparse and inconclusive. It suggests that changing the racial attitudes of adults is a herculean task. However, the *urgency* of our racial problems demands that we act on the basis of current research. To maximize the chances for successful attitude intervention programs, experiences must be designed specifically for that purpose. Programs with general or global objectives are not likely to be successful. Courses which consist primarily or exclusively of lecture presentations have little impact. Diverse experiences, such as seminars, visitations, community involvement, committee work, guest speakers, movies, multimedia materials, and workshops, combined with factual lectures, are more effective than any single approach. Community involvement and contact (with appropriate norms in the social setting) are the most productive techniques. Psychotherapy and T-grouping, if led by competent persons, are also promising strategies.[4]

Teachers must help ethnic minority students to augment their self-concepts, to feel more positively toward their own cultures, to develop a sense of political efficacy, and to master strategies which will enable them to liberate themselves from physical and psychological oppression. There is a movement among ethnic minority groups to reject their old identities, shaped largely by white society, and to create new ones, shaped by themselves. The calls for black, red, brown, and yellow power are rallying cries of these movements. However, despite the positive changes which have resulted from these identity quests, most ethnic minority youths still live in dehumanizing ghettos which tell them that black, brown, and red are ugly and shameful. They have many hostile teachers and administrators who reinforce the negative lessons which they learn from their immediate environment. Ethnic youths cannot believe that they are beautiful people as long as they have social contacts within the school and the larger society which contradict that belief. While current research is inconclusive and contradictory, the *bulk* of it indicates that recent attempts at self-determination *have not* significantly changed the self-concepts and self-evaluations of most ethnic minority children and youths.[5]

Despite the need for ethnic studies by *all* youths, ethnic content alone will not help minority youths to feel more positively about themselves and their cultures, nor will it help them develop a sense of control over their destinies. A school atmosphere must be created which values and accepts cultural differences, and ethnic youths must be taught how they have been victimized by institutional racism. They must become involved in social action projects which will teach them how to influence and change social and political institutions. One of the major goals of ethnic studies should be to help ethnic minority students become effective and rational political activists. We must provide opportunities for them to participate in social action projects so that they can become adept in influencing public policy which affects their lives. We now educate students for political apathy. They are taught that every citizen gets equal protection under the law, that racism only exists in the South, and that if they vote regularly and obey laws our benign political leaders will make sure that they will get their slice of the American Dream pie. The powerlessness and widespread political alienation among blacks, Chicanos, Indians, Puerto Ricans, and other poor peoples are deceptively evaded in such mythical lessons about our political system. We must teach ethnic youths how to obtain and exercise political power in order for them to liberate themselves from physical and psychological captivity. Their liberation might be the salvation of our confused and divided society.

There is also an urgent need for ethnic studies to help white students expand their conception of humanity. Many whites seem to believe that they are the only *humans* on earth. To the extent that a people excludes other humans from their conception of humanity, they themselves are dehumanized. Racism has dehumanized many whites and caused them to exclude ethnic minority groups from their definition of humanity. The differential reactions by the majority of whites to the killings of blacks and whites in recent years indicate how whites often consider blacks and other ethnic groups less than human. During racial rebellions that broke out in our cities in the early 1900s, the 1940s, and the late 1960s, hundreds of blacks were killed by police because they were protesting against injustices and grinding poverty. Many of these victims were innocent bystanders. In 1969, two black students were shot by police on the campus of a black college in South Carolina. The majority of white Americans remained conspicuously silent during these tragedies; a few even applauded. The tragedy at Kent State evoked strong reactions and protest by many white Americans, but no similarly strong reactions followed the tragedy at Jackson State. Reactions of the majority of white Americans to the My Lai massacre and the Attica incident were not as intense as the reaction to the Kent State tragedy.

Each of these dehumanizing events—the killings of ghetto blacks, the incidents at Kent State and Jackson State, the My Lai massacre, and the Attica tragedy—should have caused *all* Americans to become saddened, anguished, and outraged. The American dilemma which these incidents illuminated is that Americans are capable of reacting to the killings of human beings differently because of differences in their skin color and social class. While people may start treating others in dehumanizing ways because of their skin color or social class, the dehumanizing process, once started, continues unabated. Unless aggressive efforts are made to humanize white students, future incidents such as Kent State may leave the majority of Americans emotionally untouched. The issue of helping students become more humanized ultimately transcends race and social class. However, helping students see ethnic minorities as fellow humans is imperative if we are to eliminate our racial problems.

Ethnic content can serve as an excellent vehicle to help white students expand their conceptions of humanity and to better understand their own cultures. Since cultures are man-made, there are many ways of being human. The white middle-class lifestyle is one way; the Spanish Harlem culture is another. By studying this important generalization, students will develop an appreciation for man's great capacity to create a diversity of lifestyles and to adapt to a variety of social and physical environments. Most groups tend to think that their culture is superior to all others. Chauvinist ethnocentrism is especially acute among dominant groups in American society. By studying other ways of being and living, students will see how bound they are by their own values, perceptions, and prejudices. The cultures of our powerless ethnic groups, and the devastating experiences of America's oppressed black, brown, red, and yellow peoples, are shocking testimony to the criminal effects of racism on its victims. Ethnic content can serve as an excellent lens to help white America see itself clearly, and hopefully to become more humanized.

We must construct new conceptions of human intelligence and devise instructional programs based on these novel ideas to improve the education of ethnic minority groups. Brookover and Erickson have summarized the conceptions of human intelligence on which most current educational programs are based: "(1) that ability to learn is relatively fixed and unchangeable and (2) that it is predetermined by heredity. . . . These beliefs assume that ability is unaffected by external social forces. Another common assumption is that fixed ability of individuals can be measured with reasonable accuracy by intelligence tests."[6] These pervasive and outmoded assumptions have led to unfortunate practices in our schools. Ethnic minority youths are often placed in low academic tracks, classified as mentally retarded, and exposed to an unstimulating educational environment because they perform poorly on I.Q. and other tests which are standardized on a white middle-class population. These practices result in the self-fulfilling prophecy: Teachers assume that these pupils cannot learn, and they do not learn because teachers do not create the kinds of experiences which will enable them to master essential understandings and skills.

The traditional conceptions of human intelligence have been recently defended and popularized by Arthur S. Jensen. Jensen's research is based on unhelpful and faulty assumptions (he maintains, for example, that intelligence is what I.Q. tests measure). His argument is only a hypothesis, and should never have been presented to the public in a popular magazine such as Life (since it is only a hypothesis) in these racially troubled times. I believe that the hypothesis is immoral, misleading, and irrelevant. Since we have no reliable and valid ways to determine innate potential, a moral assumption is that all students have the ability to master the skills and understandings which educators deem necessary for them to function adequately in our highly technological society; we should search for means to facilitate their acquisition of these skills and understandings and not spend valuable time trying to discover which ethnic group is born with "more" of "something" that we have not yet clearly defined. As Robert E. L. Faris, the perceptive sociologist, has stated, "We essentially create our own level of human intelligence."[7]

Teachers must obtain a more liberal education, greater familiarity with ethnic cultures, and a more acute awareness of the *racist* assumptions on which much social research is based if they are to become effective change agents in minority education. Social science reflects the norms, values, and goals of the ruling and powerful groups in society; it validates those belief systems which are functional for people in power and dysfunctional for oppressed and powerless groups. Research which is antithetical to the interests of ruling and powerful groups is generally ignored by the scientific community and the society which supports it.[8] Numerous myths about ethnic minorities have been created by white "scholarly" historians and social scientists. Many teachers perpetuate the historical and social science myths which they learned in school and that are pervasive in textbooks because they are unaware of the racist assumptions on which social science research is often based. Much information in textbooks is designed to support the status quo and to keep powerless ethnic groups at the lower rungs of the social ladder.

Teachers often tell students that Columbus discovered America, yet the Indians were here centuries before Columbus. The Columbus myth in one sense denies the Indian child his past and thus his identity. Many teachers believe that Lincoln was the great emancipator of black people; yet he supported a move to deport blacks to Africa and issued the Emancipation Proclamation, in his own words, "as a military necessity" to weaken the Confederacy. Primary grade teachers often try to convince the ghetto child that the policeman is his friend. Many ethnic minority students know from their experiences that the some policemen are their enemies. Only when teachers get a truly liberal education about the nature of science and American society will they be able to correct such myths and distortions and make the school experience more realistic and meaningful for *all* students. Both pre- and in-service training is necessary to help teachers to gain a realistic perspective of American society.

The severity of our current racial problems has rarely been exceeded in human history. The decaying cities, antibusing movements, escalating poverty, increasing racial polarization, and the recent Attica tragedy are alarming manifestations of the ethnic hostility which is widespread throughout America. Our very existence may ultimately depend upon our creative abilities to solve our urgent racial problems. During the decade which recently closed, much discussion and analysis related to ethnic minority problems occurred, yet few constructive steps were taken to eliminate the basic causes of our racial crisis. Educators must take decisive steps to help create a culturally pluralistic society in which peoples of different colors can live in harmony. Immediate action is imperative if we are to prevent racial wars and chaos and the complete dehumanization of the American man.

NOTES

1 *Report of the National Advisory Commission on Civil Disorders* (New York: Bantam Books, 1968), p. 1.

2 James Baldwin, "A Talk to Teachers," *Saturday Review,* 21 December 1963, p. 42.

3 Helen H. Davidson and Gerhard Lang, "Children's Perceptions of Their Teachers' Feelings Toward Them Related to Self-Perception, School Achievement, and Behavior," *Journal of Experimental Education,* 1960, pp. 107–18; reprinted in James A. Banks and William W. Joyce, eds., *Teaching Social Studies to Culturally Different Children* (Reading, Mass.: Addison-Wesley 1971), pp. 113–27.

4 For a review of this research, *see* James A. Banks, "Racial Prejudice and the Black Self-Concept," in James A. Banks and Jean Dresden Grambs, eds., *Black Self-Concept: Implications for Education and Social Science* (New York: McGraw-Hill, 1972), pp. 5–35.

5 For a research summary and review, *see* Marcel L. Goldschmid, ed., *Black Americans and White Racism: Theory and Research* (New York: Holt, Rinehart, and Winston, 1970).

6 Wilbur B. Brookover and Edsel L. Erickson, *Society, Schools and Learning* (Boston: Allyn and Bacon, 1969), p. 3.

7 Robert E. L. Faris, "Reflections on the Ability Dimension in Human Society," *American Sociological Review* (December 1961), pp. 835–42.

8 For a perceptive discussion of this point, *see* Barbara A. Sizemore, "Social Science and Education for a Black Identity," in Banks and Grambs, *Black Self-Concept,* p. 141–70.

The Federal Courts and Faculty Desegregation

Richard S. Vacca

More than a decade has passed since the United States Supreme Court handed down its historical decisions in first *Brown* (1954)[1] and second *Brown* (1955).[2] Over the past fifteen years numerous legal problems have been faced by public school systems of the various states, particularly those in the South, as attempts were made to satisfy desegregation requirements set forth by federal governmental agencies and interpreted by federal courts.

In recent years, desegregation plans submitted by southern school systems for court approval have emphasized the racial balancing of student

From Richard S. Vacca, "The Federal Courts and Faculty Desegregation," *The Clearing House* 46 (January 1972): 312–16. Reprinted by permission of *The Clearing House* and the author.

enrollments. The concept of the *unitary school* system (as opposed to separate public school systems for the races), has emerged as the ultimate legal goal to achieve. That public school system enrollment must be balanced according to certain preconceived ratios, became a primary requirement of federal courts before desegregation plans would be approved. The recent Supreme Court decision in *Swann*[3] represents a milestone in the establishment of unitary public school systems.

THE CLASSROOM TEACHER AS A DIMENSION OF PUBLIC SCHOOL DESEGREGATION

Current research into the social and psychological dynamics of classroom interaction, and research into the effects of the teacher on the learning environment, point to the fact that not just any teacher (in academic preparation, methodology, experience, and sensitivity to human needs) can function effectively in a classroom inhabited by students from multiracial and multicultural backgrounds. Research and experience have shown that the contemporary classroom must be staffed with a particular teacher chosen because he possesses particular talents and professional attributes. As a result, public school educators realize that to implement classroom instruction successfully, within racially integrated schools, they must (1) select the ablest teachers, (2) assign them to classes and students based upon a matching of teacher differences to student needs, and (3) make effective teachers available to more students.[4] (Teacher over-supply in many areas is one factor that has helped to make this attitude possible.)

As indicated earlier, students have been, and rightfully should be, the major focus of court approved desegregation plans. A stage of development has now been reached, however, when more emphasis must be placed on vital services associated with, and directly related to, successfully implementing school integration plans. One such service involves the critical need to staff integrated schools with capable and effective classroom teachers. Until recently, the faculty dimension in public school desegregation received little if any publicity and in some cases often seemed neglected.

Cases have now reached courts of law, federal courts in particular, in which problems associated with or related to faculty desegregation are at issue. It is the purpose of this article to discuss what recent courts have said concerning faculty selection in general, and concerning faculty desegregation where it has occurred.

BOARDS OF EDUCATION AND TEACHER SELECTION IN GENERAL

Contrary to what some contemporary writers are saying, courts of law in the United States have historically maintained a *laissez-faire* attitude toward public school matters. That is to say, American courts have followed a philosophy characterized by a deliberate move away from direct intervention into school matters. As Nolte has said of the position taken by courts in reviewing the exercise of school board powers, "Ordinarily, the courts will not intervene in the peaceful exercise of those powers. . . ."[5]

The granting of extensive discretionary authority to school boards relative to matters of teacher employment, is evident in recent cases decided in federal courts. This is illustrated in a recent Wyoming case before a federal district court. In the words of the court, "School Boards should have a wide range of discretion in the management and operation of a school district, including the employment procedures of hiring and rehiring."[6]

In many instances, however, the reasonableness and propriety of school board decisions concerning teacher employment, removal, or dismissal have been challenged with the allegation that said procedures were arbitrary and discriminatory. Despite the fact that courts grant much latitude of decision making to school boards, some courts have rendered decisions overturning board action. Once such case was *Hanover Tp. Federation of Teachers* v. *Hanover Community School Corp.*[7]

District Judge Beamer, in writing the court's opinion, cited as significant the Fourth Circuit Court of Appeals decision in *Johnson* v. *Branch.*[8] In *Johnson* the Court of Appeals qualified the extent of *discretionary authority* possessed by local school boards, saying in part: "However wide the discretion of School Boards, it cannot be exercised so as to arbitrarily deprive persons of their constitutional rights."[9]

The opinion in *Hanover*[10] suggests that in such actions the burden of proof is on the board to show that all employment procedures utilized were in no way discriminatory. Moreover, clear proof and cause warranting action must be established before an employee can be removed or dismissed.

BOARDS AND CRITERIA OF TEACHER SELECTION: WHAT HAVE THE COURTS SAID?

Courts of law (in reviewing school board plans for employment, re-employment, and reassignment of teachers), have consistently emphasized the importance of selecting the "best qualified teachers." This point of view is found in a recent Ohio case, *Orr* v. *Trinter.*[11] In *Orr*, a U.S. District Court seemed to underscore the importance of providing quality education for children in a school district through faculty selection. In fact, the court cited selection of qualified teachers as a "public obligation" of school boards. In the court's opinion, providing the best education requires that a school board "exercise its best judgment as to the qualifications of individual teachers to fulfill this objective."[12]

Litigious controversies have developed, however, as a result of school boards' merging individual school faculties in an effort to achieve an acceptable degree of faculty integration. Where the faculties of two or more public schools have been merged, it has often been found that some faculty are no longer needed. What is more, it has been necessary, where court approved desegregation plans have been implemented, for boards to attempt to achieve a racial balance of faculty in proportion to the racial composition of student enrollment in each newly integrated school.

In *Teel* v. *Pitt County Board of Education,* the U.S. District Court held that "removal of race considerations from faculty selection and allocation goes hand-in-hand with the abolition of pupil segregation in public schools. . . ."[13] The court did emphasize, however, that "nonracial criteria" should be the bases upon which faculty selection and allocation is made.[14] Examples of the nonracial criteria suggested in *Teel* are as follows: educational background and qualifications (e.g., degrees earned, specialized training, teaching experience), performance on employment application tests, attitude, reputation, recommendations, and references.[15]

Hill v. *Franklin County Board of Education,*[16] a Tennessee case, was decided by the Sixth Circuit Court of Appeals in 1968. This case involved two Negro school teachers (Mrs. Scott and Mrs. Kinslow) who alleged that they, as a result of their school system's desegregation plan, had lost their jobs by reason of discriminatory procedures employed by the board.

In rendering a decision in *Hill,* the Court of Appeals ruled that Mrs. Scott's discharge was discriminatory. Speaking for the court, Circuit Judge Combs gave the following evaluation of the board's employment practices relative to Mrs. Scott's discharge: "When it became necessary to discharge a teacher because of the decrease in enrollment at the Mt. Zion school, Mrs. Scott was entitled to have her qualifications compared by definite objective standards with all other teachers in the Franklin County system."[17]

Similar emphasis on "teacher qualifications" can be found in a decision from the Eighth Circuit Court of Appeals. In its opinion in *Jackson* v. *Wheatley School District,*[18] the Appellate Court relied on *Smith* v. *Board of Education* (365 F (2d) 770, 1966, Eighth Circuit) to establish the principle that schools boards must concern themselves with the "qualifications of a teacher before making teacher assignments."[19] (*Jackson* involved action by teachers released because they were not needed for vacancies which existed in their school system.)

Horton v. *Lawrence County Board of Education*[20] is another recent case wherein a federal court emphasized the use of "objective and reasonable nondiscriminatory standards" in deciding who shall be assigned to what position within a school.[21] However, the court in *Horton* added two additional requirements to the teacher selection procedure to insure a greater degree of fairness. According to the court, the criteria used should be available for public inspection. And, the evaluations of those considered for the job on the basis of the criteria should be available to the ones not selected.[22]

A review of the cases clearly indicates that classroom teachers in public school systems, as well as other professional personnel, should not be discriminated against in hiring, assignment, promotion, reassignment, and dismissal.[23] The cases also reveal that the evaluation of each individual teacher's professional qualifications, evaluated on objective criteria and compared to all other teachers being considered by the board, is the key to practicing fairness and to avoiding discrimination. It seems evident that courts of law, as they review school desegregation plans, are extending an effort to keep the "best qualified teachers" teaching children.

RACIAL BALANCE AND FACULTY QUOTAS: A TREND?

There is an indication in some recent decisions that federal courts are seeking to achieve a racial balance among faculty in a given school based upon the racial proportion of students within that school. One such case is *Scott* v. *Winston-Salem/Forsyth County Board of Education.*[24] A North Carolina case, *Scott* went before a U.S. District Court which held, "The Board must maintain the ratio of black to white faculty members of each school in approximately the same ratio throughout the system."[25]

The Third Circuit Court of Appeals, in *Porcelli* v. *Titus,*[26] widened the scope of faculty desegregation, making it possible to consider race as a factor in teacher selection, assignment, promotion, or retention. There seemed to be little doubt in the court's mind that the integration of school faculties "is as important as proper integration of schools themselves. ..."[27] As such, said the court, "State action based partly on consideration of color, when color is not used per se, and in furtherance of a proper governmental objective, is not necessarily a violation of the Fourteenth Amendment."[28]

Despite the fact that some federal courts are suggesting a balance of faculties on the basis of race, there are not enough cases to establish that a trend exists. It should be pointed out, however, that legal precedent does exist for federal courts to order numerical quotas for faculty members according to race, in order to achieve racial balance among school faculty members—similar to percentage-based student enrollment plans now being approved.

CONCLUDING STATEMENT

As public schools move on into the decade of the 1970s, it can be said that they move farther from the concept of classroom teachers as "interchangeable parts." Thus public school boards and their administrative officers must strive, more than ever, to perfect their methods of teacher selection, placement, and reassignment. New teachers must be selected and placed, and continuing faculty must be evaluated, transferred, and sometimes replaced, all as a part of a "strategy for learning."

Based upon an examination of the recent cases, it is my opinion that most courts are still insisting that school children be taught by the most qualified teachers, no matter what the race of the teachers happens to be. And, as Circuit Judge Butzner said in *Brewer,* "The goal of faculty integration is not the allocation of teachers on either a token or a quota basis."[29]

The possibility of race being used as one criteria of evaluation in teacher selection, assignment, or reassignment has not been completely ruled out. However, it seems evident that race will not be the only criterion used. At the same time, it can not be legally used as the *sole* reason for hiring a teacher, for failing to promote a teacher, or for firing a teacher.

It can thus be concluded that courts have not substituted the ease of applying quotas and percentages to faculty members for the difficulty of selecting qualified faculty. To date, the federal courts are in general agreement that only the "most qualified" shall teach in the schools. And, that school systems must employ methods of teacher selection which insure that individuals involved are granted due process (fairness) guaranteed by the Constitution of the United States.

NOTES

[1] Brown v. Board of Education of Topeka, Kansas, 347 U.S. 483, 74 S. Ct. 686 (U.S. Supreme Court, 1954).

[2] Brown v. Board of Education of Topeka, Kansas, 349, U.S. 294, 75 S. Ct. 753 (U.S. Supreme Court, 1955).

[3] Swann v. Charlott-Mecklenburg Board of Education, 28, L. Ed. (2d) 554, 91 S. Ct. 1267 (U.S. Supreme Court, 1971).

[4] For comments on classroom staffing in schools *see* William B. Castetter, *The Personnel Function in Educational Administration* (New York, N.Y.: The Macmillan Company, 1971), p. 103.

[5] *See* Chester M. Nolte, "Powers of Board of Education are Executive, Legislative, and Quasi-Judicial in Character," *American School Board Journal,* December 1964, p. 55.

[6] Schultz v. Palmberg, 317 F. Supp. 659 (Wyoming, 1970) at 663. *See also,* Hanover Township Federation of Teachers v. Hanover Community School Corporation, 318 F. Supp. 757 (Indiana, 1970), at 760.

[7] Hanover Township Federation of Teachers v. Hanover Community School Corporation, supra, note 6.

[8] Johnson v. Branch, 364 F. (2d) 177 (Fourth Circuit, 1966).

[9] *See* Hanover Township Federation of Teachers v. Hanover Community School Corporation, supra, at 760.

[10] Ibid. at 760.

[11] Orr v. Trinter, 318 F. Supp. 1041 (Ohio, 1970).

[12] Ibid. at 1045.

[13] Teel v. Pitt County Board of Education, 272 F. Supp. 703 (North Carolina, 1967), at 708.

[14] Ibid. at 710.

[15] Ibid. at 710.

[16] Hill v. Franklin County Board of Education, 390 F. (2d) 583 (Sixth Circuit, 1968).

[17] Ibid. at 585.

[18] Jackson v. Wheatley School District, 430 F. (2d) 1359 (Eighth Circuit, 1970).

[19] Smith v. Board of Education, 365 F. (2d) 770 (Eighth Circuit, 1966). *See* Jackson supra, at 1361–1362.

[20] Horton v. Lawrence County Board of Education, 320 F. Supp. 790 (Alabama, 1970).

[21] Ibid. at 797.

[22] Ibid. at 797.

[23] Ibid. at 797.

[24] Scott v. Winston-Salem/Forsyth County Board of Education, 317 F. Supp 453 (North Carolina, 1970).

[25] Ibid. at 472.

[26] Porcelli v. Titus, 431 F. (2d) 1254 (Third Circuit, 1970).

[27] Ibid. at 1257.

[28] Ibid. at 1257.

[29] Brewer v. School Board of City of Norfolk, Virginia, 379 F. (2d) 37 (Fourth Circuit, 1968), at 39.

QUESTIONS FOR REFLECTION AND DISCUSSION

1. Green asserts that "throughout its history, the American educational systems in all regions has perpetrated the subordination of racial minorities." What evidence from your own schooling support this contention? Have you any evidence that could serve to refute it? Do you believe that Record and Banks would agree with Green?

2. Vacca discusses some of the problems that have resulted from faculty desegregation and summarizes a number of court cases which involved racially integrated faculties. Do you agree that the racial proportions of the faculty in a particular school should match the student ethnic ratios in that school? If not, then do you think that the possibility of continued discrimination exists? If so, would you accept a kind of reverse discrimination to effect the desired proportion? How does your position relate to Green's statement about "improved teacher training?"

3. Assume you agree with the five suggestions offered by Record. What kinds of specific changes in your own behavior might you anticipate if you attempted to implement these changes?

4. Banks writes of "imperatives in ethnic minority education." To what issues does he give top priority? Would Record and Green agree with him? Do you?

Chapter seven
The Future of Education

Predicting the future, whether in the political arena, at the race track, or about education, is seldom easy. It is also seldom completely accurate. Despite its difficulty and its high potential for error, future planning must go on in education and on a massive and long-range basis. Every one agrees that education changes, but often the changes are minimal: a new textbook series replaces an outdated one, a school is built to utilize space differently, team teaching or differentiated staffing or modular scheduling or individualized instruction (or all of these) is tried at this school or that. Changes of this order, however, are often the result of necessity, that ubiquitous mother of invention, and stem from a "we-have-to-do-something" mental despair. Too infrequently do these changes emerge from sound and innovative philosophical questions and answers; too infrequently do they look at the long haul, the education of a generation yet unborn, a student population yet unschooled.

The authors of the articles in this section break out of that mold. They are willing to take a look at the distant future, at education a decade or more from now. (Lest a decade seem not that distant, one must consider that, in the life of a student, a decade consumes most of his time for schooling.) Too, they have freed themselves from an overreliance on technological breakthroughs to solve all the ills of education. They realize and accept that education will always be essentially a human enterprise.

Gordon begins by asking ten seemingly simple but really quite profound questions. His answers will seem conservative to some, radical to others, but they merit consideration. In the second article Shane advocates the implementation of what he calls a curriculum continuum, "an unbroken flow of experiences planned with and for the individual learner throughout his contacts with the school." Hipple begins from the premise that today's education is too cognitively-based, too knowledge-fact-skill-centered, and argues for an education that is based more on affective concerns. Noting that "there are presently 250 new cities in various stages of development in the United States," Lieberman discusses how education might be handled in these new cities. In the final selection, Grace presents eleven conditions that must undergird twenty-first century education and provide it the moral and philosophical foundation it must have if it is to succeed.

Education in the 1970s

Ira J. Gordon

Many of the issues and needs of American education in the 1970s emerged as problems in the 1960s. Some have been with us for a considerably longer period of time. Among the pertinent issues are:

1. Who should be educated?
2. Where should education take place?
3. What should they learn?
4. How should they be taught?
5. Who should control?
6. Who should teach?
7. How should teachers be prepared?
8. What are the limits to education?
9. How should we evaluate?
10. What basic research needs to be done?

This paper, obviously, cannot deal with these in any depth. What is presented below are ideas about development of new rather than maintenance of existing programs.

First, who should be educated? We define the responsibility for free public education in the United States as extending from entry into the first grade until graduation from high school. We define the person entitled to free public education as the child between the ages of 6 and 18. The requirements of living in the 1970s suggest a redefinition. The total family will be our target population. This means an extension in both directions of the age span. Kindergarten in many states is already part of the public school system, but is not universal. Further, especially for large portions of our population, preschool programs in group settings for 18-month-olds, and other procedures beginning at 3 months, should be rapidly but

From Ira J. Gordon, "Education in the 1970s," *Peabody Journal of Education* 48 (April 1971): 228–37. Reprinted by permission of the author and George Peabody College for Teachers, copyright holder.

carefully developed so that deficiencies which presently exist as children enter school can be substantially reduced. Those youngsters who profit from earlier exposure to systematic learning must receive a sound beginning. The present system of preschool education below entry into first grade is a haphazard mix of crash *compensatory* programs, good but expensive private schools, inadequate day care and babysitting, and no program at all. A requirement in the coming decade is the organization of concerted efforts to bring some order out of the chaos of preschool education.

Movement in this direction requires an equivalent effort in adult education. Effective school programs must include parent involvement. Yet, involving a parent as an observer, visitor, or volunteer does not provide sufficient training in those roles parents can perform to enhance the intellectual and personal development of their children at home. Adult education should include training for family living and child rearing in addition to job training and retraining as job market changes, education for leisure as the work week and work year decrease, and education for personal development. If the family is the target, programs of preparation for effective family living, including provision of adequate intellectual and personal settings for children, can unite both preschool and adult education into a systematic rather than a fragmentary attack.

The requirement for the coming decade is continuous investigation into both the causes of mental retardation and exceptionality, as well as the continued development of effective programs of remediation. Much of the research shows that organizational patterns, such as special classes, will not solve the needs of these children. The use of auto-instructional devices and other individually oriented approaches within normal school settings seem to offer more effective avenues. What is required is continued federal support not only for programs training teachers for work with exceptional children, but also to enable schools to involve exceptional children as much as possible in the regular school program.

To accomplish these extensions, we need to move away from the type of state and federal funding in which a specific number of children count as a unit and are entitled to a teacher. Funding patterns must be developed which do not utilize the normal classroom counting system, but which set different amounts, on some type of cost effectiveness basis, recognizing that certain programs may be more expensive than our present classroom operations but yield more lasting results.

Second, where should education take place? Formal education has been confined to the classroom, although we know that other social agencies have educative functions. If we move toward new approaches to parent and adult education, particularly as they relate to the education of young children, the home will reemerge as a central learning institution. Present research indicates that mothers can and wish to perform educational roles when they are taught via home visit approaches. The Children's Television Workshop offers one model for the introduction of organized, systematic, learning programs beamed at a particular age level. An emerging possibility for the 1970s is the use of electronic video recording (cassettes for television) which enable the person at home to hear and see the same information as often as he wishes. The advantages of a home visit program are the personal touch and the selection of appropriate material. The advantage of television is its immediate availability to a wide section of the population. EVR offers some opportunity to combine these two approaches.

The major difficulty will be the creation of home learning materials which match the mother's background, education and motivation, the needs of the child and the family, and the goals of the program designers. Federal support will be necessary for material and curriculum development, as well as the design of delivery systems, to make the home an adequate learning setting. New ways will evolve for feedback as well as selection of materials. Users need to inform developers of materials so that efficiency can be increased. Careful evaluation and research under controlled field conditions is essential. Teams of media technicians, subject matter and child development specialists, and people from the broad spectrum of the social and behavioral sciences will need to function in a somewhat similar manner to the curriculum reformers of the 1950s, but with a more clear-cut recognition that the production of materials is only one phase of the total problem of curriculum and instruction.

The public school wil continue as the major institution for children between the ages of 6 and 18, but it must be converted into a community school with provisions for adult, technical, and vocational education and community activities. Adults should see the school as open and accessible to them for continuous learning throughout life. The procedures developed in Flint, Michigan, should be generalizable in many settings.

A phenomenon of the War on Poverty was the emergence of preschool programs not directly under the aegis of boards of education or other state agencies. On the horizon is the emergence of a day care and child development industry and a large-scale development of private, preschool programs for those able to pay. In urban settings, *street* academies which offer programs to serve a variety of the needs of adolescents not currently met in the usual academic curriculum, are emerging. The private and parochial school systems are expanding. The development of pluralistic approaches to the provision of education, in which the former dominance of the public school system may be decreased, raises a host of problems for legislation. In what ways should these agencies become available for federal funds? What controls, both over program and accounting, should be developed? What possible alternatives should be made available for all children, not just those of parents who can either afford much or those who can afford nothing? How are options to be made available to the vast middle class? I can do no more here than raise the issues.

Third, what should school-age children and preschoolers learn? With the high level of mobility of the American population and the chances of continued technological development, the issues of national curricula and national standards must move from political football to logical and substantive debate. If we can adopt as one standard that any child, growing up in any section of the country and belonging to any subculture, should be able to function as an effective citizen in any section of the country and in contact with members of other subcultures, then we will at least move the debate to a discussion of what this requires. I believe that basic competence in language, in computation, and in interpersonal relationships are common needs of all of our citizens. At the present time graduates of our high schools vary widely in their ability to speak, read, write, and handle mathematics basic to life in an urban technical world. Many lack skills for dealing with social issues. A basic requirement of American education in the area of the social studies is the development of curricula which have value overtones and commitments to American democracy along with historical, economic, and social information, so that the average American high school graduate will not be ignorant of his heritage and will be able to be an active participant in the continued development of the nation. Too many of our present students and adult population are ill-informed about even such basic American documents as the Declaration of Independence, the Constitution, and the Bill of Rights. Further, cultural pluralism will be an increasingly critical notion in the next decade. We must provide students with information and experience so that all portions of our society will understand the contributions of all others and will value regional, ethnic, and religious differences.

One can learn a set of facts without placing them in a conceptual framework and without utilizing them for action. Our present concern with ecology, for example, indicates that students will need to understand not only elements of biology but also economics, politics, social psychology, and history so that they can make wise decisions when faced with choices about engineering projects which have environmental effects. Simple knowledge of facts in any one of these fields is insufficient. Curricula must be designed to relate facts to concepts to behavior. We need to develop the types of learning materials which cut across disciplines and which develop thought patterns involved in decision making. These do not exist at the present time, nor do we presently turn out of graduate schools, in the disciplines or in education, people trained to develop such materials. Federal funds will be required for training material developers as well as for the development and assessment of learning materials. The whole delivery system needs to be reexamined.

Fourth, how should students be taught? Traditional learning theory has been sterile, but two mainstreams of psychological thought are beginning to make contributions to instruction: cognitive development and instrumental or operant learning. However, present data are insufficient to provide cues to teachers as guides for behavior in a classroom, in using media, or in working in a home. It is in the field of instruction that more basic field research must be done, in a variety of settings, with students of all ages, faced with learning a variety of materials, before we shall develop a fairly consistent set of principles. It is remarkable that this statement can be made at the beginning of 1970, after 70 years of learning research since Pavlov. Most of what is known does not apply to the classroom setting. Federal initiative for basic research in classrooms rather than in infra-human learning laboratories is a fundamental requirement.

Technology is a central issue. We have not learned how to use it. We have been deficient in training teachers to utilize electronic means in classrooms. Most of the software prepared has been inadequate. There are, in addition, a number of theoretical as well as empirical problems. What is it that programs beamed to large audiences can teach most effectively? How much repetition must be provided? How can auto-instructional means be cheaply devised, utilizing cassettes, tape recorders, and eight millimeter film? How can material be up dated? How can technology be used to allow the student some selection and control over the materials to which he is exposed? Can he check materials out like a library book? If current learning and cognitive theory suggest that the young child, especially, must be an active agent in his learning and deal with concrete objects, how can we cope with this problem?

This raises the question of *individualizing* instruction. How does individualizing *instruction* relate to the question of what should be learned? Is individualization a matter of rate or of content selection as well? It is, obviously, beyond the scope of most classroom teachers faced with thirty children to do more than mouth the slogan. How do we learn to use technology to free pupils to learn?

Fifth, where should the control of education reside? American doctrine has been local control, and fears have been expressed that federal funds mean federal control. However, in the urban centers, demands for community control and decentralization will grow stronger in the next decade. Yet, it is obvious that the smaller unit is inadequate, even at the state level, to provide sufficient funds. I oppose large nonprogrammatic grants to school districts and states because educational institutions will continue to do what they have always done. Innovation and initiative emerge when federal money is the carrot. It will not occur on the local level if money is simply awarded per number of children or number of units of instruction. This may be a harsh statement, it may be partly incorrect, but it is my view from experiences over the last twenty years.

We need some way of rewarding local initiative, encouraging variety and pluralistic programs to emerge at local levels with adequate support from government. But the skill required in proposal writing and the design of research and evaluation to accompany proposals does not exist in many local settings. The model developed in Follow Through of relating university and school systems in combined participation nationwide is a viable and desirable notion. It cannot occur readily if money is awarded to states. A program developed at a university some distance from the state may not be used because the tendency will be to turn to local institutions.

The pattern of encouraging universities and school systems to create programs in a national competition for funds, with decisions being made by scientific boards in the manner traditionally used by the National Institutes of Health, would tend to remove most of the stigma of federal control and decrease the chances of political rather than educational decision making. Patterns of federal funding should move away from quota systems, regional allocations, and head counting. After those programs which are truly pilot and *cutting edge* have been sufficiently tested and become ready for large-scale service, they should be made available as rapidly as possible to all agencies capable of applying them. Federal educational dollars for program development should be taken out of the pork barrel.

Issues six and seven concern the status of teachers. Who should teach, and how should they be prepared? We must learn to use paraprofessional manpower more efficiently in the educational process. Currently, virtually no elementary teachers are trained to work with other teachers and to use paraprofessionals effectively. Ways must be found to train professionals and paraprofessionals as teaching teams, so that each understands the other. This is particularly important when they come from different ethnic and class backgrounds. Career development for both professionals and paraprofessionals has begun for Head Start and Follow Through paraprofessionals, but needs to be enlarged and extended for people not involved in present federal programs.

The content of teacher education needs revision. Our old discussions have centered around personal development versus a set of skills, methods versus content, the internship, and the proper mix of theory and practice. Generally, these discussions have been bitter, unproductive, and unrelated to empirical data. Unfortunately, research on teaching has not demonstrated a clear-cut picture of the *effective* teacher. One reason we cannot make clear statements is that service and training programs. funded previously by the Congress have provided insufficient evaluation funds. We can never answer the question of how teachers should be prepared until we are willing to invest in investigation. We know that accumulation of credits in college subject-matter or education courses relates hardly at all to effective classroom behavior. Yet, the college course has been our traditional model. We should invest considerable funds in redesigning our teacher education programs, both at the pre- and inservice level, for all those who will function in the classroom from paraprofessional to specialist.

Federal support should go to those educational institutions and school districts which not only plan their programs in detail, but also plan to describe the relationships of program components, teacher and pupil classroom behavior, and pupil achievement. The current state of the art of multivariate statistics and research design is such that this can be done. It should be launched on a competitive proposal basis by those universities and other teacher education institutions which seriously wish to investigate the question and which presently have the capability and the responsibility for training teachers. We do not need new organizations; we need effective funding and prodding of present institutions.

Eighth, what should be the nature and scope of ancillary services? Traditionally, school boards have not been vitally concerned with medical services for pupils, psychological services beyond diagnosis, and social welfare services beyond those affecting absenteeism. The experiences of Head Start and Follow Through have indicated the tremendous value of comprehensive services for *disadvantaged* children. These comprehensive services can also be vital in the educational development of the large mass of middle-class children in the American schools. The question is: When is a frill not a frill? The family circumstances—housing, income, size, job, pattern, emotional stability—are all variables which influence the intellectual and personal development of the child. Thus, they cannot be ignored or left to chance. What should be the limits of federal support for these services for all children? Where should those legally charged with educational responsibilities stop and other agencies enter? How can we systematize the work of the various agencies? Pilot projects attempting to explore these issues and test them empirically should be funded in the coming decade. Such questions as, What are the *noneducational* needs of all American youth? How should these services be delivered? Who should be responsible? What difference does delivery make in educational achievement? can and should be attacked.

Ninth, throughout this paper I have referred to evaluation. No program should be funded without an adequate evaluation design. Until we insist that those who seek federal project funds accept the responsibility to demonstrate whether the money was used effectively, we shall waste a considerable portion of the federal education dollar. But there are a number of hard issues. In order to evaluate something, one must have yardsticks and goals. Who should determine the goals and what should be used as measuring rods? Standard achievement tests are not adequate measures for many of the goals we might seek and for many of the children in school. There has been a considerable push toward writing *behavioral objectives,* but many of these efforts use huge energies of teacher time in trivial fashion. Should our goals be personal development, intellectual achievement, social change, or a mix of all three? The former separation of cognitive (intellectual) and affective (emotional) goals with a concentration on the former in curriculum programs seems to be ending as we realize more and more that decisions and behavior embody both.

Three requirements emerge: (1) funding to develop effective processes for stating and evaluating goal attainment, (2) substantial funding for evaluation in all projects described above, and (3) continued funding for the training of evaluators at both the undergraduate and graduate level. In relation to the first requirement, if we are to urge school systems and universities to develop adequate proposals for meeting the issues of the 1970s, then their personnel need help in learning how to formulate their goals and how to think about ways to evaluate. They do not need package answers, but they need to be taught procedures involved in stating goals, programs, and measures. Very few school system personnel and few professors in our universities are able to do this at the present time. Siphoning off technically skilled personnel to R and D Centers and regional labs removed the very people from the university and school system framework who possessed a modicum of skill and isolated them from the people whom they should be serving. We should examine the policy of setting up new organizations because of the effects they have on scarce manpower. I would urge that we invest heavily in the methodology of programmatic research in substantive fields.

The tenth issue is the role of basic research. Our current knowledge is inadequate about learning and instruction, about program design, and about curriculum development. We are unable to answer with any degree of certitude questions about the effect of television on children's learning and behavior. We know even less, in any systematic fashion, about the effects of Title I programs, general school programs, computer assisted instruction, community action, etc. Our knowledge of the effects that family life variables have upon the behavior, attitudes, and development of children is meager. A recent NIMH analysis by Yarrow et al. suggests that we still know very little about the specific effects of patterns of child rearing on the behavior and development of children. Basic research, therefore, is needed, including research on methodology. Generally, purely methodological studies have not been well funded either through the U.S. Office of Education or the National Institutes of Health and Mental Health, but they are basic to the solution of many of our problems. If we cannot design adequately and measure effectively, then we will be unable to know if and why any of our efforts have succeeded.

We need careful studies embedded in the service programs as well as separate basic field research. We need to develop funding patterns so that as a part of a teacher education process, or a curriculum development design, or an investigation of a delivery system such as television, small careful bits of work can be done. In effect, this is a piggyback arrangement of research on a service program. At the present time it is extremely difficult to receive adequate support for such efforts. We should encourage research workers to utilize other programs and to build their work into ongoing field studies.

Funds are needed to train basic researchers. An effective procedure for training is the utilization of graduate students in ongoing research efforts in universities and schools. Through the allocation of federal funds we should encourage graduate assistantships and research assistantships as major training vehicles, in preference to fellowship programs. Most fellowship programs are course and theory oriented and do not provide students with practical research experience in the field setting in which they will eventually work. The training of basic education researchers should require participation in research in school settings and other educational settings off campus as a fundamental part of the program.

If we broaden our definitions and our activities as suggested in this paper beyond the classroom building, then we must increase the safeguards for noninvasion of privacy and for strict adherence to appropriate professional ethics. The National Institute of Health requirement of a careful review to be sure no possible unavoidable harm can be done in experimentation on humans in the medical field should be used as a model in education. Parents, teachers, and students should be informed as much as possible about the nature of programs and should be given as much choice as possible as to whether they wish to participate. This should be particularly true in innovative work where it is not clear what the outcomes may be. Although one can raise serious scientific objections to the use of volunteers, the concern for the person should always be primary in any of our efforts.

It is impossible here to do more than outline some of the issues. Since all relate to each other, a basic policy commitment should be made in favor of comprehensive rather than piecemeal program development. Funds should go to programs, institutions, and agencies which develop comprehensive attacks on a variety of these issues. Longitudinal, comprehensive, programmatic investigation with clear ramifications across many of the ten issues should be encouraged. Support must be given long enough, in large enough sums, so that programs can be developed and tested for a sufficient period of time to yield the best picture of just what it is they do, and what unforeseen side effects they have.

We need more interagency cooperation so that a single comprehensive project can be funded by several agencies within HEW or in combination with other departments, such as HUD and Labor, without forcing the program developers to write separate pieces using separate budgets, guidelines, and narrative styles in order to develop a comprehensive attack. To one outside of government there seems little logic in some of the high walls between agencies.

Funding policies should be developed to encourage established institutions to explore new ways of working rather than to create new *labs* which use scarce dollars and talent. Most likely, the best investigations come from an individual or from a small group of researchers who choose to work together and design efforts around their own perspectives. This is in opposition to creating a general plan for a research lab and employing *hired hands* to do the work. Clusters of interested, competent people will grow around a research effort through choice rather than through even high pressure recruiting practices. Further, fundamental lasting change has to occur in the established institutions. It is far easier for them to sluff off effects or the input from new agencies if no basic changes occur in their own organization.

Those who create policies must also recognize the fact that results are usually not instant but developmental. Requirements for quick change or large-scale growth impose obligations and hazards on program development. It is far better to recognize that good programs take time to evolve and even more time to show lasting results.

To best meet these ten issues, continued support, rather than block grants to states, will be the most effective vehicle. Federal support should be for programs rather than sprinkled in small doses to each school district. There should be a careful selection of systematic approaches rather than political or regional allocation of funds. There should, in addition, be seed and risk money for pilot projects proposed by thoughtful investigators, even though they seem quite removed from traditional approaches. The investment in brains may be even more important than the total number of dollars expended.

We enter the 1970s with a set of at least the ten issues raised at the beginning of this paper. No doubt we will leave the decade with the same set of issues. Hopefully, with sufficient programs, research, and evaluation, we may be asking these questions in newer and more sophisticated ways.

We may have some sets of answers to enable us to approach the 1980s with confidence.

A Curriculum Continuum: Possible Trends in the 70s

Harold G. Shane

For generations most education in the U.S. has been divided into arbitrary segments. It also has been given labels such as "the elementary school" and "the secondary school." A century or more ago, in view of what was then known about teaching and learning, and when the school population was expanding rapidly in urban centers, such grade-level divisions instituted for administrative purposes made a great deal of sense. However, education now has reached a level of sophistication at which serious thought can and should be given to the development of a carefully reasoned and well-designed continuum of experience for the learner, one which can replace the disjointed divisions of the past and the present.

Such a curriculum continuum presumably would provide an unbroken chain of ventures and adventures in meaningful learning, beginning with early childhood education. It would extend through postsecondary education and on into later-life education.

Urgent priority should be given to studying and experimenting with the development of genuine continuity in education for several reasons. First, learning itself is a continuous process. It begins no later than at birth and extends through time until one ultimately learns the meaning of death. Since the input of experience is continuous, there is no reason for sectioning the curriculum into four- or six- year time blocks and for "keeping school" on the basis of a nine- or ten month academic year.

Second, we have been wasting our time. Despite decades of talk about "articulating" the units of public education, this objective has never been achieved because it *cannot* be achieved. We have simply squandered our time and energy on refining the errors inherent in the graded school when we should have thrown away the "graded" and "segmented" concepts years ago.

Third, if we intend seriously to improve the psychology of teaching and

From Harold G. Shane, "A Curriculum Continuum: Possible Trends in the 70s," *Phi Delta Kappan* 51 (March 1970): 389–92. Reprinted by permission of the author and the publisher.

learning (a task which is difficult enough in itself), we need to remove the uncoordinated divisions which presently serve as barriers or hurdles to the educational progress of children and youth.

A fourth reason for giving priority to the task of bringing continuity to education is perhaps more subtle than the first three. The challenge of building a sound, well-conceived curriculum continuum is one *which can help educators to find themselves* in a confused and confusing culture. Today most educators over 30 years old are pioneers in a new, unfamiliar pedagogical world. Whether we be elementary teachers or college deans, all of us have three educational deficiencies carried over from the pre-1940 period to overcome: (1) an experientially limited, hence inaccurate, concept of the past, (2) a perception of the present diminished by our incomplete auditory and visual input related to education during the last three decades, and (3) a concept of possible educational futures which is defective because it is based on faulty, linear projections of the past into tomorrow.*

As we move toward better continuity, the implications for changes in contemporary, arbitrary segments of education (such as the secondary school) become tremendous. Indeed, as the curriculum continuum becomes a reality, such divisions as the elementary school and the secondary school will literally cease to exist as academic or administrative units. Since this may strike some persons in elementary and secondary education alike as a draconian type of educational reform, careful heed must be given to an explanation of the nature of the curriculum continuum concept, its psychological value, and the desirable changes toward which increased continuity can carry educational practice.

WHAT IS A CURRICULUM CONTINUUM?

As indicated above, an educational or curriculum continuum may be described as an unbroken flow of experiences planned with and for the individual learner throughout his contacts with the school. Much current thought and research suggests that the program should begin no later than in early childhood and should continue to provide educational opportunities as long as the school has anything to offer the learner. In other words, persons in their sixties or even older would be served methodically when the continuum concept is eventually extended to its upper ranges.

Continuity in learning implies that schooling shall extend throughout the year. Furthermore, it may begin officially at any time during the year that a child is deemed mature enough to be present (e.g., at age three), not at a legislated date such as "by the year in which he becomes six years of age on or before midnight on the 30th of November." Vacation periods would be scheduled at any time during the calendar year and for any

---

*For example, the "over-thirties" in education are likely to think of the computer as an addition to our stockpile of resources in the education warehouse rather than as the foundation for an entirely new warehouse.

length of time upon which agreement was reached. This would constitute no problem when the young learner is assigned to a team of teachers rather than to grade level or to a class. Teachers likewise could be off-duty during any interval for study, travel, rest, and so on. Deliberate "overstaffing," i.e., five teachers attached to a basic four-teacher unit or team would permit one to engage in nonteaching activities in February just as readily as in July.

In a curriculum continuum, educational experiences also are personalized. The *personalized* curriculum differs from *individualized* instruction in at least one major respect. Individualized instruction, which has been attempted for many years, was intended to help a child meet group norms or standards, but at his own rate of progress.* The personalized curriculum continuum serves as a means of making the school's total resources available to a child so that his teachers can figuratively help him to "create himself" without reference to what his "average" chronological age-mates may be accomplishing.

The meaning of a personalized continuum type of curriculum can be clarified further by means of literary allusion. The curriculum of the 1930-vintage graded school was one in which the child was forced to fit the program. That is, it was analogous to the mythological bed of Procrustes. This was an iron bedstead on which the ancient, unfriendly Greek giant bound the unwary traveler, then cut off his victim's legs or stretched them to fit.

The individualized, and sometimes nongraded, approach to instruction was a distinct improvement, since it endeavored to shorten or lengthen the Procrustean bed to fit the child. The personalized curriculum continuum, on the other hand, is one in which the child, with teacher guidance is encouraged—indeed expected—*to build his own bed.*

SOME PSYCHOLOGICAL VALUES
OF THE CONTINUUM CONCEPT

"Continuity" in education is not merely a mechanical or organizational plan for locking together or more closely articulating the present arbitrary units of education which precede and follow the secondary school years. Rather, in many ways, it is psychological concept, a way of conceiving the learner's ongoing experiences as a smoothly flowing stream with an "educational current" that is properly paced to match the skill and speed with which he can ride its eddies and rapids.

In a school characterized by the psychologically supportive qualities of the continuum, the learner begins to find answers to three questions which

---

*In the "Winnetka Plan" as begun by Carleton W. Washburne, for instance, the curriculum was basically the same for all children in a given grade, but the *rate* of progress varied. The rapid learner was kept from moving beyond the company of his age-mates by providing him with enrichment activities and similar paracurricular experiences.

during the past decade have begun to be recognized as queries of basic importance:

1. "Who am I?" (self-identity)
2. "What am I doing?" (self-orientation)
3. "Where am I going? (self-direction)

Self-awareness and, hopefully, a wholesome self-concept are developed as answers are found to question one. Through seeking and gradually acquiring an answer to point two, the learner progressively "finds himself" in the process of searching for inner integrity. He likewise develops the skills of social interaction and the coping behaviors in which self-confidence resides. Finally, in discovering answers to question three the learner establishes a personal compass course or sets in motion an inner gyroscope which, if all goes well, leads to desirable personal-social contributions, to acceptance by others, and to consequent personal happiness.

It may be conjectured that only through a personalized curriculum continuum can we construct a humane educational milieu or matrix in which the learner can safely, and with a sense of security, *discover* the world and *create* himself. We do not know enough, we cannot clearly predict enough, of the twenty-first century world (in which the infant, child, or adolescent of the 1970s will spend the larger portion of his lifetime) to gamble on a less flexible concept of the curriculum than the one proposed here. We must eschew in the realm of content the impossible dream of *what* explicit fundamentals children and youth shall learn; we must espouse the more tangible goal of teaching them *how* to learn.

And we ourselves need to unlearn the unexamined educational *beliefs* that often guide our conduct, while striving to learn the value that resides in *believing* in what education can accomplish.

NEW DIRECTIONS TOWARD WHICH CONTINUITY IN EDUCATION CAN LEAD

In the years immediately ahead, the educational world seems likely to continue to be invigorated by continued change. Probable future developments which research and trend-projection suggest include substantial increases in whatever it is that I.Q. tests measure, in the continued spread of man's 13 major languages (especially English, Spanish, Mandarin, and Russian), and the development of a phonetic English alphabet with approximately 30 consonants and 15 vowels. The schools also seem likely to be influenced by major improvements in the status of women, by legislation requiring compulsory psychiatry, by a five- or six-hour day and an eight-month working year, and by the growing need to cope with problems stemming from overbreeding, pollution, accumulating garbage and diminishing resources, and man's ancient propensity for attempting to settle his disputes through warfare.

To the exciting and sometimes unnerving educational mix of the future, bona fide continuity in the curriculum is likely to bring further vitality. To illustrate, in schools with a curriculum continuum:

There would be no failure or "double promotion." One learner would merely live differently, and at a different rate, from others.

"Special education" and "remedial work" would cease to exist. All education of all learners would be "special," regardless of whether they were handicapped, gifted, or in the wide "normal" range between.

Annual promotion would become a thing of the past. What we now speak of as promotion would become a *direction* rather than a yearly hurdle.

There would be no dropouts. At present we have created a needless dropout problem. In a personalized program, with suitable guidance resources available, the secondary school student would not drop out to accept a position. Instead, the school, employer, student, and (when possible) his family would reach a consensus that it was desirable for him to extend the flow of his curriculum continuum outside the school to include the world of work. Weeks or months later he could, if he chose, pick up the thread of his inschool experiences. The absence of grades, formal class assignment, and so on, would encourage his return with no stigma attached.

Compensatory education would terminate. There would be no need for compensating, since education in a continuum is designed to maximize talents, minimize environmental inequities; and be inherently "supportive" in the sense that it builds on and sustains the unique assets which each learner acquires because of his membership in any given U.S. subculture.

Report cards and marks would vanish. In a continuum, reporting becomes a "spot check" on where the learner appears to be rather than an invidious semestral agony foisted on individuals clumped together for purposes of comparison.

And so on. . . .

CHANGES THE CONTINUUM CONCEPT
CAN BRING TO EDUCATION IN THE FUTURE

What are some of the changes that are likely to occur in today's high school as the fact of continuity in learning and in education is more widely acknowledged and as teachers and administrators frankly face the opportunities—and problems—of a transition to an uninterrupted and personalized sequence of learning for children and youth?

Organizational Changes

For one thing, as noted earlier, a discrete secondary school program would cease to exist. But so would the elementary school on one hand and college on the other. Graduation exercises would become obsolete, since one cannot graduate from a continuum.

Almost inevitably, there would be a significant downward extension of education. Ideally, the school would establish its first contacts with the child no later than at age two during a "nonschool preschool" interval. Here children would be examined for psycho-physical or environmental impediments to learning prior to beginning direct school contacts in the "minischool," at age three, for their first methodically planned sensory input.

Patently, when schooling begins for children three to four years sooner than is now generally the rule, the structures we now call elementary and secondary schools will be dealing with a psychologically different type of client with a distinctly different background. He would not have been enrolled in kindergarten, for instance. Instead, he would have spent an indeterminate "make-ready" period in a preprimary continuum and entered the primary years anywhere between, say, five and seven or even eight years of age. By the end of the middle school era (i.e. at the close of what is now grade 8), he may have spent anywhere from 7 to 12 years in elementary education following a seamless personalized program. He has worked under teacher-team guidance, and, quite conceivably, is the beneficiary of technological developments which have helped to widen and deepen his background.

The organization of the secondary school and the nature of its curriculum, as they exist in 1970, seemingly will need to go through a complete mutation as a continuum approach spreads upward. It is not too soon to begin speculating as to how the coming splice between elementary and secondary education can be made both smoothly and so as to serve the potential new product as he moves from early to later adolescence.*

Almost certainly, there will be major changes in the traditional high school-college relationship, too. At present, the college often expects U.S. secondary school to provide a subject-content background so that the adolescent can achieve his "real education" during his university years, i.e., examine, expand, and apply the "beginnings of knowledge" presumably supplied by the time a diploma is conferred. As early childhood education becomes commonplace, as the personalized continuum becomes established, it may not be illogical to expect that, in effect, the secondary level of the 1980s will, with a more sophisticated clientele, be reorganized to replace the college years of today so that the "college-bound" secondary student of a decade hence can immediately enter upon a program at the university which is of graduate school caliber.

Changing Policies and Practices

Imbedded in the concept of continuity are various changes in policy.

*One is led to the tentative conclusion that, as education attains the continuity it has lacked, the portion of education now thought of as "secondary" will become at least as flexible as the "elementary" portion. Thus it would be of indeterminate length, without a graded structure—in short, a part of the stream of personalized, seamless education that would lead into postsecondary programs of many kinds.

Typical of these is a decrease in age homogeneity among children working together. In the absence of rigid allocations of subject matter (e.g., studying the Middle Ages in grade 6, biology in grade 10) the continuum may well draw together in year-long or in short-lived special purpose groupings children and youth who differ in age by as much as four or even six years.

Pupil interchange from school to school, district to district, and even country to country also becomes feasible if not essential when a personalized educational continuum replaces graded and nongraded schools. Teacher exchanges at an unprecedented level are a concomitant. By the 1980s it may be little more than routine to find a mature student (who today would be in high school) doing a year's work in Scotland or Ecuador. Perhaps his textual material would be transmitted from his home campus in facsimile form at appropriate intervals.

Undoubtedly, education will draw upon various instructional systems centers associated with the schools as supportive agencies for a continuum. Perhaps by the eighties some forms of computerized instruction and information retrieval will be in general use.

The practice of making adult education an integral part of what is now secondary and collegiate education comes to mind when one extends a lifelong education experience-chain to the middle years (40 to 70) and to early old age (70 years plus). With increases in leisure time, with rapid change making some skills and knowledge obsolete in a few years, and with the active lifespans of many people due to extend into the 90s within a decade or two, it seems reasonable that some people may profitably enroll in a secondary school interval appropriate to their personalized curriculum. Such re-enrollments, for as long as a year or two, might occur in the forties for the person seeking new vocational avenues and in the sixties or seventies as partial retirement draws near and new interests and hobbies are in need of cultivation. Who knows? We may have *old* married housing projects opening on the 1988 campus!

New Deployment of Faculty Members

There will probably be much more vertical deployment of teachers in the continuum school as it becomes evident that learners need access to a greater variety of stimulating faculty minds. Today's second-grade teacher may find herself on a team working with a mixed cluster of 12- to 18-year-olds twice weekly in a human development-sex education project, working with senior citizens on several afternoons, and helping to supervise paraprofessionals working with three-year-olds in a minischool complex during the remainder of the week.

The effective use of paraprofessionals seems certain to be an important challenge to the school which uses differentiated staffs to achieve personalized instruction.

Perhaps the most demanding task, and certainly one of the most important as the seamless curriculum materializes, is that of redirecting teacher education—including in-service re-education. Particularly, some secondary teachers and many college teachers who have been predominantly subject-oriented may find it difficult to become skilled in the flexible, creative use of educational resources, in identifying with interdisciplinary teams, and in working with groups of students in situations in which new criteria for group membership and for assessing success are taking form.

Selecting Content for a Curriculum Continuum

For decades, research studies have suggested that, except for central tendencies created by widely used textbooks, the U.S. curriculum has been a Joseph's coat sewn of many pieces. Even now there is little agreement as to what should be taught and when. As a result, it is unlikely that conceptualizing the curriculum as a continuum can increase the general disarray. In fact, it is likely that a continuum will bring a measure of order. One reason that much disagreement has marked curriculum development is that schools generally have grouped children chronologically, then failed to find any way of coping with problems of instruction brought about by the inevitable range in ability that ensued. The personalized curriculum reduces this problem to a minimum since it rejects, as an undesirable goal, any idea of increasing the correlation between chronological age and uniform achievement norms.

As continuity is brought to education, the scope and sequence of the child's inner curriculum, i.e., the sum of what he has internalized from his school-sponsored experience, becomes uniquely personal. In the secondary continuum school, the individual adolescent would be guided in the wise exploitation of the school's total resources. His program would be *derived* from his status and needs, not predetermined by impersonal requirements.

BETTER TOMORROWS THROUGH GREATER CONTINUITY

In a recent book, Peter F. Drucker referred to the present as an age of discontinuity. His purpose in writing was to ask *not* "What will tomorrow look like?" but "What do we have to tackle *today* to make tomorrow better?"

Likewise, in education we should not speculate about tomorrow until our speculations become an opiate that keeps us from improving the schools as they exist today. At the same time, decisions made today shape the future. Since this is so, it seems prudent for educators at all levels, including secondary education, to give consideration to the idea of an uninterrupted, personalized flow of educational experiences, a seamless curriculum. Decisions that create greater continuity are likely to lead to the distinctly better education that the U.S. has always relied on the schools to produce.

Education for the Space Age—
Cognitive or Affective

Theodore W. Hipple

Most of the people who criticized the expense of the recent Apollo Eleven moon flight did so on grounds of misdirected national priorities. Rarely was a voice heard that said we ought simply to save the money or use it to reduce the national debt; seldom did anyone argue that going to the moon was frivolous or useless. Rather, the critics asserted, the United States has pressing problems here on earth and these demand attention and solution before the nation can afford the luxury of a moon mission.

It seems reasonable to suggest, then, that few questioned whether the United States could afford its financial commitment to the space program. The question was, should we put a man on the moon before we first spend significant amounts of money, brainpower, and energy on problems of racial unrest, slum conditions, poverty and hunger, overpopulation, generational conflict and other similarly crucial domestic issues? Implicit in such a question is the assumption that, had the United States tried to solve one of these latter problems and had it elected to spend the space money, brainpower, and energy on that problem, the attempt would have been as successful as was the astronaut's space odyssey. Such an assumption ignores the major differences between putting a man on the moon and solving many of our domestic crises, differences that have enormous implications for the future of American education.

First of all, the moon voyage was a technological accomplishment, one unparalleled in the history of mankind. Its most magnificent achievement may not have been Armstrong's first step on the moon, but rather the successful blending of so many varying specialties in just the right mix to put him there. It was a triumph for the age of specialization, a vindication of those who had spent years of their lives mastering the complexities of what may have turned out to be one small, but vital, aspect of the total space program. Indeed, the few generalists in the program were best typified by the astronauts themselves, who, although they did not know as much about any of the systems as did the scientists who had designed and built them, still had to know how to use them and when to abandon them in favor of the human mind—their own, as it were. The landing of the lunar module, for example, had to be guided by Armstrong; had it been left to the NASA equipment, the craft would have landed amid boulders from which it could not have been launched.

A second aspect of the moon voyage is that the workers, from the lowliest NASA mechanic right up to the moonwalkers themselves, had essentially the same goal: to put a man on the moon. There were some who saw in the program other goals—the examination of the lunar soil comes to mind—but these were, perforce, later goals, subsidiary to the *sine qua non* of getting someone to the moon to bring the soil back. Given a common goal, the extraordinary abilities of many people, most of them highly trained, and an almost unlimited source of funds, it is not really so surprising that man did accomplish this technological tour de force in outer space.

It is but a brief jump from this point to the belief that, if man can accomplish the space trip successfully, then the same combination ought to provide answers to others of mankind's problems, among them the domestic problems, the very ones which those who criticized the space program said should have been given a higher priority in national expenditures. Even those who fully supported the space program fell victim to this intellectual wishful thinking. Ex-president Johnson, for example, confidently expressed the hope that, if we can put a man on the moon, then surely we can solve our problems here on earth.

What these people have apparently failed to consider is that many of the problems they want to solve on earth—those of racial relations or of poverty or of the generation gap—with the same methods as those used in the space problem are different kinds of problems, requiring different kinds of solutions. Just as the space trip was essentially a technological solution, so also will the solution to, say, racial inequity, if and when it comes, be essentially a behavioral solution. The race dilemma needs not new technicians or new equipment, but, rather, altered behavior on the part of man. Further, this particular domestic problem, like many of the other domestic troubles, involves not only a small, highly skilled group of people, as does the space program, but instead the whole of society, including those with considerable intellectual ability and those with almost none. Nor are the goals as commonly accepted as are the goals of most problems requiring technological solutions; in fact, in many of the domestic problems, much of the difficulty stems from disagreements about goals.

In essence, the differences between the kinds of problems are both as basic and as profound as the differences between technology and behavior. Great technological leaps forward can be brought about by the brilliance of one particular man, an Einstein perhaps, and, from his work, other, only slightly less able technologists can produce results that presently we can but barely imagine. In the area of human behavior, however, the work of any one man, no matter how brilliant or charismatic he may be, rarely can have more than marginal effects; a whole society must change its behavior, a change that is brought about by the change in all, or at least most, of the members of that society. Technology pits mind against machinery; behavior involves not only mind, but also emotions, values, attitudes, everything, really, that goes into the making of a unique human personality. Technology is tangible, machine-centered; behavior is intangible, value-centered. Technology can be supported by money, with the expectation that the greater the amount of money provided, the greater the technological feat accomplished. No amount of money, however, can produce societal changes in behavior unless and until the individual members of society collectively desire the changes. American education is the major institution of society that can, if it elects to do so, produce this collective desire.

It is just at this point that education finds itself in a bind, faced with its own problems of priority, but without a money-giving Congress or a direction-setting president to make its decision. The question can be stated simply enough: Should education continue to set as its major goal the training of skilled scientists and technicians who can use their talents in greater and greater mechanistic accomplishments or should it concentrate its efforts in achieving in its students the changes in behavior necessary to solve the nation's domestic ills? To the related question, *why can't it do both,* one has only to look at the last fifty years to see that the accomplishments of education in changing human behavior have been ones that even its staunchest supporters would have to deem minimal. Within just the last generation, however, education can point with justifiable pride at its production of the very skilled men who put the astronauts on the moon.

Yet education must achieve both aims if we are to solve both our technological problems and our behavioral ones. Society will simply not permit schools to drop as one of their purposes the attainment of technological excellence, nor should it, for the knowledges and skills gained in such attainment are going to continue to be as crucial in the days ahead as in the recent past. And not just in space; warfare, hot or cold, medical research, transportation, air and water pollution—all these and myriad other problems demand technical skill of an unprecedented amount and kind. But if the United States does hope ever to solve its racial divisiveness, its welfare problems, its urban ills, its generational difficulties, then the schools must also focus on the kind of education that fosters behavioral changes. Without such an education the gap between what William Ogburn half a century ago called the material culture of equipment and technology and the nonmaterial culture of attitudes and values by which people live and think, the cultural lag, will become increasingly wider and our domestic problems will become the greater even as we go forward on scientific frontiers.

And let there be no mistake that education is the societal institution which must not only effect the answer to its own dilemma but, by virtue of that answer, direct the energy of the nation toward future changes of a technological or behavioral kind. The evidence is in that both the home and the church, the other two institutions historically charged with the responsibility for training up the young in the ways they shall go, especially the behavioral ways, have simply ceased doing the job and, in some instances, of even trying to do it. Thus, it becomes a matter of considerable importance whether education continues along its path of creating the highly skilled craftsmen who will take their places in the future technology or it chooses also to travel, concurrently, the road toward the production of a society sufficiently humanistic to examine itself and to make those changes in behavior necessary if it is to solve those domestic problems requiring behavioral solutions.

The goals of education, like those of an individual school or even an individual teacher, can usually be classified into one of two categories. The cognitive goals, sometimes referred to as the conceptual or know-that goals, include the development in students of certain understandings of concepts, procedures, abstractions, etc. This group of goals also includes the learning of specific facts, though the trend today is away from a "facts-for-their-own-sake" approach to a methodology that suggests that the facts are useful only to the extent that they help the students acquire understandings.

Often grouped with the cognitive goals, but sometimes in school practice kept separate from them, are the skills or know-how goals, in which the objective is to teach the students to do something: bisect an angle, measure an inclined plane, blend three chemicals in certain proportions. Much of the work in today's technology demands just such skills and schools have not been at all hesitant in pointing to this need as a sort of self-serving justification for their concentration on these kinds of goals. In the hands of truly able teachers, students combine their learning of the skills with some understanding of the principles underlying the skills; hence, the frequent wedding of the conceptual objectives and the skills objectives into a larger group called "cognitive."

A second group of goals is the affective, or attitudinal, purposes. These have to do with values, attitudes, and opinions students possess and, of course, are the more important kinds of objectives if behavioral change is the desired outcome of formal schooling. Educators have long been divided on the amount and kind of tampering a school ought to engage in with respect to a student's values, but most agree on two points: that, whether they try or not, teachers are going to exert an enormous influence on the values their students hold and that it is at least an arguable proposition that the school ought deliberately to encourage its students to examine their own goals, this latter a derivative, perhaps, of the Socratic dictum: "The unexamined life is not worth living."

Given these two kinds of objectives, the schools have made choices, choices that have led to an emphasis on the cognitive goals and the resultant technological proficiency that reached its zenith, literally, in the moon shot. They have not focused their efforts on the affective goals and their failure to do so is exactly what makes the behavioral changes requisite in the solutions of many of our domestic ills seem most unlikely, at least in the near future.

The reasons for the supremacy of the conceptual and skills goals in the work a teacher does are readily apparent to anyone at all familiar with the classroom. It is easier to plan teaching lessons geared toward the satisfactions of these goals than toward the accomplishment of affective goals; it is easier to test whether the lessons have, in fact, achieved the goals. For example, when a novel is read with the purpose of identifying its plot, central characters, symbols, images, conflicts, etc. (cognitive goals), the teacher knows precisely what he wants to teach, what results he can expect and how to go about both the teaching and the assessment of his results. When that same novel is read for the purpose of having the students come to grips with some important social issue treated in it—war, for instance, or the relationship of the individual to his government—the teacher may be uncertain about how he should proceed and how he should determine whether his students have done the self-examination he hoped the novel and his teaching would encourage. Indeed, the manifestation of any self-examination may not come until long after the students have left school. It is also usually safer to teach for certain understandings or skills than to engage in the kind of class that might cause a student to question his own or his parents' values. Few teachers have ever been called on the carpet for teaching students to prove a geometry theorem, but many have been asked to tread lightly, or not at all, on such matters as the individual's role in race relations or the effectiveness of the United Nations. Other reasons within education itself exist to explain the dominance of the cognitive goals—teachers themselves have been trained more in the cognitive than in the affective domain, textbooks and other teaching materials emphasize the conceptual and skills area—but these suffice to indicate why schools stress the cognitive at the inevitable expense of the affective.

There also has been an important pressure outside education in support of the cognitive domain as the dominant objectives in our schools. The source of that pressure has been, and is, the federal government. When Sputnik I launched the space race and informed the world of America's lagging position, Congress demanded that the schools do better the task of educating the craftsmen necessary to make our own program a success. The demand was backed with money and the amount poured into certain aspects of the school program, mathematics and science especially, both of them largely concerned with the cognitive domain, was prodigious. From 1959 until 1965 virtually any math or science teacher in the secondary schools who wanted increased training in the summer could get it, expenses and salary paid for by the National Science Foundation, an agency of the government. English and social studies teachers, those whose interest in the attainment of affective objectives is usually greater than that of their colleagues in math and science, stayed home summers and competed with their students for jobs in lumber yards and drug stores. Exciting new math and science curricula were developed during these years; the old history and the old English remained about the same. In short, the schools went on a math-science binge, with the result a predictable one: Education became even more firmly entrenched in the cognitive domain. The affective goals were left behind and the problems for which they are needed if solutions are to be found remained problems and, in some instances, slum conditions and welfare for two examples, actually worsened. One of many successes of this technological push, the space program, offers compelling evidence, however, that the schools can accomplish most of the tasks set for them and suggests that, if we want to solve the domestic problems requiring behavioral solutions, we must look to the schools as the source of the trained manpower. It must, however, be manpower trained in affective, as well as in cognitive, ways.

At this moment in history it seems likely that education will continue to emphasize the cognitive goals and that America will therefore continue to have the skilled technicians to achieve solutions to what are essentially technological problems. Someday man will walk on Mars, cancer will be no more feared than polio, even air and water pollution will diminish. But, as these problems are solved, the critical dilemmas requiring changes in the behavior of people may not be moved any nearer to solution. The dream may beget the fact of racial harmony, for example, but the dream is not the fact, and will not become the fact until people change their behavior, a change that can be fostered in the schools should education add the affective domain as a full and equal partner in its objectives.

For the school can effect changes in human behavior, though such a program would require for its accomplishment a much different kind of schooling from that which we have today. To change behavior requires far more than putting a few pictures of black children on the pages of first grade primers or asking high school students to contemplate the nobility of Jim while they are reading *Huckleberry Finn*, though these measures are steps in the right direction. Of immediate necessity would be a reduction of the competitive, survival-of-the-fittest aspects of education and a concomitant upgrading of education as a period in which the rewards for learning exist in what is learned, with the most important learning that which one discovers about himself. Cooperative problem solving would replace today's intensely individualistic efforts. Simulation games and role playing would be common classroom activities. But perhaps the most striking change in an educational framework that focuses equal attention to the affective objectives and to the cognitive from one in which the major thrust is toward the cognitive only is that the student would be forced at every opportunity to examine himself: his own attitudes and values and motives for doing and thinking as he does. Knowledge of self would become as sought after in the schools as understanding of the principles of chemistry or physics. Introspection would become a hallmark of the new education. And, when an entire society spends time periodically in self-examination, that very introspection may be evidence that the climate for behavioral change is ripe; indeed, out of the introspection may come the first motion toward the change.

Even the relatively simple prescriptions set forth above suggest the major alterations necessary if education is to accomodate both its affective and the cognitive purposes. Yet, though one ought to remain cautious, there is some reason for optimism. Today's generation of college students are turning to teaching as a career in greater proportions than ever before and many of these students will take to their classrooms not only the traditional idealism of the new teacher but also a zest for changing the fabric of society by leading their students to self-discovery through self-examination. If the student revolutions have accomplished nothing else, they have forced their participants on both sides of the barricades to examine the assumptions by which they live. Today's college students will challenge tradition, not necessarily to change it, but rather to get at the assumptions presumed to undergird it. Already they are demanding relevance in education, a demand that arises out of a concern with the deficiencies of an education that has been too long cognitively centered. It is likely that they will challenge the supremacy of the cognitive. Indeed, where these teachers teach, sparks will fly, but they will ignite fires which may illuminate the hopes for a mankind that wants desperately to remove contemporary social ills.

That is, these teachers will light fires in the affective domain if they are given the opportunity to do so, an opportunity largely denied the teachers of the last decade, some of whom were anxious to make their classrooms centers of attitudinal inquiry. But for these older teachers the temper of the times demanded a cognitive emphasis. One can be optimistic, however, because the new teachers will have experienced first hand the wars of educational change on their college campuses; possibly they can change the schools and create a new teaching/learning environment that will permit affective education.

But more people than just the new teachers can help, indeed must help if the areas of affective learning are to gain an equal footing with those of cognitive learning. A few essential beginning steps for teachers, students, parents, and governmental agencies are given below:

First of all, teachers new and old must be both permitted and expected to engage their students in discussion of controversial issues. No longer can we tolerate classrooms whose most obvious characteristic is their studied avoidance of anything that might ruffle feathers or churn visceras. Presently, too many teachers mask their own insecurity about the controversial by claiming that classroom give-and-take about something like the morality of the Vietnam war or nudity in the dramatic arts may cost them their jobs. What is sad is that many of these teachers have assessed their situations correctly: to speak about something controversial may get them fired posthaste. Yet, if the schools wish to include the affective domain in their programs in a substantive way, they must engender a spirit of inquiry in their students on matters about which there are not easy answers. Letting students discover what happens when they play with the lengths of sides of right triangles is one kind of inquiry; letting them ponder the effects on individuals of different kinds of social systems (which the students have studied as part of the cognitive program) is quite another, one much more likely to lead to some classroom disagreement.

Throughout all of this attention to controversial matters, the teachers must constantly force their students to consider themselves as parts of whatever situation they are studying. Why do they feel as they do? What evidence have they? How many of their responses to issues are based more on emotion than on hard data? How often do they change their minds and why? What values underlie their choices? Such questions cause the students to look at themselves, at their own behavior, and this is the beginning of an education enterprise that can focus on the affective.

Such teaching is not necessarily indoctrination, though it is foolish to assume that it will never be. Just as we have teachers who are presently unable to handle well their cognitive tasks, so also will we encounter those equally incompetent in the affective domain, who see their roles as persuaders and not as the provokers they should be. We must do our best to remove such teachers from the profession and to train prospective teachers to handle classroom controversy in ways which, while not always neutral, are neither always propagandistic for a particular viewpoint.

Teachers must also be able to provide supportive assistance for students unwilling to express their own ideas or emotions. Not infrequently the student who will vehemently demand the right to speak on a cognitive question will clam up on an affective one, especially if the latter hits close to home. The adolescent whose father owns some slum dwellings may be justifiably confused and reticent on discussions that seek after the individual's responsibility in the eradication of urban ills. The classroom must become an open forum, where ideas, not the people who voice them, are subject to attack; it behooves the teacher to keep *ad hominem* comments to a minimum. Classroom discussion can be warm and friendly—and violent—at the same time and the teacher must, therefore, exercise care to see that the eventual outcome is an increase in self-examination, not a decrease in self-concept.

For the affective domain can be intellectually stimulating even as it is emotionally enervating. To the problem for which there is no easy answer, population control, for example, the student will seldom be able to experience the psychologically satisfying feeling of closure that accompanies his finally balancing a difficult chemical equation or solving a tricky math problem. Such a lack of closure can be frustrating and it is up to the teacher to reassure students that their debates, their inquiries, their examination of motives, their own and others, have purpose and worth, even if they fall short of ultimate solution. Such willingness to explore ideas may eventually lead to a societal persuasion to examine issues and to chart the changes in behavior necessary to combat the issues.

These changes in teacher role require similar changes in teacher preparation. Colleges and universities must lessen some of their attention to the acquisition of facts and understandings by their prospective teachers, these presumably to be passed on later once these teachers enter school rooms. Instead, the teacher-training institutions must prepare teachers to stimulate dialogues with their students, to focus in their classrooms on the unanswerable, to see their future students as people whose self-discovery is at least as crucial to the betterment of society as their cognitive accomplishment. Prospective teachers must themselves explore affective issues in college classes, not only to discover the effect on individuals of such exploration but also to witness first-hand the techniques of guiding such exploration. Teacher preparation can become an exciting time, just as teaching will be, for the realm of behavioral ideas is surely as fascinating as the realm of acquired facts and demonstrated skills.

Students, too, must change, especially those in the secondary schools and colleges where today the emphasis is so heavily on the cognitive that the more a student resembles a blotter, the greater his chances of academic success. Though he works hard, today's bright student is secure in the knowledge that he is going to do well in school. He can parrot back the lecture to the teacher better than his peers can; he can solve the problems quicker; he can demonstrate the appropriate understandings more easily. When, however, he must look at himself, at his own values and attitudes and their similarities and differences with those he sees in the larger society, his task is a different one, with a less predictable assurance of success. If the schools can foster in students this sort of introspection, then the possibility indeed exists that within a generation or two the United States can have an adult population able and willing to look hard at itself and to effect the behavioral solutions many of its problems require.

Changes in the immediate school personnel—the teachers and their students—must coincide with changes in parents if a program of affective education is going to succeed. Just as today most parents accept the dominance of cognitive goals and accomplishments, parents in the future must accept education's added emphasis on values, attitudes, feelings, and beliefs, the practical components of the affective domain. Mother must not be shocked or disappointed when she asks Johnny what he learned in school and gets a response like the following: "Nothing definite, Mom. We've been reading *Macbeth* and talking about the effects of ambition on national leaders and even on ordinary people like you and me. Pretty exciting stuff." Parents must also be willing to forgo their cocktail party bragging about Johnny's "A" average and begin to give serious thought to the teacher's statement that "Johnny is too quick to form opinions on too little evidence. He then is unwilling to alter those opinions. We need to help him collect information about problems and to question him about the 'why' of his opinions." In essence, the parents must see as worthwhile the attempts of the schools to make Johnny a person who thinks about himself as often and deeply as he thinks about physics or accounting.

Finally, government can play a significant role. Monies it would spend on education must be channeled to affective concerns as well as to cognitive ones. The teacher of literature or history ought to have his advanced education financed in the same manner that a math or science teacher now receives aid. Government must give grant support to school and college programs that search for materials and methods to be used in affective education, even though the results of such work may not bear fruit for several decades. For, by its nature, affective education is a slow process: A bright student can be taught to use the Pythagorean theorem in minutes; to teach him to examine regularly his motives and actions may take years. The government must begin to see that the solution to domestic problems cannot be handled by congressional fiat, but must be the result of an education that is affectively based; it must then support that kind of education.

The changes suggested in the preceding paragraphs are not easily effected, but neither are they so difficult as to preclude further societal and educational consideration of them. Indeed, the United States must have this consideration. No longer can we accept an education that stresses only the cognitive; to continue as we have been is ultimately self-defeating. We could have men living on the moon, but with little reason to believe that their lives would be lived any more harmoniously or richly than those they left behind on earth.

Attention to the affective domain in education is the most apparent
answer, possibly the only answer if we are to solve the many problems we
have that require behavioral solutions. That attention should have been
paid yesterday. Yesterday having passed forever (technology has not yet
permitted us to turn back the clock), we must grasp today; tomorrow
may be too late.

Education in New Cities

Myron Lieberman

In late 1970 the National Education Association announced that some of
its offices, and those of several departments and affiliated groups, would
eventually be moved into a 34-acre campus type complex in the new city
of Reston, Virginia. This decision should help focus attention on
education's immense stake in the new cities movement, i.e., the emergence
of hundreds of cities planned and developed as comprehensive new
communities from their very inception. In my judgment these new cities
constitute a development of the utmost importance, not just to education
but to all of our political and social institutions. The purpose of this article
is to explain their tremendous educational potential and clarify the stake
of the entire educational community in this particular response to
America's urban crisis.

My thesis is that new cities provide an opportunity for educational
planners to take a critical look at all aspects of education. Sometimes they
even require it. At the same time, new cities offer unique opportunities to
introduce and demonstrate educational reforms and innovations. Most of
the educational changes which are proved effective in new cities can
ultimately be introduced into existing cities, despite conventional attitudes
which assume that whatever happens in a new community is irrelevant to
existing ones.

First, let me comment briefly on the dimensions of the new cities
movement. At present there are over 250 new cities in various stages of
development in the United States. The exact number varies, depending
upon the definition of "new city" or "new community," or how strictly
the definitions are applied. As used here a new city or new community is a
planned complex that includes all of the life-support systems of a city:
government, education, transportation, law enforcement, and so on. Thus
at the outset one must recognize the difference between housing

From Myron Lieberman, "Education in New Cities," *Phi Delta Kappan* 53
(March 1972): 407–11. Reprinted by permission of the author and the publisher.

developments, no matter how large, and new cities. The former may include some attention to other life-support systems, such as transportation or recreation, if the scale of housing is large enough. They do not, however, involve a deliberate effort to plan all of the life-support systems, including plans for the options that a civilized community should enjoy.

It must be emphasized that new cities are not an attempt to program everyone or to foreclose options on housing, recreation, employment, or anything else. On the contrary, they constitute, or can constitute, a deliberate effort to build a city so as to maximize the options of its residents. Of course it may be necessary to foreclose some options in order to provide others, but this problem is not confined to new cities; it exists everywhere.

The size and location of new cities vary considerably. Columbia, Maryland, widely regarded as the most successful, covers 15,000 acres, with a population expected to increase from 6,000 in 1967 to 110,000 by 1980 (although present indications are that this rate of development will actually be accelerated). Some new cities already in the development stage are much larger. For example, the new city at Irvine, California, is planned to reach a population of 500,000 people on 88,000 acres of what is now largely ranch land. As ambitious as this may seem, the National Commission on Urban Growth has recommended "the creation of 100 new communities averaging 100,000 population each and 10 new communities of at least one million in population," to be completed by the year 2000.

Perhaps the most common misconception concerning new cities is that they are oversized Levittowns, developed at a considerable distance from one or more inner-city areas. Of course there are such communities, and there is no law to prevent a developer from labeling one of them a "new city" or "new community" if he wishes. On the other hand, the location of new cities as I have defined them varies considerably. Many are in or near metropolitan areas; e.g., two new cities are currently being developed in New York City alone. One calls for a new community of approximately 20,000 persons on Welfare Island; the other envisages a community of 450,000 on 10,600 acres in South Richmond (Staten Island) by 1992.

Before I turn more directly to education in new cities, a few words of caution may be in order. Most city builders are private corporations; sometimes the corporations are largely owned or are dominated by a single entrepreneur. By one means or another, the corporation has acquired some land on which it plans to build a city. This sounds easy, but in fact the process requires thousands of complex interrelated decisions, many of which could undermine the entire enterprise if made incorrectly.

The city builder has to decide whether a particular site is suitable for a city. Can it attract industry? If so, how and why? How will schools, colleges, hospitals, churches, parks, playgrounds, etc., be provided? Where will they be located, how will they be paid for, and how administered? What kinds of housing will be needed, in what locations, at what prices, and at what rate of construction? How do you get people to move in before there are jobs, schools, shops, roads, parks, and so on? Conversely, how do you get these facilities and amenities built so they are operational as soon as people move in? Thousands of questions like these must be answered in building a city. Perhaps the most important is: How can the developer provide a better environment while earning the kinds of profits that will persuade banks, insurance companies, and other large lenders to invest in the new city? City building is an entrepreneurial, not a charitable, activity.

At this point I want simply to emphasize the interrelated nature of these decisions, especially as they affect education. Schools have to be planned and built before people move in; otherwise, people will move in at too slow a pace for industrial, commercial, and residential development. The city builder thus faces a host of questions and constraints which do not arise in conventional situations. For the most part, educational planners for new cities do not have to contend with the citizenry for whom the schools are planned. On the other hand, the city builder cannot just say to a county school board, "I want to build a city on such and such a site; please have the following schools ready by the dates indicated, so that people will move into the houses being built and take jobs in the industry coming in." If the new city is being developed within a county school board structure, the builder must secure approval of a zoning and development plan which shows what schools will be needed, where and when they will be located, who will provide the funds to build and staff them, and how these funds are to be collected and applied. And unless the developer can show that his proposed new community will generate enough additional revenue to pay for the proposed additional facilities and services, he may never secure the permits and approvals necessary to develop the city in the first place. Obviously, taxpayers and legislators will not be eager to divert tax revenues from existing populations to proposed new communities.

The city builder is not Croesus playing God as a school planner, because the patrons haven't moved in yet. Instead, he is an entrepreneur who has to think through the problems of education because his entire investment is dependent upon the quality of the educational planning for the proposed new city.

These considerations help to explain one of the significant educational developments in new cities and the emergence of a new dimension in the community school concept. Traditionally, the community school has been one that remains open in the afternoons and evenings and provides educational, social, recreational, and cultural opportunities to the community as a whole, not just to the conventional student body.

Planning for new cities provides a sharp contrast to the traditional community school concept. Instead of planning in terms of school facilities to be made available to the community, new communities plan community facilities that will meet the needs of students. Thus, instead of asking how school auditoriums or tennis courts or libraries can be used by the community, the new cities approach plans for community auditoriums or tennis courts or libraries which can be made available to students.

The difference in approach is not just a semantic one; it is absolutely crucial. Which can provide a community with the greatest return on its investment: a school library and a branch library, with duplication of space, books, and staff; or a branch library located and staffed so that it meets educational as well as adult needs? Should the "school swimming pool" be made available to the community—or should the community swimming pool be built and operated so that it can serve the student body effectively?

One difference lies in control. Under the community-centered approach, the facilities used by students are the planning, budgetary, and administrative responsibility of a nonschool agency. This agency must take school needs into account in its operations, but its services and facilities are planned, constructed, and maintained from the very outset with due regard for the entire spectrum of community needs and resources.

Along with, or because of, differences in control and budget, there is a difference in the politics involved. Ironically, the traditional community school approach has sometimes led to a negative public reaction toward education. Typically, advocates of the community school were concerned about public involvement and support for education. They believed that the way to achieve such involvement and support was to have the school directly serve all segments of the public, not just the student body. Laudable as were these sentiments, they probably led to adverse public reactions against school budget items which did not seem quite so crucial to education.

On the other hand, a swimming pool which seems to be a fad or frill in a school budget may have an entirely different appearance in the budget of the recreation department. Certainly, the community's return on its investment is likely to be much greater where the facility was planned from the beginning to serve the entire community. Furthermore, education budgets would not be as large, and hence would be less vulnerable, if school libraries were operated as part of the city's library department, swimming pools and tennis courts as part of the city recreation department, and so on. Furthermore, the educational community might gain some valuable allies by implementing these school needs through other municipal service systems in which the schools are only one important consumer.

Actually, the location and design of schools in new cities can take into account a wide variety of relationships with the private as well as with the public sector. These relationships are particularly important in the light of the custodial nature of much secondary education. Consider a high school where the students are in school from 8:30 a.m. to 3:00 p.m. Student A is advanced in music and would be willing to use some of his school time for private music lessons at his own expense. However, there is no place in the school to accommodate him, and it is not feasible for him to take lessons during the regular school day from private teachers outside of school. One reason is that such teachers are not accessible within the time limits most students have. By the time a student leaves school, drives or uses public transportation to the place where private instruction could be given, and returns for his next class, too much time has gone by.

In a new city, it is feasible to plan commercial buildings to provide space for private teachers of music, art, dance, etc., near public schools. The students can cross the street, take a private lesson at their own expense on their study or free time, or even plan for it in their school schedules, and still not miss a regularly scheduled class of any kind. In other words, educational planning in new cities can make it possible for many students who want instruction not available in the school to get it conveniently. The student who works after school has time for private lessons that do not cost double because they require time away from his after-school job. New commercial values are created; private teachers, able to count upon opportunities to give lessons during the day, can rent space in such a building, thus making it a feasible economic venture.

This example, oversimplified as it is, nevertheless suggests another point of departure in new cities. One can find widespread concern that our schools are becoming custodial instead of educational institutions. Unfortunately, existing school locations and physical structures render it practically impossible for schools to utilize other community resources. The civic, cultural, economic, or educational resources which students need are too far away, or there is no transportation network to provide convenient transportation between the school and the resource, whatever it may be.

It is evident that not all high school students need to spend as much time in class as they do. The success of independent study experiments confirms this. But where should they go and what should they do? Where *can* they go and what *can* they do, at least between activities which should be conducted in schools? In existing school districts, this problem is usually insoluble because the other resources are simply too inaccessible.

In new cities schools can be located near other civic, cultural, and economic institutions so as to facilitate constructive relationships that are impractical in most existing districts. These relationships may relate to virtually any aspect of education. For example, school sites and sizes can be planned to take advantage of the fact that major employers can provide vocational training more effectively than the schools.

It is my hope that educational development in new cities will also stimulate educators to rethink the educational dimensions of other life-support systems. Take housing as an example. Several studies indicate that children perform better in air-conditioned than in nonair-conditioned situations. The typical schoolman sees this as an argument for air-conditioning schools, as indeed it is. But who has ever seen the education Establishment struggle for money to air-condition public housing on the ground that such expenditures might contribute more to educational achievement than remedial teachers in hot and stuffy classrooms?

Or consider a common lament in inner-city schools: The children have no place at home to study. Educators alert to the interrelationship between education and housing might be pressing for the inclusion of study rooms in new apartment buildings, especially where the families cannot afford rooms for study in their own apartments. Such communal study halls might be staffed by teachers or paraprofessionals or even on a volunteer basis by parents in the immediate neighborhood.

Much more remains to be said, not only about the foregoing matters but about many other aspects of education in new cities not mentioned. Let me conclude, however, with a comment concerning the role played by the education community in the new cities movement. This comment is based partly upon the fact that Title VII of the Housing and Urban Development Act of 1970 provides federal loan guarantees for assistance to both private and public developers of new communities through federal loan guarantees, interest grants and loans, special planning grants and loans, public service grants, technical assistance, supplementary grants, and demonstration projects. The fact that up to $500 million in loan guarantees alone was made available by Title VII illustrates the enormous scope of this assistance. That is, the full faith and credit of the federal government were made available to guarantee the obligations of developers up to a maximum of $50 million for any single new community and up to $500 million for new communities generally. This amount is likely to be increased substantially in the near future.

To secure such a federal loan guarantee, a developer must submit a plan for community development and pay a $10,000 fee to have the plan evaluated for loan purposes. To date, only seven such loan applications have been approved, so that almost four hundred million dollars in federal loan guarantees is still available for such purposes. Undoubtedly, more applications for federal guarantees will be approved during 1972.

What should be the educational criteria for approving an application for federal guarantees? Where can developers learn what educational innovations are being tried and with what success, or what innovations ought to be considered in their planning?

In view of all the rhetoric about the vested interests and the bureaucracies which allegedly stifle educational creativity and innovation, one might suppose that the foundations and federal agencies and academicians who play the innovation game would have at least made an effort to capitalize upon the enormous possibilities for innovations where the traditional roadblocks do not even exist, or exist in much weaker form. In fact, not a single educational agency or organization in the United States, governmental or nongovernmental, seems to recognize the existence, let along the potential, of the new communities movement. Neither the Office of Education nor the Department of Housing and Urban Development has any program to help new communities incorporate the most effective educational planning and design in their overall plans. Although HUD is supposed to consider education in evaluating loan guarantee applications, there is no evidence that such consideration involves a critical review by educational personnel who could upgrade the educational potential of new communities. As a matter of fact, both HUD and the Department of Health, Education, and Welfare are fumbling the opportunities provided by new cities to introduce significant innovations in a wide range of public services and life-support systems.

Similarly, the other segments of the educational community are apparently unaware of the educational opportunities provided by new cities. The 1971 convention of AERA included the usual plethora of handwringers lamenting the difficulties of innovation, but not a single part of a single program was devoted to the educational possibilities of new communities. Despite their proximity to Columbia and Reston, the National Education Association, the American Federation of Teachers, and the American Association of School Administrators have no programs or policies relating to new communities, insofar as I can determine. A few foundations have made a few small grants for educational planning in new communities, but none of them has acted to systematize and institution-alize the enormous experimentation, demonstration, and dissemination potential of new communities. To my knowledge, the only individuals aware of the educational potential new cities have for existing cities, and the only persons actively seeking a systematic, coordinated approach to utilizing this potential, are in private enterprise.

Perhaps education really has nothing new and better to offer than lame excuses and rationalizations about improvements that could be made if only this or that group ended its obstruction. In any case, the failure of educational organizations and agencies to grasp such basic opportunities raises some disturbing issues about their awareness generally in this country.

Education in the Twenty-First Century

Alonzo G. Grace

At least six important forces may be identified as being of major significance in the molding of education in the 21st century. These forces are:

1. Expansion and mobility of population.
2. Emergence of the space age.
3. Acceleration of automation.

From Alonzo G. Grace, "Education in the Twenty-First Century," *Educational Forum* 35 (May 1971): 423–29, by permission of the author and Kappa Delta Pi, an Honor Society in Education, owners of the copyright.

4. The continued ideological conflict.
5. The revolution to establish human rights and values as the accepted property of each individual.
6. The changing concept of the democratic ideal in a constitutional government.

Only the last two forces will be considered briefly in this essay.

HUMAN RIGHTS

A major social goal of the twentieth century was concerned with *civil rights.* No matter whether or not new laws are written or constitutional guarantees enforced, the untouched issue remains. This is not civil rights but human rights. We have been tinkering with the symptoms of moral degeneration and decay. We have not had the wisdom and good judgment to face head-on the real crux of the impediments to the full attainment of human rights. Unless this be accomplished the twenty-first century will emerge in an atmosphere of useless conflict, for this goal will be reached only if the proper elements are nurtured and guided.

Historically, immigration to this country reached a point of critical proportions beginning in 1880 when the search for cheap labor resulted in a horde of human beings from Southeastern Europe migrating to our country. Italian, Polish, Hungarian, and other ethnic groups in unprecedented numbers flocked into our cities. This new population settled where one would expect, viz., in communities within cities that were already or soon became the "Italian quarter" or the "Polish section" or some other ethnic settlement. The businesses, for the most part, were owned and operated by members of the particular group. The schools were populated by the children of the particular group. However, each responsible person knew that social attitudes on the part of the population in the area would not interfere with his rights or desire to live elsewhere.

This has been a different story completely with the more recent migration of thousands of Puerto Ricans who, in general occupy substandard housing and present problems with which educational systems have failed to cope. So, too, with the more recent Negro migration largely from the South and primarily from rural areas. The difference between the more recent migration from Puerto Rico and the rural areas of the South is that during the past generation people located in the central city and in a sense were locked in this limited area. School buildings are old and have been used for generations. Great difficulty is experienced in securing master teachers for these areas. The program of teacher education has been completely unrealistic—and we have not had the wisdom or courage to face the real problems.

Freedom to live where one wishes is not a universal right as far as the Negro population is concerned—*and the educational problem—integration—will not be solved morally or practically until this becomes a universal truth.* Two observations may be made here:

1. The transfer of pupils from the inner city to suburban schools via bus may lead to an improved academic opportunity but does not get at the basic education of attitudes. The suburb is merely maintaining the status quo and will continue to do so until the parents of the bussed children or others are permitted to live in the selected area. The same holds true for "regional schools," supposedly drawing from the city and suburban areas.
2. Some pointed questions require replies. Who are the landlords who are charging excessive rent for submarginal, overcrowded facilities? Why are several families permitted to live in an area designed for a single family? Who owns and conducts the businesses in these so-called ghettos? Why are urban officials reluctant or unable to investigate, control, or improve these conditions?

I am contending that while we struggle toward the attainment of full employment, education for employment and the right to live anywhere—and these are basic to the whole problem of living together—we cannot delay the provision for quality education in every school, not excluding schools in the ghetto areas. While the storm clouds have been noticeable on the horizon for these many years, only within recent years has the voice of protest, of despair and lawlessness become sufficiently loud and organized to rivet attention upon the unbelievable state of many in our midst. What, then, are some examples of the impediments to quality education?

1. In one of the great cities, population declined between 1950 and 1960 by 70,000; however, during the period from 1951 to 1963 the school population increased by 190,000. This has been a general trend in practically every great city and many others for over a generation. Another element creating a problem in a large urban center is illustrated in one high-mobility school where 50 children each day during one 40-day period moved out of or into the school—2,000 migrants in and out of this school in 40 days. These facts are not mentioned by the critics of schools.
2. The exclusive suburban school may be spending $1,000 or more per pupil on education as against $400-$500 or less per pupil in the city. The city, with all of the complex problems, requires a budget considerably greater than now is provided. A quality program is not possible at bargain rates.
3. The utter impossibility of completing homework assignments or studying in the home environment is evident to any observing citizen who will take the time to investigate the deplorable housing units occupied not by one but, in many cases, by several families. We need to think more realistically of domestic aid to underdeveloped elements in this country. The attainment of quality in the educational system is related to decent housing and the home environment.
4. The child, as previously indicated, has many teachers. The school is

but one educational opportunity. Attitudes toward others who differ with respect to race, national origin, and religion may be acquired around the breakfast table or in the home environment. Thousands of illiterate parents have migrated from rural areas in parts of our country to an urban location. The important factor is the 7,500 hours per year that the neighborhood, playground, parents, mass media, and other teachers are at work as against the 1,250 hours per year in the school.

More may be included in this consideration of quality in an educational system. However, it must be conceded that to bring an equal opportunity for education to disadvantaged children in the central city school, new educational techniques, services, and personnel requiring major financial aid from all levels of government are required. It should be said at the same moment, however, that all of the disadvantaged children and youths are not in the central city. In the suburban school and in many urban centers, there are many who come from homes where patient, understanding parental love is absent or in which the parent lives on the assumption that understanding, love, and guidance can be purchased. These children and youths also must be included under the category of "disadvantaged."

I suggest, therefore, with particular reference to the schools in the urban district, particularly the so-called ghetto schools:

1. Perhaps a most important impact on the resolution of urban problems, including education, housing, health service, employment, and others, would be a cooperative effort *by all* universities and colleges either in or near the city. It frequently happens that *one* institution is awarded a large grant for this purpose. I am recommending that several foundations provide a grant to a new community agency, viz., the *united higher education* facilities therein. Perhaps these several institutions, as for example in Chicago or New York, with sufficient financial aid and the support of private enterprise and government, could have a telling effect on the reconstruction of urban life and the integration of suburban interests.
2. Quality education with provisions for augmented salaries for master teachers, small classes where required, superior pupil-teacher services, including psychologists, social workers, a longer school day, recreation programs, and such other developments as will produce human beings able to make their contribution in a society.
3. Preschool programs for children from one year of age, if home conditions indicate the wisdom of education in a child-care center, and extending to the first year of the elementary school.
4. Elimination of the grade system as a basis for promotion year to year, as we recommended in Connecticut over 20 years ago.
5. A completely new development of secondary education.

These are only examples of needed action, needed courage to depart from the *status quo*. Whatever is said here with respect to the steps to be taken to secure the more effective integration of school populations may apply, also, to the steps essential to keep the United States a constitutional government and strong from within.

DEMOCRATIC IDEAL

1. In our zeal to make clear our concern with world affairs we have rejected the "America-first" idea. However, events indicate that without care and vision we are in the midst of adopting an "America-last" policy.

2. The observance of law and order requires education at home, in the community, and school from early childhood throughout life. The recent flagrant resort to violence is no credit to our educational system, parental guidance, or to the law enforcement function itself.

3. Too many of our people interpret freedom as license. To them it means the freedom to violate the rights and dignity of others. There is no freedom without responsibility, and there is no freedom without self-discipline. I do not recommend that we return to the authoritarian school of yesterday, but until the individual is able to control himself he is not safe for society. We have not yet abandoned our police forces or our courts. There is no reason in a school situation why we should ever believe that merely by growing older people become mature. If we cannot control ourselves, we are not fit for life in a constitutional government.

4. Moral values must supplant materialism. There is an increasing number of people in the United States who believe that the fundamental goal of all living is money—and that whatever is desired in life can be bought. This is a devastating idea that must be conquered. Making money has become a disease with many people. People have ceased to live. Their code of ethics in this matter is none too high—so-called "sharp business deals" are justified on the basis of making more money. There can be no personal happiness if others suffer and there can be no living the good life or the full life if materialism be our guiding light.

5. An effective education includes not only adequate provision for the mastering of the fundamental intellectual tools and techniques of learning, but also a thorough understanding and the capacity to control the self. Intellectual competency means fundamentally the evolution of the disciplined mind. There must be some intellectual challenge in the development of the individual, for too easy mental living may have as dire results on the race as too easy physical living. Too many people have become intellectually allergic to anything that represents effort or exertion on the part of the individual. We must not confuse equality of education opportunity and equal education for all.

6. The present concept of the social studies either should be eliminated or reorganized. While much study has been devoted to the development of a more effective social studies program, it still is largely history. I suggest that every child and youth should know the economic and political

systems, the governmental structure, the geography, and the nature of the country. He should understand the background of freedom in the Republic of the United States, and he should understand the nature of this constitutional government. We should abolish the Carnegie Unit which calls for a class period of 45 or 50 minutes for five days a week. Each of these necessary subjects could be taught on a completely different schedule—some two days a week for one semester or others one to three days per week for the school year.

Responsible American citizenship cannot be acquired through the completion of a certain specified course or courses any more than character is attained through three easy lessons or through twelve lectures by some eminent authority. Responsible citizenship is the result of the experience not only in the educational institution as such, but also in all other institutions, agencies, or actions by other agencies in the community. Within the school itself, citizenship education should not be the sole responsibility of the so-called social studies or social science department. A class in English, in mathematics, science, or the football field, the auditorium, the playground, the cafeteria, classroom organization, and the many other aspects of school life all contribute to training for responsible American citizenship.

7. The use of objective tests as a means of measuring the individual's acquisition of knowledge, perhaps his attitudes, is out of balance. The capacity of the individual to write and his ability to compete in the realm of ideas and values is depreciated in the degree that he is isolated from experience with ideas and values. I am of the opinion that we have become so dependent on tests of this type that we are losing the opportunity to write clearly, concisely, and creatively. I would hope for a more extensive return to the essay type of examination.

8. Whatever be the inevitable result of this tragedy of mankind, whatever be the power politics, the intrigue or the ambitions of the rest of the world, we, the people of the United States, not only are defending a workable ideal but more particularly an ideal constantly directed towards the improvement of the status of the individual and the society in which he moves. Let us prepare our country for an eventuality. It is better that we be prepared and be wrong than to Rip Van Winkle ourselves into a state which may mean no state.

9. While it is obvious that many units of government conceived during the pioneer era in the evolution of American democracy no longer are able independently and separately to provide all the services now required for the security of a people or devised for their security by those who seek the more perfect state, the solution does not lie in the creation of a superstate or federal government. This ultimately would lead to a people of the government, by the government, and for the government.

10. America will preserve local initiative and responsibility only if there be a willingness on the part of all elements locally to improve the governmental structure in the interests of the whole people instead of permitting aggressive minorities and political expediency to dominate the needs of the group. Unless those locally are willing to assume the

responsibility for a more effective organization, for the placement of men and women of character and capacity in positions of government, and for continuous citizen participation in the consideration of policy, the trend will be towards units of government far removed from the people.

11. The attitude of doing for a people must be replaced by an attitude of doing with and by the people. Unless there is confidence in the ability of the local unit to assume responsibility for the effective education of its citizenship, man's efforts to govern himself may succumb through passive acquiescence to the centralized interest. Democracy, on the other hand, will not function effectively until all of the people of the community recognize that all of the people are a part of the community.

It should not take a crisis to initiate the educational policies required to advance our culture and to preserve and improve our way of life. Unfortunately, this appears to be the case. Soviet penetration of outer space, irrespective of our delayed effort in this direction, had an immediate effect on the people of the United States and the educational system did not escape the impact of this accomplishment. However, abdication to fear and retreat from reason will not aid in the resolution of our problems. Hardly any educator would tolerate the return of the leisurely complacency which characterized our society a few years ago—this in spite of the fact that today's crises were plainly identifiable a decade or more ago.

The kind of educational program we need, however, will not be uncovered overnight by crash programs. The search for policy must not result in legislation by hysteria, unfounded criticism of men and institutions, or disunity through rumor. We are doing irreparable damage to ourselves without the aid of those who would destroy us. However, we shall not meet the challenge confronting educators and our educational system by clinging selfishly to old patterns, by protecting vested interests, or by resistance to needed adjustments in policy, organization, and program.

It is necessary that citizens and educators alike face the situation realistically with the view to perfecting our educational practices and procedures. This should not mean, as previously indicated, simply the addition of courses in an already overcrowded program. It is far preferable that we do fewer things better than that we undertake to teach all things to all people. It is essential, too, that the purposes of education be translated into action, that whatever happens under the jurisdiction of the educational system be reflected in the emerging product. Individuals must be better for having had the advantage of school and college. Society, too, must be better because educated men compose it. Let us be certain that what happened in countries who chose to embrace totalitarianism will not happen here.

QUESTIONS FOR REFLECTION AND DISCUSSION

1. How would you answer the questions Gordon raises? How do your answers differ from his?

2. Are the curriculum continuum Shane advocates, the affective education Hipple calls for, and the conditions Grace writes about internally consistent? That is, would the implementation of the ideas of one mesh with the ideas of the other two? If so, in what ways?

3. Can the education implied by Gordon in his answers to his own questions fit the new cities model described by Lieberman?

4. Assume you were on the planning committee for a new city. What parts of Lieberman's plan would you adopt? Reject? How much would you use the futuristic ideas of the other authors represented here?